HUMAN RIGHTS IN INTERNATIONAL LAW

HUMAN RIGHTS IN INTERNATIONAL LAW: LEGAL AND POLICY ISSUES

Edited by
THEODOR MERON

VOLUME II

CLARENDON PRESS · OXFORD
1984

Oxford University Press, Walton Street, Oxford OX2 6DP
London Glasgow New York Toronto
Delhi Bombay Calcutta Madras Karachi
Kuala Lumpur Singapore Hong Kong Tokyo
Nairobi Dar es Salaam Cape Town
Melbourne Auckland
and associated companies in
Beirut Berlin Ibadan Mexico City Nicosia

Oxford is a trade mark of Oxford University Press

Published in the United States
by Oxford University Press, New York

Library of Congress Cataloging in Publication Data

Human rights in international law.
Includes bibliographies and index.
1. Civil rights (International law) I. Meron, Theodor, 1930–
K3240.4.H835 1984 341.4'84 83-4214
ISBN 0-19-825472-5 (v. 1)
ISBN 0-19-825488-1 (v. 2)

British Library Cataloguing in Publication Data

Meron, Theodor
Human rights in International law.
Vol. 2
1. Civil rights (International law)
I. Title
341.4'81 K3240
ISBN 0-19-825488-1

Typeset by Oxprint Ltd, Oxford
Printed in Great Britain
at the University Press, Oxford

INTERNATIONAL LAW OF HUMAN RIGHTS

Summary of Contents

Volume I

Part I: The Setting

1. Teaching Human Rights: An Overview—Theodor Meron
2. International Human Rights and Rights in the United States—Louis Henkin
3. The Jurisprudence of Human Rights—Jerome J. Shestack

Part II: Global Protection of Human Rights

4. Civil Rights—Richard B. Lillich
5. Political and Related Rights—John P. Humphrey
6. Economic, Social, and Cultural Rights in the Third World: Human Rights Law and Human Needs Programs—David M. Trubek

Volume II

7. Human Rights and the International Labour Organisation—Francis Wolf
8. Race, Sex, and Religious Discrimination in International Law—Jack Greenberg
9. Human Rights in Armed Conflict: International Humanitarian Law—Yoram Dinstein
10. Human Rights: Their Implementation and Supervision by the United Nations—Louis B. Sohn
11. The Contribution of International Nongovernmental Organizations to the Protection of Human Rights—David Weissbrodt

Part III: Regional Protection

12. The Inter-American System for the Protection of Human Rights—Thomas Buergenthal
13. The European Convention on Human Rights—Rosalyn Higgins

Index

Table of Contents

Volume II

page

Chapter 7. Human Rights and the International Labour Organisation *Francis Wolf* 273

I. Legal and Policy Considerations 273

A. Introduction 273

B. Permanent Supervision of the Application of ILO Standards 276

1. Information and reports 276

a. Information on the submission of conventions and recommendations to the competent authorities 276

b. Reports on ratified conventions 277

c. Reports on unratified conventions and recommendations 278

d. Involvement of employers' and workers' organizations in the supervisory procedures 279

2. Supervisory bodies 280

a. The Committee of Experts on the Application of Conventions and Recommendations 281

b. The Conference Committee on the Application of Conventions and Recommendations 284

c. The system of direct contacts 285

C. Contentious Procedures 286

1. Representations against members 286

2. Complaints against members 288

D. Special Freedom of Association Procedures 290

1. The Committee on Freedom of Association 290

2. The Fact-Finding and Conciliation Commission on Freedom of Association 292

E. Non-Contentious Procedures 293

F. Concluding Remarks 293

II. Teaching Suggestions 294

A. Purpose of the Course 294

B. The Main Organs of the ILO 295

C. Area of ILO Activity 295

D. ILO Methods for the Promotion of Human Rights: International Labour Standards 296

E. The Nature and Scope of ILO instruments 296

F. The Supervisory Machinery 297

1. The Contentious Procedures 297

a. Representations procedure 297

b. Complaint procedure 298
c. Special freedom of association procedure 298
2. Non-contentious procedures 298
III. Syllabus 299
IV. Minisyllabus 301
V. Bibliography 301
VI. Minibibliography 304

Chapter 8. Race, Sex, and Religious Discrimination in International Law *Jack Greenberg* 307
I. Legal and Policy Considerations 309
A. The Importance of the Structures Against Discrimination 309
B. The United Nations Charter and Universal Declaration of Human Rights 309
1. U.N. Charter 310
2. Universal Declaration 311
3. Enforceability of the Charter and the Universal Declaration 313
C. The International Covenants and the Racial Discrimination Convention 318
1. Economic Covenant 319
2. Political Covenant 320
3. The Racial Discrimination Convention 322
4. Enforceability 325
D. Convention on the Elimination of All Forms of Discrimination Against Women 327
E. Declaration on Religious Discrimination 330
F. Interpretation and Applications of the Basic Instruments 332
II. Teaching Suggestions 334
III. Syllabus 339
IV. Minisyllabus 340
V. Bibliography 341
VI. Minibibliography 343

Chapter 9. Human Rights in Armed Conflict: International Humanitarian Law *Yoram Dinstein* 345
I. Legal and Policy Considerations 345
A. Introduction 345
B. The Essence of Human Rights in Armed Conflicts 348
C. The Interplay of Human Rights in Peacetime and Wartime 350

D. The Interplay of Human Rights and Corresponding Duties in Armed Conflict 354
E. Problems of Implementation and Supervision 356
II. Teaching Suggestions 362
A. A Full Course 362
B. A Module Within a General Course 364
III. Syllabus 365
IV. Minisyllabus 366
V. Bibliography 366
VI. Minibibliography 368

Chapter 10. Human Rights: Their Implementation and Supervision by the United Nations *Louis B. Sohn* 369
I. Legal and Policy Considerations 369
A. National Measures of Implementation and Supervision 369
B. International Measures of Implementation and Supervision 373
1. Periodic Reporting Systems 373
2. Procedures for Dealing with Inter-State Complaints 379
a. Reference to International Court of Justice 379
b. References to the European and Inter-American Courts of Human Rights 381
c. Fact-Finding and Conciliation 381
3. Procedures for the Consideration of Private Communications 384
4. Conflicts between Various Implementation Procedures 393
C. Conclusions 394
II. Teaching Suggestions 395
III. Syllabus 398
IV. Minisyllabus 399
V. Bibliography 400
VI. Minibibliography 401

Chapter 11. The Contribution of International Nongovernmental Organizations to the Protection of Human Rights *David Weissbrodt* 403
I. Legal and Policy Considerations 406
A. What are International Nongovernmental Organizations? 406

B. Selection of Human Rights Violations and Fact-Finding 408
C. What do International Nongovernmental Organizations do to Implement Human Rights? 410
1. Diplomatic Interventions and Missions by NGOs 412
2. Public Discussion of Human Rights Violations 415
3. The NGO Contribution to International Investigative Procedures 420
4. Aid and Human Rights 425
5. Activities at Local Levels 426
D. Contributions to the Development of Human Rights Norms 429
II. Teaching Suggestions 430
A. Problem 431
B. Materials to be Distributed to the Class 433
III. Syllabus 434
IV. Minisyllabus 435
V. Bibliography 435
VI. Minibibliography 438

Chapter 12. The Inter-American System for the Protection of Human Rights *Thomas Buergenthal* 439
I. Legal and Policy Considerations 439
A. The American Convention on Human Rights 440
1. In General 440
2. Some Problems of Interpretation 442
a. The Self-Executing Character of the American Convention 442
b. The Federal-State Clause 445
c. The Right of Derogation 448
B. The Convention Institutions 451
1. The Inter-American Commission on Human Rights .. 452
a. Its Functions 452
b. Individual and Inter-State Complaints 454
2. The Inter-American Court of Human Rights 460
a. The Inter-American Court's Contentious Jurisdiction 460
b. The Inter-American Court's Advisory Jurisdiction 467
C. The O.A.S. Charter and Human Rights 470
1. The Evolution of the Charter-Based Regime 470
a. Under the 1948 Charter 470
b. Under the Revised O.A.S. Charter 474

c. Effect of the American Convention 475
2. The Practice of the Commission as a Charter Organ .. 479
a. Country Studies and 'On-Site' Observations 479
b. Individual Communications 484
D. Conclusions 487
II. Teaching Suggestions 488
III. Syllabus 490
IV. Minisyllabus 491
V. Bibliography 491
VI. Minibibliography 493

Chapter 13. The European Convention on Human Rights
Rosalyn Higgins 495
I. Legal and Policy Considerations 495
A. Conceptual Issues 495
B. The Machinery 505
C. Case Studies 511
1. Case Study. Freedom from Torture and Inhuman or Degrading Treatment or Punishment 511
2. Case Study. Liberty of the Person 515
3. Case Study. The Rights to a Fair Trial 528
4. Case Study. The Rights to Free Speech 532
II. Teaching Suggestions 536
III. Syllabus 539
IV. Minisyllabus 546
V. Bibliography 547
VI. Minibibliography 549

Index 551

Chapter 7

Human Rights and the International Labour Organisation*

Francis Wolf[1]

I. Legal and Policy Considerations

A. INTRODUCTION

Human rights are not a separate part of the activities of the International Labour Organisation (ILO), but lie at the very heart of its mission. According to the definition of the ILO's objectives, as contained in the Declaration of Philadelphia adopted in 1944 and subsequently incorporated in the ILO Constitution,[2] all national and international policies and measures should be based on the principle that all human beings, irrespective of race, creed, or sex, have the right to pursue both their material well-being and their spiritual development in conditions of freedom, dignity, economic security, and equal opportunity. The more detailed provisions of the Declaration of Philadelphia, whether referring to such matters as freedom of expression and of association, promotion of full employment, the raising of living standards, wages and conditions of work, social security measures, or protection of the life and health of workers, all serve to direct the ILO's actions toward the realization of human rights.

A major part of ILO action to attain these objectives consists of the adoption of international labour standards in the form of conventions and recommendations. The international labour convention is the main way to deal with essential issues, especially of basic human rights, about which sustained or energetic action by member states appears to be needed. It enables ratifying states to take on formal obligations and to secure international recognition of the status of their law and practice. The role of an international labour recommendation is less formal. Sometimes it is used to deal with subjects which do not lend themselves to precise obligations, as in cases in which the diversity of

[1] This chapter was prepared with the collaboration of Ebere Osieke, a staff member of the Office of the Legal Adviser, International Labour Office, Geneva. It is a revised version of Wolf, *ILO Experience in the Implementation of Human Rights*, 10 J. Int'l L. & Econ. 599 (1975) [hereinafter cited as Wolf, *ILO Experience*], brought up to date to March 1982.

[2] 62 Stat. 3485, T.I.A.S. No. 1868, 15 U.N.T.S. 35; *amended* 7 U.S.T. 245, T.I.A.S. No. 3500, 191 U.N.T.S. 143 (1953); 14 U.S.T. 1039, T.I.A.S. No. 5401, 466 U.N.T.S. 323 (1962); 25 U.S.T. 3253, T.I.A.S. No. 7987 (1972).

national conditions prevents the establishment of rules which can be universally and fully accepted, but in which it is useful to have a set of guidelines for governments. In a great number of cases, an international labour recommendation supplements an international labour convention—the former deals with questions of detail and means of implementation while the latter deals with basic questions—and may sometimes lay down a higher standard than that contained in the corresponding convention.

Most ILO conventions and recommendations concern the promotion and protection of human rights in a broad sense, since they deal with questions such as a safe working environment, the protection of children and young persons, working hours and other conditions of work, and other aspects of the economic, social, cultural, and civil rights enunciated in the International Covenant on Economic, Social and Cultural Rights[3] and the International Covenant on Civil and Political Rights.[4] However, a number of ILO instruments deal more specifically with certain fundamental rights and freedoms, such as freedom of association,[5] freedom from forced labour,[6] and equality of opportunity and treatment in employment.[7]

[3] G.A. Res. 2200, 21 U.N. GAOR, Supp. (No. 16) 49, U.N. Doc. A/6316 (1966).

[4] G.A. Res. 2200, 21 U.N. GAOR, Supp. (No. 16) 52, U.N. Doc. A/6316 (1966). *See generally Comparative analysis of the International Covenants on Human Rights and International Labour Conventions and Recommendations*, 52 (No. 2) ILO O. Bull. 188 (1969); Valticos, *The Place of Human Rights in the Constitution and the Various Instruments of the ILO and the Legal Framework for Their Protection*, in The International Dimensions of Human Rights 407–08 (K. Vasak ed. 1979).

[5] On the subject of freedom of association, the ILO has adopted the following instruments: Right of Association (Agriculture) Convention, 1921 (No. 11); Right of Association (Non-Metropolitan Territories) Convention, 1947 (No. 84); Freedom of Association and Protection of the Right to Organise Convention, 1948 (No. 87); Right to Organise and Collective Bargaining Convention, 1949 (No. 98); Workers' Representatives Convention, 1971 (No. 135), and Recommendation, 1971 (No. 143); Rural Workers' Organisations Convention, 1975 (No. 141), and Recommendation, 1975 (No. 149); and Labour Relations (Public Service) Convention, 1978 (No. 151), and Recommendation, 1978 (No. 159).

[6] On the subject of forced labour, the ILO has adopted the following instruments: Forced Labour Convention, 1930 (No. 29); Abolition of Forced Labour Convention, 1957 (No. 105); Forced Labour (Indirect Compulsion) Recommendation, 1930 (No. 35); and Forced Labour (Regulation) Recommendation, 1930 (No. 36).

[7] On the subject of equality of opportunity and treatment in employment, the ILO has adopted the following instruments: Equal Remuneration Convention, 1951 (No. 100), and Recommendation, 1951 (No. 90); Discrimination (Employment and Occupation) Convention, 1958 (No. 111), and Recommendation, 1958 (No. 111); and Workers with Family Responsibilities Convention, 1981 (No. 156), and Recommendation, 1981 (No. 165). It should be mentioned also that during the 60th Session of the International Labour Conference in June 1975, the Conference adopted a Declaration on Equality of Opportunity and Treatment of Women Workers.

The list of instruments adopted by the ILO dealing with basic human rights may be completed by referring to the ILO's instruments concerning migrant workers including Migrant Workers' (Supplementary Provisions) Convention, 1975 (No. 143), and Migrant Workers' Recommendation, 1975 (No. 151).

These conventions and recommendations clearly demonstrate the ILO's commitment to give effect to the basic human rights principles recognized in its constitutional documents. However, the framing of instruments and their formal acceptance by member states are only the first stages of the standard-setting work of the ILO. What matters is that the instruments result in effective measures at the national level for the benefit of those whose well-being they are intended to protect and promote and, more generally, that they help to shape the social policies of member States. Thus, the utility of these instruments lies in the availability of machinery for their acceptance by States and their effective implementation.

From its inception, the ILO established precise and original rules which, as supplemented over the years, presently constitute the most developed system for securing the effective application of international standards. The component parts of this system interlock to ensure, in the vast majority of cases, that when obligations are contracted, they are respected.

The system for ensuring the implementation of ILO conventions and recommendations applies to all such instruments, but it acquires special significance when they are concerned with human rights and the 'dignity inborn in the entire human family' is at stake.[8] In his opening address to the Abidjan World Peace through Law Conference in 1973, the Honorable Earl Warren, former Chief Justice of the United States Supreme Court, emphasized the importance of the machinery of the International Labour Organisation in the implementation of human rights.[9]

> Standing before us also is the basic fact that a body of international law on human rights now exists. And because it exists we can now turn our attention to the means by which it can be implemented. . . . For the past three years, I have had the good fortune to be associated with a judicial review panel of the ILO. I have been impressed at the extent to which the basic features of effective implementation are built into the constitutional structure of the ILO—fact-finding, exposure, conciliation and adjudication. The handling of complaints, which is the heart of meaningful enforcement of human rights, has been carefully structured in a precise procedural manner. What is more important, there is a record demonstrating that these arrangements have produced concrete results . . . The ILO experience can be applied to the entire range of human rights concerns.[10]

[8] C. Jenks, The International Protection of Trade Union Freedom 37–38 (1957); *see* Jenks, *The International Protection of Trade Union Rights*, in The International Protection of Human Rights (E. Luard ed. 1957).

[9] Chief Justice Warren was a member of the ILO Committee of Experts on the Application of Conventions and Recommendations from 1970 to the time of his death in 1974.

[10] Quoted in Wolf, *ILO Experience*, *supra* note 1, at 601–02 (footnote omitted).

The machinery of the ILO for the implementation of human rights has also been favorably cited in a report submitted to the United States House of Representatives Committee on Foreign Affairs by its Subcommittee on International Organizations and Movements.[11] In testimony before the Subcommittee, it was noted that 'ILO procedures for inquiring into alleged breaches of their Conventions are probably the most sophisticated and most effective in the international sphere',[12] and that the methods of the ILO 'for the protection of human rights should be emulated by other international organizations'.[13]

The methods and procedures for the protection of human rights which exist in the ILO may be grouped under two headings. The first, that of *permanent supervision*, acts as a catalyst to obtain the widest possible application of the instruments concerned, and seeks to detect or prevent any derogation from conventions that have been ratified. Under this heading fall the submission by governments of reports on the implementation of conventions and recommendations; the examination of these reports by a committee of independent experts; and the discussion of problems of application and compliance with constitutional provisions relating to conventions and recommendations by a tripartite committee of the International Labour Conference.[14] The advantages of these methods are that they help states in the proper discharge of their obligations and that they permit the ILO to secure the application of universally valid legal rules formulated in pursuit of its aims.

In addition to reporting procedures, there exists another form of supervision based on *contentious proceedings*, following the presentation of representations and complaints.[15]

These methods and procedures—some of which are constitutional in character, while others have been progressively developed and adopted on an empirical basis—constitute the main stay of ILO experience in the implementation of standards relating to human rights. It may be useful, therefore, to examine briefly the manner in which they operate.

B. PERMANENT SUPERVISION OF THE APPLICATION OF ILO STANDARDS

1. *Information and reports*

a. *Information on the submission of conventions and recommendations to the competent authorities.* The ILO Constitution requires

[11] Human Rights in the World Community: A Call for U.S. Leadership (1974).
[12] *Id.* at 44.
[13] *Id.* at 45.
[14] For further details of this type of procedure, *see* section I.B, *infra*.
[15] For further details of this type of procedure and the cases involved, *see* section I.C. *infra*.

member States to bring any convention or recommendation adopted by the International Labour Conference before the competent authority —in most cases the national parliament[16]—for the enactment of legislation or other action. The obligation arises for each member whatever the attitude of its delegates at the Conference or the opinion of the government about ultimate ratification. The submission to the competent authority should generally be made within one year, and in no case later than eighteen months from the closing of the session of the Conference at which the convention[17] or recommendation[18] was adopted. In federal States, when a convention or recommendation contains elements on which action by the constituent units would be appropriate, arrangements must be made so that questions within the competence of the constituent units may be submitted to their proper authorities within the eighteen month period.[19]

The ILO Constitution also requires members to inform the Director-General of the International Labour Office of the measures they have taken to bring conventions and recommendations before the competent authorities, with particulars of such authorities and of the action those authorities have taken. This obligation is reinforced by the provisions of article 30 of the ILO Constitution, which authorizes a member to report to the Governing Body the failure of any other member to bring a convention or recommendation before its competent authorities.[20] If the Governing Body finds that there has been such a breach, it must report the matter to the Conference which may take whatever action it deems fit on the matter.

For purposes of convenience and uniformity, the information to be provided by members is indicated in a memorandum approved by the Governing Body of the International Labour Office in accordance with a decision by the International Labour Conference in 1953,[21] and last revised in 1980.[22]

b. *Reports on ratified conventions.* Since ratification is the act through which a convention creates binding legal obligations for member states, one of the main purposes of the system of international

[16] On the nature of the competent authority, *see* Memorandum of the Legal Adviser of the ILO, annexed to Report 1, Principles of Action, Programme and Statute of the ILO, 26th Sess. of the International Labour Conference 178 (1944); Minutes of the Governing Body of the International Labour Office 140th Sess. (Nov. 1958) at 96; ILO Doc. Appl. 19 S (Rev. 3) entitled 'Memorandum concerning the obligation to submit Conventions and Recommendations to the competent authorities' (1980).

[17] ILO Const. art 19(5)(b).

[18] *Id.* art. 19(6)(b).

[19] *Id.* art. 19(7)(b)(i).

[20] *See id.* art. 19(5)(c), 19(6)(c), 19(7)(b)(iii).

[21] 36th Sess., Proc. International Labour Conference, 393 (1953).

[22] *See* ILO Doc. Appl. 19S (Rev. 3) (1980).

labour standards is their ultimate ratification. The total number of ratifications in 1982 was over 5,000. This represents an impressive network of international commitments in the field of labour and human rights.

The constitutional obligation of a member state with respect to a convention does not terminate with ratification of the convention and the state's undertaking to make the convention effective. Members are required to submit annual reports on ratified conventions, in such form and containing such particulars as the Governing Body may request, to the International Labour Office.[23]

At the present time, detailed reports may be requested at one-year, two-year, or four-year intervals.[24] A government's first report on a ratified convention is due in the year following the date of its entry into force for the country concerned. The next two reports are then due at two-year intervals. After that, while for the majority of technical conventions reporting is at four-year intervals, reports relating to basic human rights (freedom of association, abolition of forced labour, equality of opportunity and treatment in employment, and migrant workers, among others) continue at least at two-year intervals.[25] In order to comply with the constitutional requirement that states report annually on the measures taken to give effect to ratified conventions, governments are required to supply a general report each year on those conventions for which detailed reports are not required that year.

c. *Reports on unratified conventions and recommendations.* The non-ratification of a convention is not a license for a member to ignore it. According to article 19(5)(e) of the ILO Constitution, if the competent authority fails to consent to the ratification of a convention, the government concerned must report to the Director-General of the International Labour Office, at appropriate intervals as requested by the Governing Body, the position of its law and practice in regard to the matters dealt with in the convention, and the effect which has been given, or is proposed to be given, to the instrument. Members are required to submit similar reports with respect to recommendations.[26] The practice in the application of these provisions is that every year the Governing Body chooses the conventions or recommendations for which such reports are to be requested, taking into account the importance of current interest of the instruments concerned. In doing so, the

[23] ILO Const. art. 22.

[24] For a full statement of the rules governing the reporting system, *see* 60 (No. 2) ILO O. Bull. (Ser. A) 45–46 (1977).

[25] For more detailed information on the operation of the system, *see* Samson, *The Changing Pattern of ILO Supervision*, 118 Int'l Labour Rev. 569, 570–71 [hereinafter cited as Samson].

[26] ILO Const. art. 19(6)(d).

Governing Body has in the past given a preponderant place to conventions and recommendations relating to human rights.

For instance, those governments which had not ratified the conventions dealing with forced labour were requested to supply reports in 1978 indicating the position of their law and practice in regard to the standards contained in those conventions. The receipt of these reports provided an opportunity for the Committee of Experts on the Application of Conventions and Recommendations[27] to make a general survey of the situation of the field covered by forced labour conventions in both ratifying and non-ratifying states.[28]

On the basis of a resolution adopted by the International Labour Conference at its 63rd session in June 1977, the Governing Body decided in 1979 to request member states which had not ratified the Discrimination (Employment and Occupation) Convention, 1958 (No. 111), to report at four-year intervals on their position with respect to that Convention, particularly as regards difficulty giving rise to non-ratification, steps being considered to overcome them, and prospects of ratification. The Conference resolution had stated that non-discrimination, like freedom of association, was a basic principle of the ILO and a constitutional obligation on all member states, and it requested the Governing Body to study ways and means of establishing or strengthening procedures for the supervision of this constitutional obligation.

In 1982, governments were required to report on the Freedom of Association and Protection of the Right to Organise Convention, 1948 (No. 87), on the Right to Organise and Collective Bargaining Convention, 1949 (No. 98), and on the Rural Workers' Organisations Convention, 1975 (No. 141), and Recommendation, 1975 (No. 149).

d. *Involvement of employers' and workers' organizations in the supervisory procedures*. Every year, the supervisory bodies of the ILO draw special attention to the role which employers' and workers' organizations may and should play, in the context of the supervisory procedures, in assessing whether conventions and recommendations are being satisfactorily implemented within their countries. One aspect of this role is based on article 23(2) of the ILO Constitution, which requires governments to send copies of their reports to the most representative employers' and workers' organizations in their countries. This procedure enables those organizations to submit observations concerning the measures taken by their governments to meet their obligations, particularly as regards the practical application of

[27] *See* section I.B.2a *infra*.

[28] *See* Abolition of Forced Labour, General Survey by the Committee of Experts, 65th Sess., International Labour Conference (1979).

ratified conventions. The supervisory bodies have always encouraged the submission of such observations, and there has been a steady increase in the number of observations received by the International Labour Office following the introduction of various practical measures to assist organizations in this field.[29]

The nature of these observations and the importance of the issues which they raise vary considerably from case to case. However, experience has shown that observations from employers' and workers' organizations which call for greater compliance with ratified conventions are frequently followed up by the governments concerned.[30]

In recent years, further action has been taken to strengthen tripartism in the ILO's activities. In 1971, the International Labour Conference adopted a resolution concerning the strengthening of tripartism in the overall activities of the ILO. This resolution led, on the one hand, to closer attention being paid by the supervisory bodies to observance of requirements in conventions regarding the association or consultation of employers' and workers' organizations in the implementation of ILO standards and, on the other hand, to the placing on the agenda of the conference of the question of establishing national tripartite machinery to improve the implementation of ILO standards. The latter action resulted in the adoption in 1976 of the Tripartite Consultation (International Labour Standards) Convention (No. 144) and the Tripartite Consultation (Activities of the Institutional Labour Organization Recommendation (No. 152).[31]

2. *Supervisory bodies*

The reporting system can only be used to advantage if the information and reports submitted by members are properly scrutinized in order to ascertain that conventions and recommendations are sub-

[29] Prior to 1973 when these measures were introduced, the number of observations received from employers' and workers' organizations each year was well under 20, whereas in recent years it has not fallen below 50 and has been considerably higher in some years. *See* Reports of the Committee of Experts, Report III, Part 4A, of each session of the International Labour Conference.

[30] In the year from Apr. 1974 to Mar. 1975, for example, legislative and other measures were taken, as a consequence of such observations, by the government of Barbados in respect of the Freedom of Association and Protection of the Right to Organise Convention, 1948 (No. 87), and the Right to Organise and Collective Bargaining Convention, 1949 (No. 98); and by the governments of Dahomey and the Republic of Viet-Nam in regard to the Minimum Wage-Fixing Machinery Convention, 1928 (No. 26). In other cases—relating to the application of conventions nos. 87 and 98 by Japan, and the Placing of Seamen Convention, 1921 (No. 9) by The Netherlands—measures were also taken by the governments concerned. *See also* Report of the Committee of Experts, Report III, Part 4A, at 28–29, 65 Sess., International Labour Conference (1979).

[31] As of Mar. 1982, the Convention had been ratified by 26 member states and some 13 others had indicated their intention of ratifying it. *See* Report of the Committee of Experts, Report III, Part 4B, 68th Sess., International Labour Conference (1982). *See also* Samson, *supra* note 25, at 574–75.

mitted to the competent authorities, that ratified conventions are duly complied with, and what difficulties prevent or delay ratification or implementation.

A few years after the establishment of the ILO, certain delegates to the International Labour Conference expressed concern that the reports submitted by members did not receive sufficient consideration from the Conference.[32] As a result, the Conference adopted at its 8th session in 1926 a resolution which authorized the Governing Body to appoint a Committee of Experts to make a preliminary report on the annual reports submitted by governments. The resolution also provided that every future session of the Conference should set up a special committee to consider the annual reports.[33]

a. *The Committee of Experts on the Application of Conventions and Recommendations.*[34] In accordance with the decision of the Conference in 1926, the Committee of Experts on the Application of Conventions and Recommendations was established by the Governing Body in the interval between the 1926 and 1927 sessions of the Conference. It is now composed of nineteen members appointed by the Governing Body on the proposal of the Director-General of the International Labour Office. These members are appointed in their personal capacity and not as representatives of their governments, and are chosen from among persons of recognized technical competence and complete independence—they are normally drawn from the judiciary or from academia but occasionally persons with considerable experience in public administration are appointed. Appointments are for periods of three years, which are renewable.

The primary function of the Committee of Experts is to examine the information and reports submitted by governments, in order to establish the extent to which each state has complied with its obligations under ratified conventions and under the provisions of the ILO Constitution relating to conventions and recommendations.[35] In the discharge of this task, the Committee of Experts is guided by the fundamental principles of supervision: independence, impartiality, and objectivity.

The Committee of Experts holds an annual session of about three

[32] *See, e.g.*, 7th Sess., International Labour Conference, Rec. Proc. 156–57 (1925).

[33] 8th Sess., International Labour Conference, Rec. Proc. 429, 238–44 (1926).

[34] For further details on this Committee, *see* Wolf, *Aspects Judiciaires de la Protection Internationale des Droits de l'Homme par l'O.I.T.*, 4 Revue des Droits de l'Homme, 781–87 (1971) [hereinafter cited as Wolf, *Aspects Judiciaires*].

[35] On the function of the Committee of Experts, *see generally* Valticos, *Un système de contrôle international: La mise en œuvre des Conventions internationales de Travail*, Recueil des Cours de l'Académie de Droit Internationale 311 (1968–I).

weeks on dates fixed by the Governing Body.[36] It organizes its work by assigning each of its members initial responsibility for a group of conventions; government reports and relevant documentation are sent to the expert concerned for examination prior to the Committee's session. Each member responsible for a group of conventions or a given subject submits his or her conclusions to the Committee of Experts as a whole. In addition, the Committee appoints working groups from among its members to deal with questions of principle or questions of a particularly complex nature. These working groups generally meet for a few days before the Committee's session and sometimes during the session as well. Their conclusions also are submitted to the Committee of Experts as a whole.[37] The Committee of Experts has kept its general working methods under review and in 1969, in 1971, and most recently on the occasion of its fiftieth anniversary in 1977 has set out in its report a detailed description of its principles and working methods. In the 1977 review, the Committee of Experts re-affirmed that its function is to determine whether the requirements of a given convention are being met, whatever the economic and social conditions in a given country. Subject only to any derogations which are expressly permitted by the convention itself, a convention's requirements remain constant and uniform for all countries. In carrying out this work, the Committee of Experts is guided by the standards laid down in the convention alone, mindful, however, of the fact that the modes of implementation may differ in different states.[38]

The comments of the Committee of Experts on ratified conventions take the form of observations which are incorporated in a printed report which is communicated to the member states and presented to the Conference for discussion. On points of secondary importance or calling for clarification, the Committee of Experts sends direct requests to the government involved, which are not published. The Committee of Experts also reports on and lists any specific improvements which have resulted from its previous comments.

The Committee of Experts also deals with unratified conventions and with recommendations. Basing itself on the reports submitted by

[36] The Committee elects its Chairman and Reporter at the beginning of each session and decides its procedure. It meets *in camera* and its deliberations and documents remain confidential. *See* Wolf, *Aspects Judiciaires*, *supra* note 34, at 281.

[37] Traditionally the conclusions of the Committee of Experts are unanimous. However, any minority views are recorded in its report, if the members concerned so request. The Report of the Committee of Experts is submitted to the Governing Body and presented to the following session of the Conference. *See* Report III, Part 4, at 6–15, 63d Sess., International Labour Conference (1977) (Description of the methods and procedures relating to the work of the Committee of Experts on the Application of Conventions and Recommendations).

[38] Report of the Committee of Experts, Report III, Part 4A, at 10–11, 63d Sess., International Labour Conference (1979).

governments on the instruments selected for reporting by the Governing Body, the Committee of Experts presents an overall survey of the way in which, and the extent to which, the relevant instruments are applied together with an indication of any prospects for the ratification of the conventions concerned. The Committee of Experts also explains how obstacles to full implementation of the instruments might be overcome.

The effect of the comments of the Committee of Experts depends on the kind of response they evoke from governments. With this essential purpose in mind, the Committee of Experts has endeavored not only to draw attention to any lack of conformity with a ratified convention, but also to focus on the positive steps needed to ensure better implementation. The results which have been achieved in this respect are encouraging.[39] Since 1964, over 1,400 discrepancies have been rectified by governments as a result of observations and direct requests made by the Committee of Experts, with many of these related to conventions on basic human rights.[40]

In addition to its supervisory functions with respect to ILO instruments, the Committee of Experts has assumed new responsibilities in the wider context of co-operation between international organizations in supervising the implementation of the International Covenant on Economic, Social and Cultural Rights. In November 1976, the Governing Body of the ILO decided to accede to the request of ECOSOC[41] that specialized agencies report to it on the progress made in achieving observance of the provisions of that Covenant falling within the scope of their activities, including the particulars of decisions and recommendations on implementation adopted by their competent organs. The Governing Body decided at the same time that the Committee of Experts should undertake this new task.[42] The Committee of Experts has examined these matters during each of its sessions since 1978 and has submitted reports to ECOSOC[43] relating to the implementation of articles 6 to 12 of the Economic Covenant by states parties whose reports were transmitted to the ILO by the United Nations.

[39] In 60% of cases in which divergencies were established, governments took the measures necessary to correct the situation and to eliminate, at least in part, the divergencies which had been brought to light. *See* E. Landy, The Effectiveness of International Supervision—30 Years of ILO Experience (1966). *See also* Landy, *The Influence of International Labour Conventions: Possibilities and Performance*, 101 Int'l Labour Rev. 555 (1970).

[40] *See* Report of the Committee of Experts, Report III, Part 4A, at 22–23, 68th Sess., International Labour Conference (1982).

[41] *See* ECOSOC Res. 1988 (LX) (1976).

[42] *See* 201st Sess., Minutes of the Governing Body of the International Labour Office, Agenda Item 15, § 26 (Nov. 1976).

[43] These ECOSOC reports were issued as U.N. documents E/1978/27, E/1979/33, E/1980/35, E/1981/41, and E/1982/41.

b. *The Conference Committee on the Application of Conventions and Recommendations*. During each of its annual sessions, the International Labour Conference establishes a tripartite Committee to consider and report on information and reports given by members of the ILO on the application of conventions and recommendations.[44] The Conference Committee on the Application of Conventions and Recommendations commences its work with a general discussion of questions arising out of the application of conventions and recommendations and the discharge by member states of their obligations under the ILO Constitution, based mainly on the information contained in the report of the Committee of Experts. It next discusses the general survey made by the Committee of Experts of the effect given to selected unratified conventions and recommendations. It concludes its work by examining individual cases concerning the application of ratified conventions and compliance with the constitutional obligations concerning conventions and recommendations, drawing mainly on the observations made by the Committee of Experts. In view of time constraints, the Conference Committee confines its discussion to a limited number of cases chosen from among those which have been the subject of observations by the Committee of Experts.

Over the past twenty years, the Conference Committee has adopted the practice of drawing the attention of the Conference to cases in which governments appeared to encounter serious difficulties in discharging obligations under the ILO Constitution or under conventions which they have ratified. In recent years, the Conference Committee has drawn attention to certain important cases by means of special paragraphs. In 1979 and 1980 it undertook a thorough re-examination of its methods of work and introduced certain changes in the presentation of its report. Although the form has changed—formerly attention was drawn to particular cases by means of a 'Special List'—the Conference Committee continues in its report to identify the cases of serious failure to comply with obligations relating to conventions and recommendations; to include a brief reference to special cases among those which it has discussed and to which it considers it appropriate to draw the attention of the Conference; and to list in its report any cases of continuing failure over several years to eliminate serious deficiencies in the application of ratified conventions which it has discussed in previous reports.[45]

[44] The Committee set up by the 67th Session of the Conference in June 1981 was composed of 168 members: 93 Government members, 21 Employers' members, and 54 Workers' members. It also included 11 Government deputy members, 26 Employers' deputy members, and 58 Workers' deputy members. As in the case of all the committees of the Conference, each of the three groups possesses the same number of votes and where the number of the representatives from the groups is not the same, the votes are weighted to maintain equality between the groups. *See* art. 65, Standing Orders of the Conference.

c. *The system of direct contacts.* In 1967, the Committee of Experts raised the question of whether more varied procedures might not make possible a fuller examination of certain questions and a more fruitful dialogue with governments. It then put forward a general suggestion for direct contacts with governments for the purpose of enabling it to reach its conclusions with due regard to all relevant considerations and of finding positive solutions to problems encountered in the application of conventions. The Conference Committee on the Application of Conventions and Recommendations agreed that the suggestion merited further exploration and requested the Committee of Experts to submit more precise and detailed proposals on the matter. In 1968, the Committee of Experts formulated principles and methods to be applied in initiating direct contacts with governments.[46]

According to these principles, the Committee of Experts, the Conference Committee, or the government concerned may take the initiative in suggesting such contacts. However, in the majority of cases in which direct contacts have taken place, the initiative has come from the government concerned. It sends a written communication to the Director-General of the International Labour Office, from whom an affirmative reply, also in the form of a written communication, is needed before direct contacts can be established.[47]

These contacts are intended to supplement and not to replace or limit the responsibilities of the established supervisory bodies of the ILO. Indeed, direct contacts appear to have fulfilled three essential functions. They have been used, as a form of technical assistance, to provide advice to states concerning the nature of action to be taken to meet their obligations under the ILO Constitution and international labour conventions; they have been used for fact-finding in cases where the practical application of national and international standards was at issue; and, in cases where there has been major problems or conflicting views between a government and the ILO supervisory bodies, especially in the field of basic human rights, direct contacts have provided an opportunity for fuller explanation of the positions of the parties and for the exploration of possible ways to eliminate the differences which existed.

In general, direct contacts take the form of detailed discussions between a representative of the Director-General of the International Labour Office, who visits the country in question with the consent of the government concerned, and representatives of the relevant govern-

[45] *See* Prov. Rec. No. 37, at 4–7, 12–13, 19–22, 66th Sess., International Labour Conference (June 1980). For further details on the operation of the former 'special list', *see* Wolf, *ILO Experience, supra* note 1, at 611–12.

[46] Report III, Part 4A, at 13–17, 65th Sess., International Labour Conference (1979).

[47] Report III, Part 4A, at 13, 58th Sess., International Labour Conference (1973).

ment agencies who have sufficient responsibility and experience to speak with authority about the situation in their country and about their government's attitudes and intentions in the matter and to explain all the elements of the case. Contact is also made with the employers' and workers' organizations in the course of the visit. The Committee of Experts and the Conference Committee have been able to note in many cases that governments have taken action to improve compliance with their obligations in the cases that had been the subject of these contacts.[48]

C. CONTENTIOUS PROCEDURES

Two types of contentious procedure, *i.e.*, representations and complaints, round out this discussion of methods of supervision of the application of ratified conventions. These procedures are of general application, are regulated by the ILO Constitution, and have been resorted to particularly with respect to the application of the basic human rights conventions.

1. *Representations against members*

In accordance with the provisions of article 24 of the ILO Constitution, an industrial association of employers or of workers may submit a representation to the International Labour Office that any of the members of the ILO has failed to secure in any respect the effective observation within its jurisdiction of any convention to which it is a party. After the receipt of the representation, the Governing Body may communicate it to the government concerned and may invite that government to make a statement. If no statement is received within a reasonable time from the government, or if the statement, when received, is not deemed to be satisfactory by the Governing Body, the latter can publish the representation and the statement, if any, made in reply.[49] A fundamental feature of this procedure is that it allows employers' and workers' organizations to initiate procedures to examine the implementation by members of the ILO of conventions which those states have ratified.

Very little use was made of the representations procedure for many years, but the situation appears to be changing. There has been a growing tendency to resort to the procedure in recent years, particularly with respect to the implementation of the basic human rights

[48] In the first ten years, direct contacts took place in 28 countries (15 in Latin America, 7 in Africa, 4 in Asia, and 2 in Europe). They involved discussion of some 222 cases of shortcomings in the application of ratified conventions. In 115 cases, affecting 23 countries, the Committee of Experts subsequently noted improvements. Other results have included improved compliance with various constitutional obligations and additional ratifications. *See* Report of the Committee of Experts, Report III, Part 4A, at 13–27, 65th Sess., International Labour Conference (1979).

[49] ILO Const. art. 25.

conventions. In recent years, four representations have been received by the International Labour Office alleging the non-observance of the Discrimination (Employment and Occupation) Convention, 1958 (No. 111). The first representation was submitted by the World Federation of Trade Unions (WFTU) against the countries belonging to the European Economic Community (EEC) alleging that the 'political policing' inquiry conducted by EEC authorities constituted discrimination in respect of employment against the officials affected on the grounds of political opinion, directly involving the responsibility of the then nine EEC governments both from the point of view of the international labour standards they had ratified and because of moral responsibility. The tripartite committee set up by the Governing Body to examine this representation recommended that it should be declared irreceivable.[50] The second representation was submitted by the International Confederation of Free Trade Unions (ICFTU) against Czechoslovakia alleging that it had taken repressive measures affecting the employment of authors or signatories of documents which brought to public attention criticisms of that government's policy in the field of human rights. The Governing Body concluded in this case that the government's reply was not satisfactory and decided that the representation and the reply should be published together with the report of the tripartite committee.[51] The third representation was submitted by the WFTU against the Federal Republic of Germany alleging that the many cases arising from the application of the so-called 'work ban' (*Berufsverbot*)—in particular since the adoption by the Länder Prime Ministers' Conference in January 1972 of the Anti-Radical Decree (*Radikalererlass*) which bars citizens from access to employment or exercise of their occupation, particularly in the civil service, on the grounds of their political beliefs—amounted to a gross breach of the Convention. After examining the representation, the tripartite committee recommended to the Governing Body that it declare the case closed. Lastly, in 1982 the Norwegian Federation of Trade Unions submitted a representation against the Government of Norway alleging that amendments to labour legislation adopted in 1982 contravened Convention No. 111 by permitting employers to inquire into the political, religious or cultural views of job applicants even in circumstances where such inquiry was not justified by the nature of the job. This case is still under examination.[52]

[50] *See* 205th Sess., Governing Body Feb. 28–Mar. 3, 1978), ILO. Doc. GB.205/8/17, at 4 (1978).

[51] *See* 61 (No. 3) ILO O. Bull. (Ser. A) (Supp.) 5–6 (1978).

[52] 63 (No. 1) ILO O. Bull. (Ser. A) (1980); 210th Sess., Governing Body (May–June 1979), ILO Doc. GB.210/16/27, at 8 (1979). Regarding the 1982 Norwegian representation, *see* ILO Doc. GB.220/16/28 (1982).

2. *Complaints against members*

The complaint procedure is the most far-reaching of the supervisory procedures of the ILO. Its operation is based on the provisions of articles 26 to 29 and 31 to 34 of the ILO Constitution. Any member of the ILO has a right to file a complaint with the International Labour Office that it is not satisfied that another member is securing the effective observance of any convention which both have ratified.[53] Once a complaint has been received, the Governing Body may follow several courses. It may communicate the complaint to the government against which it is made—in the same manner as a representation under article 24[54]—and may invite that government to make such statement as it thinks fit on the matter.[55] If the Governing Body does not think it necessary to communicate the complaint or if, after such communication, a satisfactory response is not received within a reasonable time, the Governing Body may appoint a Commission of Inquiry to consider the complaint and to report thereon.[56] The Governing Body may also adopt these procedures on its own motion or on receipt of a complaint from a delegate to the Conference.[57] In this way, employers and workers who are represented on the Conference delegations may make a complaint leading to the establishment of a Commission of Inquiry.

In practice, when a complaint results in the creation of a Commission of Inquiry, the Commission is composed of three independent, highly qualified persons appointed by the Governing Body on the proposal of the Director-General of the International Labour Office.[58] This practice stems from the need to ensure that matters which are often very complex and controversial are examined in a completely impartial and objective manner.[59] The procedure followed by these Commissions (assembly of documentation, hearing of parties and of witnesses, and on-the-spot visits where necessary) is carried out in a judicial and impartial manner.[60]

When the Commission of Inquiry has fully considered the com-

[53] ILO Const. art 26(1).

[54] *See* section C.1 *supra*.

[55] ILO Const. art. 26(2).

[56] *Id.* art. 26(3).

[57] *Id.* art. 26(4).

[58] These normally include at least one person who has held high judicial office. Indeed, the Chairman of the Commission of Inquiry on the complaint against Chile was José Luis Bustamante i Rivero, a former President of the International Court of Justice.

[59] The members of a commission make a declaration that they will perform their duties and exercise their powers 'honourably, faithfully, impartially, and conscientiously'—a solemn declaration which corresponds to that made by judges of the International Court of Justice. *See* Wolf, *Aspects Judiciaires*, *supra* note 34, at 809.

[60] *See* Osieke, *The Exercise of Judicial Function with Respect to the International Labour Organisation*, 47 Brit. Y.B. Int'l L. 315, 330–38 (1974–1975) [hereinafter cited as Osieke].

plaint, it prepares a report embodying its findings on all questions of fact relevant to determining the issue between the parties and containing such recommendations as it may think proper as to the steps which should be taken to meet the complaint and the time within which they should be taken.[61] The Director-General communicates the report to the Governing Body and to each of the governments concerned and arranges for its publication.[62] Each of these governments is required to inform the Director-General within three months of whether it accepts the recommendations contained in the report of the Commission and, if not, whether it proposes to refer the complaint to the International Court of Justice (ICJ).[63] The ICJ may affirm, vary, or reverse any of the findings or recommendations of the Commission of Inquiry,[64] and its decision in this respect is final.[65] If any member of the ILO fails to carry out within the time specified the recommendations contained in the report of the Commission of Inquiry or in the decision of the ICJ, the Governing Body may recommend to the Conference such action as it may deem wise and expedient to secure compliance.[66]

The complaint procedure has been used mostly in the last two decades, during which time thirteen complaints have been received, as compared to one complaint during the first forty years of the ILO's existence. It is interesting, moreover, that many of these complaints were made in connection with the observance of the basic human rights conventions. The instruments on forced labour have been the subject of four complaints;[67] seven complaints concerned the freedom of association conventions;[68] and one complaint was made with re-

[61] ILO Const. art. 28.

[62] *Id.* art. 29(1).

[63] *Id.* art. 29(2).

[64] *Id.* art. 32.

[65] *Id.* art. 31.

[66] *Id.* art. 33.

[67] *See* the complaint filed by Ghana against Portugal in 1961 concerning the observance of the Abolition of Forced Labour Convention, 1957 (No. 105); and the complaint by Portugal against Liberia in 1961 with respect to the application of the Forced Labour Convention, 1930 (No. 29). 45 (No. 2) ILO O. Bull. (Supp. 2) (1962); ILO, Report of the Portugal v. Liberia Commission of Inquiry 46 (No. 2) ILO O. Bull. (Supp. 2) (1963). *See also* Osieke, *supra* note 60, at 327–29. Complaints against the Dominican Republic and Haiti concerning the observance of several Conventions, including the two Conventions on forced labour (Nos. 29 and 105) were filed in 1981 and are at present being examined by a Commission of Inquiry; ILO Doc. GB.217/4/8, GB.217/4/9 and GB.218/6/10.

[68] All the complaints were made by worker delegates to the Conference, as follows: (a) in 1968 against Greece for the non-observance of the Freedom of Association and Protection of the Rights to Organise Convention, 1948 (No. 87); and the Right to Organise and Collective Bargaining Convention, 1949 (No. 98); 54 (No. 2) ILO O. Bull. (1972); (b) in 1975 against Bolivia for the non-observance of Convention No. 87; ILO Doc. GB.198/6/4; (c) in 1976 against Uruguay concerning the non-observance of Conventions Nos. 87 and 98; ILO Doc. GB.200/17/44; (d) in 1977 against Argentina concerning the non-observance of Convention No. 87; ILO Doc. GB.203/19/42; (e) in 1981 against the Dominican Republic and against Haiti

spect to the Discrimination (Employment and Occupation) Convention, (No. 111).[69] Several of these cases were referred to Commissions of Inquiry for examination.[70] When the Commission finds that there has been non-observance of the convention in question, it makes recommendations as to the measures that should be taken by the government concerned to fulfill its obligations under the convention. It is normally left to the regular supervisory bodies to follow-up the implementation of these recommendations.

D. SPECIAL FREEDOM OF ASSOCIATION PROCEDURES

The general procedures described above apply to the conventions on freedom of association as they do to all the others, but in view of the importance of freedom of association, the ILO has established additional machinery for its protection. This involves the examination of complaints by the Governing Body's Committee on Freedom of Association and by the Fact-Finding and Conciliation Commission on Freedom of Association. The complaints may even concern states which have not ratified the freedom of association conventions. For such states, the application of this machinery is based on their membership in the ILO and on the fact that the ILO Constitution has affirmed the principle of freedom of association; the ILO can accordingly promote the realization of this principle through procedures of investigation and conciliation.

1. *The Committee on Freedom of Association*

This Committee, which was established by the Governing Body at its 117th session in November 1951 from among its members on a tripartite basis, in the first instance examines all complaints received and reports to the Governing Body on whether the complaints appear substantiated. It also determines whether recommendations should be addressed to the governments concerned or whether, in appropriate cases, a complaint should be referred to the Fact-Finding and Concilia-

for the non-observance of Conventions Nos. 87 and 98; *see* note 67 *supra*; and (f) in 1982 against Poland for non-observance of Conventions Nos. 87 and 98; ILO Doc. GB.220/16/26.

[69] *See* the complaint initiated by the Governing Body against Chile concerning the observance of the Hours of Work Convention, 1919 (No. 1); and the Discrimination (Employment and Occupation) Convention, 1958 (No. 111). International Labour Office Report of the Commission of Inquiry in the Case of Chile (1975).

[70] In three of the cases relating to conventions on freedom of association, the Governing Body decided to refer the complaints first to its Committee on Freedom of Association prior to any decision as to the establishment of a Commission of Inquiry. *See* Samson, *supra* note 25, at 578. In some of the cases referred to a Commission of Inquiry, the members of the Commission visited the territories of the state against which the complaint was made in order to ascertain whether reasonably specific allegations were supported by current or recent facts. *See* Osieke, *supra* note 60, at 332.

tion Commission. Wide recourse has been had to this special machinery. Since its establishment in 1951, the Committee on Freedom of Association has considered about 1,100 cases, with the number of complaints increasing considerably in recent years. Whereas the Committee used to receive about 30 new complaints each year, the numbers for 1980 and 1981 were 66 and 88 respectively.[71]

In trying first to establish the facts, the Committee on Freedom of Association follows the basic rule of all contentious procedures, namely, that of giving the opposing parties an opportunity to put forward their points of view. Accordingly, the complaints are communicated to the governments against which they are made so that they may submit their observations. In a case where a doubt or contradiction exists, or if it appears useful to inform the complainants of the observations of the government, the substance of these observations is communicated to them for their comments, and questions may be put to them. The Committee on Freedom of Association has frequently reviewed its procedure to introduce improvements, expedite the examination of cases, and ensure the follow-up of its recommendations. Over the years, a number of measures have been adopted by the Committee, and approved by the Governing Body, in order to achieve this purpose. Most recently, the Committee has started in certain cases to invite the government concerned to send a representative to provide oral information at its meetings. Increasing use has also been made of the procedure of direct contacts, described above, in order to permit an on-the-spot examination and discussion of certain cases.[72]

The influence of the Committee on Freedom of Association is primarily a moral one, deriving from the objectivity of its procedures, the persuasive effect and authority of its unanimous conclusions, and the publicity given its work. The Committee has succeeded—and this is in fact one of its main achievements—in gaining wider recognition for the international value of the principles of freedom of association. A substantial proportion of the cases examined by the Committee have raised issues relating to fundamental human rights, particularly in connection with the arrest, detention, or exile of trade unionists. In many of these cases, including in particular cases where the measures complained of had not been taken within the context of judicial proceedings, the governments concerned have finally released the persons in question or allowed their return from exile. There is no

[71] *See* von Potobsky, *Protection of Trade Union Rights: Twenty Years Work by the Committee on Freedom of Association*, Int'l Labour Rev. 69 (1972). *See generally* International Labour Office, Digest of the decisions of the Freedom of Association Committee of the Governing Body of the ILO (1974); Samson, *supra* note 25, at 579.

[72] On the Committee on Freedom of Association's procedures *see* Comm. on Freedom of Association, 193d Report, 62 (No. 1) ILO O. Bull (Ser. B) 155 (1979).

doubt that the action and efforts of the Committee on Freedom of Association in these matters have contributed to a large extent in obtaining the desired results from governments.

2. *The Fact-Finding and Conciliation Commission on Freedom of Association*

This Commission was established in 1950 by an agreement between the ILO and the United Nations. Its function is to examine such cases of alleged infringements of trade union rights as may be referred to it, to ascertain the facts, and to discuss the situation with the government concerned with a view to securing by agreement the adjustment of difficulties.

The Fact-Finding and Conciliation Commission is composed of independent persons appointed by the Governing Body on the proposal of the Director-General of the International Labour Office. The Governing Body refers cases to the Commission on the recommendation of the Committee on Freedom of Association. Complaints may also be referred to the Fact-Finding and Conciliation Commission at the request of the United Nations when the complaints concern member states of the United Nations which are not members of the ILO. In principle, no complaint may be referred to the Commission without the consent of the government concerned, except in cases covered by article 26 of the ILO Constitution.[73]

Four cases have so far been referred to the Fact-Finding and Conciliation Commission. These concerned respectively Japan,[74] Greece,[75] Lesotho,[76] and Chile.[77] The procedure followed by the Commission in dealing with these cases has been analogous to the procedure of the Commissions of Inquiry which are responsible for examining complaints with respect to ratified conventions.[78]

After examining the allegations, the Fact-Finding and Conciliation Commission normally recommends the measures to be adopted by the government concerned in order to ensure observance of the principles of freedom of association enshrined in the ILO Constitution. In certain cases, the implementation of the recommendations of the Commission may not be sufficient to restore confidence and trust between the parties, or even to ensure free trade union rights, and the government may be expected to take other measures beyond the field of trade

[73] *See* section C.2 *supra*

[74] 54 (No. 1) ILO O. Bull. (Spec. Supp.) (1966).

[75] 54 (No. 3) ILO O. Bull. (Spec. Supp.) (1966).

[76] *See* ILO Doc. GB.197/3/5 (1975).

[77] International Labour Office, The Trade Union Situation in Chile: Report of the Fact-Finding and Conciliation Commission on Freedom of Association (1975) [hereinafter cited as Trade Union Situation in Chile].

[78] *See* section C.2 *supra.*

union rights as such in order to fully meet the situation. This appeared to be the situation in the case concerning Chile, where the Fact-Finding and Conciliation Commission stated that while the implementation of its recommendations

> will contribute towards the normalisation of the trade union movement . . . [it] will not suffice to ensure the free exercise of trade union rights. Many trade unionists will continue to be pursued by a feeling of constraint, and even of fear, until they are assured that there will be respect for the human rights which are essential to the normal pursuit of trade union activities, and in particular the right to freedom and personal safety, and to protection from arrest and arbitrary imprisonment, the right to a proper trial before an independent and impartial court, and freedom of opinion and expression.[79]

E. NON-CONTENTIOUS PROCEDURES

This chapter would not be complete without reference to some of the non-contentious methods by which the ILO promotes the implementation of its standards. These methods, which are less spectacular than, but supplementary to, the supervisory procedures, include regional discussions and reviews;[80] *ad hoc* investigations at the request of government and assistance to governments, and employers' and workers' organizations;[81] collaboration with other international organizations as well as nongovernmental organizations and institutions of higher learning;[82] research and promotional activities;[83] and technical cooperation with member states in the field of human rights.[84] These forms of action are designed to deal with situations and problems which prevent or delay the application of conventions and recommendations, and to make the standards and procedures of the ILO better known to those they are intended to serve. Thus, they play an essential supporting role in bringing about the implementation of the standards adopted by the ILO.

F. CONCLUDING REMARKS

An attempt has been made in this chapter to highlight the contribution which the ILO has been making in the promotion of human

[79] *See* Trade Union Situation in Chile, *supra* note 77 at 121. For the recommendations of the Fact-Finding and Conciliation Commission, *see id.* at 118–21.

[80] *See, e.g.*, Report of the Committee of Experts, Report III, Part 4A, at 8, 61st Sess., International Labour Conference (1975).

[81] *See* Rossillion, *ILO Examination of Human Rights Situation*, Rev. Int'l Comm'n Jurists (No. 12, June 1974) [hereinafter cited as Rossillion].

[82] *See* Report of the Committee of Experts, Report III, Part 4A, at 7, 61st Sess., International Labour Conference (1975). For a detailed examination of the collaboration between the ILO and all other specialized agencies in the U.N. system, *see* Samson, *supra* note 25, at 580–82.

[83] *See* In-Depth Review of International Labour Standards, 194th Sess., Governing Body, ILO Doc. GB.194/PFA/12/5, at 41 (Nov. 1974) [hereinafter cited as In-Depth Review].

[84] *See* Rossillion, *supra* note 81, at 41.

rights. The basis of this contribution is the adoption of international labour conventions and recommendations in the areas of basic human rights and the effective implementation of these instruments by decision-making and executing agencies at both the national and international levels. The ILO has adopted important instruments on forced labour, freedom of association, and discrimination; the machinery for the supervision of the implementation of these standards is contentious in some cases and non-contentious in others.

Although credit cannot be given to the instruments adopted by the ILO for all measures at the national level, there has been ample evidence of the direct influence of these standards. It is known that in addition to the influence of ratified conventions, certain conventions which have been relatively sparsely ratified and recommendations have had considerable influence on the law and practice of many countries and have acted as the inspiration for the formulation of national policies.[85] Furthermore, it has been pointed out recently that

> the mere existence of a standard has led to universal recognition of the legitimacy and validity of certain fundamental principles which, in spite of many difficulties of application, have come to constitute a kind of common law whose effective application is sought through continuous action on both the national and international levels. Freedom of association standards are the most obvious example.[86]

Despite their undoubted influence, international labour standards have not always been as decisive as desired in reducing inequality, improving working and living conditions, and increasing respect for human rights. No one can expect these standards to provide a universal remedy, but in order to ensure that they fulfill their role, it is essential to examine their limitations and ways to overcome those limitations. Standards are proposed to states for their acceptance and can be effective only to the extent that they secure the interest, support, and action needed at the state level for their implementation. To provide a continuing stimulus to that end is the justification for the various supervisory procedures and the range of supplementary measures of advice and assistance developed by the ILO.

II. Teaching Suggestions

A. PURPOSE OF THE COURSE

The purpose of a course on the ILO should be to examine its activities in the field of human rights in order to evaluate its contri-

[85] *See* International Labour Office, The Impact of International Labour Conventions and Recommendations (1976), and the extensive number of monographs cited therein.

[86] *See* In-Depth Review, *supra* note 83, at 2.

bution to the protection of fundamental human rights. As such, the course should cover the ILO's area of competence; the nature of its rules and standards; the machinery for supervising the implementation of the rules; and the results achieved. The course could be taught at undergraduate or postgraduate level. For the undergraduate programme, it would be sufficient to study the subject in a general way, but a detailed analysis and evaluation would be necessary in the postgraduate programme.

B. THE MAIN ORGANS OF THE ILO

It would be useful to begin the course with a brief study of the main organs of the ILO in order to understand fully the basis of ILO activities in the field of human rights. There are three main organs in the ILO, namely the International Labour Office, the Governing Body of the International Labour Office, and the International Labour Conference.[87] The International Labour Office is the administrative organ, the Governing Body the main executive body, and the International Labour Conference the legislative organ. The International Labour Office is composed of international public officials, with a Director-General as the administrative head; the Governing Body is composed of a total of 56 regular members made up of 28 government, 14 employer, and 14 worker representatives; each state member of the ILO is entitled to nominate four delegates to the International Labour Conference, two government delegates, one representing the employers, and one representing the workers of the member. The tripartite structure of the ILO is one of its fundamental features and distinguishes it from the other international organizations and specialized agencies of the United Nations which are purely governmental.

C. AREA OF ILO ACTIVITY

Since the primary purpose of the ILO is to promote social welfare, its contribution to the field of human rights should necessarily be related to the area of its general competence. Although most of the instruments adopted by the ILO relate to human rights in general, particular attention has been given to the areas of freedom of assocation, freedom from forced labour, and freedom from discrimination in employment. In discussing this subejct, it would be important to establish the meaning of each of these basic freedoms and its relationship to the other freedoms. For instance, what does 'freedom of association' mean, and what place should be given to this freedom in the general hierarchy of fundamental freedoms?

[87] *See* ILO Const. arts, 3, 7, 10.

It would be important also to examine the relationship between these freedoms and other norms or principles in national society, *e.g.*, national security and the general national interest. In other words, the question of the extent to which these basic freedoms should be given primacy over other rules and principles in the national society may be examined.

D. ILO METHODS FOR THE PROMOTION OF HUMAN RIGHTS: INTERNATIONAL LABOUR STANDARDS

The ILO's primary method to promote basic human rights is the adoption of international labour standards in the form of conventions and recommendations. While examining this question it would be important to establish the circumstances which call for the adoption of a convention and/or recommendation. Similarly, when is it more appropriate to adopt a convention than a recommendation?

It would also be essential to examine the nature of the obligations which arise for members of the ILO as a result of the adoption of these instruments. A convention is open to ratification and ratifying members are under an obligation to implement its provisions.[88] On the other hand, a recommendation is not open to ratification and its adoption does not create any legal obligation to implement its provisions, but does give rise to some constitutional obligations for members.[89]

Finally, the legal character of conventions and recommendations could be compared to that of other international agreements. In doing so, it should be noted that a 'reservation' cannot be made to ILO conventions[90] and that they create legal obligations for members whether or not those members voted for their adoption.

E. THE NATURE AND SCOPE OF ILO INSTRUMENTS

The ILO has adopted a large number of conventions and recommendations in the fields of freedom of association, forced labour, and discrimination in employment.[91] It would be useful to examine the provisions of some of these instruments in order to determine how adequately they deal with the problems which they were designed to resolve. Particular attention could be paid in this respect to Conventions Nos. 87 and 98 on freedom of association; Conventions Nos. 29

[88] *See id.* art. 19(5).

[89] *See id.* art. 19(6).

[90] *See* Valticos & Wolf, *L'OIT et les pays en voie de développement; technique d'élaboration et mise en œuvre des normes universelles*, in Pays en Voie de Développement et Transformation du Droit International 127, 131 (Société Française pour le Droit International 1974).

[91] *See* notes, 8, 9, & 10 *supra.*

and 105 on forced labour; and Convention No. 111 on discrimination in employment.

In appropriate cases, the provisions of these instruments could be compared with those of national legislation on the same subject. In such cases, it would be appropriate to determine the influence, if any, of the ILO Convention on the national legislation.

F. THE SUPERVISORY MACHINERY

The activities of the ILO do not end with the adoption of conventions and recommendations. The ILO has highly developed machinery for the supervision of observance by member states of their obligations under international labour conventions and recommendations as well as under the ILO Constitution. In examining this machinery, it would be important to distinguish the contentious from the non-contentious procedures.

1. *The contentious procedures*

The contentious procedures are normally applied in cases where there is an alleged breach by a member state of a convention which it had ratified. In examining this subject, special attention should be paid to three different procedures, namely representations and complaints under the ILO Constitution and the special freedom of association procedure.

a. *Representations procedure.* A representation is the main action that can be taken by employers' and workers' organizations against a member of the ILO for the non-observance of a convention which it has ratified. In examining this very important procedure, particular attention should be paid to the manner in which a representation can be initiated, the procedure for the examination of a representation, and the sanction available under the procedure. It should be noted that under this procedure, employers' and workers' organizations have been given a right to seek enforcement of a convention to which they are not parties. This situation could be compared with the general situation in the law of treaties, and even in the municipal law of contracts.

The main sanction available under this procedure is the publication of the representation and the statement, if any, made in reply to it.[92] It should be considered whether 'publication' constitutes an effective sanction for the non-observance of a convention by a member state, or whether another form of sanction could be envisaged. The case of Czechoslovakia in 1977 should be examined in this respect.

[92] *See* ILO Const. art. 25.

b. *Complaint procedure.* The complaint procedure is another method by which the non-observance of a convention can be investigated. In examining the procedure, it would be important to consider the circumstances that could give rise to a complaint and the entities that may initiate the procedure.

Over the years, the ILO has established very effective machinery for the examination of complaints, *i.e.*, the Commission of Inquiry. It would be important to examine the composition and procedure of a Commission of Inquiry, its role in the determination of disputes, and its contribution to the development of international jurisprudence.[93]

c. *Special freedom of association procedure.* The ILO has established a special freedom of association procedure to supplement the procedures provided for under the ILO Constitution. It involves the examination of complaints by the Governing Body Committee on Freedom of Association and by the Fact-Finding and Conciliation Commission on Freedom of Association. It would be necessary to examine the origins, terms of reference, and working methods of these two bodies, as well as the results that have been achieved. In the latter respect, a number of recent cases handled by the Committee and Commision could be examined and analyzed.

2. *Non-contentious procedures*

Various procedures which are non-contentious also exist for the supervision of the observance of conventions and recommendations. Special mention should be made of the Committee of Experts on the Application of Conventions and Recommendations; the Conference Committee on the Application of Conventions and Recommendations; the system of reporting on ratified and unratified conventions and on recommendations; direct contacts; and the special role of employers' and workers' organizations.

In the teaching of this section, emphasis should be placed on the origin, composition, methods of work, and powers of the Committee of Experts and the Conference Committee on the Application of Conventions and Recommendations. These two Committees could be compared and evaluated. It would be useful also to examine the methods of work of the Conference Committee before and after the changes introduced in 1980 with regard to the 'special list'. The role of the Governing Body in the 'reporting system' should also be examined, as should the nature of the response from member states to requests from the Governing Body.

The usefulness of the direct contacts procedure should be considered and, wherever possible, the results achieved under this system

[93] *See* Osieke, *supra* note 60.

should be evaluated. Some attention should be paid to the role of employers' and workers' organizations and the utility of the 'observations' which they submit to the International Labour Office.

Finally, the other non-contentious procedures could also be examined and evaluated on the basis of the results that have been achieved in recent years.

III. Syllabus

1. Purpose of the course.
2. The main organs of the ILO: the International Labour Office; the Governing Body of the International Labour Office; the International Labour Conference.
3. The tripartite structure of the ILO: Representation of employers and workers in the main organs of the ILO such as the Conference, the Governing Body, and important committees. The role of the nongovernmental bodies in the adoption of conventions and recommendations. (The text of the ILO Constitution should be consulted.)
4. ILO's competence in the field of human rights as defined in the ILO Constitution and the Declaration of Philadelphia.
5. ILO's area of activity in the field of human rights: particularly freedom of association; freedom from forced labour; freedom from discrimination in employment; the meaning of these freedoms and their relationship to other fundamental freedoms.
6. ILO methods for the promotion of basic human rights: international labour conventions and recommendations; essential characteristics of these instruments.
7. Nature and scope of ILO instruments on human rights, particularly on freedom of association, forced labour, and discrimination in employment.
8. The ILO machinery for the supervision of international labour standards.
   a. Contentious procedures: representations and complaints—the special freedom of association procedures.
   b. Non-contentious procedures: Committee of Experts and the Conference Committee on the Application of Conventions and Recommendations—direct contacts, role of employers' and workers' organizations, reports on ratified and unratified conventions and on recommendations.

Case Studies

1. Ghana v. Portugal, *in re* Observance of the Abolition of Forced Labour Convention, 1957 (No. 105); 45 (No. 2) ILO O. Bull. (Supp. 2) (Apr. 1962).

2. Portugal v. Liberia, *in re* Application of the Forced Labour Convention, 1930 (No. 29); International Labour Office Report of Commission of Inquiry, 46 (No. 2) ILO O. Bull. (Supp. 2) (1963).

3. Complaint against Chile, *in re* Observance of the Hours of Work Convention, 1919 (No. 1), and the Discrimination (Employment and Occupation) Convention, 1958 (No. 111); International Labour Office Report of the Commission of Inquiry (1975).

4. Representation by ICFTU v. Czechoslovakia, *in re* Observance of the Discrimination (Employment and Occupation) Convention, 1958 (No. 111); 61 (No. 3) ILO O. Bull. (Ser. A) (Supp.) (1978).

Suggested Subjects for Discussion

1. What is the basis of the competence of the ILO in the field of human rights?

2. What is the principle of tripartism and how does it affect the structure and decision-making process in the ILO?

3. What is the scope and content of ILO activities in the field of fundamental human rights?

4. The ILO Constitution contains provisions for (a) submission of newly adopted conventions and recommendations to the competent authorities, and (b) reporting by governments in respect of unratified conventions and of recommendations. Discuss the scope and nature of these obligations. What purpose do they serve? To what extent are workers' organizations involved?

5. What is meant by 'ratification' and what are the effects of ratification?

6. Discuss the respective roles of (a) the Committee of Experts, and (b) the Conference Committee on the Application of Conventions and Recommendations.

7. Describe the procedures for 'direct contacts'.

8. Discuss the role of workers' and employers' organizations within the framework of the ILO's regular supervisory procedures.

9. The ILO has established special procedures for the protection of freedom of association: (a) the Fact-Finding and Conciliation Commission on Freedom of Association, and (b) the Governing Body Committee on Freedom of Association. Discuss the origins, terms of reference, and working methods of these two bodies. What results have they achieved?

10. Representations and complaints procedures supplement the

regular supervisory procedures of the ILO. Discuss the workings of these procedures. Why are they useful? What is the role of workers and their organizations in initiating or contributing to action under these procedures?

IV. Minisyllabus

The following syllabus may be used for a two-hour lecture:

1. The competence of the ILO in the field of human rights—ILO Constitution, the Declaration of Philadelphia.
2. The structure of the ILO, including tripartism.
3. The measures adopted by the ILO for the promotion of human rights.
   a. International labour conventions—nature and legal character.
   b. International labour recommendations—nature and legal character.
   c. Declarations, such as 1964 Declaration on Apartheid, revised in 1980.
4. The main areas of activities of the ILO.
   a. Freedom of association.
   b. Freedom from discrimination in employment.
   c. Freedom from forced labour.
   d. Co-ordination with other international organizations.
5. Implementation of basic human rights conventions.
   a. Permanent supervisory machinery.
      (i) Reports on ratified and unratified conventions and on recommendations.
      (ii) Committee of Experts on the Application of Conventions and Recommendations.
      (iii) Conference Committee on the Application of Conventions and Recommendations.
   b. Contentious procedures.
      (i) Representations and complaints under articles 24–26 of the ILO Constitution.
      (ii) Special human rights procedures—the Governing Body Committee on Freedom of Association, and the Fact-Finding and Conciliation Commission.

V. Bibliography

A. ILO INSTRUMENTS ON BASIC HUMAN RIGHTS

Freedom of association

Freedom of Association and Protection of the Right to Organise Convention, 1948 (No. 87).

Right to Organise and Collective Bargaining Convention, 1949 (No. 98).
Workers' Representatives Convention (No. 135), and Recommendation (No. 143), 1971.
Rural Workers' Organisations Convention (No. 141), and Recommendation (No. 149), 1975.
Right of Association (Agriculture) Convention, 1921 (No. 11).
Right of Association (Non-Metropolitan Territories) Convention, 1947 (No. 84).
Labour Relations (Public Service) Convention (No. 151), and Recommendation (No. 159), 1978.

Forced labour

Forced Labour Convention, 1930 (No. 29).
Abolition of Forced Labour Convention, 1957 (No. 105).

Discrimination and employment

Equal Remuneration Convention (No. 100), and Recommendation (No. 90), 1951.
Discrimination (Employment and Occupation) Convention (No. 111), and Recommendation (No. 111), 1958.
Employment Policy Convention (No. 122), and Recommendation (No. 122), 1964.

B. ILO PUBLICATIONS

Freedom by dialogue: Economic development by social progress—The ILO contribution. Report of the Director-General, Part 1, 56th Sess., International Labour Conference, (1971).

Freedom of association: Digest of decisions of the Freedom of Association Committee of the Governing Body of the ILO (2d ed. 1976).

International Labour Office, International Labour Conventions and Recommendations, 1919–1981 (1982).

The ILO and human rights. Report of the Director-General, Part 1, 52d Sess., International Labour Conference (1968); report presented by the International Labour Organisation to the International Conference on Human Rights.

The ratification and implementation of international labour conventions by American countries, with special reference to conventions relating to freedom of association, minimum wages, labour inspection and indigenous populations. Report of the Director-General, Report I, Part 2, Tenth Conference of American States Members of the International Labour Organisation (Nov.–Dec. 1974).

The ratification and implementation of international labour conventions in Africa, with special reference to conventions relating to employment policy, forced labour, social policy and labour inspection. Report of the Director-General, Report I, Part 2, Fourth African Regional Conference (Nov.–Dec. 1973).

International Labour Standards: A Workers' Educational Manual (1978).

The Impact of International Labour Conventions and Recommendations (1976).

Manual on Procedures Relating to International Labour Conventions and Recommendations (1980).

C. OTHER PUBLICATIONS

E. Haas, Human Rights and International Action: The Case of Freedom of Association (1970).

C. Jenks, The International Protection of Trade Union Freedom (1957).

—— Human Rights and International Labour Standards (1960).

—— Social Justice in the Law of Nations: The ILO Impact after Fifty Years (1970).

G. Johnston, The International Labour Organisation: Its Work for Social and Economic Progress (1970).

E. Landy, The Effectiveness of International Supervision: Thirty Years of ILO Experience (1966).

—— *The Influence of International Labour Conventions: Possibilities and Performance*, 101 Int'l Labour Rev. 555 (1970).

Osieke, *The Exercise of Judicial Function with Respect to the International Labour Organisation*, 47 Brit. Y.B. Int'l L. 315 (1974–1975).

Rossillion, *ILO Examination of Human Rights Situation*, Rev. Int'l Comm'n Jurists 40 (No. 12, June 1974).

Samson, *The Changing Pattern of ILO Supervision*, 118 Int'l Labour Rev. 569.

Valticos, *The International Labour Organisation: Its Contribution to the Rule of Law and the International Protection of Human Rights*, 9 J. Int'l Comm'n Jurists 3 (1968).

—— *The Place of Human Rights in the Constitution and Various Instruments of the ILO and the Legal Framework for their Protection*, in The International Dimension of Human Rights 407 (K. Vasak ed. 1979).

—— *La Commission d'Investigation et de Conciliation en Matière de Liberté Syndicale et le Mécanisme de Protection Internationale des Droits Syndicaux*, 13 Annuaire Français de Droit International 445 (1967).

—— *Une Nouvelle Expérience de Protection des Droits de*

l'Homme: Le Groupe d'Étude, de l'OIT Chargé d'Examiner la Situation en Espagne, 16 Annuaire Français de Droit International 567 (1970).

—— *Les Normes de l'Organisation Internationale de Travail en Matière de Protection des Droits de l'Homme*, 4 Revue des Droits de l'Homme 691 (1971).

—— *La Protection Internationale de la Liberté Syndicale Vingt-Cinq ans Après*, 7 Revue des Droits de l'Homme 5 (1974).

—— *Les Méthodes de la Protection Internationale de la Liberté Syndicale*, Recueil des Cours 79 (1975-I).

—— *The Role of the ILO: Present Action and Future Perspectives*, in Human Rights Thirty Years After the Universal Declaration 211 (B. Ramcharan ed. 1979).

—— International Labour Law (1979).

—— *The Future Prospects for International Labour Standards*, Int'l Labour Rev. 679 (1979).

—— & Wolf, *L'Organisation Internationale du Travail et les Pays en Voie de Développement: Techniques d'Élaboration et Mise en Oeuvre des Normes Universelles*, in Pays en voie de Développement et Transformation du Droit International 127 (Société Française pour le Droit International 1974).

Vincent-Davis, *Human Rights Law: A research Guide to the Literature—ILO and UNESCO*, 15 N.Y.U. J. Int'l L. & Pol. 000 (1982).

Wolf, *Les Conventions Internationales du Travail et La Succession d'États*, 7 Annuaire Français de Droit International 742 (1961).

—— *L'Interdépendance des Conventions Internationales du Travail*, 121 Recueil des Cours 114 (1967-II).

—— *Aspects Judiciaires de la Protection Internationale des Droits de l'Homme par l'OIT*, 4 Revue des Droits de l'Homme 773 (1971).

—— *L'Application des Conventions Internationale du Travail par Voie de Conventions Collectives*, 20 Annuaire Français de Droit International 103 (1974).

—— *ILO Experience in the Implementation of Human Rights*, 10 J. Int'l L. & Econ. 599 (1975).

—— *At the Apex of the Value Hierarchy: An International Organization's Contribution*, 24 N.Y.L.S. L. Rev. 179 (1978).

VI. Minibibliography

ILO, International Labour Standards: A Workers' Educational Manual (1978).

—— The Impact of International Labour Conventions and Recommendations (1976).
C. Jenks, Human Rights and International Labour Standards (1960).
E. Landy. *The Influence of International Labour Conventions: Possibilities and Performance*, 101 Int'l Labour Rev. 555 (1970).
N. Valticos, International Labour Law (1979).
—— *The International Labour Organisation: Its Contribution to the Role of Law and the International Protection of Human Rights*, 9 J. Int'l Comm'n Jurists 3 (1968).
F. Wolf, *Aspects judiciaires de la protection internationale des droits de l'homme par l'OIT*, 4 Revue des Droits de l'Homme 773 (1971).
—— *Human Rights and the International Labour Organisation*, in this volume.

Chapter 8

Race, Sex, and Religious Discrimination in International Law*

Jack Greenberg[1]

A U.S. civil rights lawyer in 1982, surveying the international human rights vista, experiences mixed feelings of despair (at how little can be achieved through employing international means) and *déjà vu* (at how international human rights resembles our domestic scene of the not too distant past). The U.S. law of race relations today is complex and rich, articulated in a superstructure of leading U.S. Supreme Court decisions, like *Brown v. Board of Education*,[2] which held unconstitutional racial segregation in education, and an infrastructure of thousands of high and low court pronouncements on what constitutes discrimination and what does not, as well as what are appropriate or necessary means of uprooting it. The explication in education alone continues in national legislation, such as Title VI of the Civil Rights Act of 1964,[3] and in regulations of the Department of Education, secretarial decisions, administrative law judge determinations, state and local implementing legislation, and local school board rules. Similar proliferation of law, in its various modes of expression, is replicated in employment, health care, housing, voting, prison conditions, capital punishment, and almost every conceivable area of human activity.[4] The most important legal issues, moreover, continue to change in form and substance.

Contrast this with the body of international human rights law. It is somewhat, but not a great deal, more detailed than basic U.S. constitutional texts. Confining ourselves for the moment to the Universal Declaration of Human Rights,[5] it consists principally of declarations like those of article 1 ('All human beings are born free and equal in dignity and rights.') and article 16 ('Men and women of full age,

[1] I am grateful to Linda Poon, New York University School of Law, Class of 1981, for her able research assistance in the preparation of this chapter.

[2] 347 U.S. 483 (1954).

[3] 28 U.S.C. §§ 2000d–2000d-3.

[4] Citation of various cases, statutes, rules, etc. for these propositions could be endless and not very edifying. But it may be noted that subspecialities of American civil rights law, *e.g.*, housing, employment, today are reported in multivolume services and the number of volumes in such services steadily increases.

[5] G. A. Res. 217A, U.N. Doc. A/810, at 71 (1948).

without any limitations due to race, nationality or religion, have the right to marry and to found a family.'). The international covenants[6] explicate these great principles somewhat, but as to detail only remotely resemble the corpus of U.S. civil rights law. A U.S. civil rights lawyer who would like to employ international human rights principles, for example, to assist black South Africans, Soviet Jews, or blacks in the United States must naturally wonder whether it is possible to convert the majestic international accords into concrete relief for victims of discrimination. The problem is partly one of means of implementation,[7] but also one of the jurist's task of translating general principles into precise application. With this there has been scant experience in the international human rights domain.

Similarly, teachers must wonder how to teach about general principles which have been relatively little applied and whose exegesis appears mostly in scholarly articles, which usually have none of the interest of concrete cases. Too often those articles resemble philosophical disputation more than conventional legal materials.

But if we look a quarter century back into U.S. law we find it was then little more developed than international human rights law today. Indeed, the U.S. law slightly over a century ago was not even nominally as advanced as the international documents we shall discuss. Only in 1868 did the fourteenth amendment pronounce that no state shall 'deny to any person within its jurisdiction the equal protection of the laws'. That provision and others of like purpose adopted after the Civil War were at best enforced in desultory fashion until the mid-twentieth century. Up to that time the country showed considerable disposition *against* according racial equality. Such landmark decisions as *Plessy v. Ferguson*[8] and the *Civil Rights Cases*,[9] which denied to blacks basic civil rights by restrictively interpreting the reconstruction amendments, were the norm. Great jurists like Holmes, Brandeis, and Stone joined in decisions denying rights which today the amendments are held to grant.[10]

Domestic civil rights law was virtually not taught at all until the 1960s. This author's *Race Relations and American Law*, published in 1959, stood alone as a text in its area; Emerson and Haber's *Political and Civil Rights in the United States* (1952) was the only case book in that field for many years. Now books and articles on civil rights are

[6] International Covenant on Economic, Social and Cultural Rights, G. A. Res. 2200, 21 U.N. GAOR, Supp. (No. 16) 49, U.N. Doc. A/6316 (1966); International Covenant on Civil and Political Rights, G. A. Res. 2200, 21 U.N. GAOR, Supp. (No. 16) 52, U.N. Doc. A/6316 (1966).

[7] Discussed in detail in ch. 10 *infra* and elsewhere in this volume.

[8] 163 U.S. 537 (1896).

[9] 109 U.S. 3 (1883).

[10] *See, e.g.*, Gong Lum v. Rice, 275 U.S. 78 (1927); Berea College v. Kentucky, 211 U.S. 45 (1908).

numerous, reflecting greater activity by human rights proponents. Teaching of international human rights law, similarly, will capture more interest as activity in this area increases.

The application, interpretation, and teaching of domestic human rights law developed in the United States when underlying political, economic, and social relations in the country changed. The new rules in turn permitted institutionalization of change and helped bring about further growth. Similarly, it seems not unreasonable to hope for change in international human rights doctrine and, particularly, in implementation as underlying conditions develop. As Professor Sohn has pointed out: 'We must measure the accomplishments of the last thirty years not against utopian dreams but against the accomplishments of the last 3,000 years of recorded history.'[11]

I. Legal and Policy Considerations

A. THE IMPORTANCE OF THE STRICTURES AGAINST DISCRIMINATION

Mere inspection of the basic international human rights documents demonstrates that racial, sexual, and religious discrimination are, certainly in terms of attention paid on the face of the agreements, the overarching human rights concern of the international community. If one only considers the outlook of the United States, where coping with racial discrimination has been central to our constitutional development, and former colonial peoples' preoccupation with racial domination, it becomes clear why the U.N. Charter, the Universal Declaration, the international covenants, and the various conventions[12] devote more attention to preventing discrimination than to any other single category of human rights. The paragraphs that follow describe those antidiscrimination principles in some detail and reflect on their meaning and efficacy, particularly in U.S. law.

B. THE UNITED NATIONS CHARTER AND UNIVERSAL DECLARATION OF HUMAN RIGHTS

The basic provisions of international human rights law are the U.N. Charter and the Universal Declaration of Human Rights. Both ensure freedom from racial, sexual, and religious discrimination in a variety of ways.

Detailed explication of the general principles of the Charter and the

[11] Sohn, *The Human Rights Law of the Charter*, 12 Tex. Int'l L.J. 129, 138 (1977).

[12] *See, e.g.*, International Convention on the Elimination of All Forms of Racial Discrimination, 660 U.N.T.S. 195; Convention on the Elimination of All Forms of Discrimination Against Women, *opened for signature* Mar. 1, 1980, G. A. Res. 180, 34 U.N. GAOR, Supp. (No. 46) 193, U.N. Doc. A/34/46 (1979).

Universal Declaration has been made in the International Covenant on Civil and Political Rights,[13] the International Covenant on Economic, Social, and Cultural Rights,[14] the International Convention on the Elimination of All Forms of Racial Discrimination,[15] and the Convention on the Elimination of All Forms of Discrimination Against Women,[16] while certain aspects have been provisionally defined in preliminary efforts to draft a Convention on the Elimination of All Forms of Religious Intolerance.[17] Other agreements deal with slavery,[18] genocide,[19] *apartheid*,[20] and various practices which are peculiar manifestations of discrimination. Specialized agencies, such as the International Labour Organisation (ILO) and the United Nations Educational, Scientific, and Cultural Organization (UNESCO) have promulgated strictures against discrimination.[21] Regional, *e.g.*, European[22] and inter-American,[23] and other applications of the same principles, *e.g.*, the Helsinki Accords,[24] adopt the U.N. standards or formulate them somewhat differently. In these pages, however, we shall consider the substantive rules of only the principal documents, their applicability, and perhaps useful means of teaching about them.

1. *U.N. Charter*

The keystone international legal document, the U.N. Charter,

[13] *See* note 6 *supra.*

[14] *See* note 6 *supra.*

[15] *See* note 12 *supra.*

[16] *See* note 12 *supra.*

[17] *See* text accompanying notes 161–72 *infra.*

[18] Slavery Convention, 46 Stat. 2183, T.S. No. 778, 60 L.N.T.S. 253; Protocol Amending the Slavery Convention, 7 U.S.T. 479, T.I.A.S. No. 3532, 182 U.N.T.S. 51; Supplementary Convention on the Abolition of Slavery, the Slave Trade, and Institutions and Practices Similar to Slavery, 18 U.S.T. 3201, T.I.A.S. No. 6418, 266 U.N.T.S. 3; Forced Labour Convention, 1930 (ILO No. 29), *reprinted in* Basic Documents on Human Rights 176 (2d ed. I. Brownlie 1981) [hereinafter cited as Brownlie]; Abolition of Forced Labour Convention, 1957 (ILO No. 105), *reprinted in* Brownlie, *supra*, at 187.

[19] Convention on the Prevention and Punishment of the Crime of Genocide, 78 U.N.T.S. 277, *reprinted in* Brownlie, *supra* note 18, at 31.

[20] International Convention on the Suppression and Punishment of the Crime of *Apartheid*, *opened for signature* Nov. 30, 1973, G.A. Res. 3068, 28 U.N. GAOR, Supp. (No. 30) 75, U.N. Doc. A/9030 (1973), *reprinted in* Brownlie, *supra* note 18, at 164.

[21] Discrimination (Employment and Discrimination) Convention, 1958 (ILO No. 111), *reprinted in* Brownlie, *supra* note 18, at 204; [UNESCO] Convention Against Discrimination in Education, 429 U.N.T.S. 93, *reprinted in* Brownlie, *supra* note 18, at 234.

[22] Convention for the Protection of Human Rights and Fundamental Freedoms, 213 U.N.T.S. 221, *reprinted in* Brownlie, *supra* note 18, at 242. *See* arts. 4, 9, 12, and 14.

[23] *See* art. 43, Charter of the Organization of American States, 2 U.S.T. 2394, T.I.A.S. No. 2361, 119 U.N.T.S. 3; Protocol of Amendment, 21 U.S.T. 607, 721 U.N.T.S. 324; American Convention on Human Rights, O.A.S. T.S. No. 36, *reprinted in* Brownlie, *supra* note 18, at 391.

[24] *See* arts. I(a) & VII of the Final Act of the Conference on Security and Co-operation in Europe, *signed* Aug. 1, 1975, 73 Dep't State Bull. 323, 325 (1975), *reprinted in* Brownlie, *supra* note 18, at 320.

makes clear at its outset the international community's basic commitment to equality. Its preamble asserts a reaffirmation of faith 'in the equal rights of men and women . . .' Among the purposes of the United Nations, it states, are 'develop[ing] friendly relations among nations based on respect for the principle of equal rights and self-determination of peoples'[25] and 'promoting and encouraging respect for human rights and fundamental freedoms for all without distinction as to race, sex, language, or religion'.[26] 'The United Nations shall place no restrictions on eligibility of men and women to participate in any capacity and under conditions of equality in its principal and subsidiary organs.'[27]

Among the powers of the General Assembly are initiating studies and making 'recommendations for the purpose of . . . assisting in the realization of human rights and fundamental freedoms for all without distinction as to race, sex, language, or religion'.[28] The United Nations shall 'promote . . . universal respect for, and observance of, human rights and fundamental freedoms for all without distinction as to race, sex, language, or religion'.[29] Similarly, the Economic and Social Council 'may make recommendations for the purpose of promoting respect for, and observance of, human rights and fundamental freedoms for all.[30] Furthermore, the basic objectives of the international trusteeship system include assuring 'equal treatment in social, economic, and commercial matters for all Members of the United Nations and their nationals, and also equal treatment for the latter in the administration of justice . . .'[31] In connection with *apartheid* in South Africa, this provision, and the feelings underlying it, have been the basis of a great deal of international expression and activity.

2. *Universal Declaration*

The Universal Declaration of Human Rights elaborates the Charter's equal rights prescriptions and, indeed, is suffused with the notion of equality. The preamble recognizes the inherent dignity and 'the equal and inalienable rights of all members of the human family' as the 'foundation of freedom, justice and peace in the world',[32] and reaffirms 'faith . . . in the equal rights of men and women'.[33] Ten of the thirty articles which constitute the International Bill of Human Rights

[25] U.N. Charter art. 1(2).
[26] *Id.* art. 1(3).
[27] *Id.* art. 8.
[28] *Id.* art. 13(1)(b).
[29] *Id.* art. 55(c).
[30] *Id.* art. 62(2).
[31] *Id.* art. 76(d).
[32] Universal Declaration, preamble, para. 1.
[33] *Id.* para. 5.

are in one way or another explicitly concerned with equality, and others implicitly so. Following is a summary of the specific references:

Article 1. All human beings are born free and equal in dignity and rights.

Article 2. Everyone is entitled to all the rights and freedoms set forth in the Universal Declaration without distinction of any kind, such as race, color, sex, language, religion, political or other opinion, national or social origin, property, birth, or other status.

Article 4. No one shall be held in slavery or servitude.

Article 7. All are equal before the law and are entitled without any discrimination to equal protection of the law.[34]

Article 10. Everyone is entitled in full equality to a fair and public hearing in the determination of rights and of any criminal charges.

Article 16. Men and women of full age, without any limitation due to race, nationality, or religion, have the right to marry and to found a family and are entitled to equal rights as to marriage, during marriage, and at its dissolution.

Article 18. Everyone has the right to freedom of thought, conscience, and religion.

Article 21. Everyone has the right of equal access to public service. The will of the people shall be expressed by universal and equal suffrage.

Article 23. Everyone, without any discrimination, has the right to equal pay for equal work.

Article 26. Higher education shall be equally accessible to all on the basis of merit.

In addition to these numerous explicit references to equality, the concept is implicit in repeated references to 'everyone' having the right to liberty,[35] to effective remedies before competent tribunals,[36] to freedom of movement,[37] to nationality,[38] and other rights.

As a component of an international human rights law curriculum it would be interesting to reflect briefly on the requirement of article 26 that higher education be 'equally accessible to all on the basis of merit'. 'Merit' is not defined; but, at the least, this standard would prohibit exclusion from higher education because of the inability to pay for it. At a minimum, 'merit' would seem to preclude admissions policies based on wealth, social standing, race, or similar factors. But the use of the term awakens interest today in the United States in what is referred

[34] *Compare* Universal Declaration, art. 7 *with* Political Covenant, art. 26, *discussed in* Lillich, ch. 4 *supra*, text accompanying notes 93, 96–102.

[35] Universal Declaration, art. 3.

[36] *Id.* art. 8.

[37] *Id.* art. 13.

[38] *Id.* art. 15.

to as the *Bakke*[39] issue. That subject is now of high interest on American campuses, but in 1948 the provision obviously was adopted without reference to a future U.S. dispute over affirmative action. Although 'merit' may be interpreted variously, and it would not be incompatible with affirmative action policies to admit minorities with grades and scores below those of white competitors, the word *today* has been captured by opponents of such admissions. Today in the United States, admission on 'merit' ordinarily means admission on the basis of superior tests and scores. Perhaps reflecting changing perceptions, the Economic Covenant, adopted a generation later, uses different language to deal with higher education.[40] The tension between a view of nondiscrimination which prohibits any distinctions and a view which permits discrimination in favor of disadvantaged groups for the purpose, for example, of compensating them for past discrimination pervades a number of the documents we are considering,[41] just as it does U.S. civil rights law.

3. *Enforceability of the Charter and the Universal Declaration*

What is the legal effect of these equal rights provisions of the Charter and the Universal Declaration? That is a question of particular interest to U.S. lawyers because the Charter is the only one of the U.N. human rights instruments which the United States has ratified, and many scholars argue persuasively that the Universal Declaration has the force of customary international law because of its universal recognition. The contending positions have been marshalled by Professor Schachter in a comprehensive article published in 1978,[42] which echoes positions that he had taken as early as 1951.[43]

Professor Schachter describes the 'long standing controversy, dating

[39] Bakke v. Regents of the Univ. of Calif., 438 U.S. 265 (1978).

[40] Economic Covenant, art. 13(2)(c) provides: 'Higher education shall be made equally accessible to all, on the basis of *capacity* . . .' (emphasis added). Those with adequate or superior 'capacity' may not have demonstrated 'merit', at least as some have used that term.

See text accompanying note 77 *infra*.

Many countries incorporate affirmative action policies in their basic law. *See*, *e.g.*, Constitution of India, pt. III, § 15(4) ('Nothing in this article . . . shall prevent the State from making any special provision for the advancement of any socially and educationally backward classes of citizens or for the scheduled castes and the scheduled tribes.'). *See also* Karpem, *University Admission Criteria: Some German–American Comparative Observations*, Int'l Rev. Educ. 203, 204–05 (1976); Hahn, *West German Higher Education*, 58 Educ. 403, 408 (1977). (Quotas required for different groups in German universities; no one who has qualifications may be excluded, although admission may be deferred.) Comparative treatment of this issue may be of interest in arriving at the meaning of art. 26 of the Universal Declaration, art. 13 of the Economic Covenant, and cognate provisions.

[41] *See* text following note 96 *infra*; text accompanying notes 130–32 *infra*.

[42] Schachter, *International Law Implications of U.S. Human Rights Policies*, 24 N.Y.L.S. L. Rev. 63 (1978) [hereinafter cited as Schachter, *International Law Implications*].

[43] Schachter, *The Charter and The Constitution, The Human Rights Provisions in American Law*, 4 Vand. L. Rev. 643 (1951).

back to the beginnings of the United Nations, as to the legal effect of these articles.[44] The United States, he writes, for many years, 'tended to avoid characterizing those Charter provisions as obligatory on states, preferring instead to treat them as statements of general purposes . . .'[45] Some scholars, he continues, characterized them as too vague to be enforceable.[46] This position, of course, coincided with the basic political stance, dominant in Congress in the 1950's and quite powerful even today, opposed to undertaking international obligations which would supersede domestic jurisdiction. But, Schachter argues, at least since 1977 when President Carter addressed the United Nations General Assembly, 'the U.S. Government now acknowledges both the obligatory character of the human rights articles of the Charter and its corollary that member states are internationally accountable for the observance of human rights in their countries'.[47] He traces the evolution from the period of non-acknowledgement through the present, including acceptance of such international declarations as the Helsinki Accords of 1975, which specify rights and freedoms embraced by the Charter. He concludes that 'the American policy on the rights of states to censure violations of human rights by other states rests on a well-founded premise that all states are under an international obligation to observe and promote human rights.[48] Furthermore, he asserts:

> [T]he American position is also in keeping with, and lends support to, the legal conclusion that the obligations relating to human rights are obligations *erga omnes* (in the sense expressed by the International Court) and that, in consequence, every state has a legal interest in the protection of such rights everywhere and a corresponding right to raise the matter of non-observance and to censure grave violations by other governments.[49].

The Universal Declaration has been universally approved, and scholars seem to agree that it is valid international law. Saario and Cass point out that 'even the small number of member states which abstained from voting for the Universal Declaration have apparently reconsidered their position, since all have voted affirmatively on many subsequent resolutions making reference to the Universal Declaration.'[50] They write:

> [A]s new nations have referred to it or incorporated it into their constitutions or fundamental law; as national judicial decisions have cited it approv-

[44] Schachter, *International Law Implications*, *supra* note 42, at 66.

[45] *Id.*

[46] *Id.* at 67.

[47] *Id.*

[48] *Id.* at 74.

[49] *Id.*

[50] Saario & Cass, *The United Nations and the International Protection of Human Rights: A Legal Analysis and Interpretation*, 7 Calif. W. Int'l L.J. 591, 596 (1977).

ingly; and as it has been acknowledged by or incorporated into a wide range of international conventions, declarations, and recommendations; its justifiable principles at least have been elevated with considerable authority to the status of customary international law.[51]

Professor Humphrey concurs: '[W]hatever its drafters may have intended in 1948', the Universal Declaration 'is now part of the customary law of nations' and therefore binding on all states.[52] The Universal Declaration and the principles enunciated in it have been officially invoked on many occasions both inside and outside the United Nations.[53]

For the U.S. civil rights practitioner, the Charter's obligatory nature and the Universal Declaration's legal validity raise the question of the means by which they may be applied to particular instances of abuse. Of course, as Professor Schachter points out, states may raise the matter of non-observance by other states and may censure each other.[54] And, as Professor Sohn discusses in chapter 10 of this volume, international bodies established to implement the various conventions and covenants may receive and, in a variety of ways, respond to complaints. But are there more direct remedies capable of application to discrete cases utilizing legal means which are ordinarily employed within domestic legal orders? In a study of the relationship of the human rights provisions of the Charter to domestic legal orders of member states, Bernard Schlüter has concluded that '[s]elf execution of the human rights clauses is . . . a *possibility* in almost all civil law member states, the United States, the socialist countries and some Third World countries'.[55] But, in an intricate analysis of particular provisions, potential modes of enforcement, legal doctrines in a variety of nations, and other factors, he seems to conclude no more than that 'human rights clauses, or at least some of their parts, are likely to have some domestic legal effect in *many* states'.[56]

There have been attempts to apply domestically the Universal Declaration or the Charter's human rights provisions. Those aspects which deal with racial discrimination, particularly, have been urged upon U.S. courts from shortly after the Charter's adoption to the present. The results have been uniformly discouraging, except to those who find hope in a fragment of affirmative dictum, the occasional less

[51] *Id.* at 607 (footnotes omitted).

[52] Humphrey, *The Implementation of International Human Rights Law*, 24 N.Y.L.S. L. Rev. 31, 32 (1978).

[53] *Id.* 33. On the question of the status under customary international law of particular provisions of the Universal Declaration dealing with civil rights, *see* Lillich, ch. 2 *supra*.

[54] Schachter, *International Law Implications*, *supra* note 42.

[55] Schlüter, *The Domestic Status of the Human Rights Clauses of the United Nations Charter*, 61 Calif. L. Rev. 110, 114 (1973) (emphasis added).

[56] *Id.* at 162 (emphasis added).

than conclusive scope of rejection, and the mere fact that the provisions have been advocated at all.

The case with which most discussion begins is *Sei Fujii v. California*,[57] as decided by a California intermediate appellate court in 1950. It involves the validity of the California Alien Land Law, which denied to plaintiff the right to own land in California because he had been born in Japan. Among the grounds of invalidity urged against the statute was that it was 'inconsistent with the declared principles and spirit of the United Nations Charter'.[58] The court agreed and held that '[t]he Charter has become the "Supreme Law of the Land; and the Judges in every State shall be bound thereby, any Thing in the Constitution or laws of any State to the Contrary notwithstanding". U.S Const., Art. VI, sec. 2'.[59] Citing various provisions of the Charter and the Universal Declaration, the court stated that 'restrictions contained in the Alien Land Law are in direct conflict with the plain terms of the Charter . . . [and] with Article 17 of the Declaration of Human Rights which proclaims the right of everyone to own property'.[60] The opinion concluded that 'The Alien Land Law must therefore yield to the treaty as superior authority. The restrictions of the statute based on eligibility to citizenship, but which ultimately and actually are referable to race or color, must be and are therefore declared untenable and unenforceable.'[61]

If this had remained the law, international human rights jurisprudence would have been off to a good start in the United States. But the California Supreme Court took a contrary view, holding that 'the provisions of the preamble and of Article 1 of the charter which are claimed to be in conflict with the alien land law are not self-executing'.[62] It also held that '[t]he language used in Articles 55 and 56 is not the type customarily employed in treaties which have been held to be self-executing and to create rights and duties to individuals'.[63] The Court concluded:

> The charter represents a moral commitment of foremost importance, and we must not permit the spirit of our pledge to be compromised or disparaged in either our domestic or foreign affairs. We are satisfied, however, that the charter provisions relied on by plaintiff were not intended to supersede existing domestic legislation, and we cannot hold that they operate to invalidate the alien land law.[64]

[57] 217 P.2d 481 (Cal. Dist. Ct. App. 1950).
[58] *Id.* at 483.
[59] *Id.* at 486.
[60] *Id.* at 488.
[61] *Id.*
[62] Sei Fujii v. California, 38 Cal. 2d 718, 722–23, 242 P.2d 617, 620 (1952).
[63] *Id.*
[64] *Id.* at 724–25, 242, P.2d at 622.

But, it would be incorrect to conclude that the requirements of the Charter, as invoked in that case, were not honored in U.S. Law. The opinion held that the Alien Land Law, as an instrument effectuating racial discrimination, violated the fourteenth amendment. In a sense, therefore, the Charter was observed, arguably in the way preferred above all others: by a domestic prohibition of such discrimination embodied in the national constitution.[65]

The interesting question is: what would have been the obligation of the United States under international law as a signatory of the Charter if the California Supreme Court or the U.S. Supreme Court had concluded that domestic constitutional law tolerated racial discrimination? Or what if the *School Segregation Cases*,[66] for example, had been decided in a way which validated racial segregation? Would the United States have owed a Charter-imposed obligation to the international community to correct the condition? How would it have been enforced? Would the world's response have been the same as it is to *apartheid* in South Africa, with the same international expressions of disapproval?

The Charter and the Universal Declaration remain theoretically applicable to other issues which arise in U.S. courts, not only with regard to conditions in the United States, but with regard to situations in other countries which are claimed to be adjudicable in U.S. courts. Nevertheless, efforts to employ them have been unsuccessful. Professor Lillich has observed that while it is not often today that courts refer to efforts to employ the Charter and other international human rights doctrine as 'tommyrot' or 'junk and gobbledygook',[67] cases regularly have been resolved 'on as narrow and technical a basis as possible. As a consequence, the possibility for a legitimate, innovative role for United States domestic courts in the area of human rights has been ignored.'[68]

One problem in applying the basic provisions of the Charter and the

[65] *See* Bitker, *Application of the United Nations Universal Declaration of Human Rights Within the United States*, 21 De Paul L. Rev. 337 (1971). For an analysis of U.S. obligations, national and international, with regard to school desegregation, *see* Yudof, *International Human Rights and School Desegregation in the United States*, 15 Tex. Int'l L.J. (1980).

[66] *See, e.g.*, Brown v. Board of Education, 347 U.S. 483 (1959). Subsidiary arguments made by plaintiffs and *amici* in this and related cases referred to the Charter and the Universal Declaration, but evoked no response from the Court.

[67] Lillich, *The Role of Domestic Courts in Promoting International Human Rights Norms*, 24 N.Y.L.S. L. Rev. 153, 154 (1978).

[68] *Id.* at 176. Among cases which declined to apply U.N. human rights standards to claims in the nature of racial discrimination are Kemp v. Rubin, 188 Misc. 310, 69 N.Y.S. 2d 680 (1947); Sipes v. McGhee, 316 Mich. 614, 25 N.W. 2d 638 (1947); Namba v. McCourt, 185 Ore. 579, 204 P.2d 569 (1949); Boyer v. Garrett, 183 F.2d 582 (4th Cir. 1950); Camp v. Recreation Board, 104 F. Supp. 10 (D.D.C. 1952); Rice v. Sioux City Cemetery, Inc., 245 Iowa 147, 60 N.W.2d 110 (1953), *aff'd* 348 U.S. 880 (1954); Hitai v. Immigration and Naturalization Service, 343 F.2d 466 (2d Cir. 1965); Diggs v. Richardson, 555 F.2d 848 (D.C. Cir. 1976). These and related cases

Universal Declaration to contemporary U.S. racial, sexual, or religious discrimination issues is that at this stage the issues in the United States have transcended generality and deal mostly with particulars of implementation. The Charter and the Universal Declaration were relevant to the 1954 *School Segregation Cases* issues and to California's Alien Land Law prohibitions. However, they offer no help with whether busing children to promote school integration and whether reassigning blacks to formerly forbidden lines of seniority in an industrial plant rights past wrongs or inflicts unjustifiable present harm on whites. Of course, women's rights issues in the United States today are more open than racial ones, but even as to these the treaties offer no guidance on how to eliminate sex discrimination in pension systems or the armed forces, for example, two subjects with which the country is grappling. As discussed below, the covenants and conventions spell out some guidance. But it is harder (if not impossible) to argue their applicability to domestic disputes in view of the United States' failure to ratify the international covenants and the Discrimination Against Women Convention. Moreover, should ratification occur, proposed reservations would purport[69] to make ratification meaningless if it would require changes in U.S. law.

C. THE INTERNATIONAL COVENANTS AND THE RACIAL DISCRIMINATION CONVENTION

Just beneath the Charter and the Universal Declaration in importance are the two international covenants which unfold their general terms into some detail and provide means of implementation. The Economic Covenant entered into force 3 January 1976 and the Political Covenant entered into force 23 March 1976, both having been

are discussed in R. Lillich & F. Newman, International Human Rights: Problems of Law and Policy 100–22 (1979).

One recent case which points in the direction of enforceability is Filartiga v. Peña-Irala, 630 F.2d 876 (2d Cir. 1980). *Filartiga* held that United States district courts have jurisdiction under the Alien Tort Statute, 28 U.S.C. § 1350, of civil actions by aliens for torts committed in violation of the law of nations, even though the torts occurred in another country. In *Filartiga*, torture was held to be such a tort. The case poses interesting questions concerning racial discrimination which might give rise to similar conclusions and questions regarding jurisdiction and choice of law issues. For example, could a South African black bring suit in a U.S. court for redress against a South African official or private person who injured her by racial discrimination in South Africa? The injury probably woud be irremediable under South African law, but could have been in violation of international standards which are not recognized in South Africa (or quite possibly in the United States, at least as enforceable international obligations). The theoretical exercise is intriguing, but at least at this point in history probably without practical utility.

[69] It may be, however, that these reservations are ineffectual, or that ratification subject to such reservation is ineffectual. *See* Schachter, *The Obligation of the Parties to Give Effect to the Covenant on Civil and Political Rights*, 73 Am. J. Int'l L. 462, 464–65 (1979), [hereinafter cited as Schachter, *Obligations of the Parties*].

opened for signature ten years earlier. On 13 May 1968, the International Conference on Human Rights announced the Proclamation of Teheran which reiterated the basic precepts of both covenants, the Racial Discrimination Convention, and the Universal Declaration, and urged all peoples and governments to redouble their efforts to 'provide for all human beings a life consonant with freedom and dignity and conducive to physical, mental, social and spiritual welfare'.[70]

1. *Economic Covenant*

The Economic Covenant recognizes that political and civil rights can be exercised effectively only under conditions of material, social, and cultural security.[71] For example, if one is poor and illiterate, the right to vote is relatively uninformed, and power to persuade others in the political process relatively ineffective. A pauper charged with a crime cannot afford to employ effective counsel. For the poor, the right to own property, as asserted in the Universal Declaration, is as empty as the right to participate in the cultural life of the community, also affirmed in the Universal Declaration. Hence while the economic rights are asserted for their own sake and for the material security they would afford, they have been guaranteed also to give real meaning to civil and political rights.

Like the Charter and Universal Declaration, the Economic Covenant repeatedly asserts a right to racial, sexual, and religious equality. The preamble commences, '*Considering* that . . . recognition of the inherent dignity and of the equal and inalienable rights of all members of the human family is the foundation of freedom, justice and peace . . .'[72] and the Covenant continues 'the rights enunciated in the present Covenant will be exercised without discrimination of any kind as to race, colour, sex, language, religion, political or other opinion, national or social origin, property, birth or other status'.[73] The parties 'undertake to ensure the equal right of men and women to the enjoyment of all economic, social and cultural rights' set forth in the Covenant.[74] Fair and equal remuneration for work is assured and 'in particular women [are] guaranteed conditions of work not inferior to those enjoyed by men, with equal pay for equal work'.[75]

Equal opportunity to be promoted is also assured. But this particular provision evokes, as did a provision in the Universal Declaration,[76]

[70] U.N. Doc. A/CONF.32/41 (1968).
[71] Economic Covenant, preamble, para. 3.
[72] *Id.* para. 1 (emphasis in original).
[73] *Id.* art. 2(2).
[74] *Id.* art. 3.
[75] *Id.* art. 7(a)(1).
[76] *See* text accompanying notes 39–41 *supra*.

the U.S. dispute over affirmative action: promotion is ensured 'subject to no considerations other than those of *seniority* and *competence*'.[77] International human rights law is a long way from grappling with the details of implementation, but were it doing so, two contending camps would exist on this point of the Economic Covenant. One, like its counterparts among many U.S. labour unions, would argue that blacks (or other disadvantaged groups) are not entitled to compensation for past discrimination and must move from the end of the line into promotional opportunities, even if that long delays their rise to equality. The opposing group would argue the case of affirmative action advocates, that if conventional seniority rules result in perpetuating discrimination, they must be overruled.

It is perhaps interesting while considering affirmative action to observe that article 13(2)(c) of the Economic Covenant, which deals with higher education, uses a different formula than does the Universal Declaration to describe the basis of access to higher education. Article 13(2)(c) prescribes that '[h]igher education shall be made equally accessible to all, on the basis of *capacity*,[78] by every appropriate means, and in particular by the progressive introduction of free education' (emphasis added). As has been observed,[79] 'capacity', 'merit', and 'competence' are terms susceptible to various meanings. How they are employed reflects—in these contexts—policies which may advance, retard, or exclude disadvantaged groups in connection with opportunities they seek. The U.S. controversy over 'quotas' and 'affirmative action' expresses these differences.

As with the Universal Declaration, various designated rights under the Economic Covenant shall be afforded 'everyone', thereby prohibiting race, sex, and religion as criteria to be used to discriminate. For example, cultural life, the benefits resulting from scientific progress, and other gains of civilization must be afforded to 'everyone'.[80]

2. *Political Covenant*

The Political Covenant also elaborates in various ways the prohibitions against racial, sexual, and religious discrimination. The parties undertake to ensure to all individuals the rights recognized in the Political Covenant 'without distinction of any kind, such as race, colour, sex, language, religion, political or other opinion, national or

[77] Economic Covenant, art. 7(c) (emphasis added).

[78] Art. 26(1). Universal Declaration reads in part: 'Technical and professional education shall be made generally available and higher education shall be equally accessible to all on the basis of *merit*.' (Emphasis added.)

[79] *See* text accompanying notes 39–41 *supra*.

[80] Economic Covenant, art. 15.

social origin, property, birth or other status',[81] the precise language also found in the Economic Covenant. Furthermore, '[t]he States Parties . . . undertake to ensure the equal right of men and women to the enjoyment of all civil and political rights . . .'[82] Even when the life of the nation is threatened by public emergency, although the parties may take steps derogating from certain obligations under the Political Covenant, such measures may 'not involve discrimination solely on the ground of race, colour, sex, language, religion or social origin'.[83] One wonders how the Japanese relocation cases[84] would have been decided if this provision had been applicable. Without doubt, the word 'solely' would have been a principal focus of dispute. Were the Japanese Americans evacuated from the West Coast *solely* because of ancestry or because of a belief that in case of invasion they would have aided the invaders? Was that belief reasonable? How would that be decided under wartime conditions?

The Political Covenant contains other relevant provisions. Article 8 forbids slavery. Article 14(1) states: 'All persons shall be equal before the courts and tribunals.' In the determination of criminal charges, 'everyone shall be entitled to . . . minimum guarantees, in full equality'.[85] 'Everyone shall have the right to recognition everywhere as a person before the law.'[86] 'Everyone', the treaty continues, 'shall have the right to freedom of thought, conscience and religion.'[87] Article 20 provides that '[a]ny advocacy of national, racial or religious hatred that constitutes incitement to discrimination, hostility or violence shall be prohibited by law', thereby raising serious issues under the first amendment to the U.S. Constitution.[88]

The states parties to the Political Covenant undertake to take 'appropriate steps to ensure equality of rights and responsibilities of spouses as to marriage . . .'[89] 'Each child shall have without any discrimination as to race, colour, sex, language, religion, national or social origin, property or birth, the right to such measures of protection as required by his status as a minor . . .'[90] The factors mentioned in article 2, *viz.*, race, color, sex, etc., may not bar persons from participating in public affairs.[91] Adverting to U.S. constitutional language,

[81] Political Covenant, art. 2(1).
[82] *Id.* art. 3.
[83] *Id.* art 4(1).
[84] *See, e.g.*, Korematsu v. United States, 323 U.S. 214 (1944).
[85] Political Covenant, art. 14(3).
[86] *Id.* art. 16.
[87] *Id.* art 18(1).
[88] *See, e.g.*, National Socialist Party v. Skokie, 432 U.S. 43 (1977); Terminiello v. Chicago, 337 U.S. 1 (1949).
[89] Political Covenant, art. 23(4).
[90] *Id.* art. 24(1).
[91] *Id.* art. 25.

the Political Covenant provides that '[a]ll persons are equal before the law and are entitled without any discrimination to the equal protection of the law'.[92] The treaty further provides that the law must prohibit and effectively protect against 'discrimination on any ground such as race, colour, sex, language, religion', and so forth.[93] Ethnic, religious, and linguistic minorities are assured the right to enjoy their own culture, religion, and language.[94]

3. *The Racial Discrimination Convention*

The Racial Discrimination Convention entered into force on January 4, 1969, well in advance of the international covenants. Although it largely repeats the discrimination provisions of the covenants, its existence as a separate instrument underscores the vast importance which the nations of the world place on non-discrimination. The preambular paragraphs of the Racial Discrimination Convention reiterate basic concepts of the Charter: 'dignity and equality', 'fundamental freedoms for all, without distinction as to race, sex, language or religion', 'all human beings are born free and equal in dignity and rights', 'all human beings are equal before the law and are entitled to equal protection of the law'. Note, once again, the incorporation of language reminiscent of the fourteenth amendment to the U.S. Constitution.

Article I commences with a definition of racial discrimination as 'any distinction, exclusion, restriction or preference based on race, colour, descent, or national or ethnic origin which has the *purpose* or *effect* of nullifying or impairing the recognition, enjoyment or exercise, on an equal footing, of human rights . . .' (emphasis added). The use of the standards of 'purpose' and 'effect' anticipated the full-blown controversy in the U.S. law of racial discrimination which became important after the U.S. Supreme Court decision in *Washington v. Davis*,[95] that mere discriminatory effect without the *purpose* of discriminating does not violate the Constitution. Some *statutes*, however, have been held to forbid discriminatory *effect*.[96] One may speculate whether the Racial Discrimination Convention, had it been in force in the United States at the time *Washington v. Davis* was decided, would have brought about a different result.

Article 1 of that Convention concludes by addressing affirmative action, referred to above several times:

[92] *Id.* art. 26; *cf.* U.S. Const. amend. XIV, § 1.

[93] Political Covenant, art. 26.

[94] *Id.* art. 27.

[95] 426 U.S. 229 (1978). *See also* Village of Arlington Heights v. Metropolitan Housing Development Corp., 429 U.S. 252 (1977).

[96] *See, e.g.*, Board of Education of the City of New York v. Harris, 444 U.S. 130 (1979).

> Special measures taken for the sole purpose of securing adequate advancement of certain racial or ethnic groups . . . shall not be deemed racial discrimination, provided, however, that such measures do not, as a consequence, lead to the maintenance of separate rights for different racial groups and that they shall not be continued after the objectives for which they were taken have been achieved.

While this provision authorizes, but does not require, affirmative action, article 2(2) goes further:

> States Parties *shall*, when the circumstances so warrant, take, in the social, economic, cultural and other fields, special and concrete measures to ensure the adequate development and protection of certain racial groups or individuals belonging to them, for the purpose of guaranteeing them the full and equal enjoyment of human rights and fundamental freedoms. (emphasis added)

However, such separate rights may not be continued after the objectives for which they were taken have been achieved.[97]

The Racial Discrimination Convention not only condemns racial discrimination, but its states parties undertake to pursue, by all appropriate means, and without delay, a policy of eliminating it in all of its forms.[98] The affirmative steps set forth in article 2 include repeal of laws and regulations which have the effect of creating or perpetuating discrimination,[99] and prohibition by all appropriate means, including legislation, of racial discrimination by persons, groups, and organizations.[100]

A commentary is suggested by U.S. experience. Article 2(1)(e) of the Racial Discrimination Convention, which looks away from ethnocentricity and towards integration, provides that the states parties to the Convention undertake to encourage 'integrationist multiracial organizations and movements and other means of eliminating barriers between races . . .' The provision therefore looks with favor on the policies of such U.S. organizations as the National Association for the Advancement of Colored People (which believes in integration) as compared to, for example, CORE (now a black nationalist group). Clearly, the terms 'where appropriate' and 'other means of eliminating barriers between races' in article 2(1)(e) could arguably include nationalist organizations which have integration as an ultimate purpose.

Article 4 poses the contradiction between international human rights concepts and U.S. constitutional principles of free expression,

[97] Racial Discrimination Convention, art. 2(2).
[98] *Id.* art. 2(1).
[99] *Id.* art. 2(1)(c).
[100] *Id.* art. 2(1)(d).

even for groups which preach race hatred, which frequently arises. Article 4 provides that the parties to the Convention 'condemn all propaganda and all organizations which are based on ideas or theories of superiority of one race or group of persons of one colour or ethnic origin, or which attempt to justify or promote racial hatred . . .' Parties shall declare it an offense punishable by law to disseminate 'ideas based on racial superiority . . . as well as all acts of violence or incitement to such acts against any race or group of persons of another colour or ethnic origin . . .'[101] In addition, they are required to 'declare illegal and prohibit organizations, and also organized and all other propaganda activities, which promote and incite racial discrimination . . .'[102] Combating racial discrimination in these ways would contradict U.S. first amendment doctrine in many situations. With some regularity, cases of Ku Klux Klansmen or Nazis or similar groups reach U.S. courts, and, nearly uniformly, their activities based on racial, ethnic, or religious hatred are permitted to continue.[103] This is not the place to pursue the dichotomy further, except to note that in other parts of the world, legal and political traditions are different than in the United States. Activities based on racial hatred are viewed with greater alarm by states which fear the inability of society to contain their evil consequences. Perhaps in many circumstances in the United States such activities present no clear and present danger, whereas elsewhere they may.

The most comprehensive provision of the Racial Discrimination Convention is article 5. It provides that 'States Parties undertake to prohibit and to eliminate racial discrimination in all its forms and to guarantee the right of everyone, without distinction as to race, colour, or national or ethnic origin, to equality before the law, notably in the enjoyment of . . .' a long catalog of rights. These include the 'right to equal treatment before . . . tribunals',[104] '[t]he right to security of person',[105] and '[p]olitical rights'.[106] Other civil rights which the article includes are freedom of movement and residence, the right to leave any country, the right to nationality, the right to marriage, to own property, to inherit, to freedom of thought, conscience, and religion, to freedom of opinion and expression, and to peaceful assembly and association.[107] Article 5 also lists '[e]conomic, social and cultural rights' whose enjoyment parties are to protect without dis-

[101] *Id.* art. 4(a).
[102] *Id.* art. 4(b).
[103] *See, e.g.*, cases cited in note 88 *supra*.
[104] Racial Discrimination Convention, art. 5(a).
[105] *Id.* art. 5(b).
[106] *Id.* art. 5(c).
[107] *Id.* art. 5(d).

crimination, including the right to work, to form and join trade unions, to housing, public health, education, and training, and to participation in cultural activities.[108] Finally, article 5 protects equal access to public accommodations.[109] As Partsch has written,

> [t]he unresolved question is whether the States Parties, in ratifying this treaty, become obligated to positively enact legislative measures which guarantee the rights listed in Article 5, or whether States Parties agree only to bar racial discrimination in the enjoyment of these rights to the extent that these rights are safeguarded by a particular State Party.[110]

To make these rights meaningful, article 6 requires states parties to assure everyone within their jurisdiction effective remedies against human rights violations and article 7 requires states parties to undertake affirmative measures of teaching and education to combat racial prejudice.

4. *Enforceability*

The Political Covenant, the Economic Covenant, and the Racial Discrimination Convention are all in force. The United States has not ratified any of them, and the proposal of ratification which President Carter submitted to the Senate[111] contains reservations providing that ratification would require no modification of U.S. Law.[112] Ratification subject to such limitations, however, raises the question of why the United States, or any state making similar reservations, should ratify at all. In addition, there may be a question of whether such wholesale reservation is valid, or whether ratification subject to such reservation is valid.[113] After all, the most oppressive and racist government could ratify any international human rights instrument if it contained reservations which would not require it to make any changes in its policies. Moreover, the United States proposes to make a declaration accompanying ratification which would deny to the treaties self-executing effect, so that they will not in and of themselves become effective as domestic law.[114]

On the other hand, ratification would forbid regression which, in the United States, is unlikely anyway. Furthermore, while reservations could perhaps be repealed one by one, a step by step method of

[108] *Id.* art. 5(e).

[109] *Id.* art. 5(f).

[110] Partsch, *Elimination of Racial Discrimination in the Enjoyment of Civil and Political Rights*, 14 Tex. Int'l L.J. 191, 193 (1979). His answer is very complex.

[111] *See* Message of the President Transmitting Four Treaties Pertaining to Human Rights, S. Exec. Doc. No. 95–C, D, E, and F, 95th Cong., 2d Sess. (1978) [hereinafter cited as Message of the President].

[112] *See* relevant discussions in Henkin, ch. 2 *supra*.

[113] *See* Schachter, *Obligation of the Parties*, *supra* note 69, at 464–65.

[114] *See* Message of the President, *supra* note 111.

ratification does not seem to exist. Given the history of the United States' reluctance to join in international human rights compacts, ratification with wholesale reservations was apparently fastened upon as the most feasible political means of securing any U.S. acquiescence at all.

In the United States today, the foregoing three treaties are no more enforceable in domestic law than the Charter (which the United States has ratified) and the Universal Declaration. But what if the treaties were ratified? What would their effect be on domestic law? That, of course, would depend upon the particular provisions in question. In response to questions posed by Senator Jacob K. Javits concerning the effect of the human rights treaties, Professor Schachter replied that while certain provisions of the Economic Covenant, *e.g.*, the right 'to the continuous improvement of living conditions',[115] necessarily require legislative attention, prohibition of racial and related discrimination would be capable of judicial application without new legislation. In support of his conclusion, Professor Schachter cited provisions of the Political Covenant[116] which also need not be implemented legislatively before judicial application would become possible. In contrast, he argued that articles 20 and 23(1) of the Political Covenant would require further legislation because they are too general. Similarly, with respect to the Racial Discrimination Convention, articles 5 and 6 would be self-executing, but 3, 4, and 7 would not. Nevertheless, he concluded that the State Department's proposed declaration would render the treaties non-self-executing, although the United States would not thereby immunize itself from the international obligation to adopt legislation permitting implementation of the treaties. Although in that situation U.S. courts could not enforce the treaties, they could use the treaties as standards for interpreting domestic constitutional and statutory provisions.[117]

Given the paucity of international enforcement and the practical limitations on effecting change through international bodies, the U.N. Commission on Human Rights' Sub-Commission on Prevention of Discrimination and Protection of Minorities decided in 1977 'to consider, as a major part of its own contribution to the Decade for Action to Combat Racism and Racial Discrimination, ways and means of using domestic forums, including legislative forums, to help implement United Nations resolutions on racism, racial discrimination, *apartheid*, decolonization and self-determination and related

[115] Economic Covenant, art. 11.

[116] Political Covenant, arts. 6, 7, 9, 10, 11, 14, & 15.

[117] *International Human Rights Treaties: Hearings Before the Senate Comm. on Foreign Relations*, 96th Cong., 1st Sess. 84 (1979) (statement of Oscar Schachter).

matters'.[118] The report contains replies by a number of countries listing a variety of measures available in domestic forums.

The Committee on the Elimination of Racial Discrimination was established pursuant to article 8 of the Racial Discrimination Convention. Among the functions assigned to the Committee by the Convention is the review of reports which states parties to the Convention are required to submit on the measures they have taken to implement the Convention.[119] The Committee has found that although many of the principles contained in the Racial Discrimination Convention are reflected in the constitution and laws of a great many countries, some countries have failed to adequately report on the measures they have adopted to give effect to the Convention's provisions because they have had no problems of racial discrimination.[120] The Committee has maintained that the absence of discrimination in a state does not absolve the latter of the obligation to enact and report on anti-discrimination legislation. In a formal ruling in 1972, the Committee stated that its request for information, made pursuant to article 9 of the Convention, was 'addressed to all States Parties without distinction, whether or not racial discrimination exists in their respective territories'.[121]

D. CONVENTION ON THE ELIMINATION OF ALL FORMS OF DISCRIMINATION AGAINST WOMEN

The most recent addition to the body of United Nations equal rights jurisprudence is the Discrimination Against Women Convention, opened for signature March 1, 1980. The states parties commenced by noting that the Charter and the Universal Declaration proclaim that 'all human beings are born free and equal in dignity and rights',[122] but that despite these instruments and various U.N. resolutions, discrimination against women continues.[123] The Convention defines 'discrimination against women' as 'any distinction, exclusion or restriction made on the basis of sex which has the effect or purpose of impairing or nullifying the recognition, enjoyment or exercise by women, irrespective of their marital status, on a basis of equality of men and women, of human rights and fundamental freedoms'.[124]

[118] Sub-Commission on Prevention of Discrimination and Protection of Minorities (Prov. Agenda Item 4), U.N. Doc. E/CN.4/Sub.2/L.679 (1978).

[119] Racial Discrimination Convention, art. 9.

[120] *See* Report of the Committee on the Elimination of Racial Discrimination, 27 U.N. GAOR, Supp. (No. 18) 22–23, U.N. Doc. A/8718 (1972).

[121] *Id.* at 38; Buergenthal, *Implementing the UN Racial Convention*, 12 Tex. Int'l L.J. 187, 190–91 (1977). On the practice of the Committee, *see generally id.*

[122] Discrimination Against Women Convention, preamble, para. 2.

[123] *Id.* para. 6.

[124] *See* text accompanying notes 95–96 *supra.*

The states parties agree to pursue immediately 'all appropriate means' to eliminate all discrimination against women.[125] They undertake, among other things, to 'embody the principle of equality of men and women in their national constitutions',[126] to 'adopt appropriate legislation and other measures ... prohibiting all discrimination against women',[127] to 'establish legal protection of the rights of women on an equal basis with men' through the country's national tribunals or other public institutions,[128] as well as to 'take all appropriate measures ... to modify or abolish existing laws, regulations, customs and practices', which, in effect, discriminate against women.[129]

Just as other international human rights agreements have, the Discrimination Against Women Convention addresses the affirmative action question. The '[a]doption by State Parties of temporary special measures aimed at accelerating *de facto* equality between men and women shall not be considered discrimination as defined in the Convention ...'[130] These steps, it continues, will be discontinued when equality of opportunity and treatment have been achieved. But, special measures 'aimed at protecting maternity shall not be considered discrimination'.[131]

To change 'social and cultural patterns', states parties will take appropriate measures to eliminate all prejudices and practices which are grounded upon ideas of 'inferiority or the superiority of either of the sexes ...'[132] 'States Parties shall take appropriate measures ... to suppress all forms of traffic in women ...'[133] Women must be assured the right of suffrage on equal terms with men[134] and equal opportunity to represent their governments at the international level.[135]

Discrimination against women in education must be eliminated and women must be provided 'the same conditions for career ... guidance, for access to studies',[136] 'the same curricula, the same examinations,'[137] 'the same opportunities to benefit from scholarships',[138] and

[125] Discrimination Against Women Convention, art. 2.
[126] *Id.* art. 2(a).
[127] *Id.* art. 2(b).
[128] *Id.* art. 2(c).
[129] *Id.* art. 2(f).
[130] *Id.* art. 4(1). *See* text accompanying notes 39–41 and 77–79 *supra.*
[131] Discrimination Against Women Convention, art. 4(2).
[132] *Id.* art. 5(a).
[133] *Id.* art. 6.
[134] *Id.* art. 7(a).
[135] *Id.* art. 8.
[136] *Id.* art. 10(a).
[137] *Id.* art. 10(b).
[138] *Id.* art. 10(d).

the same opportunities to participate in sports activities.[139] Moreover, nations must take steps to eliminate 'any stereotyped concept of the roles of men and women' through education, reduce female drop-out rates and organize programs for females who have left school prematurely.[140]

Since the right to work is 'an inalienable right of all human beings',[141] the states parties must strive to eliminate discrimination in the workplace by ensuring women the 'same employment opportunities,'[142] '[t]he right to free choice of profession and employment,'[143] 'equal remuneration,'[144] 'social security,'[145] and 'protection of health and . . . safety'.[146] Most importantly, in order to 'prevent discrimination against women on the grounds of marriage or maternity',[147] parties shall act to 'prohibit, subject to the imposition of sanctions, dismissal on the grounds of pregnancy or of maternity leave and discrimination in dismissals on the basis of marital status',[148] to 'introduce maternity leave with pay . . . without loss of former employment, seniority or social allowances',[149] and to 'provide special protection to women during pregnancy in types of work proved to be harmful to them'.[150]

Women shall be treated equally with men in the economic world, with the same right to family benefits, bank loans, mortgages, and other forms of financial credit,[151] and shall be accorded equality with men before the law and exercise a legal capacity identical to men.[152] The parties shall ensure that women have the same rights as men 'to enter into marriage',[153] 'freely to choose a spouse',[154] and to acquire the 'same rights and responsibilities during marriage and at its dissolution'.[155] Change of nationality by a husband during marriage shall not automatically change the nationality of the wife.[156]

The Discrimination Against Women Convention came into force on

139 *Id.* art. 10(g).
140 *Id.* art. 10.
141 *Id.* art. 11(1)(a).
142 *Id.* art. 11(1)(b).
143 *Id.* art. 11(1)(c).
144 *Id.* art. 11(1)(d).
145 *Id.* art. 11(1)(e).
146 *Id.* art. 11(1)(f).
147 *Id.* art. 11(2).
148 *Id.* art. 11(2)(a).
149 *Id.* art. 11(2)(b).
150 *Id.* art. 11(2)(d).
151 *Id.* art. 13.
152 *Id.* art. 15.
153 *Id.* art. 16(1)(a).
154 *Id.* art. 16(1)(b).
155 *Id.* art. 16(1)(c).
156 *Id.* art. 9(1).

September 3, 1981. Like all fundamental instruments written in general terms, it leaves unanswered many questions which will be resolved only when concrete applications are attempted. For example, at some point there will have to be resolved conflict between the Discrimination Against Women Convention and the declaration on religious discrimination.[157] If a religion relegates women to a certain societal or familial status which otherwise would be deemed discrimination on the basis of sex, which convention governs? Or, as with the Racial Discrimination Convention, how does one ascertain whether equality has been achieved so that affirmative action must be discontinued? The equality in sports provision[158] has its counterpart in U.S. law and has there given rise to questions of implementation such as whether girls and boys must play on the same teams or whether the same amount of money must be spent on men's and women's sports? If men and women are to have 'equality' in deciding spacing of children,[159] may a man require his pregnant spouse to undergo, or may a father-to-be prohibit the woman who is pregnant by him from undergoing, an abortion?

Some of these questions may be fanciful. Others will surely arise. When the Discrimination Against Women Convention is implemented the world community will find some guidance in the U.S. cases which have addressed sex discrimination issues. It will be some time, however, before U.S. lawyers can find guidance in international sex discrimination norms.[160]

E. DECLARATION ON RELIGIOUS DISCRIMINATION

As with racial discrimination and women's rights, existing international accords secure the right to be free from religious discrimination. Nevertheless, a further, more detailed charter of religious equality has been adopted. On November 25, 1981, the General Assembly adopted the Declaration on the Elimination of All Forms of Intolerance and of Discrimination Based on Religion or Belief.[161] The Declaration provides that everyone shall have the right to freedom of thought, conscience, and religion;[162] that no one shall be subject to

[157] *See* text accompanying notes 161–72 *infra*.

[158] Discrimination Against Women Convention, art. 10(g).

[159] *Id.* art. 16(1)(e).

[160] Counsel in Reed v. Reed, 404 U.S. 71 (1971), arguing discrimination against women, cited the U.N. Charter preamble, para. 2, in a footnote. Brief for Petitioner at 55 n.52. The U.S. Supreme Court in its decision made no reference to this argument. *See also* Guggenheim, *Implementation of Human Rights by the U.N. Commission on the Status of Women*, 12 Tex. Int'l L.J. 239 (1977); Taubenfeld & Taubenfeld, *Achieving the Human Rights of Women: The Base Line, The Challenge, The Search for a Strategy*, 4 Human Rights 125 (1975).

[161] G.A. Res. 36/55, U.N. Doc. A/RES/36/55 (1981).

[162] *Id.* art. 1(1).

coercion which would impair his or her freedom to have a religion or belief of his or her choice;[163] and that freedom to manifest one's religion or beliefs may be subject only to such limitations as are prescribed by law and are necessary to protect public safety, order, health, or morals, or the fundamental rights and freedoms of others.[164]

The Religious Discrimination Declaration asserts also that parents shall have the right to organize family life in accordance with their religion or belief[165] and that every child shall enjoy the right to have access to religious education[166] and, conversely, no child may be compelled to receive religious teaching if it would be against the wishes of his or her parents.[167] However, adopting a phrase which has currency in the U.S. law of domestic relations, the Declaration states that 'the best interests of the child' shall be the guiding principle in determining the kind of religious education the child receives.

The Declaration lists a number of freedoms, including the right to worship, to maintain charitable or humanitarian institutions, to acquire materials related to religious rights, to issue publications, to teach, to solicit financial contributions, to train leaders, to observe holidays, and to communicate with others regarding religion.[169] It calls for national legislation which would enable persons to avail themselves of such freedoms.[170]

In recognition of potential confict between this Declaration and other human rights instruments, the Declaration states that nothing in it shall derogate from or restrict any right declared in the Universal Declaration and the international covenants.[171] We have already seen such conflict in U.S. law, for example, in the case of educational institutions with religious affiliations which discriminate on the basis of race. Undoubtedly, similar conflicts in other states involving religious requirements will have an effect on race, national origin, and sex discrimination issues. The international community, probably at some time well in the future, will be called upon to resolve such differences.[172]

[163] *Id.* art. 1(2).
[164] *Id.* art. 1(3).
[165] *Id.* art. 5(1).
[166] *Id.* art. 5(2).
[167] *Id.*
[168] *Id.*
[169] *Id.* art. 6.
[170] *Id.* art. 7.
[171] *Id.* art. 8.
[172] For material on earlier drafts of the Religious Discrimination Declaration, *see* Commission on Human Rights, 1979 U.N. ESCOR, Supp. (No. 6) 125, U.N. Doc. E/1979/36, E/CN.4/1347 (1979); Draft Report of the Commission on Human Rights, U.N. Doc. E/CN.4/L. 1500/Add.20 (1980).

F. INTERPRETATION AND APPLICATIONS OF THE BASIC INSTRUMENTS

We already have observed the scarcity of material bearing on the application and interpretation of the basic documents on equality, apart from scholarly exegesis. In this lies the greatest difficulty in understanding what the documents may require in particular circumstances. Of course, international agreements may be implemented differently from domestic law and some flesh may be observed on the bare bones of the texts by looking beyond judicial determinations or decisions by international bodies at, for example, unilateral censure by one government of another. But extrapolating from text alone has its limits. As any lawyer knows, general language, particularly that which deals with moral or social questions, is susceptible of various meanings which may change with circumstances. Witness the evolution in U.S. law from 'separate but equal' to the prohibition of segregation to the development of questions arising from affirmative action.

Nevertheless, there are a few opinions which should be noted. Perhaps the most important is Judge Tanaka's dissenting opinion in the *South West Africa Cases (Second Phase)*.[173] In his conclusion he stated:

> The principle of equality does not mean absolute equality, but recognizes relative equality, namely different treatment proportionate to concrete individual circumstances. Different treatment must not be given arbitrarily; it requires reasonableness, or must be in conformity with justice, as in the treatment of minorities, different treatment of the sexes regarding public conveniences, etc. In these cases the differentiation is aimed at the protection of those concerned, and it is not detrimental and therefore against their will.[174]

Along with racial discrimination, discrimination on the basis of language is forbidden by the international guarantees. The *Belgian Linguistic Case*,[175] therefore, may illuminate other prohibitions of discrimination. While that case involved application of the European Convention on Human Rights and not the treaties discussed above, the European Convention does stem from the resolve of 'European countries which are like-minded and have a common heritage of political traditions, ideals, freedom and the rule of law, to take the first steps for the collective enforcement of certain of the Rights stated in the Universal Declaration'.[176]

Belgian law had divided the country into a Dutch-speaking region,

[173] [1966] I.C.J. 4.
[174] *Id.* at 311.
[175] [1967] Y.B. Eur. Conv. on Human Rights 594 (Eur. Ct. of Human Rights).
[176] European Convention on Human Rights, preamble, para. 5.

Flanders, and a French-speaking area, Wallonia. Those who spoke French, but lived mainly in Dutch speaking areas, were required to send their children to nearby schools where they were taught in Dutch. To attend French-speaking schools required travelling a considerable distance. A case was submitted to the European Commission on Human Rights from which it went to the European Court of Human Rights. The European Court held that distinctions based on language are illegal if they do not have objective and reasonable justification in relation to the aims and effects of the measures concerned. But, as in U.S. courts making constitutional decisions bearing on state legislation, considerable deference would be given to national authority. Accordingly, the Court held that dividing the country into linguistic regions did not violate the European Convention.

Yet, while the European Commission and Court are virtually unique as international bodies which have explicated judicially the elements of substantive international equal rights jurisprudence, they have not issued a great many decisions on the subject. Most have been decided on technical or procedural grounds.[177]

Even though they rarely result in clear cut decisions, unilateral

[177] Following are some of the issues and cases before the European Court and Commission which have treated race, sex, religion, and similar discrimination: Bruggeman v. Federal Republic of Germany, [1978] Y.B. Eur. Conv. on Human Rights 638 (Comm. of Ministers) (A German statute regulating when and whether abortions may be performed did not violate the European Convention; it is cited here because in U.S. law the question of abortion is a species of women's rights litigation, although it may be characterized in other ways.); X v. United Kingdom, [1978] Y.B. Eur. Conv. on Human Rights 354 (Eur. Comm'n of Human Rights) (Applicant was sentenced to two and a half years imprisonment for homosexual relationships. The Commission accepted the application, framing the issue as to whether the view that eighteen to twenty-one year olds ought to be protected, expressed twenty years ago by the Wolfenden Commission, remains valid in a significantly changed moral climate.); X v. Netherlands, [1971] Y.B. Eur. Conv. on Human Rights 224 (Eur. Comm'n of Human Rights) (Applicant disputed a pension law which differentiated between married and unmarried women. The Commission found the legislation appreciates the difference of situation between single persons and married couples and was not out of proportion to the general purpose of the legislation. Accordingly, the application was dismissed.); X v. United Kingdom, [1967] Y.B. Eur. Conv. on Human Rights (Eur. Comm'n of Human Rights) (Because the right to be admitted to a particular country is not guaranteed by the Convention, discrimination with regard to admission does not violate the Convention; inadmissible).

There are various cases claiming denial of religious rights and/or religious discrimination by adherents of groups which refuse to comply with health, taxation, pension, or military requirements of national legislation. These claims have been rejected. *See, e.g.*, X. v. Netherlands, [1967] Y.B. Eur. Conv. on Human Rights 472 (Eur. Comm'n of Human Rights) (compulsory automobile insurance program allegedly violative of Convention; inadmissible); Grandath v. Federal Republic of Germany, [1967] Y.B. Eur. Conv. on Human Rights 626 (Eur. Comm'n of Human Rights) (legislation concerned exempted members of certain religious groups from military or alternative service; held refusal to grant same exemptions to Jehovah's Witnesses not violative of Convention); X v. Netherlands, [1962] Y.B. Eur. Conv. on Human Rights 278 (Eur. Comm'n of Human Rights) (farmer contesting health regulations pertaining to cattle; application inadmissible); Reformed Church of X v. Netherlands, [1960] Y.B. Eur. Conv. on Human Rights 648 (Eur. Comm'n of Human Rights) (contested pension program; application inadmissible).

efforts at human rights implementation also deserve a brief review. Some involve governmental action, *e.g.*, the Jackson–Vanik Amendments[178] which restrict United States trade with the Soviet Union for the purpose of influencing Jewish emigration, or the Country Reports[179] prepared by the U.S. State Department.[180]

NGO activities are discussed elsewhere in this volume.[181] However, private agencies which do not have formal NGO status may have influence. For example, the Helsinki Watch, a U.S. group which corresponds to similar bodies in other countries, including the Soviet Union, reports on domestic and Eastern European compliance with the human rights standards of the Helsinki accords. The Lawyers Committee for International Rights has participated in domestic litigation in the United States seeking to secure human rights and has appeared before international bodies. The Association of the Bar of the City of New York has sent a mission to study human rights in Argentina.[182] The National Conference on Soviet Jewry has sent missions to the Soviet Union on behalf of the Soviet Jews who seek to emigrate and has made representations in domestic and international forums around the world. A study of such groups, whose number is growing, and of what they have accomplished or failed to accomplish would be useful. There is good reason to believe that they have had some influence; how much and under what circumstances is difficult to say.

II. Teaching Suggestions

The following discussion contemplates devoting perhaps a semester to the subject matter of this chapter. If, however, an instructor has only two or three hours, it would seem best to focus on racial discrimination to the exclusion of sex and religious issues, which are not as maturely developed either in international or domestic law. And perhaps only one of the domestic aspects of the subject, such as affirmative action, might be treated when comparisons are being made. Moreover, the class could be limited to only U.S. enforcement of international standards, omitting other materials. The minisyllabus and minibiblio-

[178] 19 U.S.C. § 2432 (Countries which deny their citizens the right to emigrate or deter exercise of such rights are ineligible for most-favored-nation treatment.) Increase in Jewish emigration from the Soviet Union is thought by many to be attributable to Jackson-Vanik and like efforts.

[179] *See*, *e.g.*, Country Reports on Human Rights Practices for 1981, Report Submitted to the House Comm. on Foreign Affairs and the Senate Comm. on Foreign Relations, 97th Cong., 2d Sess. (1982) (status reports which examine the human rights policies of various countries for the purpose of aiding in determining their eligibility for assistance from the United States).

[180] On U.S. policy and its influence on other countries' human rights practices, *see* Derian, *Human Rights in American Foreign Policy*, 55 Notre Dame Law. 264 (1979).

[181] *See* ch. 11 *infra*.

[182] Mission of Lawyers to Argentina, *Report*, 34 Rec. A.B. City N.Y. 473 (1979).

graphy at the end of this chapter indicate materials which may be favored for brief consideration.

The basic international law of racial, sexual, and religious equality is set forth in the texts of the U.N. Charter, the Universal Declaration, the international covenants, both conventions, and the Religious Discrimination Declaration, all discussed in the foregoing pages. Interpretive materials, as noted above, may be found principally in scholarly commentary, a few committee or commission reports, and opinions of the European Commission and Court of Human Rights. Ordinarily, one would not consider an advocate's assertion of what the law requires to be an authoritative interpretation, but unilateral censure, criticism, or imposition of conditions (for example, as prerequisite to trade) sometimes are as effective as judicial or political decisions. Therefore, it is instructive to consider these sources as well.

The manner of teaching the subject, of course, is largely determined by the available sources and time which the instructor has to allocate. The bare rules should be mentioned, but, in this instance, they are relatively straightforward and with a few exceptions consist of what one might expect to find in a catalog of equal rights prescriptions. Of particular interest are rules which conflict with or are controversial in U.S. law. For example, affirmative action in employment and education merits discussion, not only in comparison to U.S. law, but with regard to the practice of other countries. So, too, does conflict between first amendment law and the international prohibition of activity or propaganda to incite racial hatred. The prohibition of discriminatory 'purpose' and 'effect' also bears comparison to U.S. law which in some situations only forbids conduct with discriminatory purpose, and other times may only prohibit discriminatory 'effect', and at yet other times combines 'purpose' and 'effect'.

For teaching purposes, a catalog of rights secured under the international accords might be drawn up and compared to protections of domestic law in order to ascertain the extent to which the United States in fact complies with international norms. This exercise would provide a useful background discussion of the United States' reluctance to ratify or its inclination to make reservations to international instruments on human rights. Specifically assigned projects might call for research into similar compliance issues in other countries. While U.S. constitutional law offers useful, highly articulated standards for comparison and guidance, so does the jurisprudence of the European Commission and Court of Human Rights. The law of other nations, *e.g.*, Great Britain and other English- or partially English-speaking countries such as Australia, Canada, South Africa, and India, may be readily accessible even at U.S. law schools with only modest library facilities. Students with language skills may possibly be able to venture further afield, as into German law, where there is a considerable human rights jurisprudence.

Finally, instruction may benefit from a clinical or quasi-clinical component—or at least a simulated one. Students might establish relationships with NGOs or private organizations and prepare complaints, briefs, memoranda, or other documents dealing with actual or alleged violations of human rights accords. Such techniques tend to reduce abstract propositions to concrete reality.

After reviewing the rules, domestic and international, and the judicial, political, and private activities which may achieve redress, it might be interesting and instructive to put them to use in simulated cases. One might select a number of issues of race, sex, or religious discrimination which have been decided by the U.S. Supreme Court and consider the means by which international human rights law could be brought to bear on them if they were to occur under various hypothetical circumstances. For example, one might consider what could be done if a particular situation were to occur in the United States and it had ratified the relevant conventions and covenants. There might be additional assumptions concerning whether ratification had occurred without qualification or whether the proposed reservations and declarations concerning non-self-execution had been adopted—and of course what weight, if any, domestic or international bodies would accord ratification hedged in this manner. The same cases might be viewed from a different perspective, as having occurred somewhere in the world other than the United States.

The range of cases which might be specimens for such exercises is vast. A teacher might engage classroom interest by using as the subject cases which are in the news as the semester develops. Or one might refer back to famous classic cases of U.S. equal rights law, *e.g.*, the School Segregation Cases, the Flag Salute Cases, the Abortion Cases, and so forth. All are available in any law library and in most general libraries. Moreover, most undergraduates constitutional law casebooks and, of course, law school casebooks contain much grist for this mill.

Cases

As an example of what might be done for an exercise of this sort, brief descriptions follow of three cases—race, sex, and religion—susceptible to such analysis, followed by reference to standards and procedures which might be brought to bear.

The first case is *Mclaughlin v. Florida*[183] in which defendants had been convicted of having violated a Florida statute which made it a

[183] 379 U.S. 184 (1964).

criminal offense for a white person and a black person of different sexes, not married to each other, to habitually live in and occupy in the night-time the same room. Florida sought to justify the law as a means of preventing breaches of the basic concepts of sexual decency. But the Supreme Court held that there was nothing in the suggested legislative purpose which made it essential to punish promiscuity between members of different racial groups and not that between members of the same group. The Court asserted that there was no suggestion that a white person and a black person are any more likely habitually to occupy the same room together than a white couple or a black couple, or to engage in illicit intercourse if they do. The Court concluded that Florida had trenched upon the constitutionally protected freedom from invidious official discrimination based on race. In the course of the opinion the Court expressed no view on the validity of laws prohibiting racial intermarriage, although several years later it declared them unconstitutional. It is interesting also that the Court implicitly upheld the notion of general state laws, which do not mention race, which punish sexual intercourse out of marriage.

The international ramifications will be discussed below, after posing some additional cases for consideration. But, for the moment, several general observations are in order: first, one might note the gingerly fashion in which the Court approached the issue in 1964. Today, a U.S. court and most judicial bodies with which this author is acquainted at least in the Western world, would have rejected the Florida law out of hand. But inter-racial sex was vastly more controversial in 1964 than it is today, although even today the subject can stir up rancorous argument.

McLaughlin might also be looked at for issues of sexual autonomy. Implicit in the decision is acceptance of the state's right to make sexual intercourse among nonmarried persons illegal. It is not clear whether most Americans would reject such a law today. Anti-fornication laws remain on the books and are enforced only very rarely. Nevertheless, they have not been held unconstitutional by the Supreme Court. In any event, it is worth noting that the subject matter of the *McLaughlin* case will lead to lively classroom discussion.

The second case for consideration is *Dothard v. Rawlinson*,[184] which involved an Alabama law specifying a minimum height of 5′2″ and a minimum weight of 120 pounds for eligibility for employment as a state prison guard. At issue also was a state regulation prohibiting the hiring of women as prison guards at maximum security male penitentiaries in 'contact positions', *i.e.*, those which require close physical proximity to inmates. These rules made it impossible for a great many

[184] 433 U.S. 321 (1977).

women to become prison guards and excluded them from many such jobs even if they were able to meet the height and weight requirements. The U.S. Supreme Court held the height and weight regulations invalid under the Equal Employment Opportunity Act of 1964, but upheld the exclusion from contact positions.

In the course of the opinions, a majority of Justices observed that the height–weight rule excluded 41% of women from prison guard jobs, but only 1% of men. Moreover, it had not been established that the height–weight requirements bore any relationship to ability to do the job. There had not been proof that some small women did not have the strength to do what was required of them. But a majority also held that the contact position exclusion bore a reasonable relationship to security problems in view of the fact that there was a great deal of violence in the prisons and that many prisoners were sex offenders.

Dissenting views included the observation that appearance of strength is often necessary to maintain discipline and that small women were therefore properly excluded. On the other hand, Justices who dissented from the contact position determination argued that general violence was unrelated to the sex of the guards and that women ought not to be required to pay the price for the depraved conduct of some prisoners which should be controlled in other ways.

Finally, the class could look at *Trans World Airlines v. Hardison*[185] which dealt with religious discrimination. In that case, an employee whose religion required him to observe his Sabbath on Saturday was discharged when he refused to work on Saturdays. He charged religious discrimination in violation of the 1964 Civil Rights Act. A majority of the U.S. Supreme Court held that the employer had made reasonable efforts to accommodate the religious needs of the employee, that the employer was not required to violate its collective bargaining contract with the union to accommodate the employee by breaching the seniority system, and that alternative plans, which would have permitted the employee to work only four days a week, would have unduly burdened the employer.

As a teaching exercise, consider these cases in terms of the U.N. Charter, the Universal Declaration, the international covenants, the two conventions, and the Religious Discrimination Declaration.

What provisions of these instruments would one invoke against laws prohibiting inter-racial sex as in *McLaughlin v. Florida*, unduly limiting employment of women in circumstances detailed in *Dothard v. Rawlinson*, or discriminating on the basis of religion as asserted in *Trans World Airlines v. Hardison*?

How would those rules be advanced in U.S. courts if the United

[185] 432 U.S. 63 (1977).

States were to ratify various international instruments? What difference would it make if there were reservations and requirements of further execution?

What if the cases arose in some other country which had ratified? What would be the domestic law consequences there?

How would the cases be presented to the international bodies discussed in chapter 10? What sort of evidentiary presentation would be persuasive? What would the likely outcome be?

Consider chapter 13 on the European Convention: what does its jurisprudence suggest concerning possible outcomes?

What unilateral means might there be of achieving the complainant's goals? Could censure of one country's practice by another (consider Jackson-Vanik) make a difference?

Which of the three cases summarized above is likely to muster sufficient national sentiment in one country to move it to criticize another?

Are there not probably only a handful of highly egregious, universally or near universally condemned practices which could form the basis of unilateral international action? In the area of discrimination, what are they?

What sort of unilateral NGO or private action is likely to have an effect? Again, what are likely to be the subjects which might evoke such expressions?

These exercises, of course, need not be limited to issues of discrimination. Other fundamental freedoms are apt specimens. Out of such specific case studies is likely to come an appreciation of how the international rules may be applied in particular circumstances, which techniques or combination of techniques may be productive, and, unfortunately, how limited the utility of international standards is at present. But from that realism may stem further resolve to devise remedies and, better, develop political consensus.

III. Syllabus

The following syllabus contemplates moderately thorough consideration of the subject matter of this chapter, perhaps as much as 10 to 15 hours.

1. The basic accords' provisions dealing with race, sex, and religious discrimination
   a. Charter.
   b. Universal Declaration.
   c. Political Covenant.
   d. Economic Covenant.

   e. Racial Discrimination Convention.
   f. Discrimination Against Women Convention.
   g. Religious Discrimination Declaration.
2. Other agreements concerned with the same issues.
   a. Slavery, genocide, *apartheid*.
   b. ILO, UNESCO.
   c. European Convention on Human Rights.
   d. Organization of American States.
   e. Helsinki Final Act.
3. Analogous provisions in U.S. law, their interpretation and application: a passing view of the fourteenth amendment, Title VII of the 1964 Civil Rights Act.
   a. Text of fourteenth amendment.
   b. Summaries of selected cases on race, sex, religion (*see*, *e.g.*, cases cited in text).
   c. Summary of substantive provisions of Title VII.
4. Analogies and conflicts in U.S. and international human rights law.
   a. Affirmative action.
   b. 'Purpose' and 'effect'.
   c. First amendment vs. prohibitions against racist propaganda.
5. Efforts to employ international standards in domestic law.
   a. U.S. experience; *Sei Fujii* and other cases cited in text.
   b. Other national experience, to the extent such materials are available.
6. Consideration of selected U.S. Supreme Court cases on the assumption of their presentation to an international forum.
   a. *McLaughlin* (*see* text).
   b. *Dothard* (*see* text).
   c. *Hardison* (*see* text).

IV. Minisyllabus

The following minisyllabus indicates priorities for teachers who devote only 2 or 3 hours to the subject.

1. The basic accords' provisions dealing with race, sex, and religious discrimination.
   a. Charter.
   b. Universal Declaration.
   c. Political Covenant.
   d. Racial Discrimination Convention.
2. Analogous provisions in U.S. law, their interpretation and application: a passing view of the fourteenth amendment.

  a. Text of fourteenth amendment.
  b. Summaries of selected cases on race, sex, and religion (*see, e.g.*, cases cited in text).
3. Analogies and conflicts in U.S. and international human rights law: affirmative action.

V. Bibliography

The following are extensive bibliographies on the subject matter of this book and chapter:

Reynolds, *Highest Aspiration or Barbarous Acts . . . The Explosion in Human Rights Documentation: A Bibliographic Survey*, 71 L. Lib. J. 1 (1978).

Vincent-Daviss, *Human Rights Law: A Research Guide to the Literature—Part I: International Law and the United Nations*, 14 N.Y.U. J. Int'l L. & Pol. 209 (1981); *Part II: International Protection of Refugees, and Humanitarian Law*, 14 N.Y.U. J. Int'l L. & Pol. 487 (1981); *Part III: Protection of Human Rights by the ILO and UNESCO*, 15 N.Y.U. J. Int'l L. & Pol. 000 (1982).

Books

Consult pertinent chapters of the following:

T. Buergenthal, Human Rights, International Law (1977).

J. Carey, International Protection of Human Rights (1968).

A. Henkin, Human Dignity (1978).

R. Lillich & F. Newman, International Human Rights: Problems of Law and Policy (1979).

M. McDougal, H. Lasswell & L. Chen, Human Rights and World Public Order (1980).

Articles

Bitker, *Application of the United Nations Universal Declaration of Human Rights Within the United States*, 21 De Paul L. Rev. 337 (1971).

Clark, *The United Nations and Religious Freedom*, 11 N.Y.U. J. Int'l L. & Pol. 264 (1979).

Guggenheim, *Implementation of Human Rights by the U.N. Commission on the Status of Women*, 12 Tex. Int'l L.J. 239 (1977).

Krishnaswami, *Study of Discrimination in the Matter of Religious Rights and Practices*, 11 N.Y.U. J. Int'l L. & Pol. 227 (1978).

Lillich, *The Role of Domestic Courts in Promoting International Human Rights Norms*, 24 N.Y.L.S. L. Rev. 153 (1978).

Mission of Lawyers to Argentina, *Report*, 34 Rec. A.B. City N.Y. 473 (1979).

Partsch, *Elimination of Racial Discrimination in the Enjoyment of Civil and Political Rights*, 14, Tex. Int'l L. J. 191 (1979).

Saario & Cass, *The United Nations and the International Protection of Human Rights: A Legal Analysis and Interpretation*, 7 Calif. W. Int'l L.J. 591 (1977).

Schachter, *International Law Implications of U.S. Human Rights Policies*, 24 N.Y.L.S. L. Rev. 63 (1978).

Schachter, *The Charter and the Constitution: The Human Rights Provision in American Law*, 4 Vand. L. Rev. 643 (1951).

Schachter, *The Obligation of the Parties to Give Effect to the Covenant on Civil and Political Rights*, 73 Am. J. Int'l L. 462 (1979).

Schlüter, *The Domestic Status of the Human Rights Clauses of the United Nations Charter*, 61 Calif. L. Rev. 110 (1973).

Sohn, *The Human Rights Law of the Charter*, 12 Tex. Int'l L.J. (1977).

Taubenfeld & Taubenfeld, *Achieving the Human Rights of Women: The Baseline, The Challenge, The Search for a Strategy*, 4 Human Rights 125 (1975).

Principal Texts and their Articles

United Nations Charter

Articles: preamble, 1, 8, 13, 55, 62, and 76.

Universal Declaration of Human Rights, G.A. Res. 217A U.N. Doc. A/810, at 71 (1948)

Articles: preamble, 1, 2, 3, 4, 7, 8, 10, 13, 15, 16, 17, 18, 21, 23, and 26.

International Convention on the Elimination of All Forms of Racial Discrimination, 660 U.N.T.S. 195.

Articles: preamble, 1, 2, 4, 5, and 6.

International Covenant on Economic, Social and Cultural Rights, G. A. Res. 2200, 21 U.N. GAOR, Supp. (No. 16) 49, U.N. Doc. A/6316 (1966).

Articles: preamble, 2, 3, 7, and 13.

International Covenant on Civil and Political Rights, G.A. Res. 2200, 21 U.N. GAOR, Supp. (No. 16) 52, U.N. Doc. A/6316 (1966).

Articles: 2, 3, 4, 8, 14, 16, 20, 23, 24, 25, 26, and 27.

Convention on the Elimination of All Forms of Discrimination Against Women, U.N. Doc. A/RES/34/180 (1979).

Articles: 2–10, 13, 15, and 16.

Declaration on the Elimination of All Forms of Intolerance and of Discrimination Based on Religion or Belief, G.A. Res. 36/55, U.N. Doc. A/RES/36/55 (1981).

Articles: 1, 5, 6, 7, and 8.

[European] Convention for the Protection of Human Rights and Fundamental Freedoms, 213 U.N.T.S. 221.
Articles: preamble, 4, 9, 12, and 14.

VI. Minibibliography

Bitker, *Application of the United Nations Universal Declaration of Human Rights Within the United States*, 21 De Paul L. Rev. 337 (1971).

Lillich, *The Role of Domestic Courts in Promoting International Human Rights Norms*, 24 N.Y.L.S. L. Rev. 153 (1978).

M. McDougal, H. Lasswell, & L. Chen, Human Rights and World Public Order (1980) (pertinent chapters).

Schachter, *International Law Implications of U.S. Human Rights Policies*, 24 N.Y.L.S. L. Rev. 63 (1978).

Schachter, *The Obligation of the Parties to Give Effect to the Covenant on Civil and Political Rights*, 73 Am. J. Int'l. L. 462 (1979).

Chapter 9

Human Rights in Armed Conflict: International Humanitarian Law*

Yoram Dinstein

I. Legal and Policy Considerations

A. INTRODUCTION

International law is primarily an inter-state legal system. That is to say, the rights and the duties that it creates devolve mainly on states. In this cardinal respect, there is very little difference between the special rules governing the law of armed conflict and the international legal norms applicable in general in peacetime. Nevertheless, more and more rights are being conferred by modern international law directly on individual human beings *per se*. Again, this is equally true in general as in the particular case of armed conflict. In other words, both in peacetime and in wartime, international law creates human rights.

The laws of armed conflict, like the rest of the international legal system, are partly customary and partly conventional. Many of the customary norms have been codified and now form parts of declaratory conventions. But there are still quite a few customary rules which are not reflected in any *jus scriptum*. Thus, for instance, the right of angary[1] is based on customary rather than conventional international law.[2]

As far as conventions are concerned, whether declaratory or constitutive by nature, there are two main sets of treaties. One consists of more than fifteen conventions adopted by the Hague Peace Conferences of 1899 and 1907.[3] The other comprises the four Conventions for the Protection of War Victims concluded in Geneva in 1949,[4] and two Additional Protocols done in 1977 also in Geneva.[5]

It is common practice to refer to the Geneva Conventions and Protocols as international humanitarian law. This appellation underlines the humanitarian motives that impelled the international com-

[1] Angary is the right of a belligerent, when in imperative need, to requisition neutral ships in its territory or in an occupied territory against full compensation. *See* G. Schwarzenberger, The Law of Armed Conflict 636 (1968).

[2] *See* G. von Glahn, Law Among Nations 753 (4th ed. 1981).

[3] The Hague Conventions of 1899 and 1907 are *reprinted in* 1 The Law of War: A Documentary History 204, 270 (L. Friedman ed. 1972) [hereinafter cited as Documents].

[4] The Geneva Conventions of 1949 are *reprinted in id.* at 525.

[5] *Reprinted in* 16 Int'l Legal Materials 1391 (1977).

munity to adopt them. It must be observed, however, that all the laws of war—whether formulated in Geneva, The Hague, or elsewhere—are an outcome of a realistic compromise between humanitarian considerations, on the one hand, and the requirements of military necessity, on the other. It is arguable that the Geneva Conventions reflect the tilting of the scales in favor of humanitarian considerations, whereas in other instances (principally, the Hague Conventions) there is a more balanced equilibrium between such considerations and the demands of military necessity. But, historically, many of the provisions of the Geneva Conventions are derived from the Hague Conventions. This is particularly true of the Geneva Convention for the Amelioration of the Condition of Wounded, Sick, and Shipwrecked Members of the Armed Forces at Sea of 12 August 1949 (Second Geneva Convention).[6] It replaces the Tenth Hague Convention of 1907,[7] which for its part was an adaptation to maritime warfare of the principles of the Geneva Convention for the Amelioration of the Condition of the Wounded and Sick in Armies in the Field of 6 July 1906.[8] The latter is the precursor of the Geneva Convention for the Amelioration of the Condition of the Wounded and Sick in Armed Forces in the Field of 12 August 1949 (First Geneva Convention).[9] Needless to say, the mere transposition of stipulations from one instrument drafted at The Hague to another formulated in Geneva does not by itself modify their nature. Legal norms do not acquire a humanitarian nature simply because they are incorporated in one series of conventions rather than another. Their character must be determined by substance and not by purely technical criteria.

In any event, international humanitarian law must not be confused with international human rights. First, it must be borne in mind that some wartime international human rights exist not as part of international humanitarian law but as a component of the ordinary (Hague-type) law of armed conflict. For instance, the protection of private property in occupied territories is governed, for the most part, not by the Geneva Conventions or Protocols but by the Hague Regulations (annexed to the Second Convention of 1899[10] and the Fourth Convention of 1907)[11] Respecting the Laws and Customs of War on Land.[12]

Secondly, international humanitarian law bestows rights not only

[6] 6 U.S.T. 3217, T.I.A.S. No. 3363, 75 U.N.T.S. 85.
[7] 36 Stat. 2371, T.S. No. 543.
[8] *Reprinted in* 1 Documents, *supra* note 3, at 257.
[9] 6 U.S.T. 3114, T.I.A.S. No. 3362, 75 U.N.T.S. 31.
[10] 32 Stat. 1803, T.S. No. 403.
[11] 36 Stat. 2277, T.S. No. 539.
[12] *See* G. Von Glahn, The Occupation of Enemy Territory 185–91 (1957).

on human beings as such, but also (and chiefly) on states. The adjective 'humanitarian' describes the contents of the norms and not the subject bound by them. There is one segment of international humanitarian law that applies directly to individuals, but there is another that applies only to states. Thus, article 7 of the First, Second, and Third Geneva Conventions,[13] as well as article 8 of the Fourth Convention,[14] explicitly refer to rights secured to persons protected by the Geneva Conventions. These are obviously human rights. On the other hand, many provisions in the four Geneva Conventions clearly create rights of states. By way of illustration, under article 16 of the First Convention and article 19 of the Second Convention, each belligerent is obligated to keep a record of particulars identifying wounded, sick, shipwrecked, or dead persons of the adverse party falling into its hands, and forward the information to the adverse party through the medium of a central Bureau. The corresponding right is accorded not to the individual victim of war (who may not even be alive), but to his or her state.

To the extent that international humanitarian law—and even more so the Hague Conventions—engender human rights, it is interesting to note the dates when the central instruments were formulated. Whereas the development of the international human rights of peacetime began in earnest only after World War II, some fundamental freedoms of wartime had a seminal existence even before World War I. Insofar as many peacetime human rights are concerned, 1948—the year in which the U.N. General Assembly adopted the Universal Declaration of Human Rights[15]—was the *dies a quo* from which they first started to crystallize in international law. By contrast, as regards numerous wartime human rights, 1949—the year in which the Geneva Conventions were opened for ratification—was the *dies ad quem* which finalized their consolidation as binding legal norms. It is thus safe to state that, generally speaking, wartime human rights preceded those of peacetime in the international arena. This should not be surprising, given the fact that historically the law of war is the most ancient part of international law.

For the most part, international humanitarian law deals with problems generated by inter-state wars. Thus, most of the stipulations of the four Geneva Conventions (some 400 articles) and the entire Protocol Additional to the Geneva Conventions of 12 August 1949, and Relating to the Protection of Victims of International Armed Conflicts

[13] Geneva Convention relative to the Treatment of Prisoners of War of 12 August 1949, 6 U.S.T. 3316, T.I.A.S. No. 3364, 75 U.N.T.S. 135.

[14] Geneva Convention relative to the Protection of Civilian Persons in Time of War of 12 August 1949, 6 U.S.T. 3516, T.I.A.S. No. 3365, 75 U.N.T.S. 287.

[15] G.A. Res. 217A, U.N. Doc. A/810, at 71 (1948).

(Protocol I)[16] (more than 100 articles) are devoted to international armed conflicts. However, to some extent intra-state, *i.e.*, internal, armed conflicts are also regulated by international humanitarian law. The subject is covered by article 3 common to the four Geneva Conventions and by the entire Protocol Additional to the General Conventions of 12 August 1949, and Relating to the Protection of Victims of Non-International Armed Conflicts (Protocol II).[17] Protocol II augments the protection afforded to the victims of internal wars, but it has a narrower scope of application than common article 3.[18] The human rights which are in force during internal armed conflicts raise a number of legal, psychological, and practical problems because of the unique circumstances of a conflict in which one of the parties is not a government but a group of rebels.[19] Yet, civil wars can be as devastating as inter-state wars, and the challenge that they pose to human rights must not be underrated.

B. THE ESSENCE OF HUMAN RIGHTS IN ARMED CONFLICTS

Broadly speaking, wartime human rights can be divided into two categories: (i) rights granted to lawful or privileged combatants, *i.e.*, combatants respecting the laws of war and meeting the conditions which that body of law establishes;[20] and (ii) rights accorded to civilians.

In essence, the human rights of lawful combatants are two-fold:

(a) They have the right to the status of prisoners of war once they are placed *hors de combat* by force of circumstances (being wounded, sick, or shipwrecked) or by choice (laying down their arms). A series of specific subrights relating to the humane treatment of wounded, sick, and shipwrecked combatants is incorporated in the First and Second Geneva Conventions. However, it is primarily the Third Geneva Convention which details the protection that must be rendered to all prisoners of war, the injured as well as the able-bodied.

(b) Lawful combatants also have the right not to be targets of

[16] *Reprinted in* 16 Int'l Legal Materials 1391 (1977).

[17] *Reprinted in* 16 Int'l Legal Materials 1442 (1977).

[18] *See* Dinstein, *The New Geneva Protocols: A Step Forward or Backward?*, 33 Y.B. World Aff. 265, 279–80 (1979) [hereinafter cited as Dinstein]. *Cf.* Boyd, Digest of United States Practice in International Law 1977, at 924–30 (while the 'scope of application of the Protocol' is 'its Achilles heel' the 'Protocol nevertheless accomplishes much in developing the law . . .').

[19] *See* Dinstein, *The International Law of Civil War and Human Rights*, 6 Isr. Y.B. on Human Rights 62, 66–69 (1976).

[20] On the conditions laid down by the Geneva Conventions, *see* Meron, *Some Legal Aspects of Arab Terrorists' Claims to Privileged Combatancy*, in Of Law and Man 225 (S. Shoham ed. 1971), *reprinted in* 40 Acta Scandinavica Juris Gentium 47 (1970). On the changes introduced by the Additional Protocols, *see* Dinstein, *supra* note 18, at 269–73.

biological, bacteriological, or chemical weapons, poison, and several types of bullets or projectiles. Each forbidden item entails a separate subright and the *corpus juris* is to be found in instruments such as the 1868 St. Petersburg Declaration Renouncing the Use in War of Certain Explosive Projectiles,[21] the Hague Regulations,[22] and the 1925 Geneva Protocol for the Prohibition of Poisonous Gases and Bacteriological Methods of Warfare.[23]

The human rights of civilians in time of war relate to (a) the civilian population anywhere; (b) civilian enemy aliens in the territory of a belligerent state; and (c) the civilian population in occupied territories. The main legal provisions on which the protection of civilians is based are articles 42–56 of the Hague Regulations,[24] which relate to occupied territories, the Fourth Geneva Convention, pertaining to civilians generally but especially to enemy aliens and occupied territories, and Part IV of Protocol I, relevant to the civilian population as a whole. Under Protocol I, the civilian population as such, as well as individual civilians, enjoy the right to general protection against dangers arising from military operations.[25] Specifically, they are granted subrights against indiscriminate attacks,[26] reprisals,[27] destruction of cultural objects and places of worship,[28] starvation,[29] and so forth.[30] A Convention on Prohibitions or Restrictions on the Use of Certain Conventional Weapons which May Be Deemed to Be Excessively Injurious or to Have Indiscriminate Effects, concluded in 1980, protects civilians against incendiary weapons and mines.[31]

Traditionally, the rights of civilians are especially safeguarded under belligerent occupation. The laws of war establish a minimum international standard of due process of law for securing life, liberty, and property of civilians in occupied territories.[32] But it must be understood that civilians in occupied territories are not absolutely protected. Indeed, in certain circumstances, they may be deprived of their lives, liberty, and property. However, due process of law is a *conditio sine qua non* to such deprivation. Hence, the taking of hostages, an arbitrary measure *par excellence*, is prohibited,[33] whereas capital punish-

[21] *Reprinted in* 1 Documents, *supra* note 3, at 192.
[22] *See* notes 10 & 11 *supra*.
[23] *Reprinted in* 1 Documents, *supra* note 3, at 454.
[24] *See* notes 10 & 11 *supra*.
[25] *See* Protocol I, art. 51(1).
[26] *Id.* art. 51(4).
[27] *Id.* arts. 51(6) & 52(1).
[28] *Id.* art. 53. [29] *Id.* art. 54(1).
[30] *See generally id.* arts. 51–56.
[31] Int'l Rev. Red Cross No. 220, Jan.–Feb. 1981, at 42.
[32] *See* Dinstein, *The International Law of Belligerent Occupation and Human Rights*, 8 Isr. Y.B. on Human Rights 104 (1978).
[33] *See* Fourth Geneva Convention, art. 34.

ment (if not abolished prior to the war within a territory subsequently occupied) may be pronounced by a competent court of the occupying state.[34] Civilians in occupied territories may be detained, even as a preventive-administrative measure, but a required procedure must be followed.[35] 'Contributions', which are involuntary, can be levied from the inhabitants of occupied territories provided that prescribed conditions are met.[36] Numerous other examples could be cited.

As for intra-state wars, the aforementioned article 3 common to the four Geneva Conventions establishes certain minimal human rights for persons taking no active part in the hostilities and for members of armed forces who are *hors de combat*. They are protected against murder, mutilation, cruel treatment, torture, taking of hostages, and the like. Nevertheless, humane treatment in the case of prisoners does not mean that they can only be kept captive and may not be executed. The execution of a prisoner on a charge of treason is perfectly permissible, provided that it follows a fair trial. What is disallowed is execution without due process of law. Protocol II supplements the human rights applicable during civil wars by detailed provisions relating to the protection of civilians in general,[37] children,[38] detainees,[39] the wounded, sick, and shipwrecked,[40] and persons facing penal prosecution.[41]

C. THE INTERPLAY OF HUMAN RIGHTS IN PEACETIME AND WARTIME

To appreciate the precise nature and the full complexity of the manifold human rights which are in force under international law in time of armed conflict, it is useful to compare them to the ordinary human rights that exist in peacetime. With such a comparison as a yardstick, six variations come into focus. These can be schematically presented as follows, with X representing a human right and O representing its absence (see table opposite).

Variation 1

This is the typical position of most human rights: they exist in peacetime, but may *disappear completely* in wartime. Thus, the fact that an armed conflict exists has a crucial significance for the average

[34] *See id.* art. 68.
[35] *See id.* art. 78.
[36] *See* Hague Regulations, *supra* notes 10 & 11, art. 49.
[37] Protocol II, arts. 4, 13–17.
[38] *Id.* art. 4(3).
[39] *Id.* art. 5.
[40] *Id.* arts. 7–12.
[41] *Id.* art. 6.

	Human Rights Applicable	
	In Peacetime	*In Wartime*
1	X	O
2	X	X
3	O	X
4	O	O
5	X	X minus
6	X	X plus

human right, which is suspended for the duration of the conflict. The suspension is not however automatic, but is left to the discretion of the involved state. For example, the [European] Convention for the Protection of Human Rights and Fundamental Freedoms states:

> In time of war or other public emergency threatening the life of the nation any High Contracting Party may take measures derogating from its obligations under this Convention to the extent strictly required by the exigencies of the situation, provided that such measures are not inconsistent with its other obligations under international law.[42]

A similar provision appears in article 30 of the European Social Charter,[43] article 4 of the International Covenant on Civil and Political Rights[44] (although it avoids the explicit term 'war'), and article 27 of the American Convention on Human Rights.[45]

The impact of an emergency situation on human rights was elucidated in the first judgment of the European Court of Human Rights, delivered in 1961, in the *Lawless Case*.[46] Lawless was a member of the Irish Republican Army (IRA) which employs terrorist methods with a view to joining the Northern Ireland part of the United Kingdom to the independent Republic of Ireland. Lawless was arrested by the Irish authorities and held for several months in administrative detention without trial in accordance with a special statute which vested in those authorities emergency powers for the suppression of acts of terrorism. Lawless petitioned the European Commission of Human Rights, which brought the case before the European Court of Human Rights. Even though the European Court held that, in general, administrative detentions are incompatible with the human rights guaranteed by the European Convention, it decided that in this

[42] 213 U.N.T.S. 221, art. 159(1), *reprinted in* Basic Documents on Human Rights 242 (2d ed. I. Brownlie 1981) [hereinafter cited as Brownlie].

[43] Europ. T.S. No. 35, *reprinted in* Brownlie, *supra* note 42, at 301.

[44] G.A. Res. 2200, 21 U.N. GAOR, Supp. (No. 16) 52, U.N. Doc. A/6316 (1966).

[45] O.A.S. T.S. No. 36, *reprinted in* Brownlie, *supra* note 42, at 391.

[46] Lawless Case (Merits), 3 Judgments Europ. Ct. of Human Rights 27 (1961).

instance Ireland had acted lawfully in view of the emergency and in the light of article 15 of the European Convention.[47] The result would of course be the same in wartime. Thus, if freedom from arbitrary detention in peacetime is represented by X, in time of armed conflict a government may suspend X and the individual is faced with O.

Variation 2

Exceptionally, some human rights are not subject to suspension even in wartime. That is, despite the fact that an armed conflict is being waged, the human rights in question are left intact. Each of the four derogation clauses mentioned under variation 1 lists a number of human rights which are excepted from its applicability. Foremost among the rights which cannot be suspended in wartime is freedom from torture. Indeed, the existence of this specific freedom in wartime is derived not merely from its not being subject to derogation; it is also, and independently, guaranteed under international humanitarian law. Thus, in noninternational armed conflicts, torture is expressly forbidden in the common article 3 of the four Geneva Conventions, as well as in article 4 of Protocol II. In international conflicts, torture is proscribed in articles 12 of the First and Second Geneva Conventions, article 17 of the Third Convention, and article 32 of the Fourth Convention.[48] It is also prohibited by article 75(2) of Protocol I. Consequently, if freedom from torture is represented by X, X is equally valid in wartime as in peacetime.

Variation 3

It is important to take into account the fact that the scope of wartime human rights is not limited to a partial list of peacetime human rights which cannot be or have not been suspended. In some instances, the special circumstances of an armed conflict engender new human rights which are valid in particular *vis-à-vis* an enemy state or an occupying power where no such rights existed before in the peaceful relationship between a person and the state of nationality or residence. For example, in peacetime there is no human right to avoid military service or alternative national service in the state of residence. Admittedly, freedom from forced or compulsory labour is recognized in article 4 of the European Convention, article 8 of the Political Covenant, and article 6 of the American Convention. Yet, all three clauses exclude from that freedom compulsory military service or, in the case of conscientious objectors, alternative national service. By contrast, in occupied terri-

[47] *Id.* at 54–62.

[48] Torture is a grave breach of the Geneva Conventions. *See* First Convention, art. 50; Second Convention, art. 51; Third Convention, art. 130; Fourth Convention, art. 147.

tories in wartime article 51 of the Fourth Geneva Convention bans compulsion of civilians to serve in the armed or auxiliary forces of the Occupying Power. If freedom from military service under belligerent occupation in wartime is represented by X, in peacetime there is no counterpart human right.

Variation 4

For the sake of the completion of the analysis, it should be noted that certain rights advocated by humanitarian activists and lawyers have not attained the status of recognized human rights either in peacetime or in wartime. They must, therefore, be represented by O on both sides of the diagram.

A case in point is that of freedom of immigration. Whereas international law vouchsafes to every person freedom of emigration, *i.e.*, the right to leave any country, including his or her own, on a permanent basis,[49] there is no parallel rule of general international law sanctioning freedom of immigration, *i.e.*, the right to enter a foreign country with a view to settling there.[50] This freedom is equally non-existent in peacetime as in wartime.

Variation 5

Often a human right which is full-fledged in peacetime continues to exist in wartime, but due to the exigencies of the armed conflict its scope of application is *severely limited*. Let us take as an illustration freedom of assembly. This right is enshrined in article 20 of the Universal Declaration, article 11 of the European Convention, article 5(d)(ix) of the International Convention on the Elimination of All Forms of Racial Discrimination,[51] article 21 of the Political Covenant, and article 15 of the American Convention. Freedom of assembly is admittedly subject to the derogation clauses referred to above, and may, therefore, be suspended altogether in wartime.

However, as indicated above, suspension of human rights in the course of an armed conflict is a right and not a duty. Suppose, for the sake of argument, that freedom of assembly is not suspended altogether by a belligerent state. Freedom of assembly is not an absolute right even in peacetime. As the provisions of the Political Covenant, the European Convention, and the American Convention enunciate in no uncertain terms, restrictions may be placed on the exercise of freedom of assembly if imposed in conformity with the law and where necessary

[49] *See* Dinstein, *Freedom of Emigration and Soviet Jewry*, 4 Isr. Y.B. on Human Rights 266 (1974).

[50] *See* G. Goodwin-Gill, International Law and the Movement of Persons between States 196–97 (1978).

[51] 660 U.N.T.S. 195, *reprinted in* Brownlie, *supra* note 42, at 150.

in the interests of, *inter alia*, national security. National security considerations in the course of an armed conflict could legitimately dictate a severe curtailment of freedom of assembly, in terms of the nature of the gathering, its size, etc., even where a similar limitation is peacetime would be viewed as unjustifiable. It follows that if freedom of assembly in peacetime is represented by X, in wartime (assuming that it does not go down to O) we are confronted with X minus.

Variation 6

The reverse also happens in some cases so that the position in wartime of a human right is X plus. Freedom from medical experimentation may exemplify this. In peacetime, there is only a general provision in article 7 of the Political Covenant which provides that no one shall be subjected without free consent to medical or scientific experimentation. In wartime there are also general injunctions against biological experiments[52] as well as medical or scientific experiments of any kind which are not necessitated by the medical treatment of the protected person and carried out in his interest.[53] But, moreover, article 11 of Protocol I incorporates a much more detailed provision which rules out removal of tissue or organs for transplantation even with the consent of the donor, though an exception is made for voluntary donations of blood for transfusion or of skin for grafting. In peacetime, too, there is a grave problem of 'engineering of consent', particularly by exploiting the condition of necessitous men.[54] Nevertheless, there is no peacetime counterpart to the sophisticated stipulation of Protocol I.

D. THE INTERPLAY OF HUMAN RIGHTS AND CORRESPONDING DUTIES IN ARMED CONFLICT

The concept of a right connotes the existence of a corresponding obligation. When international human rights are involved, the rights are bestowed directly on individuals, but the corresponding obligations are generally incurred by states. From the viewpoint of those corresponding obligations, human rights may be subsumed under three headings depending on the states implicated. The duties corresponding to human rights may be imposed (a) on all the states of the world; (b) only on the state of which the individual is a national; or (c) solely on the states of which the individual is not a national. Most peacetime human rights, whether or not suspended in wartime, come within the bounds of the first two categories. On the other hand,

[52] First Geneva Convention, art. 12; Second Geneva Convention, art. 12.

[53] Third Geneva Convention, art. 12; Fourth Geneva Convention, art. 32. Biological experiments are grave breaches of the Convention. *See* note 48 *supra*.

[54] *See* E. Cahn, Confronting Injustice 366–67 (1966).

wartime human rights afforded to lawful combatants and to the civilian population belong primarily to the third category. In fact, the obligations corresponding to these human rights are incumbent not on an ordinary foreign state but on a very special one, an enemy state.

It goes without saying that the relationship between an individual and an enemy state in wartime is entirely different from the relationship between an individual and his or her state (or any other state) in peacetime. If in peacetime one may presume that a certain degree of goodwill characterizes the relations between the state and at least many of the individuals to which it owes certain obligations, in wartime no such presumption is valid *vis-à-vis* enemy subjects. The situation is abnormal and it calls for a special legal mechanism.

This special legal mechanism is based on a duality of rights. The obligations are binding on the enemy state. The dual rights, which exist simultaneously, are granted to the individual, as lawful combatant or civilian, as well as to the state to which he or she owes allegiance. The human right, of the lawful combatant or civilian, and the state right, of his or her state of nationality, consequently correspond to a single obligation imposed on the enemy state. This duality of rights has beneficial results from both a practical and a theoretical standpoint.

From a practical angle, since the state right and the human right exist contemporaneously yet independently, a more effective protection of the individual is made feasible. The lawful combatant or civilian may stand on his or her right without having to rely on the goodwill of the state of nationality and, by the same token, the state of nationality may stand on its right without depending on a call for help from the individual. If, for instance, a prisoner of war is tortured, the right of the prisoner and the right of the state of nationality are violated at one and the same time. Each is entitled to take whatever steps are available and deemed appropriate by virtue of their separate rights. Moreover, neither one of them is capable of waiving the other's independent right. The fact that the prisoner may not be willing to take action on the basis of his or her human right does not restrict the state of nationality. Similarly, the fact that the state of nationality is prepared to forgive and forget the incident does not bind the prisoner.

From a theoretical perspective, the fact that the state of nationality is waging a war of aggression, constituting a crime against peace,[55] does not detract from human rights which are not its own rights. This is particularly significant in the light of the fundamental principle *ex*

[55] For a definition of crimes against peace, *see* art. 6(a), Charter of the International Military Tribunal, annexed to the Agreement for the Prosecution and Punishment of Major War Criminals of the European Axis, *reprinted in* 1 Documents, *supra* note 3, at 885, 886–87 [hereinafter cited as Nuremberg Charter].

injuria jus non oritur. In accordance with that principle, it is possible to argue that the offending state, having perpetrated a crime against international law, cannot reap the benefits which ordinarily accrue to belligerents under the laws of war, and that a distinction must be made between it and the state which was the victim of aggression.[56] But, even if the argument is plausible, it would not affect the human rights of lawful combatants and civilians who were not accomplices to the crime.[57] Crimes against peace can be committed only by high-ranking persons (organs of the state) responsible for the formulation and execution of state policies.[58] Other individuals, below policy level, may not be regarded as criminals against peace. As a result, they are entitled to enjoy the human rights which are granted to them directly by the laws of war irrespective of the criminal conduct of their state.

In some instances, the special legal structure of wartime human rights produces not only a duality of rights, but also a duality of corresponding duties. Thus, if soldier *X* of state *A* tortures prisoner of war *Y* from state *B*, not only has state *A* violated an international legal obligation corresponding to the human right of *Y* and the state right of *B* but *X* himself concurrently contravenes a duty which devolves directly on him under international law. By torturing a prisoner of war, *X* commits a war crime,[59] and he is personally liable to prosecution and punishment regardless of the sanctions which may or may not be applied to state *A*.

E. PROBLEMS OF IMPLEMENTATION AND SUPERVISION

The problem of implementation and supervision plagues international law as a whole because of the absence of a permanent international police force and an international court with universal compulsory jurisdiction. The problem is particularly acute where violations of human rights are concerned inasmuch as the relations between an individual victim of such violations and the state are characterized by enormous inequality. If this is true generally of human rights, it is especially true of wartime human rights.

There is no time like wartime in which passions are inflamed and even civilized persons, steeped in humanitarian values which appear to be self-evident in peacetime, are apt to show no restraint and to defend the indefensible out of devotion to the national cause and a conviction that the end (victory over the enemy) justifies the means. The extreme

[56] *See* Lauterpacht, *The Limits of the Operation of the Law of War*, 30 Brit. Y.B. Int'l L. 206, 212 (1953); Wright, *The Outlawry of War and the Law of War*, 47 Am. J. Int'l L. 365, 370–71 (1953).

[57] *See id.* at 373.

[58] *See* Dinstein, *International Criminal Law*, 5 Isr. Y.B. on Human Rights 55, 58 (1975).

[59] For a definition of war crimes, *see* art. 6(b), Nuremberg Charter, *supra* note 55, at 887.

barbarism of World War II, epitomized by the Holocaust, was admittedly unprecedented in the modern age, but violations of human rights occur in every war.

When such violations take place, it is not only the victim of the violation and its perpetrator who are involved. The whole international community has a definite interest that the legal structure of human rights should not crumble. The interest of the world at large in the observance of human rights in wartime is reflected in the fact that many of these rights are now viewed as emanating from peremptory norms of general international law, *i.e.*, *jus cogens*. Under article 53 of the Vienna Convention on the Law of Treaties,[60] any conflicting treaty will therefore be void. In other words no 'contracting out' from imperative human rights is possible. As pointed out by Sir Gerald Fitzmaurice:

> If two countries were to agree that, in any future hostilities between them, neither side would be bound to take any prisoners of war, and all captured personnel would be liable for execution, it is clear that even though this was intended only for application as between the parties, and not *vis-à-vis* any other country that might be involved in hostilities with either of them, such an arrangement would be illegal and void.[61]

It is noteworthy that a common provision of the Geneva Convention[62] expressly provides that parties may not conclude special agreements adversely affecting the situation of protected persons. This prohibition follows primarily from the duality of rights referred to above: protected persons are entitled to human rights independently of state rights, and states may not renounce rights which do not belong to them. Under the aforementioned common provision, protected persons, for their part, may in no circumstances renounce in part or in whole the rights secured to them.

Another result of the duality of rights in wartime is that reprisals cannot be freely used with a view to safeguarding the observance of legal norms. Ordinarily, the implementation of the law of armed conflict hinges, to a very large degree, on practical considerations of reciprocity and the fear of reprisals. That is to say, whereas in peacetime states are often prepared to sleep on their infringed rights, wartime is marked by an absence of moderation with retaliation following swiftly. The prospect of reprisals serves as a sobering and inhibiting factor on a state which contemplates a departure from accepted norms of behavior. However, when state *A* commits an

[60] U.N. Doc. A/CONF.39/27 (1969), *reprinted in* 8 Int'l Legal Materials 679 (1969).

[61] Fitzmaurice, Third Report on Law of Treaties, U.N. Doc. A/CN.4/115, *reprinted in* [1958] 2 Y.B. Int'l L. Comm'n 20, 40, U.N. Doc. A/CN.4/SER.A/1958/Add. 1.

[62] Arts. 6 of the First, Second, and Third Geneva Conventions; art. 7 of the Fourth Geneva Convention.

illegal act against state *B* warranting reprisals, state *B* is not allowed to retaliate by performing an act which constitutes a violation of the independent human rights of persons who had nothing to do with the original illegality. Thus, if state *A* kills prisoners of war of state *B*, state *B* (while entitled to retaliate in other ways) may not kill prisoners of war of state *A*. Article 13 of the Third Geneva Convention expressly proclaims: 'Measures of reprisal against prisoners of war are prohibited.' Similar prohibitions of reprisals against protected persons appear in the other Geneva Conventions[63] and in Protocol I.[64]

Should wartime human rights be violated by a belligerent state or persons forming part of its armed forces, that state bears full international responsibility for the violation. If the case demands, the state must pay compensation in accordance with article 3 of the Fourth Hague Convention of 1907[65] and article 91 of Protocol I. The State may not absolve itself from international responsibility on the grounds that it has already punished the persons who committed the violation.[66]

On the other hand, the person who committed the violation may be punished by the state of his or her own nationality, under its domestic legal system, or even by any other state, under international law. As far as the state of nationality is concerned, it is required to ensure observance of the laws of war by issuing appropriate instructions to its armed forces and supervising their execution.[67] It must also enact any legislation necessary to provide effective penal sanctions for grave breaches of the Geneva Conventions.[68]

If the violation of wartime human rights constitutes a crime under international law, *i.e.*, a war crime or a crime against humanity,[69] so that there is a duality of duties corresponding to the duality of rights, the offender may be prosecuted and punished by any state, particularly, though not necessarily, by the enemy state. Jurisdiction over such crimes is universal.[70] Moreover, as the judgments of the International Military Tribunals in *Nuremberg*[71] and *Tokyo*[72] palpably demon-

[63] *See* art. 46, First Geneva Conventions art. 47, Second Geneva Convention; art. 33, Fourth Geneva Convention.

[64] Arts. 20 & 51(6).

[65] *Reprinted in* 1 Documents, *supra* note 3, at 310.

[66] *See* Third Geneva Convention: Commentary 630 (J. Preux ed. 1960).

[67] *See, e.g.*, art. 1, Fourth Hague Convention; art. 80, Protocol I.

[68] *See* art. 49, First Geneva Convention; art. 50, Second Geneva Convention; art. 129, Third Geneva Convention; art. 146, Fourth Geneva Convention.

[69] For a definition of crimes against humanity, *see* art. 6(c), Nuremberg Charter, *supra* note 55, at 887.

[70] *See* Baxter, *The Municipal and International Law Basis of Jurisdiction over War Crimes*, 28 Brit. Y.B. Int'l L. 382, 392 (1951).

[71] *Reprinted in* 2 Documents, *supra* note 3, at 922.

[72] *Reprinted in* 2 Documents, *supra* note 3, at 1029.

strate, war criminals (in the broad sense of the term) can be brought to justice even before an international criminal court. As the *Nuremberg* judgment proclaims:

> Crimes against international law are committed by men, not by abstract entities, and only by punishing individuals who commit such crimes can the provisions of international law be enforced.[73]

The trouble is that no permanent international criminal court has yet been established. National proceedings against enemy war criminals are often tainted with lack of objectivity and, more often than not, take place only at the end of war when they are usually limited to trials of the vanquished by the victors.

Can something be done during an armed conflict to prevent violations of human rights, instead of simply waiting and punishing violators after the end of the conflict? The solution furnished by international law lies in the appointment of a Protecting Power, *i.e.*, a neutral country which undertakes to protect the interests of one party to the conflict and its nationals *vis-à-vis* another party. A common provision of the Geneva Conventions[74] stipulates that the Conventions shall be applied with the cooperation and under the scrutiny of Protecting Powers. Article 5 of Protocol I declares that it is the duty of parties to the conflict to secure the supervision and implementation of international humanitarian law by the application of the system of Protecting Powers.

However, the appointment of a Protecting Power is unfortunately contingent on acquiring the trilateral consent of all concerned, both belligerents as well as the neutral country selected, and in practice such consent proves elusive. In order to facilitate the process, article 5 of Protocol I provides that if the required consent has not been attained, the International Committee of the Red Cross (ICRC) shall, and any other impartial humanitarian organization may, offer its good offices in order to designate a Protecting Power. The ICRC may, *inter alia*, ask each party to the conflict to proffer a list of at least five states considered acceptable to act as Protecting Powers on its behalf and another five which it would accept as Protecting Powers of the adverse party, the assumption being that a comparison of the two lists will reveal some overlap.

Another common provision of the Geneva Conventions[75] declares that the appointment of a Protecting Power does not constitute an obstacle to the humanitarian activities which the ICRC or any other

[73] *Supra* note 71, at 940.

[74] Arts. 8 of the First, Second, and Third Geneva Conventions; art. 9 of the Fourth Geneva Convention.

[75] Arts. 9 of the First, Second, and Third Geneva Conventions; art. 10 of the Fourth Geneva Convention.

impartial humanitarian organization may undertake, subject to the consent of the parties to the conflict, for the benefit of protected persons.

The ICRC (which consists exclusively of Swiss citizens and must be distinguished from national Red Cross societies) plays a major role in the implementation of international humanitarian law. It has numerous specific functions under the Geneva Conventions and Protocol I which are independent of the operation of Protecting Powers. For instance, under article 126 of the Third Convention, whether or not there is a Protecting Power, ICRC delegates are allowed to visit all places in which there are prisoners of war, including places of internment, imprisonment, and labour, and to interview the prisoners without witnesses.

Moreover, another common provision of the Geneva Conventions[76] creates a legal edifice of protection with three layers. According to the first paragraph of the common article, parties to the conflict may, by mutual consent, entrust to an impartial and efficacious organization the duties incumbent on Protecting Powers by virtue of the Geneva Conventions. The correct interpretation of this vague paragraph is not that the organization in question substitutes for a Protecting Power, but rather that they share responsibility. The organization will concentrate on discharging the protective duties imposed by the Geneva Conventions, while the Protecting Power will perform the traditional functions which exist under customary international law irrespective of the Conventions.[77]

The second paragraph of the common article sets up a substitute for a Protecting Power. It states that, when protected persons do not or cease to benefit from the services of a Protecting Power or an organization as provided for in the first paragraph (services which require the consent of the two adversaries), the Detaining Power shall unilaterally request a neutral state or such an organization to undertake the functions performed by a Protecting Power under the Geneva Conventions. It must be stressed again that a Protecting Power in the full sense of the term can only be appointed on the basis of the consent of both adverse parties. Here only one party is involved in the process. Consequently, the state or organization appointed is not a genuine Protecting Power, although it carries out the tasks of one in conformity with the Geneva Conventions. Such duties are distinct from other duties under customary international law.[78]

If no protection can be arranged even on this basis, the third para-

[76] Arts. 10 of the First, Second, and Third Geneva Conventions; art. 11 of the Fourth Geneva Convention.

[77] *See* First Geneva Convention: Commentary 118–19 (J. Pictet ed. 1952).

[78] *See id.* at 120–21.

graph of the common article requires that the Detaining Power request on its own initiative, or accept the offer of, the services of a humanitarian organization such as the ICRC to assume the humanitarian functions performed by Protecting Powers under the Geneva Conventions. In this case only a humanitarian organization, rather than a neutral state, may be selected. The Detaining Power has freedom of choice as regards the organization: it need not accept the services offered by one organization if it prefers those of another. On the other hand, the paragraph resorts to binding language as far as the appointment of some (unspecified) organization is concerned. However, the binding nature of this language has not been borne out by the practice of states.[79] While article 5 of Protocol I reiterates that parties to the conflict shall accept without delay an offer which may be made by the ICRC or any other impartial organization to act as a substitute for a Protecting Power, it unequivocally adds that the functioning of such a substitute is subject to the consent of all parties to the conflict.

The Geneva Conventions stipulate that every party to the conflict may request an inquiry concerning any alleged violation of the Conventions' terms, but the parties must reach an agreement regarding the procedure for the inquiry.[80] In the absence of an agreement, it is recommended that the parties appoint an umpire who will decide upon the procedure to be followed.[81] Needless to say, as there is no clear legal obligation in the matter, a party which so desires may frustrate the inquiry. Article 90 of Protocol I lays the ground for the creation of a permanent International Fact-Finding Commission consisting of fifteen members serving in their personal capacity, provided that at least twenty High Contracting Parties have agreed in special declarations to accept the competence of this Commission on a reciprocal basis. The Commission is competent to inquire into any facts alleged to constitute a 'grave breach' as defined in the Geneva Conventions or Protocol I, or any other serious violation of those instruments, and to offer its good offices to restore an attitude of respect for those instruments. Unless otherwise agreed, inquiries are to be undertaken by a Chamber consisting of seven members, and the Commission must submit to the parties a report on the findings of fact of the Chamber, with such recommendations as it may deem appropriate.

The implementation of human rights is even less satisfactory for internal conflicts. All that article 3 common to the four Geneva Conventions provides is that an impartial humanitarian body, such as the ICRC,

[79] *See* Forsythe, *Who Guards the Guardians: Third Parties and the Law of Armed Conflict*, 70 Am. J. Int'l L. 41, 45–48 (1976).

[80] *See* art. 52, First Convention; art. 53, Second Convention; art. 132, Third Convention; art. 149, Fourth Convention.

[81] *Id.*

may offer its services to the parties to the conflict. The parties are not bound to accept these services,[82] and there is no place for the functioning of a Protecting Power. Article 18 of Protocol II also permits local relief organizations, *e.g.*, national Red Cross societies, to offer services for the peformance of traditional functions on behalf of the victims of the armed conflict. But, again, no obligation is imposed on the parties to accept those services and, in any case, the services to be rendered have nothing to do with supervision.

II. Teaching Suggestions

A. A FULL COURSE

The teaching of a special course on the subject of human rights in armed conflict is not an easy undertaking if conducted without any basic knowledge on the part of the students of international law, the laws of war and human rights. As a matter of fact, even if students have already studied the last three subjects, it is desirable to refresh their memory by a brief résumé of fundamentals with an emphasis on the sources of international law (particularly, the relationship between customary and conventional law), the unique features of the law of war (especially, the quintessential distinction between combatants and civilians), and the singular nature of international human rights (as rights established directly for individuals without the interposition of the legal personality of the state).

It is preferable to incorporate into the course specific problems relating to concrete armed conflicts occurring at the time of teaching. This enables students to view legal norms not *in abstracto* but in their application to real events. Background materials should be selected from the abundant legal literature in the field. Of the many authorities cited in the footnotes and listed in the selected bibliography, it is recommended to use three treatises as general guides: 2 L. Oppenheim, *International Law* (H. Lauterpacht ed. 1952); G. Schwarzenberger, *The Law of Armed Conflict* (1968); and J. Stone, *Legal Controls of International Conflict* (1954). Other books and articles should be consulted in relation to specific themes of discussion. It is also useful to resort to the two principal military manuals: U.S. Army, Field Manual 27–10, *The Law of Land Warfare* (1956); and the U.K. War Office, *Manual of Military Law*, Pt. III: The Law of War on Land (1958).

The foremost pedagogic problem faced by instructors in the sphere of wartime human rights is the need to uphold the inarticulate major premise that such rights have a meaning not only in the classroom but also in the world of reality and, more specifically, in the battlefield.

[82] *See* Draper, *The Geneva Conventions of 1949*, 114 Recueil des Cours 63, 91 (1965).

Instructors usually have to contend with no less than five prevalent preconceptions which are, in fact, popular misconceptions. It is frequently maintained that: (i) In time of war there is no room for the application of legal norms, or, as Cicero put it, *silent enim leges inter arma.*[83] (ii) The laws of war, such as they are, are all in a 'chaotic' state.[84] (iii) In an era of 'total war', the basic distinction between civilians and combatants is more apparent than real.[85] (iv) With the threat of a thermonuclear disaster looming large on mankind's horizons, attempts to deal with the conduct of warfare are inconsequential. (v) Efforts to develop a workable *jus in bello* are inconsistent with the prohibition of war under the present *jus ad bellum.*

These are all psychological hurdles which must be surmounted if wartime human rights are to be taken seriously. It is necessary to impress upon students that:

(a) Far from resting dormant, international law is very active in the midst of arms. Unlike natural disasters, such as earthquakes or floods, war is a man-made cataclysm: it is a manifestation of human behavior.[86] All human behavior is subject to regulation by legal norms. The international community has always tried to check the basic human urge to brutalize war. In fact, historically, the laws of war were the most important component of international law.

(b) The laws of war, like all law, require constant revision: law reform is a perennial problem. Law almost always lags behind reality. After every major war, the modification of the laws of war appears to be more urgent than ever. Nevertheless, numerous provisions of international humanitarian law have survived many wars. In some respects, the first three Geneva Conventions are better entrenched today—more widely respected and more generally recognized—than quite a few legal instruments pertaining to the law of peace. They are actually viewed, by and large, as declaratory of customary international law.

(c) The distinction between civilians and combatants is still the cornerstone of the law of armed conflict. Even those who deny the existence of many juridical principles in this sphere are compelled to concede that civilians are entitled to some protection.[87] To be sure, the phenomenon of 'total war' creates profound problems affecting the

[83] Cicero, Pro Milone, IV, 11, at 16 (Loeb Classical Library ed.).

[84] This misconception is often perpetuated by well-intentioned jurists advocating the revision of the *lex lata. See, e.g.*, Kunz, *The Chaotic Status of the Laws of War and the Urgent Necessity for their Revision*, 45 Am. J. Int'l L. 37 (1951).

[85] This thesis is developed in an erudite paper which, however, carries a partly valid point to exaggerated lengths. *See* Nurick, *The Distinction between Combatant and Noncombatant in the Law of War*, 39 Am. J. Int'l L. 680 (1945).

[86] *See* Tucker, *The Interpretation of War under Present International Law*, 4 Int'l L.Q. 11, 13 (1951).

[87] *See* Lauterpacht, *The Problem of the Revision of the Law of War*, 29 Brit. Y.B. Int'l L. 360, 364, 368 (1952).

protection of the civilian population. Some solutions have been found in Protocol I, though there still are many unresolved or poorly resolved questions.[88] The imperfections and shortcomings should not overshadow the tangible fact that, at least in part, the law is clear.

(d) The argument that thermonuclear devices, if used in a future world war, may bring about the annihilation of the human race commands efforts to ban such weapons. But the balance of terror, which has so far safeguarded humanity from a repetition on a larger scale of the experience of Hiroshima and Nagasaki, has not proved effective when it comes to the use of conventional weapons in conventional warfare. Our era is characterized by little wars in which much blood is shed and in which even Big Powers are occasionally embroiled. All in all, millions of human beings have lost their lives in a large number of conventional wars since the end of World War II. It is incongruous to overlook this present evil merely because of the much greater potential of the thermonuclear menace.

(e) The prohibition of war (except in cases of self-defense or collective security) under current international law does not mean that humanity can ignore with impunity its incidence. Even if war breaks out in flagrant violation of fundamental precepts, international law must cope with problems generated by such a violation. In point of fact, there has not been a single year of outright peace since the legal interdiction of war. While efforts 'to save succeeding generations from the scourge of war'[89] must continue, the present generation cannot escape from the reality of war.

B. A MODULE WITHIN A GENERAL COURSE

When a special course on the subject of human rights in armed conflict is not offered, it is desirable to incorporate the topic as a two or three hour module within a broader course devoted to human rights in general. The brief time frame will not permit more than a short discussion covering some elements of the subject. Since no serious exposition of the topic is possible, it is recommended that instructors concentrate on a single issue encapsulating the main aspects of interaction between human rights and armed conflict. While one can conceive of several such issues, the one which may illuminate the salient points best is the protection of prisoners of war. Prisoners of war benefit from a number of human rights (the right to life, freedom from torture, etc.), yet are denied other fundamental freedoms which are taken for granted in peacetime (freedom from detention without trial, freedom from forced labour, etc.). The whole matter is now

[88] *See* Dinstein, *supra* note 18, at 273–75.
[89] U.N. Charter preamble, para. 1.

thoroughly covered by Levie's study, *Prisoners of War in International Armed Conflict*, consisting of one volume of text and another of source materials.

III. Syllabus

It is proposed that an elective (one term) course on human rights in armed conflict should cover the following elements.

1. Introduction A: international law.
   a. Definition.
   b. The interrelationship between customary and conventional international law.
   c. The distinction between the laws of peace and the laws of war.
2. Introduction B: the laws of war.
   a. The nature of war.
   b. The Hague Conventions, 1899–1907.
   c. The Geneva Conventions, 1949–1977.
   d. The distinction between combatants and civilians.
   e. Prohibited weapons and legitimate methods of warfare.
3. Introduction C: international human rights.
   a. The Universal Declaration of Human Rights, 1948.
   b. The [European] Convention for the Protection of Human Rights and Fundamental Freedoms, 1950.
   c. The International Covenant on Civil and Political Rights; the International Covenant on Economic, Social, and Cultural Rights, 1966.
   d. The American Convention on Human Rights, 1966.
   e. The unique nature of rights conferred directly on individuals under international law.
4. The suspension of ordinary (peacetime) human rights in time of armed conflict.
5. Human rights which are not subject to derogation in armed conflict.
6. International and internal armed conflicts.
   a. The distinction between inter-state and intra-state wars.
   b. Article 3 common to the Geneva Conventions.
   c. Protocol II.
   d. The special problems affecting the protection of human rights in the course of a civil war.
7. The meaning of international humanitarian law and its differentiation from the law of human rights.
8. The special (wartime) human rights of lawful combatants and the status of prisoners of war.

9. The special (wartime) human rights of civilians.
   a. The protection of the civilian population in general.
   b. The protection of enemy aliens.
   c. The protection of the civilian population in occupied territories.
10. The simultaneous coexistence of human rights and state rights.
11. Measures of supervision and implementation.
    a. State responsibility.
    b. Individual responsibility (war crimes).
    c. The Protecting Power.
    d. The ICRC.
    e. Fact-finding inquiries.
12. Conclusion.

IV. Minisyllabus

1. Introduction: the laws of war.
   a. The Hague Conventions, 1899–1907.
   b. The Geneva Conventions and Protocols, 1949–1977.
2. Protection of prisoners of war.
   a. Human rights protected.
   b. Fundamental freedoms denied.
   c. Implementation and supervision.

V. Bibliography

In addition to the sources referred to in the footnotes accompanying the text of this chapter, the following authorities should be consulted as background reading.

Books

G. Draper, The Red Cross Conventions (1958).

L. Greenspan, The Modern Law of Land Warfare (1959).

F. Kalshoven, The Law of Warfare (1973).

H. Levie, Prisoners of War in International Armed Conflict (Naval War College, 59 International Law Studies, 1978).

—— Documents on Prisoners of War (Naval War College, 60 International Law Studies, 1979).

L. Oppenheim, International Law (7th ed. H. Lauterpacht 1952).

E. Rosenblad, International Humanitarian Law of Armed Conflict (1979).

J. Stone, Legal Controls of International Conflict (1954).

Articles

Aldrich, *Remarks: Human Rights and Armed Conflict*, 67 Proc. Am. Soc'y, Int'l L. 141 (1973).

—— *New Life for the Laws of War*, 75 Am. J. Int'l L. 764 (1981).
Baxter, *So-Called 'Unprivileged Belligerency': Spies, Guerrillas, and Saboteurs*, 28 Brit. Y.B. Int'l L. 323 (1951).
—— *Ius in Bello Interno: The Present and Future Law*, in Law and Civil War in the Modern World 518 (J.N. Moore ed. 1974).
—— *Humanitarian Law or Humanitarian Politics? The 1974 Diplomatic Conference on Humanitarian Law*, 16 Harv. Int'l L.J. 1 (1975).
Bindschedler-Robert, *Problems of the Law of Armed Conflicts*, in 1 International Criminal law 295 (M. Bassiouni & V. Nanda eds. 1973).
Blix, *Remarks: Human Rights and Armed Conflict*, 67 Proc. Am. Soc'y Int'l L. 149 (1973).
Burwell, *Civilian Protection in Modern Warfare: A Critical Analysis of the Geneva Civilian Convention of 1949*, 14 Va. J. Int'l L. 123 (1973).
Dinstein, *Another Step in Codifying the Laws of War*, 28 Y.B. World Aff. 278 (1974).
—— *The International Law of Inter-State Wars and Human Rights*, 7 Isr. Y.B. on Human Rights 139 (1977).
Draper, *The Relationship between the Human Rights Regime and the Law of Armed Conflicts*, 1 Isr. Y.B. on Human Rights 191 (1971).
—— *The Status of Combatants and the Question of Guerilla Warfare*, 45 Brit. Y.B. Int'l L. 173 (1971).
Forsythe, *The 1974 Diplomatic Conference on Humanitarian Law: Some Observations*, 69 Am. J. Int'l L. 77 (1975).
Green, *The Geneva Humanitarian Law Conference 1975*, 13 Can. Y.B. Int'l L. 295 (1975).
—— *Humanitarian Law and the Man in the Field*, 14 Can. Y.B. Int'l L. 96 (1976).
—— *The New Law of Armed Conflict*, 15 Can. Y.B. Int'l L. 3 (1977).
—— *Derogation of Human Rights in Emergency Situations*, 16 Can. Y.B. Int'l L. 92 (1978).
Greenspan, *The Protection of Human Rights in Time of Warfare*, 1 Isr. Y.B. on Human Rights 228 (1971).
Gutteridge, *The Geneva Conventions of 1949*, 26 Brit. Y.B. Int'l L. 294 (1949).
Krafft, *The Present Position of the Red Cross Geneva Conventions*, 37 Trans. Grotius Soc'y 131 (1951).
Kunz, *The Geneva Conventions of August 12, 1949*, in Law and Politics in the World Community 279, 368, (G. Lipsky ed. 1953).
Pictet, *The New Geneva Conventions for the Protection of War*

Victims, 45 Am. J. Int'l L. 462 (1951).
Rubin, *The Status of Rebels under the Geneva Conventions of 1949*, 21 Int'l & Comp. L.Q. 472 (1972).
Schwarzenberger, *Human Rights and Guerrilla Warfare*, 1 Isr. Y.B. on Human Rights 246 (1971).
—— *The Law of Armed Conflict: A Civilized Interlude?*, 28 Y.B. World Aff. 293 (1974).
Smith, *The Geneva Prisoner of War Convention: An Appraisal*, 42 N.Y.U. L. Rev. 880 (1967).
Von Glahn, *The Protection of Human Rights in Time of Armed Conflicts*, 1 Isr. Y.B. on Human Rights 208 (1971).
Yingling & Ginnane, *The Geneva Conventions of 1949*, 46 Am. J. Int'l. L. 393 (1952).

* * *

Bibliography of International Humanitarian Law Applicable in Armed Conflicts (T. Huynh ed. 1980).
Vincent-Daviss, *Human Rights Law: A Research Guide to the Literature—Part II: International Protection of Refugees, and Humanitarian Law*, 14 N.Y.U. J. Int'l L. & Pol. 487, 517 (1981).

VI. Minibibliography

Aldrich, *New Life for the Laws of War*, 75 Am. J. Int'l L. 764 (1981).
Dinstein, *Human Rights in Armed Conflict: International Humanitarian Law*, in this volume.
H. Levie, *Prisoners of War in International Armed Conflict* (Naval War College, 59 International Law Studies, 1978).
—— *Documents on Prisoners of War* (Naval War College, 60 International Law Studies, 1979).

Chapter 10

Human Rights: Their Implementation and Supervision by the United Nations*

Louis B. Sohn

International protection of human rights implies at least two different processes. In the first place, it is necessary to achieve an international agreement on the human rights standards to be applied throughout the world (or in a particular region); in the second place, methods of implementation and supervision need to be developed.

The United Nations has been successful in constantly broadening the number and increasing the depth of international instruments containing general and specific international human rights standards. By 1978 some fifty such instruments had been adopted by the United Nations and its specialized agencies,[1] and several additional ones have been adopted since or are in various stages of completion. In addition, parallel instruments on particular human rights have been adopted by regional organizations in Europe, the Americas, and Africa.[2] Similar instruments are being prepared by the League of Arab States.[3]

But standards are not enough. One cannot expect an automatic respect of these standards by all governments, authorities, public and private entities, and, most importantly, individuals. In fact most violations of human rights are committed by individuals, whether acting in their official or private capacity. It is important, therefore, to make sure, as far as possible, that human rights are actually respected by all concerned. In order to achieve this result, most of the instruments mentioned above provide for measures of implementation and supervision. Some measures are national, others are international.

I. Legal and Policy Considerations

A. NATIONAL MEASURES OF IMPLEMENTATION AND SUPERVISION

In principle, most international agreements on human rights leave

[1] For their texts, *see* United Nations, Human Rights: A Compilation of International Instruments, U.N. Doc. ST/HR/1/Rev. 2 (1978) [hereinafter cited as U.N. Compilation]. Some of these documents are discussed in chs. 4, 5, 6, 7, & 8 *supra*.

[2] Some of these documents are discussed in chs. 12 & 13 *infra*. For the African Charter on Human Rights and Peoples' Rights, *see* Rev. Int'l Comm'n Jurists 76–86 (No. 27, Dec. 1981).

[3] *See, e.g.*, U.N. Doc. E/CN.4/1229, at 29 (1976).

the question of implementation to states parties, which are supposed to enact the necessary legislative and other measures.

For instance, article 2 of the International Covenant on Civil and Political Rights[4] imposes on states parties several obligations of this kind. First, if a state party does not already have sufficient legislative or other measures for the implementation of the Political Covenant in its domestic law, it must take the necessary steps to adopt such measures in order to give effect to the rights recognized therein. Second, a state party has the duty to ensure that any person whose rights or freedoms are violated shall have an effective remedy, even when the violation has been committed by a government official. Third, while a state party has the option to make these remedies available through judicial, administrative, legislative, or other competent authorities, it shall provide a judicial remedy as soon as possible. Fourth, a state party shall ensure that the competent authorities shall enforce such remedies when granted.

As soon as the Political Covenant came into effect states parties were asked, pursuant to article 40 of that treaty, to submit reports on the measures they had adopted to give effect to their obligations under Article 2. These reports have been carefully scrutinized by the Human Rights Committee which is in charge of supervision of the implementation of the Political Covenant. For instance, the government of Denmark reported that before ratifying the Covenant it introduced the necessary legislation, but where it was not possible at that time to remove the discrepancies between the Political Covenant and Danish legislation, it had submitted appropriate reservations when ratifying the Covenant. It also noted that in Denmark there is a rule allowing the administrative authorities to interpret domestic law in such a way as to comply to the maximum extent possible with existing treaty obligations. Similarly, the Danish courts, when faced with a discrepancy between the Political Covenant and subsequent Danish legislation, apply the presumption that it has not been the intention of the Parliament to pass legislation contrary to Denmark's international obligations. The Danish representative before the Human Rights Committee pointed out that it was possible to invoke before a court the provisions of a treaty that were relevant to the case and that this has been done on some occasions. Nevertheless, the Human Rights Committee raised various questions about the implications of these general Danish statements and requested further information on several specific issues where some discrepancies between the Political Covenant and the provisions of Danish legislation were detected by some members of the Committee.[5]

[4] G. A. Res. 2200, U.N. GAOR, Supp. (No. 16) 52, U.N. Doc. A/6316 (1966).

[5] Report of the Human Rights Committee, 33 U.N. GAOR, Supp. (No. 40) 16–19, U.N. Doc. A/33/40 (1978).

Similarly, the Constitution of the International Labour Organisation (ILO)[6] contains both an obligation of member states to bring each convention adopted by the International Labour Conference before the competent authority for the enactment of legislation or other action and an obligation to report on the measures taken to give effect to the provisions of the conventions which they have ratified. The implementation of these obligations is carefully scrutinized not only by the Committee of Experts on the Application of Conventions and Recommendations but also by a Committee on the Application of Conventions and Recommendations, which is set up by the International Labour Conference at each session and which is a more political body, composed of representatives of governments and of organizations of employers and workers. In many cases the observations of these two Committees have led to important changes in national legislation.[7]

Some international human rights instruments are rather detailed with respect to national measures to be taken with respect to the ratified convention. Thus, the International Convention on the Elimination of All Forms of Racial Discrimination[8] obliges each state party: to 'take effective measures to review governmental, national and local policies, and to amend, rescind or nullify any laws and regulations which have the effect of creating or perpetuating racial discrimination wherever it exists';[9] and to 'prohibit and bring to an end, by all appropriate means, including legislation as required by circumstances, racial discrimination by any persons, group or organization'.[10] In addition, any state party which accepts the jurisdiction of the Committee on the Elimination of Racial Discrimination to receive communications from individuals or groups of individuals,[11] may establish or indicate a domestic body to which petitions must be submitted prior to their reference to the Committee.[12] Thus, in addition to the exhaustion of other local remedies, the individual or group concerned would be required to try to obtain satisfaction from the domestic body, and only in the event of failure to obtain

[6] 62 Stat. 3485, T.I.A.S. No. 1868, 15 U.N.T.S. 35; *amended* 7 U.S.T. 245, T.I.A.S. No. 3500, 191 U.N.T.S. 143 (1953); 14 U.S.T. 1039, T.I.A.S. No. 5401, 466 U.N.T.S. 323 (1962); 25 U.S.T. 3253, T.I.A.S. No. 7987 (1972).

[7] ILO Const. arts. 19(5) & 22. For ILO practice, *see, e.g.*, International Labour Office, The Impact of International Labour Conventions and Recommendations 37–56 (1976); N. Valticos, International Labour Law 234–38, 240–45 (1979). *See also* E. Landy, The Effectiveness of International Supervision: Thirty Years of ILO Experience (1967) [hereinafter cited as Landy]; ch. 7 *supra*.

[8] 660 U.N.T.S. 195, *reprinted in* U.N. Compilation, *supra* note 1, at 24 (hereinafter cited as Racial Discrimination Convention).

[9] *Id.* art. 2(c).

[10] *Id.* art. 2(d).

[11] *Id.* art. 14(1).

[12] *Id.* art. 14(2).

such satisfaction would it be permissible to move into the international plane.[13]

A seminar organized by the United Nations in Geneva in 1978 considered reports on various national and local institutions for the promotion and protection of human rights, and recommended a set of guidelines for the functioning and structure of such institutions. For instance, the seminar recommended that such institutions: should be authorized to receive complaints from individuals and groups concerning human rights violations; should possess independent fact-finding facilities for the investigation of complaints alleging deprivations of human rights; and should provide appropriate remedies through conciliation or other means of redress. In particular, the seminar noted that the ombudsman system is being increasingly adopted in developing countries, with modifications to suit local needs. It was pointed out that an ombudsman is a most useful official, often selected by and answerable only to the national parliament; that he or she usually has extensive powers to investigate complaints of individuals whose rights may have been infringed by a public authority; and that he or she may even be authorized to institute criminal proceedings against public officials for breach or abuse of governmental functions entrusted to them. Similar officials function in other countries under various names, such as Procurator, Protector of the People, or Mediator, or such investigatory powers are vested in a national committee on human rights or civil rights.[14]

While national means of implementation are often commanded by international instruments, they also have another role to play on the international plane. Several international instruments require exhaustion of local remedies before a complaint, petition, or communication can be submitted to an international institution. Only when there are no effective local remedies or they are unreasonably prolonged can a complainant approach an international institution without exhausting such remedies.[15]

[13] *Id.* art. 14(5).

[14] United Nations, Seminar on National and Local Institutions for the Promotion and Protection of Human Rights, Geneva, 18–29 Sept. 1978, reported in U.N. Doc. ST/HR/SER.A/2 (1978). *See also* United Nations, Seminar on the Effective Realization of Civil and Political Rights at the National Level, Kingston, Jamaica, 25 Apr.–8 May 1967, U.N. Doc. ST/TAO/HR/29 (1967).

[15] For a study of the subject of exhaustion of local remedies by the International Law Commission, *see* Report of the International Law Commission, 32 U.N. GAOR, Supp. (No. 10) 67–116, U.N. Doc. A/32/10 (1977), *reprinted in* [1977] 2(2) Y.B. Int'l L. Comm'n 67–116, U.N. Doc. A/CN.4/Ser.A/1977/Add.1 (Part 2). *See also* Law, The Local Remedies Rule in International Law (1961); Hoesler, The Exhaustion of Local Remedies in the Case Law of International Courts and Tribunals (1968); Amerasinghe, *The Rule of Exhaustion of Local Remedies in the Framework of International Systems for the Protection of Human Rights*, 28 Zeischrift für ausländisches öffentlisches Recht und Völkerrecht 257 (1968); Chappez, La règle de l' epuisement des voies de recours internes (1972); Adede, *A Survey of Treaty Provisions on the Rule of Exhaustion of Local Remedies*, 18 Harv. Int'l L. J. 1 (1977).

B. INTERNATIONAL MEASURES OF IMPLEMENTATION AND SUPERVISION

The Charter of the United Nations requires the United Nations not only to promote human rights and their universal respect, but also to promote their observance.[16] For this purpose, the Economic and Social Council was empowered by the Charter to set up a commission for the protection of human rights,[17] and in fact established a Commission on Human Rights in 1946 in one of its first decisions.[18] The Commission, which is composed of representatives of member states, in turn established a group of experts to assist it, the Sub-Commission on the Prevention of Discrimination and Protection of Minorities.[19] A separate Commission on the Status of Women was established simultaneously to deal with problems of sex discrimination and the rights of women.[20] In addition, many special committees have been established by the United Nations to deal with special problems (such as *apartheid* or the violations of human rights in Chile or in Israeli-occupied territories) or with the implementation of particular conventions (*e.g.*, the Committee on the Elimination of Racial Discrimination). Various international supervisory organs have also been established by specialized agencies and regional organizations.[21] Some roles may also be played in international supervision by judicial organs such as the International Court of Justice, the European Court of Human Rights, and the Inter-American Court of Human Rights.[22]

Shifting from organs of supervision to international supervisory procedures, there seem to be three main methods of securing universal observance of human rights: various systems of periodic reports, procedures for dealing with complaints by one state against another state, and procedures for the consideration of communications by individuals and private organizations (national and international).

1. *Periodic Reporting Systems*

Article 64 of the U.N. Charter provides that the Economic and Social Council may make arrangements with the members of the

[16] U.N. Charter arts. 1(3), 55(c), & 62(2).

[17] *Id.* art. 68.

[18] E.S.C. Res. 5(I), 1 U.N. ESCOR 163 (1946).

[19] Commission on Human Rights, Report on the First Session, 4 U.N. ESCOR, Supp. (No. 3) 4, U.N. Doc. E/259 (1947).

[20] At first the Economic and Social Council established a Sub-Commission on the Status of Women, by Res. 5(I), *supra* note 18; but soon, by Res. 11(II), the Council changed that Sub-Commission to a full Commission. *See* 2 U.N. ESCOR 405 (1946).

[21] With respect to the ILO and the inter-American and European organizations, *see* ch. 7 *supra* and chs. 12 & 13 *infra* respectively. Concerning the Conciliation and Good Offices Commission established by UNESCO in 1962 to implement the Convention against Discrimination in Education, *see* U.N. Compilation, *supra* note 1, at 37.

[22] The last two courts are considered in chs. 12 & 13, respectively *infra*; the treaties providing for a reference to the International Court of Justice are discussed in subsection B.2.a *infra*.

United Nations or with the specialized agencies 'to obtain reports on the steps taken to give effect to its own recommendations and to recommendations on matters falling within its competence made by the General Assembly'. On October 31, 1947, the General Assembly called upon all member states 'to carry out all recommendations of the General Assembly passed on economic and social matters', and recommended that:

in fulfilment of Article 64 of the Charter of the United Nations the Secretary-General report annually to the Economic and Social Council and that the latter report to the General Assembly on steps taken by the Member Governments to give effect to the recommendations of the Economic and Social Council as well as to the recommendations made by the General Assembly on matters falling within the Council's competence.[23]

Various steps were taken by the Economic and Social Council to implement this resolution, but the general biennial reporting procedure was discontinued in 1952 and the Council decided instead 'to include in the future, wherever practicable, in its resolutions specific indications of the timing of the report expected from governments in implementation of the resolutions concerned'.[24]

In 1953 the United States suggested that, taking into consideration the obligations under articles 55 and 56 of the Charter, 'each Member [should] transmit each year to the Secretary-General a report on developments and achievements in the field of human rights in its country'.[25] After considerable discussion, the Commission on Human Rights decided in 1956 to recommend to the Economic and Social Council that it request 'each State Member of the United Nations and of the specialized agencies to transmit annually to the Secretary-General a report describing developments and progress achieved in the field of human rights and measures taken to safeguard human liberty' in its territories dealing with the rights enumerated in the Universal Declaration of Human Rights[26] and with the right of peoples to self-determination.[27] The Council approved this recommendation, but decided that annual reports would impose too great a burden upon the governments and the U.N. Secretariat and that, therefore, they should be transmitted 'every three years', describing developments and the progress achieved during the preceding three years.[28] In 1965 the Council approved a staggered three-year system of reporting, request-

[23] G.A. Res. 119, U.N. Doc. A/519, at 24–25 (1947).
[24] 3 Repertory of United Nations Practice 388–91 (1955); 14 U.N. ESCOR, Supp. (No. 1) 48–49, U.N. Doc. E/2332 (1952).
[25] U.N. Doc. E/CN.4/L.266 (1953).
[26] G.A. Res. 217A, U.N. Doc. A/810, at 71 (1948).
[27] 22 U.N. ESCOR, Supp. (No. 3) 4, U.N. Doc. E/2844 (1956).
[28] E.S.C. Res. 624B, 22 U.N. ESCOR, Supp. (No. 1) 12, U.N. Doc. E/2929 (1956).

ing states to report in the first year of each cycle on civil and political rights, in the second year on economic and social rights, and in the third year on freedom of information.[29] In 1971, the length of the cycle was increased to six years, the three reports being submitted at two-year intervals rather than annually.[30]

In its consideration of the periodic reports, the Commission on Human Rights had to proceed slowly, as some states considered that the reporting procedure violated the Charter's prohibition of intervention in matters which are essentially within the domestic jurisdiction of a state,[31] while others simply did not present any reports. The Commission has tried a variety of procedures and has limited its conclusions to general statements. Nevertheless, the Commission and its *Ad Hoc* Committee on Periodic Reports over the years have developed considerable expertise in this field and have found what are the positive functions and the limits of this process.[32]

In addition to these general reports, various United Nations resolutions provide for reports on special subjects. For instance, the Recommendations of the General Assembly on Consent to Marriage, Minimum Age for Marriage and Registration of Marriages asked Member States to report to the Commission on the Status of Women at the end of three years, and thereafter at intervals of five years, on their law and practice with regard to the matters dealt with in the Recommendations; in particular they were to report on 'the extent to which effect has been given or is proposed to be given to the provisions of the Recommendation and such modifications as have been found or may be found necessary in adapting or applying it'.[33]

Reporting requirements are also contained in several conventions on human rights. For instance, the Supplementary Convention on the Abolition of Slavery, the Slave Trade, and Institutions and Practices Similar to Slavery obliges the parties to the Convention 'to communicate to the Secretary-General of the United Nations copies of any laws, regulations and administrative measures enacted or put into effect to implement the provisions of this Convention'; and this documentation is to be used by the Economic and Social Council as a basis for further recommendations on this subject.[34]

[29] E.S.C. Res. 1074C, 39 U.N. ESCOR, Supp. (No. 1) 24, para. 6, U.N. Doc. E/4117 (1965).

[30] E.S.C. Res. 1596, 50 U.N. ESCOR, Supp. (No. 1) 20, U.N. Doc. E/5044 (1971).

[31] U.N. Charter art. 2(7).

[32] For a summary of the work of the Commission in this area, *see* Sohn, *A Short History of UN Documents on Human Rights*, in Commision to Study the Organization of Peace, The United Nations and Human Rights 39, 74–94 (1968); United Nations, United Nations Action in the Field of Human Rights, U.N. Doc. ST/HR/2/Rev.6, at 169–71 (1980) [hereinafter cited as U.N. Action].

[33] G.A. Res. 2018, 20 U.N. GAOR, Supp. (No. 14) 36–37, U.N. Doc. A/6014 (1965).

[34] Art. 8, 18 U.S.T. 3201, T.I.A.S. No. 6418, 266 U.N.T.S. 3.

The International Convention on the Elimination of All Forms of Racial Discrimination provides a more elaborate system of reporting. The states parties undertake to submit to the U.N. Secretary-General for consideration by the Committee on the Elimination of Racial Discrimination 'a report on the legislative, judicial, administrative or other measures which they have adopted and which give effect to the provisions of this Convention: (*a*) within one year after the entry into force of the Convention for the State concerned; and (*b*) thereafter every two years and whenever the Committee so requests'.[35] The Convention provides further that the Committee 'may make suggestions and general recommendations based on the examination of the reports and information received from the States Parties'; and that these 'suggestions and general recommendations shall be reported to the General Assembly together with comments, if any, from States Parties'.[36]

Detailed provisions on reporting are contained as well in the two international covenants. Under the International Covenant on Economic, Social and Cultural Rights,[37] the states parties undertake to submit to the Economic and Social Council 'reports on the measures which they have adopted and the progress made in achieving the observance of the rights recognized' in that Covenant.[38] These reports 'may indicate factors and difficulties affecting the degree of fulfilment of obligations' under the Economic Covenant.[39] When the Economic Covenant entered into force, the Economic and Social Council established a system of biennial reports for various parts of the Covenant, and decided to establish a sessional working group of the Council to assist it in the consideration of the reports.[40] The Council also decided that the states parties to the Economic Covenant will be henceforth excused from submitting, with respect to issues covered by that Covenant, parallel reports under the 1965 reporting system.[41] At the same time, the Council decided to rely on the cooperation of the specialized agencies in the implementation of the reporting procedure, avoiding thereby possible duplication of efforts in this area.[42]

[35] Racial Discrimination Convention, art. 9(1).

[36] *Id.* art 9(2).

[37] G.A. Res. 2200, U.N. GAOR, Supp. (No. 16) 49, U.N. Doc. A/6316 (1966).

[38] *Id.* art. 16.

[39] *Id.* art. 17.

[40] E.S.C. Res. 1988, 60 U.N. ESCOR, Supp. (No. 1) 11, U.N. Doc. E/5850 (1976); E.S.C. Dec. 1978/10, U.N. Doc. E/DEC/1978/6–40, at 5 (1978); 33 U.N. GAOR, Supp. (No. 3) 34–36, U.N. Doc. A/33/3 (1978).

[41] E.S.C. Res. 1988, *supra* note 40, para. 7.

[42] *Id.*, para. 6. For the reports of the International Labour Organisation, *see, e.g.*, U.N. Docs. E/1978/27 (1978); E/1979/33 (1979); E/1980/35 (1980).

A different system exists under the Political Covenant. The states parties to that Covenant undertake to submit 'reports on the measures they have adopted which give effect to the rights recognized [therein] and on the progress made in the enjoyment of those rights'.[43] These reports are to indicate the factors and difficulties, if any, affecting the implementation of the Political Covenant.[44] They are considered by a special Human Rights Committee, which can make general comments thereon to the states parties and can transmit them also to the Economic and Social Council.[45] Once this system of reporting came into effect, the Economic and Social Council decided to exempt states parties to the Political Covenant from submitting reports on subjects covered by that Covenant under the 1965 reporting system.[46] Finally, the Economic and Social Council decided in 1971 to terminate the 1965 reporting system.[47]

As a result of the decisions taken by the Economic and Social Council in 1976, 1978, and 1981 there are now two basic reporting systems under the international covenants. In addition there are various reporting systems relating to particular conventions or declarations, some dealing with civil and political rights, others dealing with economic, social, and cultural rights.

It would seem desirable to simplify these reporting systems and to consolidate them into one or two overall systems. Until the international covenants can be amended, it will be difficult to combine their two parallel, but slightly different, reporting systems. It might be more feasible to consolidate all the reporting in the economic, social, and cultural field in the new sessional working group of the Economic and Social Council. As the reporting system for non-parties to the Economic Covenant on these subjects is the creature of the Council, and as the Council has already changed that system several times, it could authorize the sessional working group under the Covenant to also consider reports from non-parties to the Covenant. Consequently, the Economic and Social Council would have its own sphere of action in the human rights field, encompassing all the economic, social, and cultural rights, and would be able to bring into this area the perspective gained from its work on other aspects of these fields; and all the reports on economic, social, and cultural rights would be given a uniform treatment, regardless of whether or not the

[43] Political Covenant, art. 40(1).

[44] *Id.* art. 40(2).

[45] *Id.* art. 40(2), 40(3), 40(4).

[46] E.S.C. Res. 1978/20, U.N. Doc. E/RES/1978/235, at 37 (1978); 33 U.N. GAOR, Supp. (No. 3) 65–66, 68, U.N. Doc. A/33/3 (1978).

[47] 18 U.N. Chronicle (No. 7) 21 (1981).

reporting state is a party to the Economic Covenant. To enable the sessional working group to accomplish this enlarged task, it may be necessary to provide for pre-sessional meetings of that group or even for intersessional meetings of sufficient duration.

It might be more difficult to streamline the system for civil and political rights, as the Human Rights Committee under the Political Covenant is an autonomous body established by the states parties to that Covenant. But its expenses are paid by the United Nations and its staff is provided by the U.N. Secretariat.[48] Consequently, it might be possible for the Economic and Social Council to propose to the states parties to the Political Covenant that they authorize the Committee to consider also reports from states non-parties dealing with subjects covered by the Political Covenant. The rules of the Committee already provide that a representative of a state party may be present at the meetings of the Committee at which the reports of that state are being examined.[49] The Committee could be encouraged to revise its rules to enable states non-parties to participate in the meetings on the same terms as those provided for states parties, *i.e.*, appear when their reports are being examined.

While theoretically the substance of reports based on the covenants may differ from that of the reports based on other human rights instruments, these differences are not crucial.

As far as various U.N. declarations are concerned, it would be easy for the Economic and Social Council to transfer the reporting functions to its sessional working group on the Economic Covenant, or to encourage the consideration of reports which pertain to civil and political rights by the Human Rights Committee. The situation is more difficult with respect to the reporting systems under various human rights conventions. Nevertheless, it should be possible for the Economic and Social Council to recommend to the parties to these conventions that they transfer the consideration of the reports under these conventions to the two principal bodies mentioned above. In some cases the parties may be willing to do this by an informal decision; in other cases a protocol to a particular convention may be necessary. By using an analogy to article 37 of the Statute of the International Court of Justice,[50] one might even envisage the possibility of drafting a general protocol to the effect that whenever a convention provides for

[48] Political Covenant, arts. 35 & 36.

[49] Rule 68, 32 U.N. GAOR, Supp. (No. 44) 48, 60, U.N. Doc. A/32/44 (1977).

[50] Arts. 37 provides:

> Whenever a treaty or convention in force provides for reference of a matter to a tribunal to have been instituted by the League of Nations, or to the Permanent Court of International Justice, the matter shall, as between the parties to the present Statute, be referred to the International Court of Justice.

a system of reporting on human rights, the reports under that convention shall be submitted to the appropriate system of reporting established under the international covenants.

A step of a similar character has been taken in the International Convention on the Suppression and Punishment of the Crime of *Apartheid*,[51] which provides for reports on the legislative, judicial, administrative, or other measures that the parties to the Convention have adopted and that give effect to its provisions.[52] These reports are to be submitted to a group consisting of three members of the Commission on Human Rights to be appointed by its Chairman from among those members who are representatives of states parties to the *Apartheid* Convention.[53]

It should be noted, finally, that reporting systems exist also in other international organizations dealing with human rights. The most sophisticated system exists in the International Labour Organisation, which uses its system to effectively monitor the implementation of human rights conventions.[54]

2. *Procedures for Dealing with Inter-State Complaints*

a. *Reference to International Court of Justice.* A few conventions on human rights provide for the submission of disputes between the parties to the International Court of Justice. For instance, according to the Convention on the Prevention and Punishment of the Crime of Genocide[55] disputes between the parties relating to the interpretation, application, or fulfilment of that Convention 'shall be submitted to the International Court of Justice at the request of any of the parties to the dispute'.[56] Less clearly, some conventions provide that any such dispute 'which is not settled by negotiation shall be referred to the International Court of Justice for decision unless the Contracting

[51] G.A. Res. 3068, 28 U.N. GAOR, Supp. (No. 30) 75, U.N. Doc. A/9030 (1973).

[52] *Id.* art. 7.

[53] *Id.* art. 9(1). This article provides also for other appointments if there are not enough representatives of states parties on the Commission on Human Rights. *Id.* art. 9(2).

[54] *See* Landy, *supra* note 7, at 15–211. *See also* ch. 7 *supra.*

[55] 78 U.N.T.S. 277, *reprinted in* U.N. Compilation, *supra* note 1, at 45.

[56] *Id.* art 9. Similar provisions are contained in: art. 22, Convention for the Suppression of the Traffic in Persons and of the Exploitation of the Prostitution of Others, 96 U.N.T.S. 271, *reprinted in* U.N. Compilation, *supra* note 1, at 60; art. 38, Convention relating to the Status of Refugees, 189 U.N.T.S. 137, *reprinted in* U.N. Compilation, *supra* note 1, at 86; art. 10, Supplementary Convention on the Abolition of Slavery, *supra* note 34; art. 10, Convention on the Nationality of Married Women, 309 U.N.T.S. 65, *reprinted in* U.N. Compilation, *supra* note 1, at 75; art. 34, Convention relating to the Status of Stateless Persons, 360 U.N.T.S. 117, *reprinted in* U.N. Compilation, *supra* note 1, at 80; art. 8, Convention against Discrimination in Education, 429 U.N.T.S. 93, *reprinted in* U.N. Compilation, *supra* note 1, at 35; art. 14, Convention on the Reduction of Statelessness, U.N. Doc. A/CONF. 9/15 (1961), *reprinted in* U.N. Compilation, *supra* note 1, at 76; art. 4, Protocol relating to the Status of Refugees, 19 U.S.T. 6223, T.I.A.S. No. 6577, 606 U.N.T.S. 267.

Parties agree to another mode of settlement'.[57] It is probably understood, however, that also in this case the dispute can be submitted to the International Court of Justice at the request of any of the parties. On the other hand, the consent of all the parties to the dispute seems to be required when a convention provides that any dispute concerning its interpretation or application 'shall, at the request of all the parties to the dispute, be referred to the International Court of Justice for decision, unless the parties agree to another mode of settlement'.[58]

A more elaborate procedure for dealing with inter-state complaints operates within the framework of the International Labour Organisation. Its constitution, as revised in 1946, gives each member of the ILO the right to file a complaint that another member is not effectively observing an international labour convention which both members have ratified.[59] The Governing Body of the ILO may refer the complaint to a Commission of Inquiry,[60] which prepares a report embodying its findings on questions of fact as well as its recommendations on the steps to be taken to meet the complaint.[61] A member which does not accept the report may refer the matter to the International Court of Justice[62] which may affirm, vary, or reverse any of the findings or recommendations of the Commission of Inquiry.[63] If a member fails to carry out the recommendations of the Commission or of the Court, the Governing Body may recommend to the International Labour Conference 'such action as it may deem wise and expedient to secure compliance therewith'.[64] In addition, the ILO Constitution provides that any question or dispute relating to the interpretation of any convention concluded in pursuance to the provisions of that constitution shall be referred for decision to the International Court of Justice.[65] While several cases have been submitted to Commissions of Inquiry, no case has yet been referred to the International Court of Justice.[66]

[57] Art. 5, Convention on the International Right of Correction, 435 U.N.T.S. 191, *reprinted in* U.N. Compilation, *supra* note 1, at 98. A similar provision can be found in art. 9, Convention on the Political Rights of Women, 27 U.S.T. 1909, T.I.A.S. No. 8289, 193 U.N.T.S. 135.

[58] Art. 8, Convention on Consent to Marriage, Minimum Age for Marriage and Registration of Marriages, 521 U.N.T.S. 231, *reprinted in* U.N. Compilation, *supra* note 1, at 112.

[59] ILO Const. art. 26(1).

[60] *Id.* art. 26(3).

[61] *Id.* art. 28.

[62] *Id.* art. 29(2).

[63] *Id.* art. 32.

[64] *Id.* art. 33.

[65] *Id.* art. 37(1).

[66] *See, e.g.*, report of the complaint filed by Ghana against Portugal, 45 (No. 2) ILO O. Bull. (Supp. 2) (1962); report of the complaint filed by Portugal against Liberia, 46 (No. 2) ILO O. Bull. (Supp. 2) (1963).

b. *References to the European and Inter-American Courts of Human Rights.* The [European] Convention for the Protection of Human Rights and Fundamental Freedoms[67] contains an optional clause[68] under which a state party may recognize as compulsory the jurisdiction of the European Court of Human Rights with respect to all matters concerning the interpretation and application of the European Convention. In addition, any state party may refer to the European Commission of Human Rights any alleged breach of the provisions of the European Convention by another state party.[69] If a state has accepted the jurisdiction of the European Court of Human Rights, a case can be brought before the Court by either the European Commission or one of the states concerned (the state which referred the case to the Commission, the state against which a complaint has been lodged before the Commission, or the state whose national is alleged to be a victim). While more than ten inter-state cases have been considered by the Commission, only one inter-state case—a complaint by Ireland against the United Kingdom concerning alleged violations of the European Convention which occurred in Northern Ireland—has been submitted to the European Court of Human Rights.[70]

The American Convention on Human Rights[71] also contains an optional clause under which a state party may accept the jurisdiction of the Inter-American Court of Human Rights with respect to all matters relating to the interpretation or application of that Convention.[72] Once this jurisdiction has been accepted by a state party, a case can be submitted to the Inter-American Court either by the Inter-American Commission on Human Rights or by another state party. In addition the Court has broad jurisdiction to render advisory opinions on request of any state member of the Organization of American States or an organ of that Organization.[73]

c. *Fact-Finding and Conciliation.* The UNESCO Convention against Discrimination in Education provides for reference of inter-state disputes about its interpretation or application to the International Court of Justice, 'failing other means of settling the dispute'.[74] In 1962 the

[67] 213 U.N.T.S. 221, *reprinted in* Basic Documents on Human Rights 242 (2d ed. I. Brownlie 1981) [hereinafter cited as Brownlie].

[68] *Id.* art. 46.

[69] *Id.* art. 24.

[70] For further discussion of these European cases, *see* ch. 13 *infra.*

[71] O.A.S. T.S. No. 36, *reprinted in* Brownlie, *supra* note 67, at 391.

[72] *Id.* art. 62. Under art. 62, other modalities of acceptance of jurisdiction are also possible.

[73] For further discussion of the Inter-American Court of Human Rights and the Inter-American Commission on Human Rights, *see* ch. 12 *infra.* On the Inter-American Court, *see generally* Buergenthal, *The Inter-American Court of Human Rights*, 76 Am. J. Int'l L. 231 (1982).

[74] Art. 8.

Twelfth General Conference of UNESCO decided to supplement this provision by a protocol instituting an eleven-member Conciliation and Good Offices Commission which was to be responsible for seeking an amicable settlement of disputes relating to the application or interpretation of the Convention against Discrimination in Education.[75] If a state party considers that another state party is not giving effect to a provision of the Convention, and the matter cannot be adjusted by bilateral negotiations, either state has the right to refer the matter to the Commission.[76] The Commission will ascertain the facts and make available its good offices to the states concerned.[77] The Commission may recommend that the Executive Board (or, in some circumstances, the General Conference) of UNESCO request the International Court of Justice to give an advisory opinion on any legal question connected with a matter laid before the Commission.[78] If an amicable solution is not reached 'on the basis of respect for the Convention',[79] the Commission shall draw up a report on the facts and indicate the recommendations which it made with a view to conciliation.[80]

The Racial Discrimination Convention allows a state party which considers that another state party is not giving effect thereto to bring the matter to the attention of the eighteen-member Committee on the Elimination of Racial Discrimination established under that Convention.[81] After certain preliminary proceedings, the Chairman of the Committee shall, with the unanimous consent of the parties to the dispute, appoint an *ad hoc* Conciliation Commission of five persons (who may or may not be members of the Committee);[82] or, if the parties fail to agree on the composition of that Commission, its members will be elected by secret ballot by a two-thirds majority vote of the Committee from among its own members.[83] The *ad hoc* Conciliation Commission shall prepare a report embodying its findings on all questions of fact and containing recommendations for the amicable solution of the dispute.[84] The declarations of the parties to the dispute as to whether or not they accept the recommendations contained in the report[85] are communicated by the Chairman of the Committee to all the states parties to the Convention.[86]

[75] Protocol Instituting a Conciliation and Good Offices Commission, 651 U.N.T.S. 362, *reprinted in* U.N. Compilation, *supra* note 1, at 37.
[76] *Id.* art. 12.
[77] *Id.* art. 17(1).
[78] *Id.* art. 18.
[79] *Id.* art. 17(1).
[80] *Id.* art. 17(3).
[81] Racial Discrimination Convention, art. 11.
[82] *Id.* art. 12(1)(a).
[83] *Id.* art. 12(1)(b).
[84] *Id.* art. 13(1).
[85] *Id.* art. 13(2).
[86] *Id.* art. 13(3).

While the Economic Covenant contains no provisions concerning complaints, the Political Covenant includes an optional provision enabling a party to declare that it recognizes the competence of the Human Rights Committee established by the Political Covenant to receive and consider communications to the effect that this party is not fulfilling its obligations under the Political Covenant.[87] But no such communication shall be accepted by the Committee if it has been made by a party which has not made a similar declaration recognizing the competence of the Committee in regard to itself.[88] In each case submitted to it, the Committee shall make available its good offices to the parties to the dispute with a view to a friendly solution of the matter 'on the basis of respect for human rights and fundamental freedoms as recognized in the present Covenant'.[89] If no solution is reached, the Committee shall prepare a report limited to a brief statement of the facts and the text of the written and oral submissions of the parties.[90] The Covenant provides further that, with the consent of the parties, a matter which has not been thus resolved by the Committee may be referred to an *ad hoc* Conciliation Commission similar to the one envisaged by the Racial Discrimination Convention.[91] Unlike the very limited report of the Human Rights Committee, the report of the Conciliation Commission in a case in which no solution is reached shall embody not only its findings on questions of fact but also its views on the possibilities of an amicable solution of the matter.[92] These provisions came into force on 28 March, 1979 when ten states parties accepted this optional clause.[93]

From the point of view of the new international law of human rights, it would be extremely important to have some methods for dealing with inter-state human rights complaints. As a minimum there should be provisions for fact-finding and conciliation of the kind embodied in the widely ratified Racial Discrimination Convention.[94] The General Assembly might adopt a protocol applicable to all existing human rights instruments which do not contain a more effective system for the settlement of inter-state disputes. It would provide for the establishment of a fact-finding and conciliation commission, with powers

[87] Political Covenant, art. 41(1).

[88] *Id.*

[89] *Id.* art. 41(1)(e).

[90] *Id.* art. 41(1)(h)(ii).

[91] *Id.* art. 42(1)(a).

[92] *Id.* art. 42(7)(c).

[93] *See* U.N. Doc. A/34/440 (1979). As of Dec. 31, 1981, the following 14 states had made declarations under art. 41 of the Political Covenant: Austria, Canada, Denmark, Finland, Federal Republic of Germany, Iceland, Italy, the Netherlands, New Zealand, Norway, Senegal, Sri Lanka, Sweden, and the United Kingdom. U.N. Doc. E/CN.4/1511 (1981).

[94] As of July 1, 1982, 115 states were parties to the Racial Discrimination Convention. U.N. Doc. ST/4R/4/Rev. 4 (1982).

similar to the *ad hoc* Conciliation Commission established under the Racial Discrimination Convention. In ratifying such a protocol, a state might accept the Conciliation Commission's jurisdiction for disputes relating to the interpretation or application of all human rights instruments or might accept it only for some of them, or for all of them with the exception of certain ones.

3. *Procedures for the Consideration of Private Communications*

While the European and inter-American human rights systems,[95] as well as the International Labour Organisation,[96] include effective procedures for dealing with private complaints by individuals concerned or by national or international nongovernmental organizations (NGOs),[97] the record of the United Nations in this field is rather spotty.

The U.N. Charter provides for dealing with individual complaints in only one case. The General Assembly and the Trusteeship Council were authorized to accept 'petitions' relating to trust territories and to 'examine them in consultation with the administering authority'.[98] Under this provision large numbers of petitions have been considered by the Council, and in many cases the Council has made recommendations with respect to them to the administering authorities. Petitions have been also received and petitioners heard by the Fourth Committee of the General Assembly and in some cases recommendations have been made by the General Assembly to the administering authorities.[99] After considerable controversy, the Fourth Committee in 1961 also opened its doors to petitioners from non-self-governing territories other than trust territories.[100] That same year the General Assembly established a Special Committee on Territories under Portuguese Administration and authorized it to receive petitions and hear petitioners.[101] The United Nations Special Committee of Seventeen (later Twenty-Four) on decolonization, over the objections of some administering powers, agreed in 1962 to receive written petitions and to hear petitioners;[102] and since then it has considered more than a thousand

[95] *See generally* chs. 12 & 13 *infra*.

[96] *See generally* ch. 7 *supra*.

[97] *See generally* ch. 11 *infra*.

[98] U.N. Charter art. 87.

[99] 4 Repertory of United Nations Practice 340–61 (1955); *id.* Supp. (No. 1(2)) 279–82 (1958); *id.* Supp. (No. 2(3)) 336–41 (1963); *id.* Supp. (No. 3(3)) 208–10, 226–29 (1972). *See also* Murray, The United Nations Trusteeship System 150–74 (1957); Thullen, Problems of the Trusteeship System 75–81 (1964); Zonouzi, L'évolution du régime international de tutelle 147–53 (1967).

[100] 16 U.N. GAOR, C.4 (1208th mtg.) 322–26, U.N. Doc. A/C.4/SR.1208 (1961).

[101] G.A. Res. 1699, 16 U.N. GAOR, Supp. (No. 17) 38, U.N. Doc. A/5100 (1962).

[102] Report of the Special Committee on the Situation with regard to the Implementation of the Declaration on the Granting of Independence to Colonial Countries and Peoples, 17 U.N.

petitions.[103] It may be also noted that the Committee on the Elimination of Racial Discrimination has been authorized to consider petitions from non-self-governing territories transmitted to it by other United Nations bodies and to make recommendations with respect to them.[104]

However, since 1947 the Economic and Social Council has held the view that the Commission on Human Rights and the Commission on the Status of Women have 'no power to take any action in regard to any complaints' concerning, respectively, human rights or the status of women.[105] Despite many attempts to revise that rule, it is still in force today.[106] But when in 1965 the Special Committee on decolonization drew the attention of the Commission on Human Rights to evidence submitted by petitioners respecting violations of human rights in southern Africa,[107] the Economic and Social Council asked the Commission 'to consider as a matter of importance and urgency the question of the violation of human rights and fundamental freedoms, including policies of racial discrimination and segregation and of *apartheid* in all countries, with particular reference to colonial and other dependent countries and territories'.[108] Later the Council authorized the Commission to examine information relevant to 'gross violations of human rights and fundamental freedoms' (as exemplified by the policy of *apartheid* as practiced in southern Africa) contained in communications received by the Commission, and after thorough study of 'situations which reveal a consistent pattern of violations of human rights', to report with recommendations thereon to the Council.[109] The procedural proposals for dealing with this new assignment, which were prepared by the Commission on Human Rights and its Sub-Commission on Prevention of Discrimination and Protection

GAOR, Annexes (Add. Agenda Item 25) 18, U.N. Doc. A/5238 (1962). For comments on this decision, *see id.* at 6–17. Concerning the right of petition from non-self-governing territories, *see also* Repertory of United Nations Practice, Supp. (No. 3(3)) 62–65 (1972).

---

[103] For instance, with respect to petitions 1264 and 1265 (from the New Hebrides), *see* 31 U.N. GAOR, Supp. (No. 23, vol. III) 3, U.N. Doc. A/31/23/Rev. 1 (1977).

[104] Racial Discrimination Convention, art. 15. *See also* art. 7, Optional Protocol to the International Covenant on Civil and Political Rights, G.A. Res. 2200, U.N. GAOR, Supp. (No. 16) 59, U.N. Doc. A/6316 (1966), *reprinted in* U.N. Compilation, *supra* note 1, at 16.

[105] E.S.C. Res. 75 & Res. 76, 5 U.N. ESCOR, Supp. (No. 1) 20, 21, U.N. Doc. E/573 (1947). This decision was confirmed by the Economic and Social Council in Res. 728F, 28 U.N. ESCOR, Supp. (No. 1) 19, U.N. Doc. E/3290 (1959).

[106] For a short history of these attempts, *see* United Nations Action, *supra* note 32, at 177–81. *See also* L. Sohn & T. Buergenthal, International Protection of Human Rights 746–856 (1973) [hereinafter cited as Sohn & Buergenthal].

[107] 20 U.N. GAOR, Annexes (Add. Agenda Item 23), 58–59, U.N. Doc. A/6000/Rev.1 (1965).

[108] E.S.C. Res. 1102, 40 U.N. ESCOR, Supp. (No. 1) 6, U.N. Doc. E/4176 (1966).

[109] E.S.C. Res. 1235, 42 U.N. ESCOR, Supp. (No. 1) 17–18, U.N. Doc. E/4393 (1967).

of Minorities, were codified by the Economic and Social Council in Resolution 1503.[110]

Resolution 1503 authorized a multi-step procedure, starting in a Working Group of the Sub-Commission and proceeding through the Sub-Commission to the Commission, whenever communications to the Commission appear to reveal 'a consistent pattern of gross and reliably attested violations of human rights'. The Commission can consider the situation itself or, with the express consent of the state concerned, it may refer it to an *ad hoc* committee for an investigation and to endeavor to achieve a friendly solution. After considering over 20,000 individual communications in a number of years, the Working Group drew some of the communications to the attention of the Sub-Commission.[111] As all the bodies concerned are under an injunction to keep all actions confidential until the Commission decides to make recommendations to the Council, no information on the subject has been forthcoming for several years. Starting in 1978, the Commission began to announce at each session that it had taken decisions in private sessions concerning certain specific countries; for instance, in 1978 it listed Bolivia, Equatorial Guinea, Malawi, the Republic of Korea, Uganda, Ethiopia, Indonesia, Paraguay, and Uruguay, but the content of these decisions was not revealed.[112] In 1980, for the first time, the Commission concluded the examination of a case under Resolution 1503 and recommended that the European and Social Council should express its regret that the Government of Malawi has failed 'to co-operate with the Commission on Human Rights in the examination of a situation said to have deprived thousands of Jehovah's Witnesses in Malawi of their basic human rights and fundamental freedoms between 1972 and 1975, which failure constrains the Economic and Social Council to publicize the matter'; and also that the Council should express the hope that 'the human rights of all citizens of Malawi have been fully restored and, in particular, that adequate measures are being taken to provide remedy to those who may have suffered injustices'.[113]

While the great expectations with respect to the procedure under Resolution 1503 have not yet been fulfilled, the Commission on Human Rights has been dealing with several cases of gross violations of human rights without subjecting them to this complex procedure. For instance, already in 1967, following an urgent request by the

[110] E.S.C. Res. 1503, 48 U.N. ESCOR, Supp. (No. 1A) 8–9, U.N. Doc. E/4832/Add.1 (1970).

[111] *See, e.g.*, U.N. Doc. E/CN.4/1101 (1972); E/CN.4/Sub.2/332, at 25 (1972).

[112] 1978 U.N. ESCOR, Supp. (No. 4) 47, U.N. Doc. E/1978/34, E/CN.4/1292 (1978). For a comment on this decision, *see* Rev. Int'l Comm'n Jurists 33–35 (No. 20, June 1978).

[113] 1980 U.N. ESCOR, Supp. (No. 3) 3, U.N. Doc. E/1980/13, E/CN.4/1408 (1980); *id.* at 91–92, 202–03.

General Assembly's Special Committee on the Policies of *Apartheid*, the Commission on Human Rights established an *Ad Hoc* Working Group of Experts to investigate the charges of torture and ill-treatment of prisoners, detainees, or persons in police custody in South Africa; and the Commission authorized the Working Group to receive communications, to hear witnesses, and to recommend action to be taken in concrete cases.[114] The only authority cited for this decision was Resolution 9 of the Economic and Social Council which authorized the Commission 'to call in *ad hoc* working groups of non-governmental legal experts in specialized fields', with the approval of the President of the Economic and Social Council and the Secretary-General.[115] The Economic and Social Council welcomed this decision and extended the terms of reference of the Working Group to deal also with allegations regarding infringements of trade union rights in South Africa.[116] Later, the Economic and Social Council extended these terms of reference further, covering also violations of trade union rights in Namibia and Southern Rhodesia.[117]

Similar action was taken by the Commission on Human Rights in 1969 with respect to questions of human rights in the territories occupied as a result of the 1967 hostilities in the Middle East. The Commission established a Special Working Group of Experts 'to investigate allegations concerning Israel's violations of the Geneva Convention relative to the Protection of Civilian Persons in Time of War of 12 August 1949, in the territories occupied by Israel as a result of hostilities in the Middle East', and authorized the Working Group to 'receive communications, to hear witnesses, and to use such modalities of procedure as it may deem necessary'.[118] The Working Group seems to have been discontinued after the General Assembly established a Special Committee to Investigate Israeli Practices Affecting the Human Rights of the Population of the Occupied Territories[119] and that Committee presented its first report.[120]

[114] Comm'n on Human Rights Res. 2 (XXIII), 42 U.N. ESCOR, Supp. (No. 6) 76–78, U.N. Doc. E/4322, E/CN.4/940 (1967).

[115] E.S.C. Res. 9, para. 3, 2 U.N. ESCOR 400, 401 (1946).

[116] E.S.C. Res. 1216 & Res. 1236, 42 U.N. ESCOR, Supp. (No. 1) 12, 18, U.N. Doc. E/4393 (1967).

[117] E.S.C. Res. 1302, 44 U.N. ESCOR, Supp. (No. 1) 11, U.N. Doc. E/4548 (1968). Concerning the reports of the Working Group and the actions of the General Assembly based on its recommendations, *see* U.N. Action, *supra* note 32, at 84–87, 275.

[118] Comm'n on Human Rights Res. 6 (XXV), 46 U.N. ESCOR, Supp. (No. 6) 183–84, U.N. Doc. E/4621, E/CN.4/1007 (1969). For Israel's refusal to co-operate with the Working Group, *see id.* at 76. During its first year of operation the Working Group heard 103 witnesses. 48 U.N. ESCOR, Supp. (No. 5) 48, U.N. Doc. E/4816, E/CN.4/1039 (1970). *See also* Comm'n on Human Rights Res. 10 (XXVI), *id.* at 79–82.

[119] G.A. Res. 2443, 23 U.N. GAOR, Supp. (No. 18) 50, U.N. Doc. A/7218 (1969).

[120] U.N. Doc. A/8089 (1970). For the Commission's consideration of the question in 1971, *see* 50 U.N. ESCOR, Supp. (No. 4) 33–39, 79–82, U.N. Doc. E/4949, E/CN.4/1068 (1971). The

During the 1969 discussion in the Commission on Human Rights of the situation in Israeli-occupied territories a reference was made to the death sentences carried out in Iraq against a number of persons charged with spying for Israel. In reply it was stated that 'the question was a purely domestic one, coming within the exclusive jurisdiction of a sovereign State', and that the Commission had no right to deal with it.[121] In 1970, the attention of the Commission was drawn to several situations which, in the opinion of the speakers, might constitute situations revealing a consistent pattern of violations of human rights. Among them were: the situations of the Tibetans, of Soviet Jews wishing to emigrate to Israel, of citizens of Jewish faith living in some Arab countries, of Iranians resident in Iraq, of non-Russian nationalities in the Soviet Union, of political prisoners in Cuba, and of persons of African and Jewish origin living in the United States. Again the issue was raised whether article 2(7) of the U.N. Charter precluded consideration of these situations by the Commission.[122]

Some consideration was given in 1973 to the situations in Greece and in the South-Asian sub-continent (India, Pakistan, and Bangladesh);[123] in 1974 to the situation in Chile;[124] and in 1975 to the situations in Cyprus and Chile.[125] In the latter case, the Commission had before it information supplied by several NGOs as well as by the International Labour Office, UNESCO, and the Organization of American States.[126] It appointed an *Ad Hoc* Working Group 'to inquire into the present situation of human rights in Chile', and to prepare a report on the basis 'of a visit to Chile and of oral and written

question continued to be discussed by the Commission in later years. In 1977 its title was changed to 'Question of the violation of human rights in the occupied Arab Territories, including Palestine.' 62 U.N. ESCOR, Supp. (No. 6) 9, U.N. Doc. E/5927, E/CN.4/1257 (1977).

[121] Comm'n on Human Rights, Report on the Twenty-Fifth Session, 46 U.N. ESCOR, Supp. (No. 6) 73, U.N. Doc. E/4621, E/CN.4/1007 (1969).

[122] 48 U.N. ESCOR, Supp. (No. 5) 45, U.N. Doc. E/4816, E/CN.4/1039 (1970). Later reports of the Commission, while they refer to situations in some countries which were alleged to reveal a consistent pattern of violations of human rights, do not mention these countries by name. *See, e.g.*, 50 U.N. ESCOR, Supp. (No. 4) 51–52, U.N. Doc. E/4949, E/CN.4/1068 (1971); 52 U.N. ESCOR, Supp. (No. 7) 40–41, U.N. Doc. E/5113, E/CN.4/1097 (1972). Similar general statements are contained in later reports. However, in most cases the names of the countries concerned are mentioned in the summary records of the Commission.

[123] 54 U.N. ESCOR, Supp. (No. 6) 46, U.N. Doc. E/5265, E/CN.4/1127 (1973).

[124] 56 U.N. ESCOR, Supp. (No. 5) 30–31, U.N. Doc. E/5464, E/CN.4/1154 (1974). For the telegram sent by the Commission to Chile, *see id.* at 56–57.

[125] 58 U.N. ESCOR, Supp. (No. 4) 18–19, 23–26, U.N. Doc. E/5635, E/CN.4/1179 (1975). Concerning Cyprus, *see also* Comm'n on Human Rights Res. 4 (XXXII), 60 U.N. ESCOR, Supp. (No. 3) 59–60, U.N. Doc. E/5768, E/CN.4/1213 (1976); Res. 17 (XXXIV), 1978 U.N. ESCOR, Supp. (No. 4) 120–21, U.N. Doc. E/1978/34, E/CN.4/1292 (1978).

[126] U.N. Doc. E/CN.4/1166/Add.1–15 (1974–75). For comments by Chile, *see* U.N. Doc. E/CN.4/1158; U.N. Doc. E/CN.4/1174; U.N. Doc. E/CN.4/1174/Add.1 (1974–75).

evidence to be gathered from all relevant sources'.[127] The reports of the Working Group were discussed not only in the Commission but also in the General Assembly, and led to resolutions condemning 'constant [and] flagrant violations of human rights' in Chile.[128] It may be noted that in 1977 the observer for Chile had stated in the Commission that 'his Government agreed that the Commission had authority to deal with all violations of human rights and had, therefore, never raised an objection based on the argument of interference in domestic affairs'; his objections were limited to the objectivity of the Working Group's report and the fairness of its procedure.[129] But a year later the observer for Chile stated that his country strongly objected to a study by the United Nations of the impact on human rights in Chile of foreign economic aid, which constituted 'an unwarranted interference in the internal affairs of his country', and considered the U.N. resolutions and the inquiry of the *Ad Hoc* Working Group to be an infringement of his country's sovereignty.[130] Nevertheless, after prolonged negotiation, the Working Group was allowed to visit Chile in July 1978.[131]

While no action was taken in 1977 on proposals relating to the human rights situation in Uganda,[132] the Commission decided in 1978 at least to transmit to the government of Democratic Kampuchea for comment a set of documents and the Commission's summary records relating to the human rights situation in that country.[133] As noted before, the Commission also disclosed in 1978 the names of nine countries in which there were situations under consideration by the Commission.[134]

In 1976 the procedures concerning communications became further complicated by the entry into force of the Optional Protocol to the International Covenant on Civil and Political Rights.[135] By the end of 1981, the Optional Protocol had been ratified by twenty-seven

[127] Comm'n on Human Rights Res. 8 (XXXI), 58 U.N. ESCOR, Supp. (No. 4) 66–67, U.N. Doc. E/5635, E/CN.4/1179 (1975). The Working Group was not permitted to enter Chile in 1975. U.N. Doc. A/10285, at 21–28 (1975).

[128] G.A. Res. 3448, 30 U.N. GAOR, Supp. (No. 34) 89–90, U.N. Doc. A/10034 (1976); Comm'n on Human Rights Res. 3 (XXXII), 60 U.N. ESCOR, Supp. (No. 3) 57–59, U.N. Doc. E/5768, E/CN.4/1213 (1976). Similar decisions were adopted in later years. *See, e.g.*, G.A. Res. 31/124, 31 U.N. GAOR, Supp. (No. 39) 104–05, U.N. Doc. A/31/39 (1977).

[129] 62 U.N. ESCOR, Supp. (No. 6) 35, U.N. Doc. E/5927, E/CN.4/1257 (1977).

[130] 1978 U.N. ESCOR, Supp. (No. 4) 15, U.N. Doc. E/1978/34, E/CN.4/1292 (1978).

[131] *See* U.N. Doc. A/33/331, at 5–13 (1978). Similar steps were taken in 1981, on request of the General Assembly, with respect to El Salvador and Bolivia. Comm'n on Human Rights Decs. 32 and 34 (XXXVII), 1981 U.N. ESCOR, Supp. (No. 5) 233, 235, U.N. Doc. E/1981/25, E/CN.4/1475 (1981).

[132] 62 U.N. ESCOR, Supp. (No. 6) 17–18, U.N. Doc. E/5927, E/CN.4/1257 (1977).

[133] Comm'n on Human Rights Dec. 9 (XXXIV), 1978 U.N. ESCOR, Supp. (No. 4) 48, 137, U.N. Doc. E/1978/34, E/CN.4/1292 (1978).

[134] *See* text preceding note 112 *supra*.

[135] *See* note 104 *supra*.

states;[136] and the Human Rights Committee established under the Political Covenant is therefore competent to deal with communications from individuals who are subject to the jurisdiction of a state party to the Optional Protocol and who claim to be victims of a violation by that state of any of the rights set forth in the Political Covenant.[137] After considering the communication in closed meetings,[138] the Committee shall forward its views to the state concerned and to the complaining individual.[139] The only additional publicity to be given these endeavors is by including in the annual report of the Committee a summary of its activities under the Optional Protocol.[140] In 1977 the Human Rights Committee decided to establish a Working Group to consider the communications in the light of all written information made available to it by the individual and by the state party concerned and to make recommendations to the Committee regarding the fulfilment of the conditions of admissibility laid down in the Optional Protocol.[141]

During 1977 and 1978 the Human Rights Committee considered forty communications. Seven of these were declared admissible, and another seven were declared inadmissible, while one was withdrawn by the author. The decision on admissibility was pending at the end of 1978 with respect to the remaining communications. Some of them were referred to the states concerned with a request for information and observations relevant to the question of admissibility; in some others the authors were asked to submit additional information.[142] In 1979 the Committee decided that two communications from Uruguay had disclosed violations of the Political Covenant, and expressed the view that Uruguay was under an obligation to provide effective remedies to the victims (including, in one case, compensation in accordance with article 9(5) of the Covenant).[143]

As soon as the Optional Protocol entered into force, the need to examine the relationship between the various procedures was recognized and suggestions were made for adopting a unified method for dealing with communications.[144] It was also noted, in another connec-

[136] As of 31 Dec. 1981, the following states were parties to the Optional Protocol: Barbados, Canada, Central African Republic, Colombia, Costa Rica, Denmark, Dominican Republic, Ecuador, Finland, Iceland, Italy, Jamaica, Madagascar, Mauritius, The Netherlands, Nicaragua, Norway, Panama, Peru, St. Vincent and the Grenadines, Senegal, Suriname, Sweden, Trinidad and Tobago, Uruguay, Venezuela, and Zaire. U.N. Doc. E/CN.4/1511 (1981).

[137] Optional Protocol, art. 1.

[138] *Id.* art. 5(3).

[139] *Id.* art. 5(4).

[140] *Id.* art. 6.

[141] Rules 89 & 94, 32 U.N. GAOR, Supp. (No. 44) 5, 64–65, U.N. Doc. A/32/44 (1977).

[142] 33 U.N. GAOR, Supp. (No. 40) 98, U.N. Doc. A/33/40 (1978).

[143] U.N. Press Releases HR/1854 & HR/1871 (1979).

[144] 62 U.N. ESCOR, Supp. (No. 6) 15–16, U.N. Doc. E/5927, E/CN.4/1257 (1977).

tion, that procedural difficulties have arisen as a result of the co-existence of public and confidential procedures for examining allegations of violations of human rights.[145]

It is too early to comment on the system established by the Optional Protocol, and perhaps some of its obvious limitations might be avoided in practice. It is clear, however, that the system established by the Economic and Social Council's Resolutions 1235 and 1503[146] is not working satisfactorily. After more than ten years, this system has produced only one report for public scrutiny. At the same time, in several important instances the system has been bypassed by the Commission on Human Rights. The General Assembly itself has stepped into some of these cases with far-ranging recommendations.

One has to distinguish between those gross violations of human rights which contravene the Charter itself and the important, but more technical, violations of specific international instruments on human rights. The first ones can be considered effectively only in the glare of publicity, allowing public opinion to put pressure on the offending state. The present, mostly secret, procedure of the Commission on Human Rights is completely unsuitable for this purpose, and should be replaced by the procedure utilized by the General Assembly and the Commission on Human Rights in those cases which escaped the pitfalls of the procedure under Resolution 1503. There is no provision in the Charter prohibiting the General Assembly, the Economic and Social Council, or the Commission on Human Rights from considering communications received from individuals or organizations as a basis for public discussion and recommendation. The only thing required is a request by a state or a group of states that a particular case be considered in the light if the communications received and of other information which may become available.

When the Council of the League of Nations was faced with a similar problem in connection with petitions by members of minorities under the various treaties for their protection, it decided to appoint in each case a Committee of Three for the purpose of inquiring whether there had been a violation of a treaty. The rapporteur of each Committee presented the case to the Council, without involving the responsibility of his government, and some rapporteurs became specialists on certain areas or subjects.[147] Following this example, and building also on the recent practice of the Commission on Human Rights and of the General Assembly, the Commission on Human Rights might be authorized to appoint annually one or more pre-sessional working

[145] *Id.* at 18.

[146] *See* notes 109 and 110 *supra.*

[147] *See* the report of the Committee of Three of 6 June 1929. League of Nations O. J., Spec. Supp. 73, at 42–64 (1929), *reprinted in* Sohn & Buergenthal, *supra* note 106, at 213–50.

groups, composed either of experts acting in their private capacity or of representatives of five member states, one from each main geographic region, to consider whether any communications submitted to it relate to gross violations of human rights.[148] If the reply is positive, the rapporteur of the working group would, *ex officio*, be authorized to submit the case to the parent body for discussion. Each member of the working group might be assigned either a group of countries (in his or her region or some other region) or certain topics (*e.g.*, racial discrimination, treatment of prisoners, or equality of women) and would, after a while, become a specialist on the subject. The working group might also be authorized to submit to the parent body a draft recommendation for further action. The report of the working group and its recommendations would then be discussed in public and the pressure of public opinion could be mobilized to support the proposed action. Once this possibility is at the disposal of the working group, the state concerned might be more willing to discuss with it ways and means of settling the matter, thus avoiding exposure to public scrutiny. In such a case the working group would merely report that the case had been settled in conformity with the relevant international human rights instruments.

The procedure under the Political Covenant and its Optional Protocol is less likely to involve gross violations of human rights, and is probably destined to deal primarily with the difficulties caused by the imperfect introduction of international human rights provisions into domestic legal systems. As the European countries have realized, no legal system is flawless and the right to complain to an international institution helps to remove the blemishes. The changes which may be required by an international decision in such a case are not likely to interfere drastically with the domestic legal system and the decision can be easily, if sometimes reluctantly, obeyed.

Once it is shown that this is the case, one can hope that the Optional Protocol will be widely ratified and that it will not be necessary to devise some substitute system for states which are not bound by the Protocol. However, should such a substitute prove desirable it would not be too difficult for the General Assembly to come up with an adequate system. Alternatively, another optional protocol might be prepared allowing a state to accept the jurisdiction of the Human Rights Committee (or of another appropriate body) with respect to international instruments (other than the Political Covenant) to which it is a party which do not themselves provide for a system of handling communications relating to their violation.

[148] Alternatively, that function might be conferred upon the Bureau of the Commission on Human Rights. *See* 1978 U.N. ESCOR, Supp. (No. 4) 40, 42, U.N. Doc. E/1978/34, E/CN.4/1292 (1978).

4. *Conflicts between Various Implementation Procedures*

The entry into force of the Political and Economic Covenants has also raised the possibility of conflicts between their implementation provisions and the various procedures which already exist under instruments relating to specialized agencies or regional organizations. Both Covenants provide in general terms that nothing in them 'shall be interpreted as impairing the provisions of the Charter of the United Nations and of the constitutions of the specialized agencies which define the respective responsibilities of the various organs of the United Nations and of the specialized agencies in regard to matters dealt with' in these Covenants.[149] In addition, article 44 of the Political Covenant stipulates expressly that its provisions 'shall apply without prejudice to the procedures prescribed in the field of human rights by or under the constituent instruments and the conventions of the United Nations and of the specialized agencies'. More specifically, according to the same article, the Political Covenant's implementation procedures shall not prevent the states parties to it 'from having recourse to other procedures for settling a dispute in accordance with general or special international agreements in force between them'. Finally, the Optional Protocol, which relates to communications from individuals, prohibits the consideration by the Human Rights Committee of any communication when 'the same matter' is being examined under another 'procedure of international investigation or settlement'.[150]

This liberal attitude might be contrasted with the more exclusive approach of the European Convention, the states parties to which have agreed that 'they will not avail themselves of treaties, conventions or declarations in force between them for the purpose of submitting, by way of petition, a dispute arising out of the interpretation or application' of that Convention to 'a means of settlement' other than those provided in the European Convention.[151]

The provisions of the Political and Economic Covenants show clear preference for applying U.N. procedures only in cases where other procedures are not available. In particular, the procedures developed by the specialized agencies, such as the International Labour Organisation and UNESCO, are given triple protection. This seems to be justified when these procedures result in a settlement; but if no settlement has been reached under the procedure resorted to by the parties

[149] Political Covenant, art. 46; Economic Covenant, art. 24.

[150] Optional Protocol, art. 5(2)(a).

[151] European Convention, art. 62. For comments, *see* Eissen, *The European Convention on Human Rights and the United Nations Covenant on Civil and Political Rights: Problems of Coexistence*, 22 Buffalo L. Rev. 181 (1972); Tardu, *Quelques questions relatives à la coexistence des procédures universelles et regionales de plainte individuelle dans le domaine des droits de l'homme*, 4 Revue des Droits de l'Homme 589 (1971).

to the dispute, and if this procedure has not resulted in a final and binding decision, it should be possible to resort to the Human Rights Committee or some other available U.N. procedure. On the other hand, it would seem undesirable to provide for an appeal to the United Nations from a final and binding decision rendered under the auspices of a specialized agency.

As far as regional organizations are concerned, they are not mentioned expressly in the relevant articles of the Political and Economic Covenants. The Optional Protocol, however, may be interpreted as giving precedence to regional procedures. It is less clear whether the reference to examination under another procedure[152] is to be construed as an absolute prohibition of submission to the Human Rights Committee, or, more likely, a merely temporary restriction while the case is pending before another international body. Perhaps this provision might be treated similarly to the rule about exhaustion of local remedies;[153] regional remedies should also be exhausted unsatisfactorily before the matter can be submitted to the U.N. Human Rights Committee.

A clarification by the General Assembly or the Economic and Social Council of these relationships between the various U.N. procedures and the parallel procedures of specialized agencies and regional organizations would be desirable.

C. CONCLUSIONS

The preceding survey shows that important progress took place in the last thirty years with respect to the protection of human rights, and that a sometimes-bewildering variety of procedures has been devised for implementing those rights and for supervising that implementation.

The momentum achieved through the entry into force of the Political and Economic Covenants, the Optional Protocol, and the procedure under article 41 of the Political Covenant should not be lost. There are many constructive steps which the United Nations can take to improve the means available to it to promote and protect human rights. Where the desired results cannot be achieved by imaginative decisions of the General Assembly or of its subsidiary bodies, a variety of instruments and optional protocols might be preferred. The pessimists might again be confounded, and these new instruments might come into force sooner than expected and might bring the peoples of the world several steps further toward an effective system of international human rights law.

[152] Optional Protocol, art. 5(2)(a).
[153] *Id.* art. 5(2)(b).

II. Teaching Suggestions

It is necessary to distinguish at the outset between domestic implementation and international supervision. Domestic implementation in the United States (and some other countries) raises in the first place issues concerning the self-execution character of human rights treaties. It might be useful to discuss in this connection *Sei Fujii v. California*,[154] the proposed Bricker Amendment,[155] and the proposal of the Carter Administration that in ratifying four treaties on human rights the United States should declare that they are not self-executing.[156] Once these documents are ratified, various issues will arise as to their effect in the United States courts, especially as to their use in interpreting relevant United States legislation.[157]

It should also be noted that the United States may be internationally bound by a human rights treaty, but the courts may refuse to enforce it because it violates the Constitution, has been superseded by a later statute, or is not self-executing and the necessary implementing legislation has not been enacted. In such a case, the United States may nonetheless be internationally responsible for having violated its treaty obligations.[158] Whether the United States can be sued in such a case before an international court would depend on the existence of a jurisdictional clause encompassing the violation in question. In this connection, reference should be made to the so-called 'Connally reservation' to the United States declaration accepting the jurisdiction of the International Court of Justice, through which the United States exempted from the Court's jurisdiction any dispute which it has determined unilaterally to be essentially within the domestic jurisdiction of the United States. But that reservation does not apply where a particular treaty contains its own jurisdictional clause referring to the International Court of Justice any dispute relating to its interpretation or application.[159]

It should be easier to deal with international supervision. Most of

[154] 217 P.2d 481 (Cal. Dist. Ct. App. 1950), *rev'd* on the point concerning the self-executing character of the U.N. Charter, 38 Cal. 2d 718, 242 P.2d 617 (1952). For a summary of other U.S. cases on the subject, *see* Sohn & Buergenthal, *supra* note 106, at 944; for foreign cases, *see id.* at 992. *See also* R. Lillich & F. Newman, International Human Rights: Problems of Law and Policy 115 (1979) [hereinafter cited as Lillich & Newman]; 14 M. Whiteman, Digest of International Law 280 (1970) [hereinafter cited as Whiteman].

[155] Sohn & Buergenthal, *supra* note 106, at 948.

[156] Four Treaties Pertaining to Human Rights: Message from the President of the United States, S. Exec. Docs. C, D, E, and F, 95th Cong., 2d Sess. viii, xi, xv, xviii(1978).

[157] *See* 2 Hyde, International Law Chiefly as Interpreted and Applied by the United States 1463 (1945); 14 Whiteman, *supra* note 154, at 316.

[158] *See* 1 G. Schwarzenberger, International Law 69 (3d ed. 1957), summarizing the practice of international courts on the subject.

[159] *See* Bishop & Myers, *Unwarranted Extension of Connally-Amendment Thinking*, 55 Am. J. Int'l L. 135 (1961).

the internationally supervised treaties are of recent origin and practice under them is scant. In comparing various reporting procedures, it might be useful to take into account the experience of the International Labour Organisation discussed in chapter 7. Similarly, the experience of the European Commission of Human Rights, discussed in chapter 13, should be taken into account when discussing complaint procedures.

Discussion of U.N. reporting procedures might concentrate on the development of procedures under the Racial Discrimination Convention.[160] In considering the complaint procedures within the U.N. system, sharp distinction must be made between ordinary communications, to which little attention is paid despite their large numbers;[161] the special procedure in cases of gross violation which has been developed, especially under Resolution 1503 of the Economic and Social Council;[162] and the *ad hoc* procedure used in some cases of special concern to the United Nations (such as South Africa, Chile, and the Israeli-occupied territories).[163]

It is necessary to deal also with two recurrent, interconnected, general questions: is the international law of human rights really enforceable? and why are the existing procedures so ineffective? It is a common belief that since states are sovereign they can disregard international law with impunity. There are various possible answers to this. In the first place, most states comply with international law on most occasions as a matter of course or as a matter of convenience. They have found by experience that it is easier to live in the world community if everybody obeys certain basic rules. For example, domestically it proved to be important to have regulations governing road traffic; if everybody could drive as they pleased, very few people would survive a trip of even a few miles. Internationally, it proved equally important to observe the rules relating to air and sea navigation. If somebody disobeys, disasters similar to that of the *Andrea Doria* are likely to happen.

Secondly, once a state agrees that a rule is binding, it ordinarily follows it. Even those who are considered as arch-villains hesitate to

[160] *See, e.g.*, Sohn & Buergenthal, *supra* note 106, at 868; Buergenthal, *Implementing the Racial Convention*, 12 Tex. Int'l L.J. 187 (1977).

[161] *See* Sohn & Buergenthal, *supra* note 106, at 746.

[162] *See id.* at 772; Lillich & Newman, *supra* note 154, at 337.

[163] As to Chile, *see id.* at 292; Kirgis, International Organizations in Their Legal Setting 822 (1977); Bossuyt, *The United Nations and Civil and Political Rights in Chile*, 27 Int'l & Comp. L.Q. 462 (1978). *See also* Ermacora, *International Enquiry Commissions in the Field of Human Rights*, 1 Revue des Droits de l'Homme 180 (1968); Kaufman, *The Necessity for Rules of Procedure in Ad Hoc United Nations Investigations*, 18 Am. U. L. Rev. 739 (1969); Miller, *United Nations Fact-Finding Missions in the Field of Human Rights*, Austl. Y.B. Int'l L. 40 (1970–73).

imitate the German statement of 1914 that the treaty guaranteeing the neutrality of Belgium was a scrap of paper. Like domestic courts which do not want to apply a particular rule, international decision-makers seldom come out boldly and assert that their sovereign state is entitled to disregard a particular rule whenever it pleases; instead, they attempt to distinguish the case at hand from past precedents and try to present a legal argument for following a different path. Thus, even when a violation of international law is committed, the violator usually defends it as an allowed deviation from the rule. This is especially common in the field of human rights, where the violator often invokes the rule that matters of domestic jurisdiction are not subject to international law nor to international scrutiny through various implementation measures. Other common excuses are connected with the need to protect national security, public order, health, or morals.[164] If everything else fails, one can claim that there is a public emergency threatening the life of the nation.[165] While the international community cannot completely close these loopholes, there is a growing tendency to diminish the self-serving character of these exceptions by submitting them to the scrutiny of the competent international body, which may decide that their invocation was not justified in a particular instance.[166]

As far as outright disregard of human rights is concerned, it is true that some governments have grossly mistreated their peoples. It needs to be pointed out, however, that very few of the villains have avoided retribution. For instance, in 1979 the rule of three gross violators of human rights in Africa was terminated—in Uganda, the Central African Empire, and Guinea-Bissau. While some such violators have been punished by special international criminal courts after they lost a war, and others were punished when they were unable to escape after a revolution against them, there is as yet no general international criminal court able to punish such violations in peacetime. Nevertheless, this idea has been considered seriously from time to time, and is likely to be considered by the General Assembly again in the 1980s.[167]

The international legal system is constantly evolving and we have seen a great amount of progress in the field of human rights since 1945. It took a long time to develop a satisfactory system of human rights

[164] The Political Covenant allows the invocation of these exceptional circumstances in certain instances. *See* arts. 12(3), 14(1), 18(3), 19(3)(b), 21, & 22(2).

[165] *See id.* art. 4.

[166] For decisions of the European Commission of Human Rights and the European Court of Human Rights on this subject, *see* ch. 13 *infra*.

[167] For a detailed, well-documented summary of efforts to prepare a draft code of offenses against the peace and security of mankind and a statute of an international criminal court, *see* B. Ferencz, An International Criminal Court: A Step Toward World Peace: A Documentary History and Analysis (1980).

protection in the most developed countries; one cannot expect to develop it internationally overnight. But through teaching this subject to an ever growing community, one can expect that progress in this field will be expedited.[168]

III. Syllabus

I. *Implementation*
  A. Differences between international and domestic implementation of human rights.
  B. Implementation in the United States: Special issues.
    1. Self-executing and non-self-executing human rights treaties.
    2. Conflicts with domestic legislation.
    3. International consequences of non-fulfillment of international obligations.
  C. Obligation to implement.
    1. Duties under article 2 of the International Covenant on Civil and Political Rights.
    2. Similar obligations under other human rights treaties.
    3. National and local institutions for the promotion and protection of human rights.

II. *International Measures of Implementation and Supervision*
  A. International supervisory commissions.
  B. Methods of supervision.
    1. Periodic reporting systems.
      a. Under U.N. resolutions.
      b. Under various U.N. conventions.
      c. Under the International Convention on the Elimination of All Forms of Racial Discrimination.
      d. Under the Political Covenant and the International Covenant on Economic, Social and Cultural Rights.
  C. Procedures for dealing with inter-state complaints.
    1. Human rights treaties providing for reference to the International Court of Justice.
    2. Submission of complaints to other international courts.
    3. Submission of complaints to fact-finding and conciliation commissions.
  D. Procedures for the consideration of private communications.
    1. Comparison between U.N. procedures and procedures developed by the European Commission of Human

[168] *See* T. Buergenthal & J. Torney, International Human Rights and International Education (1976).

Rights and the Inter-American Commission on Human Rights.
2. Effective operation of the U.N. petition and communication systems in the areas of trusteeship and non-self-governing territories.
3. Unsuccessful efforts in the U.N. to establish a regular procedure for dealing with communications in other human rights areas.
4. Development of new procedures for dealing with 'gross violations' of human rights.
5. Other *ad hoc* procedures.
6. Entry into force of the Optional Protocol to the International Covenant on Civil and Political Rights, and development of procedures for dealing with communications relating to the Political Covenant.
7. Current difficulties and possible means of improving the system.

IV. Minisyllabus

Teachers who can only devote two or three hours to the teaching of the subject dealt with in this chapter should concentrate on dealing with individual complaints, as these are of special interest to both lawyers and private persons who may find it necessary some day to file a complaint.

After a short introduction explaining the existing institutions for implementation, the teacher may wish to concentrate on the European Convention as it has a vast jurisprudence on the subject, and on the inter-American system, as it is the only one now accessible to United States citizens. Thus the teacher may wish to combine the study of this chapter with chapters 12 and 13 relating to these two regional systems.

Consequently the short syllabus might be as follows:

I. Differences between international and domestic implementation of human rights.

II. International supervisory system: commissions and courts.

III. Procedures for the consideration of private communications.
   - A. European system.
   - B. Inter-American system.
   - C. United Nations system.
     1. Gross violations.
     2. Communications under various special conventions and resolutions.
     3. Communications under the Optional Protocol to the International Covenant on Civil and Political Rights.

V. Bibliography

United Nations, United Nations Action in the Field of Human Rights, U.N. Doc. ST/HR/2/Rev.1 (1980).
—— Alternative Approaches and Ways and Means Within the United Nations System for Improving the Effective Enjoyment of Human Rights and Fundamental Freedoms: Report of the Secretary-General, U.N. Doc. A/10235 (1975).
—— Human Rights: A Compilation of International Instruments, U.N. Doc. ST/HR/1/Rev.1 (1978).
Aries, *International Human Rights and Their Implementation*, 19 Geo. Wash. L. Rev. 579 (1951).
Bilder, *The International Promotion of Human Rights: A Current Assessment*, 58 Am. J. Int'l L. 728 (1964).
—— *Rethinking International Human Rights: Some Basic Questions* 1969 Wis. L. Rev. 171.
Buergenthal, *Implementing the Racial Convention*, 12 Tex. Int'l L. J. 187 (1977).
J. Carey, UN Protection of Civil and Political Rights (1970).
R. Clark, A United Nations High Commissioner for Human Rights (1972).
A. Del Russo, International Protection of Human Rights (1970).
G. da Fonseca, How to File Complaints of Human Rights Violations: A Practical Guide to Inter-Governmental Procedures (1975).
Evans, *Self-Executing Treaties in the United States of America*, 30 Brit. Y.B. Int'l L. 178 (1953).
M. Ganji, International Protection of Human Rights (1962).
Golsong, *Implementation of International Protection of Human Rights*, 110 Recueil des Cours 1 (1963).
J. Green, The United Nations and Human Rights (1964).
Humphrey, *The Right of Petition in the United Nations*, 4 Revue des Droits de l'Homme 463 (1971).
—— *The International Bill of Rights: Scope and Implementation*, 17 Wm. & Mary L. Rev. 527 (1976).
Korey, *The Key to Human Rights—Implementation*, Int'l Conciliation, No. 570 (1968).
H. Lauterpacht, International Law and Human Rights (1950).
E. Luard, ed., The International Protection of Human Rights (1967).
Macdonald, *A United Nations High Commissioner for Human Rights: The Decline and Fall of an Initiative*, 10 Can. Y.B. Int'l L. 40 (1972).
McDougal, *et al.*, *Human Rights and World Public Order*, 72 Nw. U. L. Rev. 227 (1977–78).

M. Moskowitz, International Concern with Human Rights (1974).
Mower, *The Implementation of the UN Covenant on Civil and Political Rights*, 10 Revue des Droits de l'Homme 271 (1977).
Nanda, *Implementation of Human Rights by the United Nations and Regional Organizations*, 21 De Paul L. Rev. 307 (1971).
A. Robertson, Human Rights in the World (1972).
Rodley, *Monitoring Human Rights Violations in the 1980s*, in J. Dominguez, *et al.*, Enhancing Global Rights (1979).
Schlüter, *The Domestic Status of the Human Rights Clauses of the United Nations Charter*, 61 Cal. L. Rev. 110 (1973).
Schwelb, *Civil and Political Rights: The International Measures of Implementation*, 62 Am. J. Int'l L. 827 (1968).
—— *Some Aspects of the Measures of Implementation of the International Covenant on Economic, Social and Cultural Rights*, 1 Revue des Droits de l'Homme 363 (1968).
—— *The International Measures of Implementation of the International Covenant on Civil and Political Rights and of the Optional Protocol*, 12 Tex. Int'l L. J. 141 (1977).
Sohn, *A Short History of United Nations Documents on Human Rights*, in Commission to Study the Organization of Peace, The United Nations and Human Rights 39 (1968).
V. Van Dyke, Human Rights, the United States, amd World Community (1970).
Weston, *et al.*, *International Procedures to Protect Human Rights: A Symposium*, 53 Iowa L. Rev. 268 (1967).

VI. Minibibliography

G. da Fonseca, How to File Complaints of Human Rights Violations: A Practical Guide to Inter-Governmental Procedures (1975).
Humphrey, *The International Bill of Rights: Scope and Implementation*, 17 Wm. & Mary L. Rev. 527 (1976).
Rodley, *Monitoring Human Rights Violations in the 1980s*, in J. Dominguez, *et al.*, Enhancing Global Rights (1979).
Schwelb, *The International Measures of Implementation of the International Covenant on Civil and Political Rights and of the Optional Protocol*, 12 Tex. Int'l L. J. 141 (1977).

Chapter 11

The Contribution of International Nongovernmental Organizations to the Protection of Human Rights*

David Weissbrodt[1]

There are a considerable number of nongovernmental organizations (NGOs) engaged in the protection of human rights.[2] Working at the international[3] and/or national levels,[4] these organizations function as

[1] An earlier version of the substantive discussion appeared as Weissbrodt, *The Role of International Nongovernmental Organizations in the Implementation of Human Rights*, 12 Tex. Int'l L.J. 293 (1977), which is republished here in revised form with the permission of the editors of the Texas International Law Journal.

[2] *See* Shestack, *Sisyphus Endures: The International Human Rights NGO*, 24 N.Y.L.S. L. Rev. 89 (1978); Weissbrodt, *The Role of International Nongovernmental Organizations in the Implementation of Human Rights*, 12 Tex. Int'l L.J. 293 (1977) [hereinafter cited as *Role of International NGOs*]; Note, *Role of NGOs in Implementing Human Rights in Latin America*, 7 Ga. J. Int'l & Comp. L. 476 (1977). *See also* Green, *NGOs* in Human Rights and World Order 90 (A. Said ed. 1978). *See generally International Protection of Human Rights: The Work of International Organizations and the Role of U.S. Foreign Policy: Hearings Before the Subcomm. on Int'l Organizations and Movements of the House Comm. on Foreign Affairs*, 93d Cong., 1st Sess. (1973) [hereinafter cited as *House Hearings on International Protection of Human Rights*]; Rodley, *Monitoring Human Rights Violations in the 1930's*, in J. Dominguez, N. Rodley, B. Wood & R. Falk, Enhancing Global Human Rights 119 (1979) [hereinafter cited as Rodley]; Cassese, *How Could Non-Governmental Organizations Use U.N. Bodies More Effectively?*, 1 Universal Human Rights, 73 (No. 4, 1979). For current information on NGO human rights activities, *see* Human Rights Internat Newsletter (1976–present).

[3] Over 700 NGOs have accredited status with the U.N. Economic and Social Council. U.N. Doc. E/INF. 162 (1977). Among those organizations which have full-time international human rights programs are Amnesty International, Anti-Slavery Society, Commission of the Churches on International Affairs, International Association of Democratic Lawyers, International Commission of Jurists, International Committee of the Red Cross, International Confederation of Free Trade Unions, International Federation of Human Rights, International Indian Treaty Council, International League for Human Rights, Minority Rights Group, World Conference on Religion and Peace, and World Federation of Trade Unions. There are also numerous NGOs which devote part of their time and resources to human rights. *See* Shestack, *Sisyphus Endures: The International Human Rights NGO*, 24 N.Y.L.S. L. Rev. 89, 94–95 (1978).

[4] National Council of Churches of Christ in the U.S.A., *Human Rights in North America*, in 2 Human Rights and Christian Responsibility 80 (Commission of the Churches on International Affairs 1974). In the United States, a number of national NGOs have been in the forefront of protecting civil rights and civil liberties: American Civil Liberties Union Center for Constitutional Rights, National Association for the Advancement of Colored People, NAACP Legal Defense and Educational Fund, American Jewish Committee, and Lawyer's Committee for Civil Rights Under Law. For a description of the activities of Amnesty International national sections, *see* T. Claudius & F. Stepan, Amnesty International Portrait Einer Organisation 214–78 (3d ed: 1978). *See generally* Human Rights Periodicals (D. Christiano ed. 1977) (lists organizations and agencies active in civil liberties in the United States and Canada); Weissbrodt, *Deciding United States Policy in Regard to International Human Rights: The Role of Interest Groups*, in Dynamics of Human Rights in U.S. Foreign Policy (N. Hevener ed. 1981) [hereinafter cited as *Interest Groups*].

unofficial ombudsmen safeguarding human rights against governmental infringement, by such techniques as diplomatic initiatives,[5] reports,[6] public statements,[7] efforts to influence the deliberations of human rights bodies established by intergovernmental organizations,[8] campaigns to mobilize public opinion,[9] and attempts to affect the foreign policy of some countries with respect to their relations to states which are regularly responsible for human rights violations.[10]

These NGOs share the same basic purpose, that is, to gather information which can be effectively mustered—either directly or indirectly—to influence the implementation of human rights by governments. While the great bulk of the organizations' information may be gathered at their central offices from reading relevant laws, reviewing periodicals, studying submitted appeals or documents, interviewing occasional visitors, and corresponding with informants, the organizations may also pursue on-site investigations of human rights prob-

[5] *See, e.g.*, International Committee of the Red Cross, Annual Report 1977 (1978). The report contains, *inter alia*, accounts of diplomatic initiatives in Rhodesia/Zimbabwe, at 15, South Africa, at 17, and Indo-China, at 19.

[6] *See, e.g.*, Amnesty International, An Amnesty International Report: Political Imprisonment in the People's Republic of China (1978); A. Cook, South Africa: The Imprisoned Society (1974) (a publication of the International Defence and Aid Fund); S. Cronje, Equatorial Guinea: The Forgotten Dictatorship (1976) (Research Report No. 2 of the Anti-Slavery Society); International Commission of Jurists, Final Report of Mission to Chile, April 1974, to Study the Legal System and the Protection of Human Rights (1974); Minority Rights Group, The Sahrawis of Western Sahara: Report No. 40 (1979).

[7] For example, Amnesty International [hereinafter cited as AI] issued 76 news releases on 38 countries during the period July 1, 1977–June 30, 1978. AI, Amnesty International Report 1978 at 319 (1979); International Commission of Jurists, ICJ Protests Against the Bukovsky Trial, Jan. 11, 1972.

[8] *See, e.g.*, AI, Allegations of Human Rights Violations in Democratic Kampuchea: UN Sub-Commission on Prevention of Discrimination and Protection of Minorities: Statement Submitted by Amnesty International, a Non-governmental Organization in Consultative Status (1978); International League for Human Rights, Communication to the United Nations on a Consistent Pattern of Violations of Human Rights in the Republic of Guinea (1977).

[9] For example, Amnesty International conducted an El Salvador campaign during Oct.–Dec. 1978. It is documented by many mimeo materials. A year long campaign on specific aspects of political imprisonment in Uruguay began in Aug. 1979.

[10] Representatives from NGOs frequently appear before foreign policy committees of the U.S. Congress, *see, e.g.*, *Human Rights in the Philippines: Report by Amnesty International: Hearing Before Subcomm. on Int'l Organizations of the House Comm. on Int'l Relations*, 94th Cong., 2d Sess. (1976); *Human Rights in Uruguay and Paraguay: Hearings Before Subcomm. on Int'l Organizations of House Comm. on Int'l Relations*, 94th Cong., 2d Sess. 66–104, 154–218 (1976); *Human Rights in Iran*; *Hearings Before the Subcomm. on Int'l Organizations of the House Comm. on Int'l Relations*, 94th Cong, 2d Sess. 1–16, 63–69 (1976); *Chile: The Status of Human Rights and its Relationship to U.S. Economic Assistance Programs: Hearings Before the Subcomm. on Int'l Organizations of the House Comm. on Int'l Relations*, 94th Cong., 2d Sess. 3–13, 196–97; *Human Rights in South Korea: Implications for U.S. Policy: Hearings Before Subcomms. on Asian and Pacific Affairs and Int'l Organizations and Movements of the House Comm. on Foreign Affairs*, 93d Cong., 2d Sess. 28–50, 54–69, 104–11 (1974); Lawyers Committee for International Human Rights, Violations of Human Rights in Uganda 1971–1978: Testimony prepared for the Subcommittee on Foreign Economic Policy of the United States Senate Committee on Foreign Relations (1978).

lems.[11] Over the past twenty years, NGOs have developed a fairly substantial practice of sending fact-finding missions.[12]

Among the most prominent international NGOs in the field of human rights are Amnesty International,[13] the Anti-Slavery Society,[14] the Commission of the Churches on International Affairs,[15] the International Association of Democratic Lawyers,[16] the International Commission of Jurists,[17] the International Committee of the Red Cross,[18] the International Defense and Aid Fund,[19] the International

[11] *See, e.g.*, AI, Report on Allegations of Torture in Brazil (1972); Judicial Sub-Commission of the International Commission of Enquiry into the Crimes of the Military Junta in Chile, The Crimes of the Chilean Military Junta in the Light of Chilean Law and International Law (Sept. 1974); AI, Amnesty International Briefing: Guatemala (Dec. 1976); AI, Political Imprisonment in the People's Republic of China (1978); Minority Rights Group, The Mexican Americans: Report No. 39 (1979); *Indonesia*, Rev. Int'l Comm'n Jurists 9 (No. 15, Dec. 1973).

[12] *See, e.g.*, *Continued Absence of Democracy in Indonesia*, 27 Bull. Int'l Comm'n Jurists (Sept. 1966); AI, Report of an Amnesty International Mission to the Republic of the Philippines (2d ed. Mar. 1977); AI, The Republic of Nicaragua: An Amnesty International Report (July 1977). *See generally Role of International NGO's*, *supra* note 1, at 300–04; Wiseberg & Scoble, *The International League for Human Rights: The Strategy of a Human Rights NGO*, 7 Ga. J. Int'l & Comp. L. 289, 309–10 (1977) [hereinafter cited as *Int'l League for Human Rights*].

[13] *See* AI, Handbook (1977); T. Claudius & F. Stepan, Amnesty International Portrait Einer Organisation (3d ed. 1978); [1974] Y.B. Int'l Org. 29 (Union of International Associations). *See generally* E. Larsen, A Flame in Barbed Wire (1978); J. Moreillon, Le Comité International de la Croix-Rouge et la protection des detenus politiques 199–218 (1973) [hereinafter cited as Moreillon]; Scoble & Wiseberg, *Amnesty International: Evaluating Effectiveness in the Human Rights Arena*, Intellect, Sept.–Oct. 1976; Scoble & Wiseberg, *Human Rights & Amnesty International*, 413 Annals 11 (1974).

[14] *See* Anti-Slavery Society, Human Rights and Development, A 3-year research and action programme, 1978–1981 (unpublished manuscript, 1977).

[15] *See generally* Commission of the Churches on International Affairs, Human Rights and Christian Responsibility 2–12 (May 1974); N. MacDermot, Human Rights and the Churches (1976).

[16] *See generally* International Association of Democratic Lawyers, IXth Congress of the International Association of Democratic Lawyers (1970). *XXth Anniversary of the I.A.D.L.*, Int'l Assoc. Democratic Law. Bull. (1967). The IADL also publishes a journal, Revue de Droit Contemporain.

[17] *See generally* International Commission of Jurists, Objectives, Organizations, Activities (1972); MacDermot, *The Work of the International Commission of Jurists*, 1 Index on Censorship 15 (1972). The general principles advocated by the ICJ are found in International Commission of Jurists, The Rule of Law and Human Rights (1966).

[18] *See* M. Veuthey, Red Cross; D. Tansley, Final Report: An Agenda for Red Cross (1975); International Committee of the Red Cross, Le CICR, La Ligue et Le Rapport Tansley (1977); D. Forsythe, Humanitarian Politics: The International Committee of the Red Cross (1977) [hereinafter cited as Forsythe, Humanitarian Politics]; J. Freymond, Guerres, Revolutions, Croix-Rouge, Reflexions sur le rôle du Comité International de la Croix-Rouge (1976); M. Vauthey, Guerilla et droit humanitaire 48–61, 262–64, 319–33 (1976); Bissell, *The International Commission of the Red Cross and the Protection of Human Rights*, 1 Revue des Droits de l'Homme 255 (1968).

[19] The International Defense and Aid Fund (IDAF), headquartered in London, has regularly issued reports about human rights violations in South Africa and other African countries. *See, e.g.*, R. Ainslie, Masters and Serfs: Farm Labour in South Africa (rev. ed. 1977); IDAF, The Sun Will Rise (M. Benson ed. 1976); IDAF, Boss: The First 5 Years (1975); A. Hepple, Press Under Apartheid (1974); A. Cook, South Africa: The Imprisoned Society (1974); IDAF, South African Prisons and the Red Cross Investigation (1967) [hereinafter cited as IDAF, Prisons].

Federation of Human Rights,[20] the International League for Human Rights,[21] the Minority Rights Group,[22] Survival International,[23] and the World Peace Council.[24]

Section I.A. of this chapter sketches the structure and characteristics of NGOs. The subject of section I.B. is the fact-finding techniques of NGOs, while I.C. considers their work, including diplomatic efforts, public discussions of human rights violations, contributions to international investigative procedures, aid to human rights victims, and local activities. Section I.D. discusses the contribution of NGOs to the development of human rights norms. Section II suggests an overall approach to the teaching of human rights through the work of NGOs with a description of two classes on how NGOs contribute to the protection of human rights, and includes a hypothetical which might serve as the basis for class discussion, as well as suggestions for issues which should be raised by the teacher. Section III contains a syllabus outlining the topics which a teacher might cover in dealing with NGOs. Section IV presents a bibliography on nongovernmental human rights organizations; the remaining two sections suggest a shorter syllabus and bibliography for more abbreviated treatment of the subject.

I. Legal and Policy Considerations

A. WHAT ARE INTERNATIONAL NONGOVERNMENTAL ORGANIZATIONS?

Most NGOs have consultative status with such intergovernmental bodies as the U.N. Economic and Social Council (ECOSOC),[25] the

[20] *See* Fédération Internationale des Droits de l'Homme Bull. No. 2 (Dec. 1977–Feb. 1978).

[21] *See* International League for Human Rights, Annual Review (1976–1977) (undated); [1974] Y.B. Int'l Org. 399 (Union of International Associations); *Int'l League for Human Rights*, *supra* note 12; Scoble & Wiseberg, *Human Rights as an International League*, in Human Rights and World Order 100 (A. Said ed. 1978).

[22] The Minority Rights Group is an international research and information group headquartered in London which publishes its research findings about minority groups suffering discrimination. *See*, *e.g.*, Minority Rights Group, The Sahrawis of Western Sahara: Report No. 40 (1979); The Mexican Americans: Report No. 39 (1979); The Hungarians of Rumania: Report No. 37 (1978); Australia's Policy Towards Aborigines, 1967–1977: Report No. 35 (1978).

[23] *See* Survival International Rev. (Spring 1978).

[24] *See* [1974] Y.B. Int'l Org. 634 (Union of International Associations); *see*, *e.g.*, World Peace Council, Violations of Human Rights in Haiti, El Salvador, and Nicaragua (undated).

[25] *See* note 3 *supra*. As of July 1974 there were over 600 NGOs with accredited relationships to the ECOSOC. Twenty held Consultative Status Category I; 192 held Consultative Status Category II. In addition, over 400 were listed on the Roster of the Office of Public Information by action of ECOSOC (86) or of the Secretary-General (27) or by virtue of their status with other U.N. bodies or specialized agencies. U.N. Doc. E/INF/144 (1974). The 1974 Yearbook of International Organizations lists over 4,000 international organizations, most of which are nongovernmental, and also suggests a definition, at 15, which supplements the distinctions

International Labour Organisation (ILO), the U.N. Educational, Scientific and Cultural Organization (UNESCO),[26] the Council of Europe,[27] and the Organization of American States (OAS).[28] Although they are founded upon a membership of people, rather than of governments, NGOs are most often structured so that there exists an international secretariat which more or less represents national sections in various countries.[29] The national sections often vary considerably. For example, the International League for Human Rights has its international secretariat in New York City near the U.N. building and counts among its sections the National Council for Civil Liberties in the United Kingdom, the Canadian Civil Liberties Association, the Moscow Human Rights Committee, the American Civil Liberties Union, and the New Zealand Democratic Rights Council,[30] P.E.N., which is an international association of poets, playwrights, essayists, editors, and novelists, and which possesses a total world membership of some 10,000, has its headquarters in London, and also has an American Center in New York City.[31] The International Commission of Jurists has national sections of lawyers and judges in over fifty countries.[32] The Commission itself is comprised of about forty dis-

between NGOs in Category I, Category II, and on the ECOSOC Roster, as set forth in E.S.C. Res. 1296, 44 U.N. ECOSOC, Supp. (No. 1), at 21, U.N. Doc. E/4548 (1968). *See also* note 71 *infra.*

Nongovernmental organizations are specifically recognized by art. 71 of the U.N. Charter and frequently are called upon to help execute, publicize, or contribute to U.N. decisions. *See Preparatory Conference of Experts on the Role of Nongovernmental Organizations—Report*, 27 Int'l A. 35–36 (1975); U.N. Doc. E/C.2/603 (1963); E. Brock, Representation of Non-Governmental Organizations and the United Nations (1955); J. Robb, The Historical Background of Article 71, Charter Review Study Group, Sixth General Conference of Consultative NGOs, U.N. Doc. GC/SG/WP-NY/2/Rev. 1, at 2 (1955); U.N. Doc. E/43 (1946).

---

[26] UNESCO, Directives Concerning UNESCO's Relations with International Non-Governmental Organizations (1960); *see* American Council of Learned Societies, The Role of Non-Governmental Organizations in International Intellectual Cooperation (1964).

[27] *See* Council of Europe, The Consultative Assembly Procedure and Practice 372–81 (1969). *See also* notes 101–02 *infra.*

[28] Organization of American States, Directory of Organizations with Which the OAS Has Agreements for Cooperative Relations (1973); Standards on Cooperative Relations Between the Organization of American States and the United Nations, its Specialized Agencies, and Other National and International Organizations, O.A.S. Doc. AG/Res. 57 (1971).

The Organization of African Unity also grants observer status to NGOs. *See, e.g.*, O.A.U. Doc. CM/Res. 330 (XXII) (1972); O.A.U. Doc. CM/Res. 289 (XIX) (1974).

[29] *See* B. Stosic, Les Organisations Non Gouvernmentales et Les Nations Unies 21–120 (1964); L. White, International Non-Governmental Organizations: Organizations; Their Purposes, Methods and Accomplishments (1968). *See also* Potter, *Non-Governmental Organizations Viewed by a Political Scientist*, 14 Int'l A. 403 (1962); *Draft Convention Aiming at Facilitating the Work of International Non-Governmental Organizations*, 11 Int'l A. 520 (1959).

[30] International League for the Rights of Man, Annual Report 23 (1973); 15 Y.B. Int'l Org. 399 (1974); *Int'l League for Human Rights, supra* note 12.

[31] *See* P.E.N. American Center, P.E.N., What it is—What it does 1 (1974).

[32] International Commission of Jurists, Objectives, Organization, Activities (1972); *see* 15 Y.B. Int'l Org. 283–85 (1974).

tinguished jurists from many states in Africa, Asia, Western Europe, and the Americas, with a secretariat in Geneva and an office in New York City for its representatives to the United Nations.

One of the largest and newest of the NGOs concerned with human rights is Amnesty International.[33] There are Amnesty International sections in forty-one countries, but its main working arms are the international secretariat with its 50 researchers and other staff of 120 in London, as well as the approximately 2,700 groups principally located in Western Europe, the United States, Canada, Japan, and elsewhere—each group working for adopted prisoners of conscience, on country-oriented campaigns, or on urgent appeals for prisoners in imminent danger of torture or execution.

Considering what needs to be done, none of these organizations is very large. With rare exceptions the central offices are staffed by only a handful of people. Almost all the organizations rely heavily on voluntary work by members and subsist on meager budgets.

B. SELECTION OF HUMAN RIGHTS VIOLATIONS AND FACT-FINDING

Amnesty International, the International Commission of Jurists, the International League for Human Rights, the Commission of the Churches on International Affairs of the World Council of Churches, the Pontifical Commission Justice and Peace, the International Committee of the Red Cross, and other international NGOs gather information in more or less the same way. At their international centers they collect information about human rights problems from newspapers, magazines, professional journals, U.N. publications, members, relatives of prisoners, escaped or freed victims, expatriot groups, disgruntled public officials, incidental travelers, and from each other. The reports are of widely varying reliability, though some care is taken to check sources and contradictions. The older organizations may have clipping files and dossiers about human rights violations going back ten or twenty years. For example, the treatment of Jehovah's Witnesses in Malawi; Kurds in Iraq, Iran, and Turkey; ministers and priests in Poland, Afghanistan, and China; and the indigenous peoples in Australia, New Zealand, Norway, Canada, Brazil, and the United States raise recurrent problems.[34] Often it is very useful to see the

[33] AI, Amnesty International Report 1982, at ii, 7 (1982).

[34] *See, e.g.*, Minority Rights Group, Jehovah's Witnesses in Central Africa (1976); The Kurds (1975); What Future for the Amerindians of South America (1973); Canada's Indians (1974). The Anti-Slavery Society—one of the oldest nongovernmental organizations, originally founded in 1823—has particularly concerned itself with the rights of indigenous peoples. So has Survival International, based in London. More recently, the Indian Treaty Council has obtained consultative status with ECOSOC and other North American Indian groups have become interested in activity at the United Nations.

newest outbreak of oppression or violence in the light of previous incidents and the governmental responses to them.

Quite frequently, the NGO must first determine whether it would be useful to intervene in a particular situation in which human rights are being violated. Might intervention help or hurt the victims? What sort of intervention would be most effective? Have interventions with this country or with respect to this type of problem been successful in the past? Are the officials of the country receptive to initiatives from outsiders? Are the facts sufficiently well established to permit diplomatic intervention or publicity? Which NGO would be most effective in raising the issue?

The standard of care of the various organizations differs considerably. Also, limited resources of the organizations require allocation of effort. There is sometimes a risk that an NGO will choose to investigate and pursue a particular violation only because the state concerned is an easy target. NGOs may avoid pursuing violations because that might upset influential friends, sources of financial support, friendly governments, etc. The possibilities for abuse in the selection of test cases are legion. It is a tribute to most of the organizations that they do remain remarkably independent despite their small size and impecunious position.

To a degree the nongovernmental organizations concerned with human rights remain subject to Cold War differences.[35] The International Association of Democratic Lawyers (IADL), the World Peace Council, and the World Federation of Democratic Youth find a large part of their members and support in socialist countries and in allied groups in nonsocialist nations. In the United States, for example, the National Conference of Black Lawyers and the National Lawyers Guild are affiliated with the International Association of Democratic Lawyers. The International Commission of Jurists and Amnesty International find most of their strength outside of the socialist countries. Accordingly, in the United States, the American Bar Association has a Committee of its International Law Section which cooperates with the International Commission of Jurists.

During periods of detente, joint action among the various organizations grows and differences are diminished.[36] The IADL is, however,

[35] *See* Epps, *Human Rights: General Reflection*, in 1 Human Rights and Christian Responsibility 13–14 (Commission of the Churches on International Affairs 1974).

[36] Governments may use friendly NGOs to test ideas in international discussion or to carry out political positions. For example, the representative of the People's Republic of China urged the expulsion of all NGOs with ties to Taiwan as a way of continuing political pressure on the Taiwan Government. U.N. Doc. E/SR.1944, at 3, 21–22 (1975); *cf.* E.S.C. Res. 2/3, 2 U.N. ESCOR, Annex 8a, at 360, para. 3, U.N. Doc. E/43/Rev. 2 (1946) (discredited fascist organizations excluded).

more restrained in its criticism of human rights violations in socialist countries than is the International Commission of Jurists.[37] Amnesty International, the Commission of the Churches on International Affairs, the Friends World Committee for Consultation, the Pontifical Commission Justice and Peace, Pax Romana, and the World Conference on Religion and Peace are far more willing to discuss such issues as conscientious objection and religious freedom[38] than are the World Peace Council and the World Federation of Democratic Youth.[39]

C. WHAT DO INTERNATIONAL NONGOVERNMENTAL ORGANIZATIONS DO TO IMPLEMENT HUMAN RIGHTS?

Most governments seem to be sensitive to any criticism by these organizations. The USSR has been very concerned about discussion concerning the emigration of Jews and the imprisonment of Ukrainians, Baptists, and Soviet human rights leaders. Guatemala has been at times highly sensitive to criticism of torture, imprisonment, and killing of *campesinos*, Indians, journalists, lawyers, and unionists.[40] The United States has considered its image in the world community to be very delicate with respect to the treatment of its black citizens and indigenous peoples.[41] Most countries are proud of the humanitarian ideals which form one basis for the legitimacy of the state. Almost every country's constitution prominently sets forth the fundamental rights of its citizens. If a government—whether democratic or dictatorial—acts tyranically towards its citizens, it violates the basic trust which permits it to continue ruling. It appears that even most dictatorships attempt to show at least a façade of democratic trappings or an appearance of enlightenment.

Governments do not wish to be reminded that they are ignoring the fundamental rights of their citizens. They particularly do not like to be

[37] *Le Congres de l'Association internationale des juristes democrates est marque par l'entre' enforce des pays du tiers-monde*, Le monde, Apr. 8, 1975, at 13, col. 3.

[38] *E.g.*, U.N. Doc. E/CN.4/NGO/176 (1974); U.N. Doc. E/CN.4/NGO/179 (1974); U.N. Doc. E/CN.4/NGO/181 (1974). *See also* Schaffer & Weissbrodt, *Conscientious Objection to Military Service as a Human Right*, Rev. Int'l Comm'n Jurists 33 (No. 9, 1972) [hereinafter cited as *Conscientious Objection*].

[39] Somewhat similar observations might be made about the Cold War origins and changing relations of the International Confederation of Free Trade Unions (ICFTU), on the one hand, and the World Federation of Trade Unions, on the other. *See* Boggs, *The ILO's Rocky Road*, Free Trade Union News, Sept. 1974, at 1, 11–12.

[40] AI, Briefing on Guatemala (1976); AI, Violence in Rural Guatemala (1979); AI, Repression of Journalists in Gautemala (1979); AI Repression of Lawyers in Guatemala (1979); AI, Repression of Trade Unions in Guatemala (1979).

[41] National Council of the Churches of Christ in the U.S.A., *Human Rights in North America*, in 2 Human Rights and Christian Responsibility 80–101 (Commission of the Churches on International Affairs 1974); National Conference of Black Lawyers, *et al.*, Petition to the United Nations Commission on Human Rights . . . Human Rights Violations in the United States, Dec. 17, 1978.

criticized in the openness of international debate.[42] Also, the International Bill of Human Rights[43] has attained such broad acceptance in the international community that a government cannot violate basic human rights without some fear of exposure. The pointed finger of shame, particularly when directed by an organization with some appearance of impartiality and political independence, has caused executions to be stayed, death sentences to be commuted, torture to be stopped, prison conditions to be ameliorated, prisoners to be released, and more attention to be paid to the fundamental rights of many citizens.[44]

Although some countries are not as sensitive as others and some resist pressure for many years, the pressure has some effect. For example, the racist government of South Africa is isolated from the world community.[45] It is not asked to participate in international

[42] For example, the Chilean Government considered it necessary to respond to criticism in International Commission of Jurists reports by paying for a series of half-page advertisements in the New York Times and the Washington Post. *See* McCarthy, *The Chilean Junta's Advertising Campaign*, Washington Post, Dec. 10, 1974, at A20, col. 3. *See also* U.N. Doc. E/SR.1944, at 8–9 (remarks of representative of Egypt), at 13–14 (remarks of representative of USSR) (1975). Sensitivity of countries to criticism caused UNESCO to ask AI not to hold its Paris Conference on Torture in UNESCO facilities in Dec. 1973 because of the issuance of a report which discussed allegations of torture in 65 countries. *UNESCO Ban Fails to Halt Conference*, AI Newsletter, Jan. 1974, at 2. *See also* Permanent Mission of India to the United Nations, *Groundless Charges Against India by League of Human Rights*, Press Release, June 7, 1976.

[43] *See* note 130 *infra.*

[44] For example, hesitant internal political liberalization and international human rights pressure apparently have combined to result in the release of some political detainees after others were executed. *Morocco*, Rev. Int'l Comm'n Jurists 19 (No. 13, 1974); AI, Morocco Background Paper (1974); AI, Recent Developments in Morocco (1974); H. Woesner, Report on Mission to Morocco (1973). Shortly after the International Commission of Jurists article, *Dents in the Image of Indonesia*, Rev. Int'l Comm. Jurists 16 (No. 13, 1974), appeared, the Indonesian government freed some of the 42 detainees mentioned in the article. *Cf. Amnesty Welcomes Commutation of Death Sentence of Pole*, AI News Release, Jan. 23, 1973. A Bulgarian economist was allowed to leave his country in Aug. 1974 after AI joined a worldwide campaign for his release from a death sentence. *Spetter Thanks Amnesty*, 1 AI Matchbox 26 (Winter 1975). *See also AI Appeals to India to Release 30,000 Detainees During Strike Crisis*, AI Newsletter, June 1974, at 2; *India Frees Rail Strike Leaders*, AI Newsletter, July 1974, at 2.

[45] Ndoh, *Violation of Human Rights in Africa* 8–11 (Commission of the Churches on International Affairs Background Information No. 3 1975); Carlson, *South Africa Today: The Security of the State vs. The Liberty of the Individual*, 2 Human Rights 125 (1972); U.N. Doc. A/8770 (1972); Davis, *Infringements of the Rule of Law in South Africa*, Rev. Int'l Comm'n Jurists 22 (No. 7, 1971); *A Vast Prison House*, Objective: Justice, Jan. 1970, at 15–16, U.N. Doc. ST/OPI/371 (1970); *The Lawless Laws of South Africa*, *id.* at 17–19; *Southern Africa*, Rev. Int'l Comm'n Jurists 19, 21–25 (No. 3, 1969); International Commission of Jurists, Erosion of the Rule of Law in South Africa (1968); U.N. Doc. ST/PSCA/SER.A/2 (1967); International Commission of Jurists, South Africa and the Rule of Law (1960), *Namibia: The United Nations and U.S. Policy, Hearings Before the Subcomm. on Int'l Organizations of the House Comm. on Int'l Relations*, 94th Cong., 2d Sess. (1976); AI, Annual Report 1975–76, at 67–68 (1976), AI, Annual Report 1974–75, at 49–50 (1975); U.N. Press Release HR/219 (Aug. 22, 1974) (report from International Student Movement for the United Nations concerning floggings in Namibia); *Freedom to Namibia*, International Defense and Aid Fund for Southern Africa News, Nov. 1974, at 7; Minority Rights Group, The Namibians of Southwest Africa (1974); *Military Interests and Decolonization*, Objective: Justice. Apr. 1970, at 34, U.N. Doc. ST/OPI/372 (1970).

sporting events. It is subjected to trade sanctions and arms embargoes. Its citizens often are shunned or questioned when they travel abroad. For a time Greece under the Colonels was morally, economically, and politically isolated from European allies because it tortured and illegally imprisoned its citizens. Both the isolated country and to a lesser extent its supporters suffer opprobium in the eyes of world opinion—directed by the news media, international governmental organizations, and, to a considerable degree, international nongovernmental organizations.

In some ways, NGOs are far freer to criticize where criticism is due than are governments or international bodies. Most governments are concerned with keeping their bilateral relations on a friendly basis. Even where relations are quite close—or perhaps because they are close—governments hesitate to criticize one another.[46] Governments do occasionally make diplomatic interventions on issues relating to human rights (and should be doing much more in this respect), but presently they act on human rights questions infrequently and with exaggerated circumspection.

Although the setting of intergovernmental organizations permits somewhat greater scope for forthright discussion of human rights problems, governments remain reluctant to talk about such issues openly. When they do mention human rights issues, they are often accused of political bias. For example, the United States may mention violations of human rights in Eastern Europe, while the USSR and the Arab countries insist upon debates concerning human rights in Israel.

In most circumstances, NGOs are more independent of political forces and thus are able to identify and criticize human rights violations wherever they may occur. NGOs do not need to wait for the coming into force and active enforcement of international conventions or the development of acceptable implementation procedures in the U.N. Commission on Human Rights or other intergovernmental organizations. When those principles and procedures are available, the NGOs make use of them, but there is already an ample delineation of human rights standards in the International Bill of Human Rights for much NGO activity.

1. *Diplomatic Interventions and Missions by NGOs*

Having investigated and selected a case, the NGO may decide to seek a visit with representatives of the government concerned. Unless there is a need for immediate cessation of the human rights violations, *e.g.*, torture or impending execution, the initial contact may only

[46] *See generally* Weissbrodt, *Human Rights Legislation and U.S. Foreign Policy*, 7 Ga. J. Int'l & Comp. D. 231, 232–40, 281–83 (1977) [hereinafter cited as *Human Rights Legislation*].

apprise the government that a violation has been noted and the NGO may propose inquiry by appropriate officials. Such contacts generally are made discreetly, *i.e.*, with no publicity. Often the NGO functions as a much-needed intermediary between the highest officials in a government and human rights victims. In the absence of an effective right of *habeas corpus*, a free press, and/or an ombudsman, high officials may not know what is happening within their own prisons or may try to avoid knowing. But once an NGO brings a problem to the government's attention it becomes more difficult to ignore human rights violations. Also, interventions are made mostly with diplomatic personnel who have little to do with prisons or secret police and who are familiar with the governing international standards of conduct. When made aware of the problem and the possible risk of embarrassment, these diplomatic officers may take steps to help remedy the situation.

In addition, the NGO may offer or ask to send a mission to the country, to interview alleged victims, lawyers, and government officials, to witness trials, or to attempt to mediate disputes. Some countries are sufficiently concerned about their image (or sufficiently confident that the accusations are unfounded) that they accept NGO visits.[47] For example, Iran in 1972 received several visits from distinguished lawyers representing the IADL, the International Federation of Human Rights, and the International Commission of Jurists.[48] Chile received missions from Amnesty International and the International Commision of Jurists in 1973 and 1974.[49] The International League for Human Rights sent observers to trials in Yugoslavia during 1975 and in Spain during 1973. Amnesty International sent an observer

[47] *See, e.g.*, AI, Report of an Amnesty International Mission to Israel and the Syrian Arab Republic to Investigate Allegations of Ill-Treatment and Torture 10–24 October 1974 (1975). Sometimes an NGO is invited by a government to visit the country and to act as an impartial international fact-finding body on allegations of human rights violations. *See, e.g.*, *W.C.C. Team's Visit to Iraq*, Commission of the Churches on International Affairs, Newsletter No. 5 (1975); International Commission of Jurists, Report on the Events in Panama January 9–12, 1964 (1964); International Commission of Jurists, Report on the British Guiana Commission of Inquiry (1965).

[48] The International Federation for the Rights of Man, centered in Paris, has also sent numerous missions to Iran. *See also* AI, Briefing on Iran (1976); W. Butler & G. Levasseur, Human Rights and the Legal System in Iran (1976); *Iran*, Rev. Int'l Comm'n Jurists 5 (No. 8, 1972); AI, Iran: Trial Procedures for Political Prisoners (1972); Y. Baudelot, Prison Conditions for Political Detainees in Iran (1974). *See also* Simons, *Shah's 'Phobia' Pushes Iran*, Washington Post, 27 May 1974, at AI, col. 2; *More Executions in Iran*, 1 AI Matchbox 13 (Spring/Summer 1974).

[49] *See Human Rights in Chile, Hearings Before the Subcomm. on Inter-American Affairs of the House Comm. on Foreign Affairs*, 93d Cong., 2d Sess., at 1, 2–28, 51–84 (1974). The International Association of Democratic Lawyers, the International Association of Catholic Lawyers, and the International Federation for the Rights of Man also sent a combined mission to Chile in Fall 1973.

to a post-trial hearing in South Dakota in 1979,[50] and Afghanistan received an Amnesty International representative in 1979.[51] South Africa has accepted International Commission of Jurists observers for trials for over ten years.[52]

The International Committee of the Red Cross (ICRC), as one of the oldest and largest of the NGOs concerned with human rights, has the most extensive program of visiting places of detention with the permission of the respective governments.[53] The ICRC is composed almost exclusively of Swiss nationals; its international character is based on aims and activities which include visits to prisoner of war and civilian internment camps pursuant to the four Geneva Conventions of 1949 and the two Protocols of 1977.[54] For example, in 1978 the ICRC visited prisoners of war in Chad, Mauritania, Morocco, and Western Sahara.[55] In the same year, the ICRC also visited a number of persons detained for offenses or reasons of a political nature in Afghanistan, Argentina, Chile, Indonesia, Iran, Nicaragua, Paraguay, Portugal, Rhodesia, South Africa, Yemen Arab Republic, and Zaire.

The ICRC provides detailed findings of its missions only to host governments. Because of its considerable resources and reputation for independence it has less difficulty in obtaining permission to send missions than do other NGOs. In cases where governments misrepresent the findings, the ICRC reserves the right to release its results. Such was the situation with respect to the ICRC visits to Greek places of detention in 1969. Similarly, in 1980 the ICRC released full reports of earlier visits to Iranian prisons after the new Iranian régime released partial reports.[56] But the ICRC annual reports, monthly bulletins, occasional press releases, and the *ICRC Review* also reveal very significant information about the number of prisoners visited.

The recommendations of the NGO missions—particularly the ICRC missions—have substantial impact upon the treatment of political offenders. With the partial exception of the ICRC, most NGOs publicly report the results of their missions and thus provide invaluable first-hand information about violations of human rights.

[50] AI, Annual Report 1979, at 74 (1979).

[51] AI, Violations of Human Rights and Fundamental Freedoms in the Democratic Republic of Afghanistan (1979).

[52] *See* note 45 *supra*.

[53] *See* T. Bissell, The International Committee of the Red Cross and the Protection of Human Rights (1963); A. Milani, Les Organisations Non Gouvernmentales Des Nations Unies 63–73 (1952).

[54] International Committee of the Red Cross, Activities, Principles, Organization (1971); *see* Moreillon, *supra* note 13. *See also* ch. 9. *supra*.

[55] International Committee of the Red Cross, Annual Report 1978, at 20–23, 43 (1978).

[56] *Red Cross Found Jail Better in Shah's Last Year*, Washington Post, 10 Jan. 1980, at A23, cols. 1–4.

2. *Public Discussion of Human Rights Violations*

Publicity is clearly an important factor in the implementation of human rights law by NGOs. For example, in December 1971, the International Commission of Jurists issued an article entitled *Condemned without hope in California* on the use of indeterminate sentences in that state.[57] The article was the result of a visit by a representative of the Commission and was distributed to the justices of the California Supreme Court. They probably were a bit dismayed to find California discussed in the same journal with Guinea, Greece, Northern Ireland, Paraguay, Spain, Taiwan, and the USSR. Certainly the article drew international attention to California's sentencing practices and added to the growing criticism of the indeterminate sentence law and of the California Adult Authority which administered the law. The indeterminate sentence law has been repealed in California and questioned elsewhere. It is worthy of note also that the Supreme Court of California subsequently made at least one decision declaring the law cruel and unusual punishment as applied.[58]

Similarly, Amnesty International's 1972 report on allegations of torture in Brazil contained a listing of more than one thousand torture victims and demonstrated a consistent pattern of gross violations of human rights in Brazil.[59] P.E.N. has issued reports on the suppression of writers and intellectuals in Czechoslovakia.[60] The International Commission of Jurists has issued thoroughly researched reports on violations of human rights in Uganda,[61] Uruguay,[62] and Chile.[63] In addition, the Commission produces a *Review* twice each year which describes and comments upon human rights problems throughout the world. The International League for Human Rights and the Lawyers Committee for International Human Rights have produced reports on Argentina, Burundi, Greece, the USSR, Northern Ireland, and Yugoslavia. The ICRC and Amnesty International produce annual reports and some individual reports, which, taken together with the *Review of the International Commission of Jurists*, constitute an illuminating picture of human rights problems for each year.[64]

[57] Rev. Int'l Comm'n Jurists 17 (No. 7, 1971).

[58] *In re* Lynch, 8 Cal. 3d 410, 438–39, 503 P.2d 921, 940 (1973) (citing the International Commission of Jurists article). The California legislature has now abolished indeterminate sentencing in that state. Cal. Pen. Code §§ 667.5, 1168, 1170 *et seq.*, 12022 *et seq*; Oppenheim, *Computing a Determinate Sentence . . . New Math Hits the Courts*, 51 Cal. St. B.J. 604 (1976).

[59] AI, Report on Allegations of Torture in Brazil (1972).

[60] P.E.N. American Center, Czechoslovakia (Country Report No. 1, 1973).

[61] International Commission of Jurists, Violations of Human Rights and the Rule of Law in Uganda (1974, Supp. 1974).

[62] International Commission of Jurists, ICJ and Amnesty International Mission Report on Continuing Torture and Ill-Treatment of Political Suspects in Uruguay (1975).

[63] M. MacDermot, Final Report of International Commission of Jurists Mission to Chile (1974, Supp. 1975).

[64] Nevertheless, an NGO concerned with human rights might well consider the need for a

Often, press releases and other statements are issued jointly by NGOs. For example, in March 1971 Amnesty International, the Commission of the Churches on International Affairs, the Committee on Society, Development and Peace (SODEPAX, a joint organization of the World Council of Churches and the Pontifical Commission Justice and Peace), the International Federation of Human Rights, the International Association of Democratic Lawyers, the International Commission of Jurists, the International Youth and Student Movement for the United Nations, the Women's International League for Peace and Freedom, the World Federation of Trade Unions, the World Muslim Congress, and other NGOs made a united appeal to the Brazilian government to end the detention of political prisoners and the use of torture.[65] The U.S. Conference of Bishops[66] and the National Conference of Brazilian Bishops[67] made similar appeals to the Brazilian government.

In recent years the World Jewish Congress, the American Jewish Committee, and the American Israel Public Affairs Committee have mounted remarkably successful campaigns with respect to Jews in the Soviet Union, Iraq, and Syria.[68] In 1974, the International Commission of Jurists, the Women's International League for Peace and Freedom, and a number of other NGOs obtained the release of a lawyer from a South Vietnamese prison by convincing universities to invite her to teach and by fostering public discussion of her case by the press and by members of the U.S. Congress. The International League for Human Rights was successful in obtaining permission for Valery Chalidze to leave the USSR by similar methods. Despite the passing of International Women's Year in 1975, however, relatively few organizations have begun to work particularly and effectively for the release of women political prisoners or started to work in the

thorough annual or biannual review of the human rights situation in each country of the world. *See* Amnesty International, Report on Torture (2d ed. 1975); *Conscientious Objection*, *supra* note 38; International Commission of Jurists, *The Legal Protection of Privacy*, 24 Int'l Soc. Sci. J. 417 (1972). AI has begun to fill this need by issuing briefings on various countries. *See, e.g.*, AI, Briefing on Taiwan (Republic of China) (1976); AI Briefing on Malawi (1976). In addition, the U.S. State Department was initially required to publish reports on the human rights situation of all countries receiving U.S. aid and has begun to publish reports on all nations in the world. *See* *Human Rights Legislation*, *supra* note 46, at 263–74 (1977).

[65] *Study of the Situation in Brazil which Reveals a Consistent Pattern of Violations on Rights*, in *House Hearings on International Protection of Human Rights*, *supra* note 1, at 673–75. In order to promote cooperation and coordination among those NGOs particularly concerned with international human rights matters in the U.N. about 65 of these organizations meet and work regularly under the aegis of the Committees of NGOs on Human Rights in New York and Geneva.

[66] *Id.* at 671–73.

[67] *Id.* at 675–80; *see* Rev. Int'l Comm'n Jurists 15 (No. 11, 1973).

[68] *See, e.g.*, American Jewish Committees, Current Situation of Jews in Arab Lands (1973).

international arena to eradicate more structural discriminations against women.[69]

Reports, studies, bulletins, newsletters, and press releases of such NGOs as the Commission of the Churches on International Affairs, the International League for Human Rights, the Carnegie Endowment for International Peace, the American Committee on Africa, the International Press Institute, Writers and Scholars International, the Minority Rights Group, and P.E.N. are further disseminated by newspapers, magazines, and other media which may report upon human rights violations.[70]

Consultative status permits NGOs to contribute to the work of the U.N. Commission on Human Rights and its Sub-Commission on Prevention of Discrimination and Protection of Minorities.[71] Representatives of Amnesty International, the Anti-Slavery Society, the Commission of the Churches on International Affairs, the International Commission of Jurists, the International League for Human Rights, and the Minority Rights Group often make written

[69] *See, e.g.*, 2 ISIS Int'l Bull. 16 (Oct. 1976); 10 ISIS Int'l Bull. 17 (Winter 1978/79). *See also* U.N. Doc. E/CN.6/CR.25 (1980) (Non-confidential list of communications concerning the status of women from numerous individuals, as well as such organizations as the International Council of Social Democratic Women, the International Association of Democratic Lawyers, the World Council of Churches, ISIS, International Federation of University Women, International Alliance of Women, Socialist International, Lutheran World Federation, etc.).

[70] *See* J. Carey, UN Protection of Civil and Political Rights 130 (1970).

[71] Nongovernmental organizations in Consultative Status Category I may suggest items for the agenda of the Economic and Social Council and its appropriate subordinate bodies. E.S.C. Res. 1296, para. 23, 44 U.N. ESCOR, Supp. (No. 1), at 22. U.N. Doc. E/4548 (1968); U.N. Doc. E/5677, rule 83, at 28 (1975); *see* Prasad, *The Role of Non-Governmental Organizations in the New United Nations Procedures for Human Rights Complaints*, 5 Denver J. Int'l L. & Pol. 460 n.84 (1975). Representatives of NGOs in Category I or Category II may sit as observers at public meetings of the Economic and Social Council, its committees, and sessional bodies. NGOs on ECOSOC's Roster may send representatives when matters within their field of competence are being discussed. *See* Rules of Procedure of the Functional Commissions of the Economic and Social Council, U.N. Doc. E/4767, rule 75, at 16 (1970). Representatives of NGOs in Category I and Category II may submit communications to the Economic and Social Council and its subsidiary organs. U.N. Doc. E/5677, rules 82–83, at 27–28 (1975); E.S.C. Res. 1296, paras. 23–24, *supra*; Epps, *NGO Interventions at the ECOSOC Committee on NGO's*, 26 Int'l A. 454 (1974); White, *United Nations Consultation with Nongovernmental Organizations*, 24 Int'l A. 539 (1972). *See also* U.N. Doc. E/C.2/INF/2 (1971); G. Riegner, Consultative Status (1969); Brief History of the Consultative Relationship of Non-Governmental Organization with the Economic and Social Council, U.N. Doc. E/C.2/R.35 (1968). There has continued to be some controversy over the right of NGOs to mention individual countries during open sessions of the U.N. Commission on Human Rights or its Sub-Commission. *See, e.g.*, note 80 *infra*. While oral statements are subject to the government's right of reply, NGOs are relatively free to discuss human rights 'situations' around the world, so long as they do not overtly criticize governments. The U.N. Secretariat staff will not generally circulate written statements under E.S.C. Res. 1296, however, unless the NGOs purport to discuss general human rights phenomena or regional world-wide problems, mentioning country situations only by way of example. These unwritten rules of interpreting E.S.C. Res. 1296 are subject to political considerations, depending upon the countries mentioned.

and oral presentations during discussions of human rights issues.[72] Some of the NGO presentations add significantly to the debates.[73] At the 1974 session of the Commission on Human Rights, Mrs. Salvador Allende was able to speak as a special representative of two NGOs.[74] Her speech, along with reports of violations from other NGOs and from delegates,[75] prompted an extraordinary telegram from the Commission to the Chilean government.[76] This step then led the Sub-Commission, *inter alia*, to request NGOs in consultative status 'to submit reliable information on torture and other, cruel, inhuman or degrading treatment or punishment in Chile' so that additional information could be studied by the Commission as a basis for future action.[77] The great bulk of the documentary information on Chile that

[72] For example, all but one of the five NGO written statements circulated at the Commission Human Rights session in 1974 were made jointly. U.N. Doc. E/5464, E/CN.4/1154, at 89–90 (1974); *see, e.g.*, U.N. Doc. E/CN.4/NGO/176 (1974) (urging a declaration on the elimination of all forms of religious intolerance; twenty-two NGOs participated in the statement, including organizations from most of the world's major faiths). *See also* U.N. Doc. E/5265, E/CN.4/1127, at 140–43 (1973) (six of eight NGO statements were joint); 58 U.N. ESCOR Supp. (No. 4), Annex V, at 7, U.N. Doc. E/5635, E/CN.4/1179 (1975) (two of five NGO statements were joint). Since individual NGOs are limited by E.S.C. Res. 1296 to very brief statements (500 words for Category II organizations and 2,000 words for Category I organizations), joint statements are very useful.

[73] Nongovernmental organizations contributed significantly to the drafting of the human rights provisions of the U.N. Charter and the International Bill of Rights. *J. Marie*, La Commission Des Droits de l'Homme de L'ONU 23–27 (1975); O. Nolde, Free and Equal (1968); Humphrey, *The U.N. Charter and the Universal Declaration of Human Rights*, in The International Protection of Human Rights 39 (E. Luard ed. 1967); J. Blaustein, Human Rights—A Challenge to the United Nations and to Our Generation 6–7 (1963); D. Robins, United States Non-Governmental Organizations and the Educational Campaign from Dumbarton Oaks, 1944 Through the San Francisco Conference, 1945 (1960); J. De Groote, American Private Organizations and Human Rights—1940–1945 (1954); L. White, International Non-Governmental Organizations 10 (1951).

In 1968, U.N. Secretary-General U Thant addressed an NGO Conference convened to commemorate the twentieth anniversary of the Universal Declaration of Human Rights and observed:

> This may be an appropriate moment for recalling once again the decisive role of non-governmental organizations in obtaining the inclusion in the United Nations Charter of appropriate references to the international obligation of States to promote respect for human rights through national measures supported and encouraged by the action of the international community, effectively organized for that purpose. Subsequently, during 1947 and 1948, non-governmental organizations participated at every stage in the strenuous process of preparing the Universal Declaration of Human Rights . . .

U.N. Doc. SG/SM/999, at 2 (1968).

[74] The International Association of Democratic Lawyers and the Women's International Democratic Federation. *See* U.N. Doc. E/CN.4/SR.1271 & 1274 (1974).

[75] *See* U.N. Doc. E/CN.4/SR.1274 & 1275 (1974).

[76] On 1 Mar. 1974, the U.N. Commission on Human Rights sent a telegram to the Government of Chile expressing concern about violations of human rights in that country and calling particular attention to the cases of five prominent detainees. E.S.C. Res. 1873, 56 U.N. ESCOR, Supp. (No. 5) 56–57, U.N. Doc. E/5464, E/CN.4/1154 (1974).

[77] Sub-Comm'n on Prevention of Discrimination and Protection of Minorities Res. 8 (XXVII), U.N. Doc. E/CN.4/1160, E/CN.4/Sub.2/354, at 53–54 (1974). *See also Protection of Human Rights in Chile*, G.A. Res. 3219, 29 U.N. GAOR, Supp. (No. 31) 83, U.N. Doc. A/9631 (1974).

was made available to the Commission in February 1975 came from NGOs.[78] Moreover, the Commission directed a working group of five members to mount an official inquiry into the human rights violations in Chile and to report the results of its inquiry.[79]

Indeed, because many national delegations lack the resources to do thorough human rights research, NGOs often provide delegates with information and even draft documentation for use in U.N. bodies. Hence, NGOs are not dependent entirely upon their rights to make oral and written interventions. Their influence may be felt even more strongly in informal cooperation with governmental representatives.

Because some of the NGOs tend to be activist and because the NGO's work is of uneven quality, some U.N. personnel and some delegates to the United Nations share a certain degree of suspicion about the motives and reliability of NGOs.[80] It is very difficult to

[78] U.N. Doc. E/5636, E/CN.4/1179, at 23 (1976). *See also* U.N. Doc. A/10295, at 11 (1975).

[79] Human Rights Comm'n Res. 8 (XXXI), 56 U.N. ESCOR, Supp. (No. 4) 66, U.N. Doc. E/5625, E/CN.4/1179 (1975). The first progress report of the *Ad Hoc* Working Group on the Situation of Human Rights in Chile was issued in Oct. 1975. U.N. Doc. A/10285 (1975). The second substantial report of the *Ad Hoc* Working Group was issued on Oct. 8, 1976. U.N. Doc. A/31/253 (1976). In an unsuccessful attempt to blunt U.N. criticism of its human rights practices, Chile released several hundred prisoners in Nov. 1976. Kandell, *Chile Trying to Better Image Abroad of Its Visible Repression*, Minneapolis Trib., Dec. 19, 1976, at 18A, cols. 1–6. Nevertheless, the U.N. General Assembly on Nov. 22, 1976, passed an extremely strong resolution condemning the constant and flagrant violations, deploring Chile's failure to cooperate with the Working Group, calling for further scrutiny by the Working Group, and raising the possibility of humanitarian or legal aid to victims. U.N. Doc. A/C.3/31/L.26/Rev. 1 (1976). *See also* U.N. Doc. A/C.3/31/6 (1976); U.N. Doc. A/C.3/31/6/Add. 1 (1976); U.N. E/CN.4/1221 (1977); U.N. Doc. A/33/331 (1978); U.N. Doc. A/34/583/Add. 1 (1979); U.N. Doc. A/34/829, at 23–30 (1979); U.N. Doc. A/C.3/34/L.61 (1979) (U.N. Trust Fund for Chile).

[80] For example, following a resolution by the Economic and Social Council, E.S.C. Res. 1225, 42 U.N. ESCOR, Supp. (No. 1) 24, U.N. Doc. E/4393 (1967), the Committee of Non-Governmental Organizations of ECOSOC initiated an investigation by questionnaire of NGOs, which focused on covert government financing of NGOs, involvement of NGOs in South Africa, relations of NGOs to Zionism, and criticism by NGOs of human rights violations in socialist countries. *See* U.N. Doc. E/C.2/ST.224 (1968); U.N. Doc. E/2361 (1968).

After the responses to the questionnaire were received, the ECOSOC Committee on Non-Governmental Organizations considered the responses and decided which organizations should be accorded consultative status. *See* U.N. Doc. E/C.2/R.38/Add. 1 & 2 (1968); U.N. Doc. E/C.2/R.39/Add. 1–11 (1968). AI, for example, was maintained as a Category II organization by a vote of eight for, none against, with four abstentions. U.N. Doc. E/4647 (1969). The consultative status of one organization—the Co-ordinating Board of Jewish Organizations—was particularly attacked for its relation to Israel, U.N. Doc. E/4799 (1970); U.N. Doc. E/SR.1691–92 (1970). No NGOs were deprived of their status as a result of this investigation, but several of the more active NGOs faced attempted exclusion by governments that had previously been criticized for human rights violations. S. Liskovsky, The U.N. Reviews its NGO System (unpublished manuscript 1970). *See also* Ascher, *The Economic and Social Council Reviews Consultative Status of Non-Governmental Organizations*, 20 Int'l A. 27 (1968).

Another eruption of suspicion about NGOs in the protection of human rights came at the 1975 session of the Commission on Human Rights, when governmental representatives expressed concern about supposed breaches by NGOs of the confidentiality requirements of E.S.C. Res. 1503, 48 U.N. ESCOR, Supp. (No. 1A) 8, para. 8, U.N. Doc. E/4832/Add. 1 (1970), which established a procedure for consideration of complaints about human rights violations. *See* U.N.

discern the factual basis for these suspicions, and despite the undercurrent of doubt, the United Nations and its members constantly rely upon NGOs for information and for dissemination as well as implementation of U.N. decisions.[81] The doubts and political opposition to the work of NGOs have, however, created some limitations on the contributions NGOs may make to the consideration of issues in U.N. bodies.[82]

3. *The NGO Contribution to International Investigative Procedures*

Nongovernmental organizations also have used the developing procedures for individual communications about human rights violations in the U.N. Commission on Human Rights, the International Labour Organisation, the Inter-American Commission on Human Rights, and the European Commission of Human Rights.[83]

Doc. E/5635, E/CN.4/1179, at 19 (1975); Shestack & Cohen, *International Human Rights: A Role for the United States* 14 Va. J. Int'l L. 591 (1974). *See also* U.N. Doc. E/CN.4/1070, E/CN.4/Sub. 2/323, at 24 (1971). Also, an oral statement on February 11, 1975, by Dr. Homer A. Jack, Secretary-General of the World Conference on Religion and Peace, alleging violations of religious freedom in the Philippines, Northern Ireland, Pakistan, Syria, Cyprus, Egypt, Czechoslovakia, the USSR, and Zaire evoked a storm of criticism. *Id.*; *see* U.N. Doc. E/L.1652 (1975). *See also* U.N. Doc. E/SR.1944 and 1947 (1975). Liskofsy, *Coping with the Question of the Violation of Human Rights and Fundamental Freedoms*, 8 Revue des Droits de l'Homme 883, 896–900 (1975).

Yet another such episode occurred in 1978, when all NGOs were asked to submit quadrennial reports of their activities pursuant to E.S.C. Res. 1296, *supra* note 24. This request was aimed at the more activist human rights NGOs, but in the end only NGOs which failed to respond were placed in any real jeopardy.

---

[81] NGOs often are asked to disseminate views of the United Nations. *See*, *e.g.*, U.N. Doc. E/4476 (1968). The General Assembly has invited NGOs in consultative status to submit material on alternative approaches and ways and means for improving the effective enjoyment of human rights and fundamental freedoms. G.A. Res. 3221, 29 U.N. GAOR, Supp. (No. 31) 84, U.N. Doc. A/9631 (1974). It also has urged them to assist victims of *apartheid* and to help end military, economic, political, and other support for *apartheid*. G.A. Res. 3223, 29 U.N. GAOR, Supp. (No. 31) 85, U.N. Doc. A/9631 (1974). *See also Contribution of Non-Governmental Organizations to the Implementation of the Declaration of the Granting of Independence to Colonial Countries and Peoples*, E.S.C. Res. 1740, 54 U.N. ESCOR, Supp. (No. 1) 36, U.N. Doc. E/5367 (1973); G.A. Res. 2785, 26 U.N. GAOR, Supp. (No. 29) 8, U.N. Doc. A/8429 (1971) (NGOs' measures against racism and racial discrimination); G.A. Res. 2716, 25 U.N. GAOR, Supp. (No. 28) 81, U.N. Doc. A/8028 (1970) (NGOs called upon to consider ways and means to promote the status of women); G.A. Res. 2588, 24 U.N. GAOR, Supp. (No. 30) 60, U.N. Doc. A/7630 (1969) (NGOs' contribution to the International Year of Human Rights); Excerpts from General Assembly Resolutions Concerning Non-Governmental Organizations, U.N. Doc. SP/OPI (1972); U.N. Doc. E/5257/Add. 1 (1973).

[82] *See* E.S.C. Res. 1296, *supra* note 24, paras. 23, 24, & 36. When NGOs are asked to submit material on human rights issues they are frequently reminded not to submit anything which is 'politically motivated contrary to the principles of the Charter of the United Nations'. *See*, *e.g.*, G.A. Res. 3221, 29 U.N. GAOR, Supp. (No. 31) 84, U.N. Doc. A/9631 (1974); U.N. Doc. A/9767, Annex I, at 12 (1974).

[83] One of the challenges ahead for NGOs will be the determination of what role, if any, they might play in the enforcement of the two most recently activated safeguards for international human rights: the International Covenant on Civil and Political Rights, G.A. Res. 2200, 21 U.N. GAOR, Supp. (No. 16) 52, U.N. Doc. A/6316 (1966), and the International Covenant on

The procedures of the Sub-Commission on the Prevention of Discrimination and Protection of Minorities of the Commission on Human Rights state that communications may originate from:

a person or group of persons who, it can be reasonably presumed, are victims of the violations . . . , any person or group of persons who have direct and reliable knowledge of those violations, or non-governmental organizations acting in good faith in accordance with recognized principles of human rights not resorting to politically motivated stands contrary to the provisions of the Charter of the United Nations and having direct and reliable knowledge of such violations[84]

Economic, Social and Cultural Rights, G.A. Res. 2200, 21 U.N. GAOR, Supp. (No. 16) 49, U.N. Doc. A/6316 (1966). *See* AI, Memorandum NS 60/76 (9 Apr. 1976). *But see* U.N. Doc. W/5764 (1976). For example, art. 2 of the Optional Protocol to the International Covenant on Civil and Political Rights, G.A. Res. 2200, 21 U.N. GAOR, Supp. (No. 16) 59, U.N. Doc. A/6316 (1966), establishes procedures for the receipt of communications from 'individuals who claim that any of their rights enumerated in the [Political] Covenant have been violated . . .' Just as with the [European] Convention on Human Rights and Fundamental Freedoms, 213 U.N.T.S. 221, *reprinted in* Basic Documents on Human Rights (2d ed. I. Brownlie 1981), this language does not appear to allow for direct NGO communications. *See also* note 101 *infra*. But there does not appear to be any reason why the Human Rights Committee, established pursuant to the Political Covenant, could not utilize NGO information in considering communications under the Optional Protocol. NGOs have begun to represent and assist human rights victims in preparing communications. Furthermore, NGOs should have consultative status with the working group established by ECOSOC for reviewing reports filed pursuant to the Economic Covenant.

---

[84] Sub-Commission on Prevention of Discrimination and Protection of Minorities Res. 1 (XXIV), para. (2)(a), U.N. Doc. E/CN.4/1070, E/CN.4/Sub. 2/323, at 50–51 (1971); *see* E.S.C. Res. 1503, *supra* note 79. *See also* E.S.C. Res. 728F, 28 U.N. ESCOR, Supp. (No. 1) 19, U.N. Doc. E/3290 (1939); Commission on Human Rights Res. 8 (XXIII), 42 U.N. ESCOR, Supp. (No. 6) 131, U.N. Doc. E/4322, E/CN.4/940 (1967); E.S.C. Res. 1235, 42 U.N. ESCOR, Supp. (No. 1) 17, U.N. Doc. E/4393 (1967); Sub-Commission on Prevention of Discrimination and Protection of Minorities Res. 2 (XXIV), U.N. Doc. E/CN.4/1070, E/CN.4/Sub. 2/323, at 52–53 (1971). *See generally* United Nations Action in the Field of Human Rights, U.N. Doc. ST/HR/2/Rev.1, at 276–77.

More recently, in 1974 the Sub-Commission established yet another procedure whereby NGOs may submit 'reliably attested information' 'in good faith', 'not politically motivated', and not 'contrary to the principles of the Charter of the United Nations', concerning 'violations of the basic human rights of persons detained or imprisoned throughout the world'. Such information is to be reviewed annually by the Sub-Commission. Sub-Commission on Prevention of Discrimination and Protection of Minorities Res. 7 (XXVII), U.N. Doc. E/CN.4/1160, E/CN.4/Sub. 2/354, at 52–53 (1974); *see* Burke, *New United Nations Procedure to Protect Prisoners and Other Detainees*, 67 Cal. L. Rev. 201 (1976). The Sub-Commission, in a 1975 resolution, specifically requested that the U.N. Secretariat 'submit timely in advance of its next session . . . a synopsis of the materials received from non-governmental organizations'. Sub-Commission on Prevention of Discrimination and Protection of Minorities Res. 1 (XXVIII), U.N. Doc. E/CN.4/Sub. 2/CRP. 3/Add.8 at para. 5 (1975) (prov.); *see* U.N. Doc. E/CN.4/Sub.2/L.635 (1975). Similarly, the Sub-Commission created a working group to review and to report to the Sub-Commission concerning 'reliable information on slavery and slave trade in all their manifestations, the traffic in persons and the exploitation or the prostitution of others' as transmitted by NGOs, as well as governments, etc. Sub-Commission on Prevention of Discrimination and Protection of Minorities Res. 11 (XXVII), U.N. Doc. E/CN.4/1160, E/CN.4/Sub. 2/354, at 57–58 (1974); Sub-Commission on Prevention of Discrimination and Protection of Minorities Res. 5 (XXVIII), U.N. Doc. E/CN.4/1180, E/CN.4/Sub.2/364 (1975). *See generally* Ermacora, *Procedure to Deal with Human Rights Violations: A Hopeful Start in the United Nations*, 7 Revue des Droits de l'Homme 670 (1974); Moller *Petitioning the United*

In 1979, the Lawyers Committee for International Human Rights submitted a communication to the Sub-Commission on the widespread violations of human rights in Argentina.[85] In the same year the International Commission of Jurists submitted a communication on Uruguay. Similarly, in 1979, Amnesty International submitted communications on Afghanistan, Argentina, the Central African Empire, Ethiopia, Indonesia, Paraguay, and Uruguay. The International League for Human Rights presented a communication on Paraguay. The National Conference of Black Lawyers presented a petition complaining about the United States. The International Conference of Free Trade Unions submitted a communication concerning Tunisia and the International Human Rights Law Group submitted one concerning Romania.[86]

Nongovernmental organizations also have had the right to and sometimes do contribute to special studies on various human rights issues conducted by the United Nations, as well as to the periodic human rights reporting formerly established by the Commission on Human Rights.[87] In addition, NGOs are entitled to submit written or oral communications in other U.N. bodies:[88] the Trusteeship Council,[89] the Special Committee against *Apartheid*,[90] the Special

Nations, Universal Human Rights 57 (No. 4, 1979); U.N. Doc. E/CN.4/1317 (1979). In 1980 the U.N. Commission on Human Rights also established a working group for disappearances, which could receive all reliable information. Much of such information will undoubtedly come from NGOs. *See* Comm'n on Human Rights Res. 20, U.N. Doc. E/CN.4/L.1501/Add.5 (1980).

---

[85] Lawyers Committee for International Human Rights, Violations of Human Rights in Argentina: 1976–1979 (1979).

[86] Since the Commission on Human Rights has not yet initiated even one thorough study or investigation as a result of a E.S.C. Res. 1503 communication, the effort of NGOs to utilize this procedure may not have been worthwhile. Furthermore, the secrecy of these procedures lessens their impact. In 1979 the Commission did remove the case of Equatorial Guinea from the Res. 1503 procedure and appointed a special rapporteur to make a thorough study, because the country refused even to respond to the Res. 1503 communication. U.N. Doc. E/1979/36, E/CN.4/1347, at 57 (1979). Accused nations seem to have usually taken the communications quite seriously and sufficient information has informally been revealed about communications to have had some incremental impact on human rights violations. *See U.N. Commission on Human Rights*, Rev. Int'l Comm'n Jurists 23 (No. 16, 1976); Newman, *The New United Nations Procedure for Human Rights Complaints: Reform, Status Quo, or Chamber of Horrors?*, 34 Annales de Droit 129 (1974). In addition, some prisoners may have been released.

[87] *E.g.*, Rannat, Study of Equality in Administration of Justice, U.N. Doc. E/CN.4/Sub.2/296/Rev.1, at 246 (1972); Study of the Right of Everyone to be Free From Arbitrary Arrest, Detention and Exile, U.N. Doc. E/CN.4/Sub. 2/200/Rev.1, at 74 (1960).

[88] The many U.N. procedures dealing with communications concerning human rights and the utilization of these procedures by NGOs are discussed in T. van Boven, Partners in the Promotion and Protection of Human Rights (unpublished manuscript 1976). *See also* G. da Foneseca, How to File Complaints of Human Rights Violations: A Practical Guide to Intergovernmental Procedures (1975); M. Tardu, Human Rights, The International Petition System (1980); U.N. Doc. E/5628 (1975); U.N. Doc. E/NGO/30 (1975).

[89] *See* U.N. Charter art. 87. An example of such a communication is Communication from Mr. Jerome J. Shestack, Chairman of the International League for the Rights of Man, Concerning the Trust Territory of the Pacific Islands, U.N. Doc. T/PET.10/101/Add.1 (1976).

[90] *See* G.A. Res. 1761, 17 U.N. GAOR, Supp. (No. 17) 9, U.N. Doc. A/5217 (1962); G.A. Res.

Committee on the Situation with regard to the Implementation of the Declaration on the Granting of Independence to Colonial Countries and Peoples,[91] the Commission on Human Rights *Ad Hoc* Working Group of Experts on Human Rights in Southern Africa,[92] and the Special Committee to Investigate Israeli Practices Affecting the Human Rights of the Population of the Occupied Territories.[93]

The International Labour Organisation provides the most formal role for nongovernmental organizations of employers and employees.[94] They are entitled to receive and to comment upon governmental reports and the measures taken to comply with the many conventions and recommendations which comprise the international law administered by the ILO.[95] The ILO has also established a special procedure for receiving complaints alleging infringements of trade union rights; these complaints may be submitted by workers' or employers' organizations or by governments to the ILO Governing Body's Committee on Freedom of Association—a tripartite group of representatives of employers, employees, and governments.[96] The

2396, 23 U.N. GAOR, Supp. (No. 18) 19, U.N. Doc. A/7218 (1968); G.A. Res. 2775C, 26 U.N. GAOR, Supp. (No. 29) 42, U.N. Doc. A/8429 (1971) (authorizing Special Committee to hold consultations with experts and representatives of the oppressed people of South Africa as well as anti-*apartheid* movements and NGOs concerned with the campaign against *apartheid*). *See also, e.g.*, U.N. Press Release GA/AP/501 (Sept. 17, 1975) (letter from Lawyers' Committee for Civil Rights Under Law concerning detentions in South Africa); Report of Special Committee on Apartheid, 28 U.N. GAOR, Supp. (No. 22) 56, para. 278, U.N. Doc. A/9022 (1973). *See generally* United Nations Action in the Field of Human Rights, U.N. Dc. ST/HR/2/Rev.1, at 349–50 (1980).

[91] *See* 17 U.N. GAOR, Annexes (Add. Agenda Item 25) paras. 16–111, U.N. Doc. A/5238. *See also, e.g.*, U.N. Doc. A/10156, at 22 (1975) (paper outlining violations of human rights in South Africa presented by the International Defense and Aid Fund for Southern Africa).

[92] *See* Comm'n on Human Rights Res. 2 (XXIII), U.N. Doc. E/CN.4/L.908 (1967), 42 U.N. ESCOR, Supp. (No. 6) 76, U.N. Doc. E/4822 (1967). The *Ad Hoc* Working Group reported to the Commission on Human Rights in 1970 that letters were sent to various NGOs and African liberation movements requesting 'relevant information, including the names and addresses of witnesses' and that 'the names of most of the witnesses who were heard by the Group or sent written information were communicated by several of these organizations'. U.N. Doc. E/CN.4/1020 (1970).

[93] *See* Report of the Special Committee, 25 U.N. GAOR, Annexes (Agenda Item 101) 19, para. 45, U.N. Doc. A/8039 (1971). *See also, e.g., id.* Annex VI, at 103 (Memorandum Received by the Special Committee from the Israeli League for Human and Civil Rights).

[94] Fischer, *Les organisations nongouvernmentales et les institutions internationales*, in 2 Les Nations Unies, Chantier De L'Avenir 113–28 (1961).

[95] *See* ILO Const. art. 24 *et seq.*, Morse, *Note on ILO Procedures for Supervising the Observance of International Labor Standards and Related Constitutional Obligations*, in *House Hearings on International Protection of Human Rights*, *supra* note 2, at 574–76.

[96] *See generally* E. Hass, Human Rights and International Action (1970); G. Weaver, The International Labor Organization and Human Rights 2 (1968); International Labour Office, Freedom of Association (1972). For a description of the procedure to be followed by the Committee on Freedom of Association in examining complaints of alleged infringements of trade union rights, *see* 34 (No. 3) ILO O. Bull. 207–10 (1951). Doc. E/4144, at 20 (1965). Allegations may originate from national and international organizations of employers or workers enjoying consultative status with the ILO or having a direct interest in the subject matter of the allegation. *See* 29th Report of Governing Body Committee of Freedom of Association, 43 (No. 2) ILO O.

International Confederation of Free Trade Unions and the World Federation of Trade Unions have made use of these procedures.[97]

Beginning in 1970, several NGOs, principally the U.S. Conference of Bishops and the International Commission of Jurists, submitted communications to the Inter-American Commission on Human Rights with respect to allegations of torture, detention of political prisoners, and political executions in Brazil.[98] Brazil refused to permit an on-site investigation but did reply to the complaint. The Inter-American Commission concluded that 'evidence collected in this case leads to the persuasive presumption that in Brazil serious cases of torture, abuse and maltreatment have occurred to persons of both sexes while they were deprived of their liberty'.[99] In addition, Amnesty International and the International Commission of Jurists in 1973 called upon the Inter-American Commission to investigate allegations of mass arrests and political executions in Chile. Inter-American Commission experts visited Chile in the summer of 1974 and issued a report in October to the Permanent Council of the Organization of American States, thus providing a thorough documentation of the continuing pattern of human rights violations in that country.[100] Also

Bull. 79, para. 9 (1960); 1st Report of Governing Body Committee on Freedom of Association, *reprinted in* International Labour Organisation: Sixth Report of the International Labour Organisation to the United Nations, App. V, para. 14 (1952); Wolf, *supra* ch. 7, section I.D.1.

If the state gives its consent, a complaint may be submitted to an independent Fact-Finding and Conciliation Commission on Freedom of Association. Unlike a Commission of Enquiry established under ILO Const. art. 26 which can only deal with complaints arising under ratified conventions, the Fact-Finding and Conciliation Commission can deal with complaints that trade union rights have been infringed even apart from alleged failures to comply with ratified conventions. *See* Report on the Establishment of a Fact-Finding and Conciliation Committee on Freedom of Association, Submitted to the Conference by the Governing Body of the International Labour Office, 33 (No. 2) ILO O. Bull. 86 (App. VI) (1950). *See also*, *e.g.*, 57 (No. 1) ILO O. Bull. 40, 114 (1974) (appointment of Fact-Finding and Conciliation Committee panel to deal with violations of human and trade union rights in Chile); Wolf, *supra* ch. 7, section I.D.2.

[97] 129th Report of the Governing Body Committee on Freedom of Association, Case No. 666 (Portugal), 55 ILO O. Bull. 92 (1972).

[98] *See* Handbook of Existing Rules Pertaining to Human Rights, Inter-American Commission on Human Rights, O.A.S. Doc. OEA/Ser.L./V/II.13, Rev. 6, at 13–15, 27, 35–37, 44–47, 60–62 (1979).

[99] Inter-American Commission on Human Rights Res. on Case 1684 (Brazil), O.A.S. Doc. OEA/Ser.L./V/II.28, doc. 14 (1972); *see* Rev. Int'l Comm'n Jurists 4 (No. 8, 1972); Inter-American Commission on Human Rights Res. on Case 1684 (Brazil), O.A.S. Doc. OEA/Ser.L/V/II.30, doc. 36 (1973) (inserting observation in annual report). The case against Brazil, however, failed to proceed to full consideration by the O.A.S. General Assembly and was apparently concluded without definitive action. *See* Diuguid, *OAS Ministers Table Study of Brazil and the United States and OAS Response*, in *House Hearings on International Protection of Human Rights*, *supra* note 2; at 897–912 (1973); *cf.* O.A.S. Doc. OEA/Ser.P/AG/doc. 409/74, at 108–11 (1974); OAS. Doc. OEA/Ser.G/CP/doc. 399/75, at 38–42 (1975); B. Wood, International Organization and Human Rights with Special Reference to the Organization of American States 18, 20–22 (unpublished manuscript 1976).

[100] *See* O.A.S. Doc. OEA/Ser.L./V/II.34, doc. 21 (1974); Hauser, *Human Rights in Latin America*, Washington Post, Mar. 5, 1975, at A15, col. 1. Having received a second report, the

in 1974, the International League for Human Rights successfully urged the Inter-American Commission to take up the case of slavery and genocide in Paraguay.[101]

Nongovernmental organizations have not been particularly active in fostering individual applications to the European Commission of Human Rights.[102] Amnesty International and other NGOs have, however, been relatively active in lobbying for consideration of human rights issues by the Consultative Assembly of the Council of Europe.[103]

4. *Aid and Human Rights*

Nongovernmental organizations that have adequate financial resources provide much needed assistance to victims of human rights violations. The ICRC provides medical supplies, blankets, clothing and food to both prisoners and civilians. Both the Program to Combat Racism of the World Council of Churches and the ICRC have given medical and educational assistance and other types of aid to the liberation movements in southern Africa. The World Council of Churches, the League of Red Cross Societies, CARE, Catholic Relief Services, Caritas, and numerous other organizations provide development, training, educational, and humanitarian assistance. The International Defense and Aid Fund for Southern Africa and the Africa Legal Assistance Project of the Lawyers' Committee for Civil Rights Under Law have provided assistance to the families of prisoners, to the victims of oppression, and to the legal defense of persons accused under the racist laws of South Africa.

O.A.S. General Assembly at its June 1976 meeting in Santiago, Chile called upon the Chilean Government to ensure full respect for human rights in Chile. O.A.S. Doc. AG/Res. 243 (1976); *see* O.A.S. Doc. OEA/Ser.L./V/II.37, doc. 19 (1976).

[101] *Paraguay: Slavery & Genocidal Acts*, The Rights of Man Bull., Sept. 1974, at 6; *see* Inter-American Commission on Human Rights, Informe Anual, O.A.S. Doc. OEA/Ser.L./V/II.37, at 172 (1976); *cf.* U.N. Doc. E/CN.4/Sub.2, 353 (1974).

[102] It should be noted that, unlike most of the U.N. procedures discussed above, NGOs may submit petitions to the European Commission of Human Rights only if they claim to be themselves victims of human rights violations. *See* art. 25, European Convention. *See, e.g.*, X (Evangelical-Lutheran Church of Sweden) v. Sweden [1969], Y.B. Eur. Conv. on Human Rights 664, 674–76 (Eur. Comm'n of Human Rights). It should also be noted, however, that the European Commission may decide to hear as a witness, expert, or 'in any other capacity any person whose evidence or statements seem likely to assist it in the carrying out of its task'. European Commission of Human Rights, Rules of Procedure, Rule 54(1), at 24 (1971). In addition, although Rule 36 of the European Commission's Rules of Procedure provides only for representation of victims by lawyers and professors of law, it appears that NGOs might under some circumstances be permitted to represent victims of human rights violations or to appear as representatives or advisors for governments. European Commission of Human Rights, Rules of Procedure, Rule 36, at 16 (1971); *see* Council of Europe, Convention for the Protection of Human Rights and Fundamental Freedoms, Case-Law Topics, *Bringing an Application Before the European Commission of Human Rights* 7–10 (1972).

[103] Cf. Golsong, *Les organisations non gouvernmentales et le Conseil de l'Europe*, in Les Organisations non Gouvernmentales en Suisse 93–106 (1973); P. Rohn, Relations Between the Council of Europe and International Non-Governmental Organizations (1957).

It is sometimes possible for general aid programs to be coordinated to achieve human rights ends. The assistance and attention given to liberation movements in Portuguese-occupied territories probably helped achieve self-determination for Mozambique, Guinea Bissau, and Angola. During 1972 the African Conference of Churches and the World Council of Churches were successful in mediating and helping to bring to an end the civil war in Sudan because of the availability of assistance to salve the wounds of war and help foster development.[104]

5. *Activities at Local Levels*

Because of greater resources, many national sections of international NGOs and, indeed, many NGOs without any direct international ties succeed in implementing international human rights law in ways unavailable to international NGOs.

In the United States there are innumerable organizations which deal with human rights on the domestic level. The American Civil Liberties Union, the National Association for the Advancement of Colored People, the NAACP Legal Defense and Educational Fund, the Lawyers' Committee for Civil Rights under Law, the American Jewish Committee, the Mexican-American Legal Defense and Educational Fund, and the Native American Rights Fund are a few of the more prominent. Very few of those organizations, however, have recognized international human rights law or have attempted to use it in dealing with domestic human rights problems.[105]

Since January 1975, about two dozen national and international organizations have become active in Washington, D.C., and have cooperated under the name of the Human Rights Working Group in promoting human rights concerns in the U.S. government.[106] One of

[104] *See Southern Sudan*, Rev. Int'l Comm'n Jurists 14–15 (No. 8, 1972); L. Niilus, Peace in the Sudan (mimeo, 12 Mar. 1973).

[105] The Africa Legal Assistance Project of the Lawyers' Committee for Civil Rights Under Law, in Washington, D.C., the Center for Constitutional Rights in New York City, the Center for Law and Social Policy in Washington, D.C., the International Human Rights Law Group in Washington, D.C., and the Lawyers Committee for International Human Rights are five U.S. NGOs which have undertaken domestic litigation to further international human rights objectives. For example, the Lawyers' Committee for Civil Rights Under Law and the Center for Constitutional Rights sought before the New York City Human Rights Commission to restrain the *New York Times* from advertising job positions in South Africa for which blacks would not be considered. Lawyers' Committee for Civil Rights Under Law, Africa Legal Assistance Project—Interim Report 36–39 (1974); Center for Constitutional Rights. Docket Report 18 (1974). *See* Lillich, *The Role of Domestic Courts in Promoting International Human Rights Norms*, 24 N.Y.L.S. L.Rev. 153 (1978); Stein, *Public Interest Litigation and United States Foreign Policy*, 18 Harv. Int'l L.J. 375 (1977); Weissbrodt, *Domestic Legal Activity in Furtherance of International Human Rights Goals*, in Implementing International Human Rights Through the Domestic Legal Process 10 (W. Raymond ed. 1976).

[106] *See Interest Groups*, *supra* note 3; Note, *Role of NGOs in Implementing Human Rights in Latin America*, 7 Ga. J. Int'l & Comp. L. 476 (1977); Coalition for a New Foreign and Military Policy, What is the Human Rights Working Group? (1976); Ottoway, *The Growing Lobby for Human Rights*, Washington Post, 12 Dec. 1976, at B1.

the most potent forms of international pressure may be exerted by professional groups such as doctors, lawyers, trade unionists, teachers, and scientists expressing their concern about the violation of the human rights of their fellow professionals or unionists.[107] In many countries such as South Africa, Namibia, and Zimbabwe, certain Christian churches have performed invaluable work for human rights, while receiving vital encouragement and support from their sister churches abroad, particularly through the World Council of Churches, Lutheran World Federation, and Pontifical Commission Justice and Peace.[108]

Amnesty International's success in recent years has been due considerably to its ability to mobilize the efforts of local groups who work for the human rights of named prisoners.[109] Normally, Amnesty groups are assigned prisoners of conscience (selected by the International Secretariat) from different countries. (Amnesty International defines prisoners of conscience as those who are imprisoned in violation of their human rights and who have neither used nor advocated violence.) Local Amnesty groups manifest a personal concern for the release of their prisoners and work toward that end by writing letters to prison officials, judges, and various government officers of the state involved, by visiting embassies, and by sending appeals to lawyers and other NGOs which might intervene. Also, groups attempt to write letters directly to their adopted prisoner or to his or her family thereby giving moral support, and to provide economic and other assistance where possible. Some Amnesty groups, in addition, send telegrams and letters to protest or prevent imminent torture or executions.

At times the groups give Amnesty International a rather amateurish image, but it cannot be doubted that its person-to-person and energetic approach can be effective when the more professional, sophisticated, better researched, and discreet efforts of its International Secretariat or of other international NGOs are not successful.[110] Since

[107] For example, a group of distinguished professors cabled a plea to the O.A.S. expressing deep concern over violations of human rights in Chile and raised particularly the case of a former head of the Technical University of Chile. *Venezuelan Minister Vows OAS Support*, Washington Post, 13 May 1975, at A3, col. 1. Similarly, the Arab Lawyers Union has worked for lawyers and judges whose rights are infringed. *See also* A.B.A. Comm. on Int'l Human Rights, Reports of the Working Group on Independence of Lawyers in Foreign Countries, June 30, 1976.

[108] *See* Pontifical Commission Justice and Peace, The Church and Human Rights (1975); F. Parakatil, Human Rights—A Summary of Actions (mimeo 1971); N. Malicky, Religious Groups at the United Nations (1971); N. MacDermot, Human Rights and the Churches 2–4 (1976); *Motu Proprio* of Pope Paul VI, *Instatiam et pacem* (1977).

[109] *See* AI, Handbook (1977).

[110] *Sole AI Adoptee in Libya is Released*, AI Newsletter, Feb. 1974, at 3; *Joint AI–ICJ Mission Visits Uruguay; Five 'Marcha' Journalists Released*, AI Newsletter, June 1974, at 2; *Freed Tanzanians Maulidi Mshangama and Ali Muhsin Barwani Thank Amnesty*, AI Newsletter, June 1974, at 3; *East German POC's Freed*, 1 AI Matchbox 25 (Winter 1975); *Two Released Rhodesian POC's Aided by AI Groups*, AI Newsletter, May 1974, at 3; *Mexico Releases Six After AI Pleas*, Amnesty Action, July–Aug. 1973, at 3.

the organization was formed in 1961, it has been estimated that Amnesty International has assisted in the release of thousands of prisoners of conscience.[111] Often, several NGOs work for the release of named prisoners and many political, military, economic, as well as human rights factors may combine to result in the release of prisoners.[112]

[111] Amnesty International has launched a campaign against the use of torture. *See* AI, Report on Torture. Two of the lastest steps in making torture an important issue of world concern came with the adoption of G.A. Res. 3218, 29 U.N. GAOR. Supp. (No. 31) 82, U.N. Doc. A/9631 (1974), and with the adoption of G.A. Res. 3453, 30 U.N. GAOR, Supp. (No. 34) 92, U.N. Doc. A/10034 (1976). *See also* U.N. Doc. A/9767 (1974); U.N. Doc. A/10158 (1975); U.N. Doc. 10260 (1975); *Torture as Policy: The Network of Evil*, Time, 16 Aug. 1976, at 31; notes 113–15 *infra* and accompanying text.

Amnesty International has similarly attempted since 1978 to make the death penalty a matter of international human rights concern. *See, e.g.*, AI, The Death Penalty (1979). But the results have been far less immediate. Several NGOs, including AI, the International Commission of Jurists, and the International League for Human Rights have also attempted to identify disappearances as another phenomenon worthy of international human rights attention. *See* AI U.S.A. 'Disappearances': A Workbook (1981). The U.N. General Assembly and Commission on Human Rights have responded promptly to this problem. G.A. Res. 33/173, 33 U.N. GAOR, Supp. (No. 45) 158, U.N. Doc. A/33/45 (1978); Comm'n on Human Rights Res. 20 (XXXVI), U.N. Doc. E/CN.4/L.1501/Add.5 (1980). *See also* U.N. Doc. E/CN.4/1362 (1980).

[112] Only very fragmentary and inconclusive data on prisoner releases are available. In 1973, *Time* magazine reported that AI had taken up the cases of some 13,000 prisoners of conscience and as a result of its efforts 7,500 had been released. *Time*, July 9, 1973, at 27. The figure of 7,500 is misleadingly high, because many of the prisoners would probably have been released in any case. In 1976 AI attempted to measure more systematically the effectiveness of its efforts, but the study failed to distinguish meaningfully between releases of adopted prisoners caused partially or wholly by AI pressure and those resulting from expiry of sentence, change of government, pardon, health reasons, acquittal at trial, successful appeal, exchange of prisoners, or other outside pressure. *See* Scoble & Wiseberg, *Amnesty International: Evaluating Effectiveness in the Human Rights Arena*, Intellect 79, 81–82 (Sept. 10, 1976).

Frequently there is an interaction between international human rights pressure and internal political sentiment to achieve the release of improperly detained persons. For example, Julio Augusto de Peña Valdez was arrested on Jan. 31, 1971, in an apartment in Santo Domingo, Dominican Republic. He was participating in a political discussion, but was accused of harboring weapons in the apartment, although he contended that no weapons were found. Afterward he was sentenced to three years in prison and served his sentence. Nevertheless, after the supreme court ordered his release the government refused to release him and the five other persons arrested at the same time. In response all 250 political prisoners at La Victoria Prison went on a hunger strike, which received considerable support among those who were opposing the re-election of the President. In retaliation, the government cut off water, light, and medical services to the prison.

AI volunteers in the United States who had been working for the release of Mr. de Peña were alerted by a telephone call from Mrs. de Peña. After a frantic day of telegrams by well-organized volunteers, a television station announced that water and light were being restored to the prison. The AI telegrams and letters gave international credence to the already existing pressure for the release of the prisoners. The relatively free press of the Dominican Republic made the Dominican people aware of the international public opinion expressed by Amnesty International. The President finally announced that the prisoners would be released, and they were released after the election. Some were later rearrested and AI has continued, where necessary, to work for the release of prisoners at La Victoria. *Dominican Prisoners Freed*, Amnesty Action, Nov.–Dec. 1974, at 3. *See also All AI-Adopted Prisoners in Metropolitan Portugal Freed After Coup*, AI Newsletter, May 1974, at 1; *AI Was 'Light of Hope' to Ex-Prisoners, Portuguese Relief Group Says*, AI Newsletter, June 1974, at 1.

D. CONTRIBUTIONS TO THE DEVELOPMENT OF HUMAN RIGHTS NORMS

In addition to their active role in implementing human rights, NGOs were instrumental in the drafting of the Universal Declaration of Human Rights.[113] The representatives of NGOs may have been influential in the drafting process as much for their personal expertise and prestige as for the importance of their organizations. By their presence in drafting sessions and by their individual contacts with national delegates or U.N. staff, NGO representatives can have even more impact than their more formal interventions in open sessions. Most diplomatic experts and staff are eager for the ideas and information which thoughtful and knowledgeable NGO representatives could provide to great advantage. Amnesty International has been credited with raising world consciousness about torture and assisting with the adoption of the U.N. Declaration on the Protection of All Persons from being Subjected to Torture and Other Cruel, Inhuman or Degrading Treatment or Punishment.[114] Amnesty International and the International Commission of Jurists have taken an active part in the preparation of the draft principles on the rights of detainees[115] and of the draft convention against torture.[116]

Similarly, eight NGOs joined in 1979 in urging the Sub-Commission on the Protection of Minorities and Prevention of Discrimination to establish a new mechanism for encouraging nations to ratify the principal human rights treaties.[117] The Sub-Commission established a working group to inquire about progress toward ratification and to offer advice to states encountering obstacles.[118]

It is clear that international NGOs provide one way by which individuals may become actively involved in the day-to-day protection of human rights. These organizations achieve so very much with their

[113] G.A. Res. 217A, U.N. Doc. A/810, at 71 (1948). *See Role of International NGOs, supra* note 2, at 306 n. 71.

[114] G.A. Res. 3452, 33 U.N. GOAR, Supp. (No. 34) 91, U.N. Doc. A/10034 (1978). *See* Cassese, *How could Nongovernmental Organizations Use U.N. Bodies More Effectively?* Universal Human Rights 73 (No. 4, 1979); Leary, *A New Role for Non-Governmental Organizations: A Case Study of Non-Governmental Participation in the Development of International Norms*, in U.N. Law/Fundamental Rights 197 (A. Cassese ed. 1979). *See also* Archer, *New Forms of NGO Participation in World Conferences*, in Non-Governmental Organizations in International Co-operation for Development (B. Andemicael ed. forthcoming).

[115] *See* U.N. Doc. E/CN.4/WG.1/WR.1 (1979); *U.N. Commission on Human Rights*, Rev. Int'l Comm'n Jurists 19 (No. 22, 1979).

[116] *See Report of the Sub-Commission*, Rev. Int'l Comm'n Jurists 21 (No. 21, 1978). *See also* G.A. Res. 36/60, U.N. Doc. A/RES/36/60 (1981).

[117] U.N. Doc. E/CN.4/Sub.2/NGO/80 (1979); U.N. Doc. E/CN.4/Sub.2/NGO/80/Add.1 (1979).

[118] *See* U.N. Doc. E/CN.4/Sub.2/L.716 (1979).

present minimal resources[119] that it is possible to foresee that they could do far more if there were adequate support.

II. Teaching Suggestions

Nongovernmental organizations are active in nearly every phase of international human rights. They have advocated and helped to draft international human rights norms in multilateral treaties and resolutions. They have assisted intergovernmental organizations and governments in the implementation of human rights norms. Nongovernmental organizations have also engaged in various measures which directly encourage improvements in human rights situations, including diplomatic approaches, publicity, letter-writing campaigns, mounting of trial observer and fact-finding missions, providing aid to human rights victims, etc.

Nongovernmental organizations are also very accessible to students and others who wish to become active in human rights work. Accordingly, a general human rights course could be taught from the perspective of how NGOs have contributed and could contribute to international human rights. Such a course would necessarily cover all the basic human rights treaties and other norms under which the NGOs work and to which the NGOs have contributed. Most of the principal intergovernmental procedures for implementing human rights permit NGOs to be petitioners directly, to represent victims, to inform decision-makers, or to otherwise influence the implementation process.

Such an approach might appear out of balance with the significance of NGOs in the human rights field.[120] But since very few students can expect to represent governments in human rights proceedings and since NGOs are quite accessible to interested students, an NGO-oriented human rights course can motivate students to learn the doctrines and procedures of human rights for possible use in real situations.[121]

Even without completely structuring a human rights course around NGOs, they are sufficiently important to justify at least a few classes. With this narrower focus, a student might be given a copy of an article describing the general role of NGOs in the implementation of human

[119] One of the most important developments in the work of human rights organizations during the period beginning in 1975 has been the increased support of the Ford Foundation and, to a lesser extent, the Rockefeller Brothers Foundation for many NGOs and for such efforts as Human Rights Internet Newsletter, *see* note 2 *supra*, and the International Human Rights Internship Program. R. Magat, Confronting Man's Inhumanity 10–14 (1978).

[120] *Cf.* L. Sohn & T. Buergenthal, International Protection of Human Rights (1973).

[121] *Cf.* R. Lillich & F. Newman, International Human Rights: Problems of Law and Policy (1979).

rights, such as provided in section I above. In addition, the student might be asked how to deal with a realistic hypothetical, such as, for example, the following problem which should be accompanied by background material about the human rights situation in Argentina:[122]

A. PROBLEM

Yesterday, Martin Johnson visited our office. He is terribly concerned about his daughter, Edna. She was expected to telephone the family on her mother's birthday, September 26th, but she did not call. Edna is 26 years old; she was born in Minneapolis, attended Minneapolis Lutheran High School, St. Olaf's College in Northfield, where she majored in history; and then entered the Ph.D. program in history at the University of Minnesota. She began a thesis on the history of the union movement in Argentina a year ago. After several months of preparation and learning Spanish, she left for Argentina six months ago. She is normally very conscientious about writing her parents and telephoning them on holidays.

Martin had been a client of ours for some time because he is the manager of the retail baking division of Peavey Company in Minneapolis. Mr. Johnson would like us to consider the steps which can be taken to find out what happened to his daughter. He does not know any of the people with whom she was working in Argentina and telephone calls and letters to her previous place of residence have been unavailing.

Your initial research has revealed that the Associated Press reporter in Cordoba had heard that Edna Johnson was visiting the office of four Argentinean lawyers on September 14. She was talking with the lawyers about their representation of the National Federation of Mine and Metallurgical Workers, when the police arrived. They arrested all the lawyers and Edna. Argentinean newspapers have reported that Edna is being held at the provincial police station in Cordoba.

How would you work for Edna's release?

The student should begin to analyze this hypothetical first as to the sort of protection Ms. Johnson might expect from her own government. The student should be given material about the State Department approach to such cases[123] and the statue which apparently requires State Department efforts in such cases,[124] but which does not, in fact, provide much aid.[125] The student should be invited to consider

[122] *See, e.g.*, Lawyers Committee for International Human Rights, Violations of Human Rights in Argentina: 1976–1979 (1979).

[123] *Protection of Americans Abroad: Hearings before the Subcomm. on Int'l Operations of the House Comm. on Int'l Relations*, 95th Cong., 1st Sess., 88–94 (1977) (testimony of Dep. Ass't Sec'y of State William P. Stedman, Jr.).

[124] 22 U.S.C. § 1732 (1979).

[125] Redpath v. Kissinger, 415 F. Supp. 566 (W.D. Tex. 1976).

what the U.S. government might or might not do for its nationals and what considerations motivate U.S. action. The student should also consider how the U.S. government can ethically request the release of its nationals, when Argentineans are incarcerated and tortured for similar 'offenses'.[126]

Having concluded that the U.S. government may be unwilling or unable to assist Ms. Johnson, the class might consider which NGOs might be motivated and well placed to help obtain Ms. Johnson's release. The students should consider what human rights provisions might provide support for any NGO activity for Ms. Johnson. The class would then consider what measures NGOs might take and compare their prospects of success with the efforts of governments or intergovernmental organizations. The class should also ponder whether Ms. Johnson's interests might in some circumstances conflict with the efforts of NGOs and how such conflicts might be resolved.

Another class on the role of NGOs might provide the student with a sample communication under ECOSOC resolution 1503,[127] such as the International League for Human Rights complaint on India,[128] or the Lawyers Committee for International Human Rights complaint on Argentina,[129] The students should then be asked to review the complaint in the light of the International Bill of Human Rights.[130] After identifying all the substantive violations arguably alleged by the complaint, students should consider each of the principal U.N.,[131] O.A.S.,[132] ILO,[133] or other procedures which are available for

[126] *See* J. Brierly, The Law of Nations 276–96 (6th ed. 1963); Murphy, *State Responsibility for Injury to Aliens*, 41 N.Y.U. L. Rev. 125 (1966).

[127] *See* note 80 *supra*.

[128] Communication from International League for Human Rights to U.N. Secretary-General Kurt Waldheim, May 31, 1976.

[129] *See* note 122 *supra*.

[130] The International Bill of Human Rights is comprised of four documents: (a) The Universal Declaration of Human Rights; (b) the Political Covenant; (c) the Economic Covenant; and (d) the Optional Protocol, 8 J. Int'l Comm'n Jurists 17 (1967); E. Schwelb, Human Rights and The International Community (1964); J. Carey, UN Protection of Civil and Political Rights 12–19 (1970); Newman, *Interpreting the Human Rights Clauses of the U.N. Charter*, 5 Revue des Droits de l'Homme 283, 285 n.7 (1972); Humphrey, *The International Law of Human Rights in the Middle Twentieth Century*, in The Present State of International Law and other Essays 75, 85 (M. Dos ed. 1973); E. Luard, The International Protection of Human Rights 53 (1967); T. Buergenthal & J. Torney, International Human Rights and International Education 163 (1976); Human Rights: A Compilation of International Instruments, U.N. Doc. ST/HR/1/Rev.1, at 1–17 (1978); American Association for the International Commission of Jurists, International Bill of Human Rights (undated); International Human Rights: Selected Declarations and Agreements, 94th Cong., 2d Sess. (1976).

[131] *See* Optional Protocol; E.S.C. Res. 1296, *supra* note 71; E.S.C. Res. 1503, *supra* note 80; E.S.C. Res. 728F, *supra* note 84; E.S.C. Res. 1235, *supra* note 84; Sub-Commision on Prevention of Discrimination and Protection of Minorities Res. 1 (XXIV), *supra* note 84.

[132] Handbook of Existing Rules Pertaining to Human Rights, Inter-American Commission on Human Rights, O.A.S. Doc. OEA/Ser.L/V/II.50, doc. 6 (1980).

[133] International Labour Office, ILO Principles, Standards and Procedures Concerning Freedom of Association (1978).

handling the complaint. Students should be given copies of the rules for each major international human rights procedure and be asked to evaluate the merits of each alternative procedure, from the standpoint of such considerations as (1) access of NGOs to the procedure, (2) prospects of success, (3) usefulness of the procedures for achieving concrete ends, (4) confidentiality and visibility problems, (5) procedural rights for complainants, etc. From this problem students should not only learn about applicable human rights doctrines and procedures, but should acquire a technique for construing U.N. resolutions.

B. MATERIALS TO BE DISTRIBUTED TO THE CLASS

For the classes on the work of NGOs in the implementation of human rights, students should receive copies of the following materials.

1. The Johnson Case (1 class—2 hours).
   a. The Johnson Hypothetical.
   b. The International Bill of Human Rights[134].
   c. The Lawyers Committee for International Human Rights communication on Argentina[135].
   d. State Department testimony of the protection of Americans abroad[136].
   e. 22 U.S.C. § 1732[137].
   f. *Redpath v. Kissinger*[138].
   g. Section I of this chapter.

2. NGO Communications Procedures (2 classes—4 hours).
   a. The Lawyers Committee for International Human Rights communication on Argentina[139].
   b. The International Bill of Human Rights[140].
   c. Principal U.N. resolutions establishing procedures to which NGOs may have access[141].
   d. Selections from the Inter-American Commission's Handbook of Existing Rules Pertaining to Human Rights[142].
   e. International labour procedures[143].

[134] *See* note 130 *supra*.
[135] *See* note 122 *supra*.
[136] *See* note 123 *supra*.
[137] *See* note 124 *supra* and accompanying text.
[138] 415 F. Supp. 566.
[139] *See* note 122 *supra*.
[140] *See* note 130 *supra*.
[141] *See* note 131 *supra*.
[142] *See* note 132 *supra*.
[143] *See* note 133 *supra*; notes 94–97 *supra* and accompanying text.

III. Syllabus

Section I of this chapter provides an overview of the ways in which NGOs contribute to the promotion and implementation of human rights. Section II proposes an activist and concrete approach to teaching how NGOs help to implement human rights. In addition to or instead of using the approach suggested by section II, the teacher might follow the outline of section I in lecture format and/or class discussion covering the following topics:

A. Structure and Characteristics of International Nongovernmental Organizations in the Human Rights Field.
   1. Consultative status with the U.N. Economic and Social Council, etc.
   2. NGO Secretariat.
   3. National sections or affiliates.
   4. Membership and constituency.
   5. Sources of financial support.

B. Relationship of NGO Characteristics to Selection of Targets for Fact-Finding and Action; How NGOs Select Their Areas of Concern.
   1. Availability of information.
   2. Financial implications.
   3. Political tendencies.
   4. Interests of constituency.

C. NGO Implementation of Human Rights.
   1. Effectiveness of NGO criticism and the sensitivity of governments.
   2. NGOs can often be more forthright and more impartial than governments and intergovernmental bodies.
   3. Aspects of the implementation process.
      a. Fact-finding.
      b. Diplomatic initiatives.
      c. Missions for fact-finding and direct contacts.
      d. Public reports.
      e. Statements to the United Nations and other international bodies.
      f. Petitions to international bodies.
         (i) E.S.C. Res. 1503.
         (ii) Optional Protocol.
         (iii) Other U.N. procedures.
         (iv) International Labour Organisations.
         (v) UNESCO.
         (vi) Inter-American Commission on Human Rights.

(vii) European Commission of Human Rights.

g. Relationship of financial aid and human rights.
h. NGOs as conciliators.
i. Relationship of international and national human rights efforts.

D. Contributions of NGOs to the Development and Elaboration of Human Rights Norms.
1. Contribution of NGOs to the U.N. Charter, Universal Declaration, Torture Declaration, etc.
2. Consultative status as a means of contributing to the formulation of norms.
3. Direct NGO assistance in drafting and pressure from NGO constituencies on government delegates.

IV. Minisyllabus

A. Structure and Characteristics of International NGOs in the Human Rights Field.

B. Relationship of NGO Characteristics to Selection of Targets for Fact-Finding and Action. How NGOs Select Their Areas of Concern.

C. NGO Implementation of Human Rights.
1. Effectiveness of NGO criticism and the sensitivity of governments.
2. NGOs can often be more forthright and more impartial than governments and intergovernmental bodies.
3. Aspects of the implementation process.
a. Fact-finding.
b. Diplomatic initiatives.
c. Missions for fact-finding and direct contacts.
d. Public reports.
e. Statements to the United Nations and other international bodies.
f. Petitions to international bodies.
g. Relationship of international and national human rights efforts.

D. Contributions of NGOs to the Development and Elaboration of Human Rights Norms.

V. Bibliography

B. Andemicael, Non-governmental Organizations in International Cooperation for Development (forthcoming).

—— & E. Rees, Non-governmental Organizations in Economic and Social Development (1975).

Archer, *Action by Unofficial Organizations on Human Rights*, in The International Protection of Human Rights 160 (E. Luard ed. 1967).

J. Bissel, The International Committee of the Red Cross and the Protection of Human Rights (1968).

E. Bock, Representation of Non-Governmental Organizations and the United Nations (1955).

Cassese, *How could Nongovernmental Organizations Use U.N. Bodies More Effectively?* 1 Universal Human Rights 73 (No. 4, 1979).

Clark, *The International League for Human Rights and South West Africa 1947–1957: The International Human Rights NGO as Catalyst in the International Legal Process*, 1 Human Rights Q. 101 (1981).

T. Claudius & F. Stepan, Amnesty International Portrait Einer Organization (1978).

E.S.C. Res. 1296, 44 U.N. ESCOR, Supp. (No. 1) 21, U.N. Doc. E/4548 (1968).

D. Forsythe, Humanitarian Politics, The International Committee of the Red Cross (1977).

—— *The Red Cross a Transnational Movement: Conserving and Changing the National–State System*, 30 Int'l Organization 607 (1976).

—— & Weisberg, *Human Rights Protection: A Research Agenda*, 1 Universal Human Rights 1, 15–19 (No. 4, 1979).

Golsong, *Les Organisations non gouvernmentales et le Conseil de l'Europe*, in Les organisations non gouvernmentales en Suisse 93 (1973).

Green, *NGOs*, in Human Rights and World Order 90 (A. Said ed. 1978).

Gunter, *Towards a Consultative Relationship Between the United Nations and Non-Governmental Organizations?* 10 Vand. J. Transnat'l L. 557 (1977).

Human Rights Internet Newsletter (1976–present).

J. Lador-Lederer, International Nongovernmental Organization and Economic Entities (1963).

E. Larson, A Flame in Barbed Wire: The Story of Amnesty International (1979).

Leary, *A New Role for Non-governmental Organizations: A Case Study of Non-Governmental Participation in the Development of International Norms on Torture*, in U.N. Law/Fundamental Rights 197 (A. Cassese ed. 1979).

—— *The Implementation of the Human Rights Provisions of the Helsinki Final Act: A Preliminary Assessment 1975–1977*, in Human Rights International Law and the Helsinki Accord, 111, 121–27 (T. Buergenthal ed. 1977).

N. MacDermot, Human Rights and the Churches (1976).

MacDermot, *The Work of the International Commission of Jurists*, 1 Index on Censorship 15 (1972).

A. Milani, Les Organisations Non Gouvernmentales des Nations Unies (1952).

J. Moreillon, Le Comité International de la Croix Rouge et la protection des détenus politiques (1973).

Note, *Role of Nongovernmental Organizations in Implementing Human Rights in Latin America*, 7 Ga. J. Int'l & Comp. L. 476 (1977).

R. Perruchoud, Les Résolutions des Conferences Internationales de La Croix-Rouge (1979).

Potter, Non-Governmental Organizations Viewed by a Political Scientist, 14 Int'l A. 403 (1962).

J. Power, Against Oblivion, Amnesty International's Fight for Human Rights (1981).

Prasad, *The Role of Non-Governmental Organizations in the New United Nations Procedures for Human Rights Complaints*, 5 Denver J. Int'l L. & Pol'y 441 (1975).

Rees, *Exercises in Private Diplomacy*, in Unofficial Diplomats 111 (M. Berman & J. Johnson eds. 1977).

D. Robins, United States Non-Governmental Organizations and the Educational Campaign from Dumbarton Oaks, 1944 Through the San Francisco Conference, 1945 (1960).

Rodley, *Monitoring Human Rights by the U.N. System and Non-governmental Organization*, in Human Rights and American Foreign Policy (D. Kommers & G. Loescher eds. 1979).

P. Rohn, Relations Between the Council of Europe and International Non-Governmental Organizations (1957).

Scoble & Weisberg, *Amnesty International: Evaluating Effectiveness in the Human Rights Area*, Intellect, Sept./Oct. 1976, at 79.

—— *The International League for Human Rights: The Strategy of a Human Rights NGO*, 7 Ga. J. Int'l & Comp. L. 289 (1977).

—— *Human Rights and Amnesty International*, 413 Annals 11 (1974).

—— *Human Rights NGOs: Notes Toward Comparative Analysis*, 9 Revue des Droits de L'Homme 611 (1976).

Sheperd, *Human Rights Theory and NGO Practice: Where Do We Go From Here*, in Global Human Rights (V. Nanda ed. 1981).

Shestack, *Sisyphus Endures: The International Human Rights NGO*, 24 N.Y.L.S. L. Rev. 89 (1978).
B. Stosic, Les Organisations non gouvernmentales et les Nations Unies (1964).
D. Tansley, Final Report: An Agenda for the Red Cross (1975).
United Nations, List of Non-Governmental Organizations in Consultative Status with the Economic and Social Council, pts. I & II (mimeo 1978).
Vincent-Daviss, *Human Rights Law: A Research Guide to the Literature—Part I: International Law and the United Nations*, 14 N.Y.J. Int'l L. & Politics 209, 313–19 (1980).
Weissbrodt, *International Trial Observers*, 18 Stanford J. Int'l L. 27 (1982).
—— *Strategies for the Selection and Pursuit of International Human Rights Objectives*, 8 Yale J. World Public Order 301 (1982).
—— *Deciding United States Policy in Regard to International Human Rights: The Role of Interest Groups*, in The Dynamics of Human Rights in U.S. Foreign Policy 229 (N. Hevener ed. 1981).
—— *The Role of International Nongovernmental Organizations in the Implementation of Human Rights*, 12 Tex J. Int'l L. 293 (1977).
—— & McCarthy, *Fact-finding by Non-governmental Human Rights Organizations*, 22 Va. J. Int'l L. 1 (1981).
L. White, International Non-Governmental Organizations: Their Purposes, Methods and Accomplishments (1968).

VI. Minibibliography

Weissbrodt, *The Contribution of International Nongovernmental Organizations to the Protection of Human Rights*, in this volume.
Leary, *A New Role for Nongovernmental Organizations: A Case Study of Nongovernmental Participation in the Development of International Norms on Torture*, in U.N. Law/Fundamental Rights 197 (A. Cassese ed. 1979).
Cassese, *How Could Nongovernmental Organizations Use U.N. Bodies More Effectively?*, 1 Universal Human Rights 73 (No. 4, 1979).
E.S.C. Res. 1296, 44 U.N. ESCOR Supp. (No. 1) 21, U.N. Doc. E/4548 (1968).
Shestack, *Sisyphus Endures: The International Human Rights NGO*, 24 N.Y.L.S. L. Rev. 89 (1978).

Part III: Regional Protection of Human Rights

Chapter 12

The Inter-American System for the Protection of Human Rights*[1]

Thomas Buergenthal

I. Legal and Policy Considerations

The inter-American system for the protection of human rights has two distinct legal sources, giving rise to a dual institutional structure of protection.[2] One has evolved directly from the Charter of the Organization of American States; the other was created by the American Convention on Human Rights. The two overlap to a certain extent and share various institutions. The Inter-American Commission on Human Rights, for example, is an organ both of the Charter-based regime and of the one derived from the American Convention. At times both regimes are applicable to one and the same case, strengthening the institutional pressures that can be brought to bear on governments charged with violating human rights.

To understand how the inter-American system for the protection of human rights functions, one has to have a very clear conception of the legal and political evolution of these two regimes. Here we shall therefore explore the manner in which these regimes have evolved, their practice, and how they interact.

A. THE AMERICAN CONVENTION ON HUMAN RIGHTS

1. *In General*

The American Convention on Human Rights[3] was adopted in 1969

[1] This study was completed in 1981.

[2] On the inter-American system for the protection of human rights, *see generally* Gros Espiell, *L'Organisation des Etats Américains*, in Les Dimensions Internationales des Droits de l'Homme 600 (K. Vasak ed. 1978); Buergenthal, *The Revised OAS Charter and the Protection of Human Rights*, 69 Am. J. Int'l L. 828 (1975) [hereinafter cited as *Revised OAS Charter*]; R. Goldman, The Protection of Human Rights in the Americas: Past, Present and Future (5 N.Y.U. Center for International Studies Policy Papers No. 2 1972). *See also* L. Sohn & T. Buergenthal, International Protection of Human Rights, ch. 8 (1973) [hereinafter cited as Sohn & Buergenthal], which contains extensive bibliographic references and primary source materials bearing on this subject.

[3] For the legislative history of the American Convention on Human Rights, *see* Conferencia Especializada Interamericana Sobre Derechos Humanos, San José, Costa Rica, 7–22 de noviembre 1969, Actas y Documentos, O.A.S. Doc. OEA/Ser. K/XVI/1.2 (1973) [hereinafter cited as Conferencia Especializada]. Additional documents and draft texts bearing on the drafting history of the American Convention can be found in the first three volumes of the

at an inter-governmental conference convened by the Organization of American States (O.A.S.). The meeting took place in San José, Costa Rica, which explains why the American Convention is also known as the 'Pact of San José, Costa Rica'. The American Convention entered into force in July 1978, after the eleventh instrument of ratification had been deposited.[4] Thereafter four more O.A.S. member states ratified. By 1981, the following states had become parties to the American Convention: Bolivia, Colombia, Costa Rica, Dominican Republic, Ecuador, El Salvador, Grenada, Guatemala, Haiti, Honduras, Jamaica, Nicaragua, Panama, Peru, and Venezuela.

Only O.A.S. member states have the right to adhere to the American Convention,[5] and barely a majority of them has done so thus far. All major O.A.S. powers—United States, Mexico, Brazil, and Argentina—are absent from the list. So too are Chile, Paraguay, and Uruguay, as well as Barbados, Trinidad and Tobago, Surinam, Dominica, and St. Lucia. The United States signed the American Convention and President Carter transmitted it to the Senate for its advice and consent to ratification,[6] but the Senate has not as yet acted on the request. If the United States ratifies the American Convention, it will join Jamaica as the only common law country to have done so. The legal systems of the other states parties adhere to the Spanish civil law tradition, although it appears that Barbados, another common law country which has already signed the American Convention, will ratify in the very near future. For the time being, the smaller and medium-sized Latin American states predominate among the parties to the American Con-

Inter-American Yearbook of Human Rights, published by the Inter-American Commission on Human Rights. The three volumes cover the period from 1960 to 1970 inclusive.

For the American Convention, O.A.S. T.S. No. 36, and other major O.A.S. human rights texts, see the O.A.S. Handbook of Existing Rules Pertaining to Human Rights [hereinafter cited as Handbook], published and annually updated by the Inter-American Commission on Human Rights. All references in this chapter are to the July 1980 edition of the Handbook. The American Convention and other O.A.S. human rights documents are also reproduced in L. Sohn & T. Buergenthal, Basic Documents on International Protection of Human Rights (1973) [hereinafter cited as Basic Documents].

On the American Convention generally, *see* Fox, *The American Convention on Human Rights and Prospects for United States Ratification*, 3 Human Rights 243 (1973) [hereinafter cited as Fox]; A. Robertson, Human Rights in the World 122–39 (1972) [hereinafter cited as Robertson]; Thomas & Thomas, *Human Rights and the Organization of American States*, 12 Santa Clara Law. 319, 349–74 (1972); Buergenthal, *The American Convention on Human Rights: Illusions and Hopes*, 21 Buffalo L. Rev. 121 (1971) [hereinafter cited as Buergenthal].

[4] See American Convention, art. 74(2).

[5] *Id.* art. 74(1).

[6] President Carter transmitted the American Convention to the U.S. Senate together with other human rights treaties. *See* Message from the President of the United States Transmitting Four Treaties Pertaining to Human Rights, S. Exec. Doc. C, D, E and F, 95th Cong., 2d Sess. (1978) [hereinafter cited as President's Message]. *See also International Human Rights Treaties: Hearings before the Comm. on Foreign Relations*, 96th Cong., 1st Sess. (1979).

vention. Within that group, Costa Rica, Venezuela, and Ecuador provide strong pro-human rights leadership.

The American Convention is patterned on the European Convention of Human Rights.[7] This is true, in particular, of the American Convention's institutional framework which is quite similar to its European counterpart.[8] But the American Convention also drew heavily on the American Declaration of the Rights and Duties of Man, adopted on 2 May 1948,[9] and on the International Covenant on Civil and Political Rights,[10] especially in formulating the catalog of rights that the American Convention incorporates.[11]

The American Convention is longer than most international human rights instruments. It contains eighty-two articles and codifies more than two dozen distinct rights, including the right to juridical personality, to life, to humane treatment, to personal liberty, to a fair trial, to privacy, to a name, to nationality, to participation in government, to equal protection of the law, and to judicial protection. The American Convention outlaws slavery; it proclaims freedom of conscience, religion, thought, and expression, as well as freedom of association, movement, and residence, besides prohibiting the application of *ex post facto* laws and penalties.

The states parties to the American Convention undertake 'to respect' and 'to ensure' the 'free and full exercise' of these rights 'to all persons subject to their jurisdiction'.[12] The American Convention defines 'person' as 'every human being',[13] which indicates that corporations and other legal persons are not protected as such. But to the extent that an injury to a corporation or association violates an individual's rights under the American Convention, it can be assumed to give rise to a cause of action under it. The outlawing of a labour union, for example, may amount to a denial of the right to freedom of association enjoyed by the union members. The union as such, as distinguished from the injured individual, does not, however, enjoy the protection of the American Convention.

The states parties to the American Convention have an obligation not only 'to respect' the rights guaranteed in the Convention, but also

[7] [European] Convention on Human Rights and Fundamental Freedoms, 213 U.N.T.S. 221, *reprinted in* Basic Documents on Human Rights (2d ed. I. Brownlie 1981) [hereinafter cited as Brownlie].

[8] *See* Buergenthal, *supra* note 2, at 122; Robertson, *supra* note 2, at 126–36.

[9] For the text of the American Declaration, *see* Basic Documents, *supra* note 3, at 187; Handbook, *supra* note 3, at 17.

[10] G.A. Res. 2200, 21 U.N. GAOR, Supp. (No. 16) 52, U.N. Doc. A/6316 (1966).

[11] Dunshee de Abranches, *Comparative Study of the United Nations Covenants on [Human Rights] and the Draft Inter-American Convention on Human Rights*, [1968] Inter-American Y.B. of Human Rights 169.

[12] American Convention, art. 1(1).

[13] *Id.* art. 1(2).

'to ensure' the free and full exercise of those rights.[14] A government consequently has both positive and negative duties under the American Convention. On the one hand, it has the obligation not to violate an individual's rights; for example, it has a duty not to torture an individual or to deprive him or her of a fair trial. But the state's obligation goes beyond this negative duty, and may require the adoption of affirmative measures necessarv and reasonable under the circumstances 'to ensure' the full enjoyment of the rights the American Convention guarantees. Thus, for example, a government of a country in which individuals 'disappear' on a massive scale might be deemed to violate article 7(1) of the American Convention,[15] even if it cannot be shown that its agents are responsible for the disappearances, provided the government is able but fails to take measures reasonably calculated to protect individuals against such lawlessness.

The catalog of rights which the American Convention proclaims is longer than that of the European Convention, and many of its provisions establish more advanced and enlightened guarantees than does its European counterpart, or for that matter, the Political Covenant.[16] But some of the provisions of the American Convention are so advanced that it may be doubted whether there is a country in the Americas that is in full compliance with all of them. This fact has not prevented the American Convention from obtaining the necessary number of ratifications to bring it into force. Most of these ratifications were unaccompanied by any reservations,[17] notwithstanding the fact that the *de jure* and *de facto* conditions in at least some of the ratifying countries should have prompted a larger number of reservations.

2. *Some Problems of Interpretation*

a. *The Self-Executing Character of the American Convention.* A number of provisions of the American Convention have a direct bearing on the manner in which this treaty will be applied on the domestic legal plane of the states that have ratified it. One of these provisions is article 2, which reads as follows:

> Where the exercise of any of the rights or freedoms referred to in Article 1 is not already ensured by legislative or other provisions, the States Parties

[14] *Id.* art. 1(1).

[15] Art. 7(1) provides: 'Every person has the right to personal liberty and security.'

[16] *See, e.g., id.* arts. 4, 5, 17(5), & 23.

[17] The only dramatic exception is the reservation of El Salvador, which declares that its ratification is 'with the reservation that such ratification is understood [to be] without prejudice to those provisions of the Convention that might be in conflict with express precepts of the Political Constitution of the Republic.' For the texts of the instruments of ratification, *see* Handbook, *supra* note 3, at 59.

undertake to adopt, in accordance with their constitutional processes and the provisions of this Convention, such legislative or other measures as may be necessary to give effect to those rights or freedoms.

Treaty provisions such as article 2 can have very important domestic legal consequences in countries which apply the so-called self-executing-treaty doctrine. In these countries, the self-executing provisions of a duly ratified treaty have the status of directly applicable domestic law and, as such, supersede prior conflicting domestic law. Non-self-executing treaty provisions, on the other hand, require implementing legislation to create directly enforceable rights in national courts. It follows that if a human rights treaty is characterized as non-self-executing, individuals will not be able to rely on it in domestic courts to override conflicting national laws, which greatly reduces the utility of such treaties.[18] While the test for judging whether a treaty provision is self-executing or not varies somewhat from country to country, depending upon national constitutional traditions and peculiarities,[19] the courts in some countries proceed on the assumption that a treaty, containing a provision such as article 2 of the American Convention, was designed to be non-self-executing. (This is the case, for example, under the law of the United States.)[20] And although this presumption appears to be rebuttable, some national courts view provisions of this type as proof that the drafters, by calling for national implementing legislation, intended the treaty to be non-self-executing. It is therefore useful to review the history of article 2 to determine what function it was designed to perform.

No comparable clause appeared in the draft text of the American Convention which was used as a working document of the San José conference.[21] The addition of this provision, which draws on the language of article 2(2) of the Political Covenant, was proposed by the Chilean delegation to the San José conference.[22] The Chileans favored this clause because they thought it important that the treaty contain an express statement that all states parties had the obligation to adopt whatever domestic laws were necessary to implement fully the rights proclaimed in the American Convention. The opposing argument

[18] *See, e.g.*, Sei Fujii v. State, 38 Cal. 2d 713, 242 P.2d 617 (1952). *See generally*, R. Lillich & F. Newman, International Human Rights: Problems of Law and Policy 68–122 (1979).

[19] Schlüter, *The Domestic Status of the Human Rights Clauses of the United Nations Charter*, 61 Cal. L. Rev. 110 (1973); Buergenthal, *The Domestic Status of the European Convention on Human Rights: A Second Look*, 7 J. Int'l Comm'n Jurists 55 (1966).

[20] *See* Fox, *supra* note 3, at 259–60; Restatement (Second) of Foreign Relations Law § 141 (1965). This matter is more recently dealt with in Restatement of Foreign Relations Law (Rev.) § 131, Comments h & i, at 46–48 (Tent. Draft No. 1, 1980).

[21] The draft Convention is reproduced in [1968] Y.B. Inter-American Comm'n on Human Rights 389.

[22] *See* Conferencia Especializada, *supra* note 3, at 38.

advanced by some delegates, who submitted that the provision was not necessary because under international law all parties to a treaty already had the obligation to take whatever domestic legal action was needed to comply with the treaty, did not persuade the Chileans to withdraw their amendment. In responding to the contention that nothing need be said about implementation on the domestic plane since in many Latin American countries duly ratified treaties acquired the status of domestic law, Chilean delegates pointed to article 18 of the Convention, which reads as follows:

> Every person has the right to a given name and to the surnames of his parents or that of one of them. The law shall regulate the manner in which this right shall be ensured for all, by the use of assumed names if necessary.

It was obvious, the Chileans contended, that even if article 18 as such was deemed to be domestic law, the 'law' referred to in it had to be enacted separately in all those countries that did not already have it. An express stipulation in article 2 that such a 'law' had to be enacted thus created an unambiguous legal obligation to do so.[23]

The soundness of the arguments advanced by the Chileans is less important than the fact that in moving the text of article 2 it was never their aim to make the American Convention non-self-executing. This fact was recognized by the U.S. delegation, which supported the inclusion of article 2, but for the opposite reason, namely, to make the American Convention non-self-executing under U.S. law.

> The United States agrees that this article should be included in the . . . Convention since it helps to clarify the legal effect of ratification on the domestic law of the respective parties. The article is sufficiently flexible so that each country can best implement the treaty consistent with its domestic practice. Some countries may choose to make the articles of the treaty directly effective as domestic law and this article would permit them to do so. The comments made by Chile suggest that its own practice may vary depending on the text of each article. Others may prefer to rely solely on domestic law to implement the articles of the treaty. In the U.S. we would interpret this article as authorizing us to follow the last course in these cases of matters within Part I, the substantive portions, of the draft convention. That will permit us to refer, where appropriate, to our Constitution, to our domestic legislation already in existence, to our court decisions and to our administrative practice as carrying out the obligations of the Convention. It will also mean that we will be able to draft any new legislation that is needed in terms that can be readily and clearly assimilated into our domestic codes. In other words, it is not the intention of the U.S. to interpret the articles of the treaty in Part I as being self-executing.[24]

[23] *Id.*
[24] *Id.* at 146–47.

The U.S. statement recognized that article 2 left the states parties free to implement the American Convention on the domestic plane as they saw fit, either by treating it as self-executing or not. The United States thus acknowledged that it was not the purpose of article 2 to make the American Convention non-self-executing. At the same time, of course, the delegation went on record that the United States would treat the American Convention as being non-self-executing. Article 2 neither compels nor prohibits this result, and the U.S. statement acknowledged as much. Given the history of article 2, a national judge sitting in a country that adheres to the self-executing-treaty doctrine might well conclude that the presence of article 2 in the American Convention does not *ipso facto* make the treaty as a whole non-self-executing.[25] But such a ruling would not necessarily foreclose a holding in one or another country finding individual provisions of the American Convention to be non-self-executing in those instances where they cannot be applied by the courts without some additional legislative action.[26]

b. *The Federal-State Clause.* Article 28 affects the domestic application of the American Convention in those states that have a federal system of government. Known as the 'federal clause', article 28 reads in part as follows:

> 1. Where a State Party is constituted as a federal state, the national government of such State Party shall implement all the provisions of the Convention over whose subject matter it exercises legislative and judicial jurisdiction.
> 2. With respect to the provisions over whose subject matter the constituent units of the federal state have jurisdiction, the national government shall immediately take suitable measures, in accordance with its constitution and its laws, to the end that the competent authorities of the constituent units may adopt appropriate provisions for the fulfillment of this Convention.

Article 28 is an anachronism which harks back to the days of the League of Nations. Few modern international human rights instru-

[25] A. U.S. judge could also reasonably reach this conclusion, although he or she would next have to decide what effect to give to the statement of the U.S. delegation 'that it is not the intention of the U.S. to interpret the articles of the treaty in Part I as being self-executing'. *Id.* the answer to this question is not easy because there is no settled U.S. law on the extent to which the courts are bound by such a statement. *Compare* Power Authority v. Federal Power Commission, 247 F.2d 538 (D.C. Cir. 1957) *with* Charlton v. Kelley, 229 U.S. 447 (1913). A somewhat different question would arise if the U.S. were to ratify the American Convention with the specific declaration that Pres. Jimmy Carter proposed when he transmitted the treaty to the Senate. The proposed declaration reads as follows: 'The United States declares that the provisions of Articles 1 through 32 of this Convention are not self-executing.' President's Message, *supra* note 6, at XVIII.

[26] Art. 18 of the American Convention would be an example of a non-self-executing provision in the sense that it would require the adoption of the 'law' referred to in it before it could be applied in full.

ments contain comparable clauses. The Political Covenant adopts precisely the opposite principle by declaring in article 50 that '[t]he provisions of the present Covenant shall extend to all parts of federal states without any limitations or exceptions'. The European Convention of Human Rights, the Convention on the Prevention and Punishment of the Crime of Genocide,[27] and the International Convention on the Elimination of All Forms of Racial Discrimination[28] contain no federal clause; they apply with equal force in unitary as in federal states. Moreover, many states which have a strong federal tradition, including Canada and the Federal Republic of Germany, have been able to adhere to these instruments without federal-state reservations.

Article 28 of the American Convention found its way into the treaty because the United States insisted on it.[29] In explaining the meaning of this provision, the U.S. delegation to the San José conference reported to the Secretary of State that

> The present Convention . . . does not obligate the U.S. Government to *exercise* jurisdiction over subject matter over which it would not exercise authority in the absence of the Convention. The U.S. is merely obligated to take suitable measures to the end that state and local authorities may adopt provisions for the fulfillment of this Convention. Suitable measures could consist of recommendations to the states, for example. The determination of what measures are suitable is a matter of internal decision. The Convention does not require enactment of legislation bringing new subject matter within the federal ambit.[30]

The U.S. delegation proposed article 28 in order to ensure that a federal state not be deemed to have assumed any international obligation to prevent violations of the American Convention involving rights or acts within the jurisdiction of any governmental entity other than the federal government. Moreover, by limiting the international obligations of the federal state to subject matter over which it *exercises* jurisdiction, the United States sought to indicate that such a state has no obligation under the American Convention in situations where the federal government, although having jurisdiction, has not previously exercised it.

Put in the context of U.S. constitutional law, the delegation believed that article 28 prevented the application of the *Missouri v. Holland*[31] principle to the American Convention. Under *Missouri v. Holland*, a

[27] 78 U.N.T.S. 277, *reprinted in* Brownlie, *supra* note 7, at 31.

[28] 660 U.N.T.S. 195, *reprinted in* Brownlie, *supra* note 7, at 150.

[29] *See* Report of the United States Delegation to the Inter-American Conference on Protection of Human Rights, San José, Costa Rica, November 9–22, 1969, at 37 (1970) [hereinafter cited as Report of the U.S. Delegation]; Fox, *supra* note 3, at 250–54.

[30] Report of the U.S. Delegation, *supra* note 29, at 37 (emphasis in original).

[31] 252 U.S. 416 (1920).

treaty concluded by the United States that is otherwise constitutional[32] gives the federal government jurisdiction over the subject matter of the treaty even if such jurisdiction previously resided in the states of the Union. Thus, in the absence of article 28, if the United States was to ratify the American Convention, the federal government would have jurisdiction under *Missouri v. Holland* to enforce the American Convention throughout the country, notwithstanding that prior to such ratification some or all subjects dealt with by the treaty were within the jurisdiction of the several states.[33] But if article 28 accomplishes the result sought by the U.S. delegation, U.S. ratification of the American Convention will not affect a shift in jurisdiction from the states to the federal government. All in all, given the purpose attributed to it by the U.S. delegation, article 28 allows federal states to ratify the American Convention without making its provisions applicable within its entire territory.

The ostensible simplicity of article 28 hides the legal complexities inherent in it. It raises difficult international and domestic law issues not fully perceived by its drafters. Whether a federal state, for example, 'exercises legislative and judicial jurisdiction' over a specific subject matter is an international law issue to the extent that it involves an interpretation of a treaty. But it can be decided in a given case only by reference to the domestic law of a particular country. This conclusion suggests the question whether and to what extent the Inter-American Court of Human Rights, which has jurisdiction to interpret and apply the American Convention,[34] is empowered to verify a defense of a state party based on article 28. Suppose, for example, that a state defends its failure to enforce the American Convention on the ground that under its domestic law it lacks jurisdiction over a specific subject matter at issue. Is the Inter-American Court in such a case bound by the *ipse dixit* of the federal authority or is it free to examine the relevant domestic law and practice and determine for itself what the domestic law provides on the subject? To illustrate the problem, let us assume that in a case involving State *X*, counsel for *X* asserts that the subject matter of the claim is one over which the federal government exercises neither legislative nor judicial jurisdiction. Assume further that the complainant points to a decision of the Supreme Court of *X*, rendered in another case a year earlier, that plainly contradicts the view of counsel for *X*. Is the Inter-American Court free to consider the effect of the Supreme Court decision and, if so, may it receive expert evidence on the subject, or is it bound by *X*'s statement as to what the law is?

[32] *See* Reid v. Covert, 354 U.S. 1 (1957).

[33] *See generally*, L. Henkin, Foreign Affairs and the Constitution 144–48 (1972). *Cf.* National League of Cities v. Usery, 426 U.S. 833 (1976).

[34] American Convention, art. 62(3).

The issues might be even more troublesome in a country which, in addition to being a federal state, determines that the Convention is non-self-executing. Here a domestic court might never get the opportunity to interpret article 28 or to apply it by reference to other provisions of the American Convention, making it more difficult for the international tribunal to ascertain what the relevant domestic law is. Sight must also not be lost of the fact that in some federal systems it is by no means easy, even as a matter of domestic law, to determine what constitutes an 'exercise of jurisdiction' or what is meant by 'subject matter' as that term is used in article 28.

c. *The Right of Derogation.* Problems relating to the domestic application of the American Convention are also likely to arise from the application of article 27, which recognizes that in certain circumstances the state parties may suspend some of the rights that the treaty proclaims. Article 27 provides:

> 1. In time of war, public danger, or other emergency that threatens the independence or security of a State Party, it may take measures derogating from its obligations under the present Convention to the extent and for the period of time strictly required by the exigencies of the situation, provided that such measures are not inconsistent with its other obligations under international law and do not involve discrimination on the ground of race, color, sex, language, religion, or social origin.
>
> 2. The foregoing provision does not authorize any suspension of the following articles: Article 3 (Right to Juridical Personality), Article 4 (Right to Life), Article 5 (Right to Humane Treatment), Article 6 (Freedom from Slavery), Article 9 (Freedom from *Ex Post Facto* Laws), Article 12 (Freedom of Conscience and Religion), Article 17 (Rights of the Family), Article 18 (Right to a Name), Article 19 (Rights of the Child), Article 20 (Right to Nationality), and Article 23 (Right to Participate in Government), or of the judicial guarantees essential for the protection of such rights.
>
> 3. Any State Party availing itself of the right of suspension shall immediately inform the other State Parties, through the Secretary General of the Organization of American States, of the provisions the application of which it has suspended, the reasons that gave rise to the suspension, and the date set for the termination of such suspension.

Although this provision resembles the derogation clauses found in the European Convention and the Political Covenant,[35] it differs from them in a number of important respects. The situations which justify derogation under the American Convention are 'war, public danger,

[35] *See* Higgins, *Derogation under Human Rights Treaties*, 48 Brit. Y.B. Int'l L. 281 (1975–76). *See also* Buergenthal, *International and Regional Human Rights Law and Institutions: Some Examples of their Interaction*, 12 Tex. Int'l L.J. 321, 324–25 (1977); Eissen, *The European Convention on Human Rights and the United Nations Covenant on Civil and Political Rights: Problems of Coexistence*, 22 Buffalo L. Rev. 181, 211 (1972) [hereinafter cited as Eissen].

or other emergency that threatens the independence or security of a State Party'. This language differs from that of article 4 of the Political Covenant which speaks of a 'time of public emergency which threatens the life of the nation'. Article 15 of the European Convention allows derogations during a 'time of war or other public emergency threatening the life of the nation'. The tests of the European Convention and the Political Covenant appear to be more stringent than that of the American Convention, which suggests that the emergency need merely threaten the 'independence or security of a State Party' to justify the derogation.

The concept of a 'threat to the security' of a state, besides being vague and subject to abuse,[36] embraces threats that are less serious than threats 'to the life of the nation' or its 'independence'. Here it is important to remember, however, that this provision, like all other provisions of the American Convention, must be interpreted consistent with the provisions of article 29, which provides:

> No provision of this Convention shall be interpreted as:
> a. permitting any State Party, group, or person to suppress the enjoyment or exercise of the rights and freedoms recognized in this Convention or to restrict them to a greater extent than is provided for herein;
> b. restricting the enjoyment or exercise of any right or freedom recognized by virtue of the laws of any State Party or by virtue of another convention to which one of the said states is a party;
> c. precluding other rights or guarantees that are inherent in the human personality or derived from representative democracy as a form of government; or
> d. excluding or limiting the effect that the American Declaration of the Rights and Duties of Man and other international acts of the same nature may have.

Of some relevance too is article 30 of the American Convention, which stipulates that '[t]he restrictions that, pursuant to this Convention, may be placed on the enjoyment or exercise of the rights or freedoms recognized herein may not be applied except in accordance with laws enacted for reasons of general interest and in accordance with the purpose for which such restrictions have been established'. Moreover, in the first preambular paragraph of the American Convention, the state parties reaffirm 'their intention to consolidate in this hemisphere, within the framework of democratic institutions, a system of personal liberty and social justice based on respect for the essential rights of man'. The concept, 'threat to the security of a state', found in article 27 of the American Convention, will therefore have to be interpreted by

[36] *See generally* H. Montealegre, La Seguridad del Estado y los Derechos Humanos (1979) [hereinafter cited as Montealegre].

reference to the values and criteria that the aforementioned provisions articulate.

Although article 27(1) appears to make derogation somewhat easier than do the corresponding provisions of other international instruments, the catalog of rights from which no derogation is permitted is much longer under article 27(2) than under the European Convention or the Political Covenant. The European Convention lists only four non-derogable rights—the right to life, freedom from torture, and the prohibitions of slavery and *ex post facto* laws.[37] The Political Covenant proclaims seven non-derogable rights: the four enumerated by the European Convention, plus the prohibition against imprisonment for nonfulfillment of contractual obligation, the right to be recognized as a person before the law, and freedom of thought, conscience, and religion.[38] By contrast, under the American Convention no derogation is permitted from eleven specific rights, including the right to nationality and the right to participate in government. The 'judicial guarantees essential for the protection' of these rights are also not derogable under article 27(2).

It might be argued that the 'long list' approach of the American Convention is unwise, because governments are unlikely to recognize all of these rights in times of national emergency. The American Convention, however, permits derogation in emergencies which are much less serious than those envisaged by the other instruments, and to that extent an expanded list of non-derogable rights is more justified. Given the political realities of the Western Hemisphere with its frequent national emergencies and states of siege,[39] it is not all that unreasonable to prohibit derogation from the right to participate in government, for example, whose suspensions for long periods of time have tended to make it easier for dictatorial regimes to remain in power.

The differences between the derogation provisions of the Political Covenant and the American Convention have some very interesting consequences. A state which is a party to both the American Convention and the Political Covenant must take account of the fact that these instruments permit a state party to take measures derogating from its obligations, provided that such measures are not inconsistent with its other obligations under international law.[40] Because of this proviso, a state which has adhered to both instruments would violate its obliga-

[37] European Convention, art. 15(2).

[38] Political Covenant, art. 4(2).

[39] *See*, *e.g.*, Inter-American Commission on Human Rights [hereinafter cited as IACHR]. Report on the Situation of Human Rights in Nicaragua, O.A.S. Doc. OEA/Ser. L/V/II.45, doc. 16, Rev. 1, at 29–30 (1978); Montealegre, *supra* note 36, at 3.

[40] American Convention, art. 27(1); Political Covenant, art. 4(1).

tions under the Political Covenant if, in a public emergency threatening the nation, it took measures suspending those rights that are non-derogable under article 27(2) of the American Convention, even though the rights in question are otherwise subject to derogation under the Political Covenant. To the extent that the suspension of these rights would violate the American Convention, it would be inconsistent with the state's obligations under international law.

If this principle applies also to the test for determining the existence of the emergency that justifies the derogation, which is a more difficult question, a state party to the American Convention might be deemed to violate its obligations under the Political Covenant if, in a derogation based on article 27(1) of the American Convention and validly founded on a threat 'to the security' of the state, it took measures suspending any of the rights that the Political Covenant guarantees. Since a threat to a state's 'security' is not a valid ground for derogation under the Covenant, its validity under the American Convention might not be legitimate under the law of the Political Covenant.

B. THE CONVENTION INSTITUTIONS

The American Convention establishes two organs to safeguard its implementation: the Inter-American Commission on Human Rights and the Inter-American Court of Human Rights. Each of these organs consists of seven experts, elected in their individual capacities and not as government representatives. The members of the Inter-American Commission are elected by the O.A.S. General Assembly with all O.A.S. member states, whether or not they are parties to the American Convention, participating in the nomination process and taking part in the vote.[41] The judges of the Inter-American Court, on the other hand, may only be nominated and elected by the states parties to the American Convention.[42] However, the judges need not be nationals of state parties. The only condition relating to nationality—and it applies equally to the members of the Inter-American Commission as to the judges—is that they must be nationals of an O.A.S. member state.[43]

The difference in the election process of the members of the Inter-American Commission and the judges may be attributed, in part at least, to the dual functions that the Commission performs. As will be

[41] The members of the Inter-American Commission are elected from a list of candidates nominated by the O.A.S. member states, with each state being allowed to nominate no more than three candidates. A state nominating three individuals must propose at least one candidate who is not its own national. American Convention, art. 36.

[42] The election of the judges must also take place in the O.A.S. General Assembly, but only the states parties to the American Convention may participate in the vote. American Convention, art. 53.

[43] *Id.* arts. 52(1) & 36(2). Of the judges now serving on the Inter-American Court, one of them—the present author—is a U.S. national who was nominated by Costa Rica.

explained in greater detail later, the Inter-American Commission is not only an institution created by the American Convention, it is also an O.A.S. Charter organ[44] with jurisdiction over all O.A.S. member states. The Inter-American Court, on the other hand, is not expressly mentioned in the O.A.S. Charter, and the functions assigned to it in relation to states not parties to the American Convention are much more limited than those of the Inter-American Commission.

The first elections of the members of the Inter-American Commission and the judges of the Inter-American Court took place in May 1979, almost a year after the entry into force of the American Convention. In the interim, the functions of the Commission were performed by its predecessor organ, the old Inter-American Commission on Human Rights, which had been established in 1960.[45] The Inter-American Court, an entirely new institution, was installed in June 1979.

1. *The Inter-American Commission on Human Rights*

a. *Its Functions.* Article 41 of the American Convention describes the functions of the Commission as follows:

> The main function of the Commission shall be to promote respect for and defense of human rights. In the exercise of its mandate, it shall have the following functions and powers:
>
> a. to develop an awareness of human rights among the peoples of America;
> b. to make recommendations to the governments of the member states, when it considers such action advisable, for the adoption of progressive measures in favor of human rights within the framework of their domestic law and constitutional provisions as well as appropriate measures to further the observance of those rights;
> c. to prepare such studies or reports as it considers advisable in the performance of its duties;
> d. to request the governments of the member states to supply it with information on the measures adopted by them in matters of human rights;
> e. to respond, through the General Secretariat of the Organization of American States, to inquiries made by the member states on matters related to human rights and, within the limits of its possibilities, to provide those states with the advisory services they request;

[44] *See* O.A.S. Charter, art. 51; Farer & Rowles, *The Inter-American Commission on Human Rights*, in J. Tuttle, International Human Rights Law and Practice 47 (1978) [hereinafter cited as Farer & Rowles].

[45] The authority of the Inter-American Commission to exercise the interim function was provided by a resolution of the O.A.S. Permanent Council, entitled 'Transition from the Present Inter-American Commission on Human Rights to the Commission Provided for in the American Convention on Human Rights.' Permanent Council Res. 253 (343/78), O.A.S. Doc. OEA/Ser.G (Sept. 20, 1978). For the debate on this resolution, *see* O.A.S. Doc. OEA/Ser.G., CP/ACTA 343/78 (Sept. 20, 1978).

f. to take action on petitions and other communications pursuant to its authority under the provisions of Articles 44 through 51 of this Convention; and
g. to submit an annual report to the General Assembly of the Organization of American States.

The first sentence of the Spanish text of this provision—the American Convention was drafted in Spanish—declares that the Inter-American Commission's main function is to promote 'la observancia y la defensa de los derechos humanos', which should have been translated as 'the observance and protection of human rights'. This is not only a more felicitous rendition of the Spanish text, it also corresponds to the English text of article 112 of the O.A.S. Charter whose Spanish version is identical to the Spanish text of article 41 of the American Convention.[46] It follows that the principal function of the Inter-American Commission is to 'promote the observance and protection' of human rights in the Americas.

In sub-paragraphs (a) through (g) of article 41, the American Convention assigns the Inter-American Commission a number of different tasks. First, article 41(a) gives the Commission very extensive promotional powers which, when supplemented by the authority granted in sub-paragraphs (c) and (e), require it to support hemisphere-wide education and research programs devoted to human rights. Secondly, the provisions of article 41(b), (c), (d), and (g), read together, empower the Inter-American Commission to take a variety of general and specific measures designed to prevent violations of human rights by any O.A.S. member state, whether or not it has ratified the American Convention. Such measures might include country studies, 'on-the-spot' investigations, and the dispatch of 'observer' missions. The exercise of these functions by the Inter-American Commission is not tied to the complaint machinery established by the American Convention, and consequently enables the Commission to act on its own motion without any specific request or petition. By giving it this power, the American Convention preserves for the Inter-American Commission the authority to perform the functions that the old Inter-American Commission on Human Rights exercised under articles 9 and 9 *bis* of its Statute[47] and to comply with its O.A.S. Charter mandate.[48] Finally, article 41(f) empowers the Commission to examine petitions and communications charging the states parties with violations of their obligations under the American Convention.

[46] Art. 112 of the O.A.S. Charter provides, in part, that 'there shall be an Inter-American Commission on Human Rights, whose principal function shall be to promote the observance and protection of human rights . . .'

[47] This topic is dealt with in section I.C. *infra*.

[48] *See* O.A.S. Charter, art. 112; section I.C. *infra*.

In performing this task, which will be described in detail in the next section, the Inter-American Commission exercises quasi-judicial functions similar to those of the European Commission of Human Rights.

In addition, the American Convention contains a very important grant of power spelled out in article 42, which stipulates:

> The States Parties shall transmit to the Commission a copy of each of the reports and studies that they submit annually to the Executive Committees of the Inter-American Economic and Social Council and the Inter-American Council for Education, Science, and Culture, in their respective fields, so that the Commission may watch over the promotion of the rights implicit in the economic, social, educational, scientific, and cultural standards set forth in the Charter of the Organization of American States as amended by the Protocol of Buenos Aires.

The O.A.S. Charter, as amended by the Protocol of Buenos Aires, proclaims a lengthy list of economic, social, and cultural principles.[49] By giving the Inter-American Commission a role in the implementation of these standards as they apply to the states parties to the American Convention, article 42 provides the legal foundation for an Inter-American system for the protection of economic, social, and cultural rights, which could have far-reaching consequences.[50] The Commission's new rules of procedure suggest that it is aware of these possibilities and that it intends to make use of its power in this area.[51]

b. *Individual and Inter-State Complaints.* The Inter-American Commission's power under article 41(f), which authorizes it to deal with complaints charging a state party with violations of human rights, differs in one important respect from the authority vested in other international human rights institutions. The American Convention stipulates that by becoming a party to it, a state has accepted *ipso facto* the jurisdiction of the Commission to deal with private complaints lodged against that state.[52] But the Inter-American Commission may only deal with so-called inter-state complaints—complaints filed by one state party against another—if both states, in addition to ratifying

[49] O.A.S. Charter, arts. 29–50.

[50] *See*, in this connection, the very interesting analysis of the Commision concerning the violation of economic and social rights in El Salvador. IACHR, Report on the Situation of Human Rights in El Salvador and Observations of the Government of El Salvador on the Report, O.A.S. Doc. OEA/Ser.P,AG/doc. 1086/79, at 162 (1979). Even though this report was prepared pursuant to the power the Inter-American Commission derives from the O.A.S. Charter, rather than from the American Convention, the analysis and approach is not likely to differ much in the future.

[51] *See* Regulations of the Inter-American Commission on Human Rights [hereinafter cited as Regulations], art. 60, *reprinted in* Handbook, *supra* note 3, at 117.

[52] American Convention, art. 44.

the American Convention, have made a further declaration recognizing the inter-state jurisdiction of the Commission.[53] The American Convention thus reverses the more traditional pattern utilized by the European Convention, for example, where the right of individual petition is optional[54] and the inter-state complaint procedure is mandatory.[55] The drafters of the American Convention apparently assumed that inter-state complaints might be used by some governments for political objectives or interventionist purposes, and that this risk existed to a much more limited extent with regard to private petitions. Whatever may be the soundness of these assumptions, it is undisputed that the availability of the right of private petition enhances the effectiveness of an international system for the protection of human rights. By enabling individuals to assert their own claims, the right of private petition makes the enforcement of human rights less dependent on the extraneous political considerations that tend to motivate governmental action and inaction.[56]

Unlike the European Convention, the American Convention does not provide that only victims of a violation may file private petitions.[57] It provides instead that:

> Any person or group of persons, or any nongovernmental entity legally recognized in one or more member states of the Organization, may lodge petitions with the Commission containing denunciations or complaints of violation of this Convention by a State Party.[58]

Moreover, although the states parties must recognize the jurisdiction of the Inter-American Commission to deal with inter-state communications before they may institute them, the states need not prove any special interest in the case to file it. They are consequently free to submit complaints alleging violations committed against their own nationals, against stateless persons, or against nationals of any other state.[59]

The admissibility of a petition is conditioned on (a) the exhaustion of domestic remedies 'in accordance with the generally recognized principles of international law',[60] and (b) the requirement that the

[53] *Id.* art. 45.

[54] European Convention, art. 25(1).

[55] *Id.* art. 24.

[56] On this subject generally, *see* Schwelb, *Book Review*, 1 Revue des Droits de l'Homme 626, 630 (1968).

[57] *Compare* European Convention, art. 25(1) *with* American Convention, art. 44.

[58] American Convention, art. 44.

[59] *See id.* art. 45(1). The same principle has been consistently adhered to under the European Convention. *See*, e.g., the case law reproduced in Sohn & Buergenthal, *supra* note 1, at 1054–62. The 'special interest' doctrine enunciated by the International Court of Justice in the South West Africa cases, [1966] I.C.J. 6, consequently does not apply to inter-state complaints filed under the American Convention or the European Convention.

[60] American Convention, art. 46(1)(a).

petition be submitted to the Inter-American Commission within a period of six months from the date on which the victim of the alleged violation was notified of the final domestic judgment in his or her case.[61] But these requirements do not prevent the admissibility of a petition whenever it can be shown that:

a. the domestic legislation of the state concerned does not afford due process of law for the protection of the right or rights that have allegedly been violated;
b. the party alleging violation of his rights has been denied access to the remedies under domestic law or has been prevented from exhausting them; or
c. there has been unwarranted delay in rendering a final judgment under the aforementioned remedies.[62]

The Commission's rules of procedure provide, moreover, that the respondent government has the burden of demonstrating the non-exhaustion of available domestic remedies if the complainant alleges that it was impossible to comply with the exhaustion requirement.[63]

Article 47(d) of the American Convention provides that the Commission shall 'consider inadmissible any petition or communication . . . [that] is substantially the same as one previously studied by the Commission or by another international organization.'[64] Article 46(1)(c) conditions the admissibility of all complaints on the requirement 'that the subject of the petition or communication is not pending in another international proceeding for settlement'. The Inter-American Commission has clarified these provisions in article 36 of its rules of procedure. The rules indicate that a case pending in another international organization will be deemed inadmissible by the Inter-American Commission only if the respondent state is a party to the other proceeding and if an effective remedy is there available to dispose of the specific claim that was submitted to the Commission. What constitutes an effective remedy will presumably be determined by reference to the American Convention.[65] Furthermore, before a complaint will be deemed inadmissible on the ground that it is 'the same as one previously studied . . . by another international organization', the Inter-American Commission must ascertain, first, whether the

[61] *Id.* art. 46(1)(b).

[62] *Id.* art. 46(2).

[63] Regulations, *supra* note 51, art. 34(3). This rule is inapplicable only when petitioner's contention is manifestly contradicted by the information contained in the petition itself. *Id.*

[64] The Spanish text of art. 47(d) speaks of any petition or communication previously 'examinada', indicating that the English 'examined' would have been a more appropriate rendition instead of the more ambiguous 'studied'.

[65] For the petition to be inadmissible it must also appear, *inter alia*, that the victim or someone authorized by him instituted the proceedings in the other organ. Regulations, *supra* note 51, art. 36(2).

case was in fact finally resolved and, secondly, whether the solution addressed the specific claim of the complaint and provided an effective remedy.[66]

Article 36 of the Inter-American Commission's rules of procedure thus indicates that the mere fact that a complaint is simultaneously submitted to it and to another international organ is not an absolute bar to its examination by the Commission; the latter will be able to deal with the case as soon as it is no longer pending elsewhere. An individual who has filed the same complaint with a number of international human rights organs might therefore be informed by the Inter-American Commission that the case will be ruled inadmissible unless the other complaints are withdrawn. In other words, we are here dealing with relative or conditional inadmissibility. By contrast, a case is absolutely inadmissible if it was previously fully and effectively resolved by another international organ. Note that here the Inter-American Commission, drawing on the universally accepted principles of *res judicata*, very wisely makes absolute inadmissibility dependent, among other considerations, on the existence of a final decision or resolution of the dispute.[67]

A complaint which is not inadmissible for one of the reasons mentioned above and which contains allegations stating a *prima facie* violation of the American Convention, will advance to the next or second stage of the Inter-American Commission's proceedings.[68] Here the Commission examines the petitioner's allegations, seeks information from the government concerned, investigates the facts, and holds hearings in which both the government and the petitioners may participate.[69] Although a complaint ruled admissible may at this stage still be rejected as 'inadmissible or out of order',[70] this ruling must be based on a finding by the Inter-American Commission that it would have been obliged to reject the complaint at the admissibility stage if the relevant facts had been known to it at that time. If after investigating a complaint, the Commission concludes, for example, that the petitioner failed to exhaust all available domestic remedies, it has the power to rule the petition inadmissible. The same result would be indicated if the evidence deduced in the case left no reasonable doubt whatsoever that the complaint was without merit.[71] In other words, the authority

[66] *Id.* arts 36(1)(a) & 36(2)(a).

[67] On this problem generally, *see* Tardu, *The Protocol to the United Nations Covenant on Civil and Political Rights and the Inter-American System: A Study of Co-Existing Petition Procedures*, 70 Am. J. Int'l L. 778 (1976). *See also* Eissen, *supra* note 35.

[68] *See* American Convention, art. 47(b) & (c).

[69] *See id.* art. 48(1)(a), (d), & (e); Regulations, *supra* note 51, arts. 40–41, 61–63.

[70] American Convention, art. 48(1)(c).

[71] Under art. 47 of the American Convention, the Inter-American Commission must rule a complaint inadmissible if it plainly appears that 'the petition or communication is manifestly groundless or obviously out of order . . .'

granted to the Inter-American Commission at this stage enables it to dismiss cases which, in retrospect, should never have been admitted.[72] But this power is clearly not to be used by the Inter-American Commission to adjudicate on the merits.

During the second stage of the proceedings, the Inter-American Commission also has an obligation to 'place itself at the disposal of the parties concerned with a view to reaching a friendly settlement of the matter on the basis of respect for the human rights recognized' in the Convention.[73] If a friendly settlement is obtained, the Commission must prepare a report, describing the facts of the case and how it was resolved. This report is transmitted by the Commission to the Secretary General of the O.A.S. 'for publication'.[74]

A case moves into the third stage of the proceedings if the parties are unable to reach a friendly settlement. At this point, the Inter-American Commission must draw up a report setting out the facts that have emerged from its investigations and the conclusions it has reached about the case. This report, which may also include whatever recommendations the Commission wishes to make regarding the resolution of the dispute, is transmitted only to the states concerned and may not be published by them.[75] After receiving the report, the state has three months within which to act on it. During that period, the case may be either settled by the parties or referred to the Inter-American Court of Human Rights by the Inter-American Commission or a state; private parties have no standing to do so.

A case reaches the fourth stage of the proceeedings before the Inter-American Commission if it has been neither referred to the Inter-American Court nor otherwise settled by the parties. At this point 'the Commission may, by the vote of an absolute majority of its members, set forth its opinion and conclusions concerning the question submitted for its consideration'.[76] If the Commission decides to adopt this report—and it is obviously under no obligation to do so in all cases—it must set out its 'recommendations' and 'prescribe a period within which the state is to take the measures that are incumbent upon it to remedy the situation examined'.[77] Once this period has expired, and if the Commission in fact adopted the aforementioned report, it 'shall decide by the vote of an absolute

[72] The European Commission of Human Rights obtained a similar authority through an amendment to the European Convention. *See* Protocol No. 3 to the European Convention, art. 1, *reprinted in* Brownlie, *supra* note 7, at 260, art. 29, as amended. On this subject, *see* Sohn & Buergenthal, *supra* note 2, at 1091.

[73] American Convention, art. 48(1)(f).

[74] *Id.* art. 49.

[75] *Id.* art. 50; *see* Regulations, *supra* note 51, art. 43.

[76] American Convention, art. 51(1).

[77] *Id.* art. 51(2).

majority of its members whether the state has taken adequate measures and whether to publish its report'.[78] This last decision concludes the Inter-American Commission proceedings in the case.

It is obvious that the American Convention establishes a very cumbersome and ambiguous procedure for the resolution of cases by the Inter-American Commission. As we have seen, it provides for two Commission reports—one at the third stage of the proceedings and the other at the fourth. From the wording of the relevant provisions of the American Convention, it is by no means easy to ascertain how these reports differ in their contents and functions. It is important to note, however, that the report to be prepared by the Inter-American Commission at the third stage of the proceedings is mandatory; it does not require a vote of an absolute majority of the Commission members; and it has to contain the Commission's conclusions indicating whether the respondent state has or has not violated the American Convention.[79] If in this report the Inter-American Commission finds that no violation of the American Convention has been committed, it will in all likelihood not draw up the fourth-stage report. That report is not mandatory and appears to be designed for cases involving a breach of the American Convention which the state has failed to remedy in the manner suggested by the Inter-American Commission in its third-stage report. Although the American Convention does not say so expressly, it would appear that the fourth-stage report, if published, should also contain the Commission's decision on the question 'whether the state has taken adequate measures' to remedy the situation which gave rise to the case. That decision, after all, is an integral and indispensable part of the case and the proceedings relating to it. Interestingly enough, the Inter-American Commission's rules of procedure contain a specific provision enabling the Commission to include the fourth-stage report in its annual report to the O.A.S. General Assembly.[80] This approach, which does not prevent the report from also being published as a separate document, gets the case on the agenda of the O.A.S. General Assembly where the state's failure to comply with the Inter-American Commission's recommendations can then be discussed and acted upon. Since an O.A.S. General Assembly debate could subject a recalcitrant government to considerable adverse publicity, many governments will take seriously the threat of the publication of a critical report by the Inter-American Commission as well as any condemnatory resolution the O.A.S. Assembly might adopt in such a case.

Although the proceedings involving cases that have not been settled

[78] *Id.* art. 51(3); *see* Regulations, *supra* note 57, art. 45.
[79] *See* American Convention, art. 50.
[80] Regulations, *supra* note 51, art. 45(2).

or referred to the Inter-American Court end with the publication of the Commission's fourth-stage report, the Commission can be deemed to have the power under the American Convention and the O.A.S. Charter to keep a serious situation 'under observation' beyond that stage and to keep the O.A.S. Assembly informed. The Inter-American Commission could provide this information on its own motion or at the request of the Assembly. In due course the Commission probably should develop appropriate formal procedures to monitor cases dealt with in fourth-stage reports. Such an approach would be particularly useful for dealing with situations requiring a substantial amount of time to assess the extent of a government's compliance with the recommendations of the Commission.

2. *The Inter-American Court of Human Rights*[81]

The American Convention vests two distinct judicial functions in the Inter-American Court of Human Rights. One involves the power to adjudicate disputes relating to charges that a State Party has violated the Convention. In performing this function, the Inter-American Court exercises its so-called contentious jurisdiction.[82] The Court's other power is to interpret the American Convention and certain human rights treaties in proceedings that do not involve the adjudication of specific disputes.[83] This is the Inter-American Court's advisory jurisdiction.

a. *The Inter-American Court's Contentious Jurisdiction.* The contentious jurisdiction of the Inter-American Court is spelled out in article 62 of the American Convention, which reads as follows:

> 1. A State Party may, upon depositing its instrument of ratification or adherence to this Convention, or at any subsequent time, declare that it recognizes as binding, *ipso facto*, and not requiring special agreement, the jurisdiction of the Court on all matters relating to the interpretation or application of this Convention.
> 2. Such declaration may be made unconditionally, on the condition of reciprocity, for a specified period, or for specific cases. It shall be presented to the Secretary General of the Organization, who shall transmit copies thereof to the other member states of the Organization and to the Secretary of the Court.
> 3. The jurisdiction of the Court shall comprise all cases concerning the interpretation and application of the provisions of this Convention that are submitted to it, provided that the States Parties to the case recognize or have

[81] [Ed. note: On the Inter-American Court of Human Rights, *see generally* Buergenthal, *The Inter-American Court of Human Rights*, 76 Am. J. Int'l L. 231 (1982).]

[82] American Convention, art. 62.

[83] *Id.* art. 64.

recognized such jurisdiction, whether by special declaration pursuant to the preceding paragraphs, or by special agreement.

This provision indicates that a state party does not subject itself to the contentious jurisdiction of the Inter-American Court by merely ratifying the American Convention. The Court acquires that jurisdiction with regard to a state party only when that state has either filed the declaration referred to in paragraphs 1 and 2 of article 62 or concluded the special agreement mentioned in paragraph 3. The declaration may be made when a state ratifies the American Convention or at any time thereafter; it may also be made for a specific case or a series of cases. To date only Costa Rica, Honduras, Peru, and Venezuela deposited the declaration for future cases. But since the states parties are free to accept the Inter-American Court's jurisdiction at any time in a specific case or in general, the Inter-American Commission's rules of procedure quite properly authorize it to invite states to permit cases being dealt with by the Inter-American Commission to be submitted to the Court.[84] It would probably make sense for the Inter-American Commission to extend that invitation in every case in which it has adopted its stage-three report.[85]

A case may also be referred to the Inter-American Court by 'special agreement'. In speaking of the 'special agreement', article 62(3) of the American Convention does not indicate who may conclude the agreement. While it is obvious that it may be concluded by and between states parties, it is less clear whether the Inter-American Commission could take the place of a state. A state might be willing, for example, to submit a case to the Inter-American Court by means of a special agreement concluded with the Commission, provided it and the Commission can agree to seek a Court judgment on only some, but not all, of the issues that the initial complaint presented. If it is assumed that the Court must adjudicate all the relevant issues raised by a case that was referred to it under a declaration accepting its jurisdiction, it would follow that the only way to obtain a more limited adjudication is to conclude a special agreement enumerating the issues to be decided. Whether the American Convention permits this solution is an issue which the Inter-American Court will no doubt have to decide one of these days.

In providing that '[o]nly the States Parties and the Commission shall have the right to submit a case to the Court', article 61(1) makes quite clear that private parties do not have standing to institute these

[84] Regulations, *supra* note 50, art. 47(3).

[85] It will be recalled that the decision whether to refer a case to the Inter-American Court must be made within a three-month period after the stage-three report has been transmitted to the states concerned.

proceedings. An individual who has filed a complaint with the Inter-American Commission cannot consequently bring that case to the Inter-American Court. A case arising out of an individual complaint can get to the Court, but it must be referred to it by the Commission or a state.

Although it is undisputed that the states parties to the American Convention have standing to submit cases to the Inter-American Court, it is less certain whether in a specific case only those states that participated in the prior proceedings before the Inter-American Commission may do so or whether all states parties have that right. Article 61(2) of the American Convention provides that a case may not be brought to the Inter-American Court until after the Inter-American Commission has dealt with it and adopted its stage-three report. But the Convention is silent on whether the standing of the states parties is otherwise restricted. In addition to various policy arguments that bear on the issue, two provisions of the American Convention appear to be relevant. One is article 50(2), which declares that the Commission's stage-three report 'shall be transmitted to the states concerned, which shall not be at liberty to publish it'. The other is article 61(1). It provides that '[o]nly the States Parties and the Commission shall have the right to submit a case to the Court'. If article 50(2) means that the stage-three report may be made available only to the 'states concerned' and if that reference embraces only states which have participated in the Inter-American Commission proceedings, then no other states will have access to the report. Other states will therefore lack the information necessary to take the case to the Inter-American Court. On the other hand, given the unambiguous language of article 61(1), it might be that 'states concerned', as used in article 50(2), refers to all states which have accepted the Inter-American Court's jurisdiction. Here it could be argued that these states must be deemed to be 'concerned' because they have standing to submit the case to the Court. The latter argument gains some support from the contention that, if the drafters had intended to limit the standing of states, they would have said so expressly in article 61(1) and they would have provided in article 50(2) that the report be transmitted only to 'the states parties to the dispute'.

As has been noted already, article 61(2) provides that '[i]n order for the Court to hear a case', the Inter-American Commission must first have dealt with it and a stage-three report must have been adopted. This provision raises at least two questions. The first is whether the states parties to a dispute may waive the proceedings before the Commission and go directly to the Court. Second, even assuming that the requirement relating to the role of the Commission cannot be waived, does it apply to all cases which might be brought to the

Court?[86] The answer to the first question will depend, in part at least, on a determination of the purpose of the requirement and whether it was designed solely for the benefit of the states parties to the dispute. The second question arises because, as will be recalled, the Inter-American Court may acquire jurisdiction either by declaration or special agreement. A case referred to the Court pursuant to a declaration will have originated in a complaint, whether inter-state or individual, charging a state with a violation of a human right proclaimed in the American Convention. That need not be true of disputes submitted to the Court under a special agreement. Such disputes might relate to any clause of the American Convention, in particular to those that are not human rights provisions as such. It is consequently entirely possible for State *X*, for example, to have a dispute with State *Y* regarding the application of article 70 of the American Convention, which accords members of the Inter-American Commission and judges of the Inter-American Court diplomatic immunity during their term of office. A hypothetical case might involve Judge *A*, who, while in *Y*, was denied the immunities to which *X* claims the judge is entitled under the Convention. If both *X* and *Y* are states parties to the American Convention, they could conclude a special agreement to submit the dispute to the Inter-American Court. Note that this would not be a dispute relating to a violation of 'a human right set forth in this Convention'.[87] For that reason, it would not be admissible if filed with the Inter-American Commission as a complaint,[88] and since the Commission has no jurisdiction to accept complaints by 'special agreement', it is clear that the dispute between *X* and *Y* could not be taken up by the Commission. This suggests that disputes between states might be referred directly to the Inter-American Court by special agreement without any intercession by the Commission, provided the disputes concern the interpretation or application of those provisions of the American Convention that do not concern individual human rights. Whether the same would be true of other disputes, that is a much more difficult question.

The judgment rendered by the Inter-American Court in any dispute submitted to it is 'final and not subject to appeal'.[89] Moreover, the 'States Parties to the Convention undertake to comply with the judgment of the Court in any case to which they are parties'.[90] The

[86] [Ed. note: The answers to these questions have been clarified by the Inter-American Court in its decision on Nov. 13, 1981, *In re* Viviana Gallardo, No. G. 101/81, *reprinted in* 20 Int'l Legal Materials 1424 (1981).]

[87] American Convention, art. 45(1).

[88] *Id.* art. 47(b).

[89] *Id.* art. 67.

[90] *Id.* art. 68(1).

American Convention does not specify that the Inter-American Commission is also bound by the judgments of the Inter-American Court. But this does not necessarily mean that the Commission is free to disregard the Court's rulings, which may be binding on it as *res judicata* or authoritative precedent. This conclusion follows from the fact that the Commission is a quasi-judicial body to which the Convention assigns a role that is hierarchically inferior to the Court for certain purposes and from the fact that the Commission participates in the proceedings before the Court.[91]

The American Convention, in article 63(1), contains the following stipulation relating to the judgments that the Court may render:

> If the Court finds that there has been a violation of a right or freedom protected by this Convention, the Court shall rule that the injured party be ensured the enjoyment of his right or freedom that was violated. It shall also rule, if appropriate, that the consequences of the measure or situation that constituted the breach of such right or freedom be remedied and that fair compensation be paid to the injured party.

This provision indicates that the Inter-American Court must decide whether there has been a breach of the American Convention and, if so, what rights the injured party should be accorded. Moreover, the Court may also determine the steps that should be taken to remedy the breach and the amount of damages to which the injured party is entitled. Let us assume, for example, that the Court finds that the trial of an individual violated the American Convention because he or she was denied various rights proclaimed in article 8 (Right to a Fair Trial) of the American Convention. After enumerating the specific rights to which the injured individual was and is entitled, the Court may also declare whether he or she should be granted a new trial and/or whether he or she should be awarded damages for the injuries sustained.

A separate provision of the American Convention deals with money damages. It provides that the 'part of a judgment that stipulates compensatory damages may be executed in the country concerned in accordance with domestic procedure governing the execution of judgments against the state'.[92] It is unclear what this provision means. If it means that an injured party is free to seek execution through the relevant domestic procedures, the provision has little significance and gives the individual no additional rights. It could also be interpreted to mean that, if there exist appropriate domestic procedures for judgments against the state, the Inter-American Court's judgment shall be

[91] On this problem generally, *see* Buergenthal, *The Effect of the European Convention on Human Rights on the Internal Law of Member States*, in The European Convention on Human Rights, Int'l & Comp. L.Q. Supp. No. 11, at 79, 94–95 (1965).

[92] American Convention, art. 68(2).

equated, for purposes of execution, to a domestic judgment. Thus interpreted, it might be a very useful remedy. Finally, the provision might be deemed to authorize a state to insist that the judgment be executed in the manner prescribed by domestic law for judgments against the state. The advantage or disadvantage of such an interpretation may well differ from country to country, depending on domestic legal procedures, including immunities, and the delays that are encountered in the execution of judgments. The provision, whatever its meaning, would have much greater significance if it expressly required full domestic law enforcement of the Court's judgment. That result could, of course, be achieved by appropriate domestic legislation.

In addition to regular judgments, the Inter-American Court also has the power to grant what might be described as temporary injunctions. This power is spelled out in article 63(2) of the American Convention, which reads as follows:

> In cases of extreme gravity and urgency, and when necessary to avoid irreparable damage to persons, the Court shall adopt such provisional measures as it deems pertinent in matters it has under consideration. With respect to a case not yet submitted to the Court, it may act at the request of the Commission.

This extraordinary remedy is available in two distinct circumstances: the first consists of cases pending before the Inter-American Court; the second involves complaints being dealt with by the Inter-American Commission that have not yet been referred to the Court for adjudication.

In the first category of cases, the request for the temporary injunction can be made at any time during the proceedings before the Court, including simultaneously with the filing of the case. Of course, the requested relief may only be granted after the Court has determined, if only in a preliminary manner, that it has jurisdiction over the parties. Although article 63(2) does not say anything about jurisdiction, it is obvious that the Court can only deal with a case, whether it calls for provisional or permanent relief, in which the states parties have accepted its jurisdiction.[93] But since jurisdictional issues may at times be extremely complex and intertwined with matters bearing on the merits of the case, the Inter-American Court should not have to resolve fully all jurisdictional issues before ordering provisional measures, assuming, of course, that such measures are otherwise plainly indicated. Given the need for urgency and the extraordinary character of the relief, the Court would certainly be justified to follow the pre-

[93] *Id.* art. 62(3).

cedent of the International Court of Justice, which requires no more than a *prima facie* showing of jurisdiction before granting provisional measures in an otherwise appropriate case.[94]

The same principle should no doubt also apply to the second category of cases, that is, cases in which a preliminary injunction appears to be indicated even before the Inter-American Commission has had a chance either to complete its examination of the complaint or to refer it to the Inter-American Court. The Commission might receive a complaint, for example, in which it is asserted that State *X*, which has ratified the American Convention and accepted the jurisdiction of the Inter-American Court, plans within the next few days to execute Mr. *B.*, who was convicted following a trial that is alleged to have violated various provisions of the Convention. The Inter-American Commission could take this type of case to the Court immediately on receipt of the complaint and seek the remedies provided for by article 63(2). The Court would here obtain jurisdiction only for purposes of dealing with the request for provisional measures. It would not acquire jurisdiction to decide the case on the merits until the proceedings before the Commission had been concluded and the complaint was thereafter referred to the Court for adjudication by the Commission or a state. But even if the case is subsequently not submitted to the Court, the provisional measures remain within its jurisdiction and can presumably be modified or revoked only by it.

Since the states parties to the American Convention are free at any time to accept the jurisdiction of the Inter-American Court for the adjudication of a specific case, the Inter-American Commission would appear to be entitled to seek provisional measures in a case in which the defendant state had not accepted the Court's jurisdiction. Of course, the Court could not comply with the demand until the state indicated, be it at the request of the Commission or the Court, that it would accept the Court's jurisdiction in the particular case. But until the state has unambiguously signaled its unwillingness to accept the Court's jurisdiction, it would be improper for the Court or the Commission to take it for granted.

Although the Inter-American Court lacks the power to enforce its judgments or preliminary rulings, one provision of the American Convention bears on this subject. It reads as follows:

> To each regular session of the General Assembly of the Organization of American States the Court shall submit, for the Assembly's consideration, a

[94] *See* Case concerning United States Diplomatic and Consular Staff in Tehran, Provisional Measures, Order of Dec. 15, 1979, [1979] I.C.J. 7, 13, where the Court declared that provisional measures ought to be granted 'only if the provisions invoked by the Applicant appear, *prima facie*, to afford a basis on which the jurisdiction of the Court might be founded'.

report on its work during the previous year. It shall specify, in particular, the cases in which a state has not complied with its judgments, making any pertinent recommendations.[95]

This provision enables the Court to inform the O.A.S General Assembly of situations involving non-compliance with its decisions, and it permits the O.A.S. Assembly to discuss the matter and to adopt whatever political measures it deems appropriate. It should be noted, moreover, that the mere fact that article 65 speaks of 'regular sessions' of the Assembly does not mean that the matter of non-compliance by a state may not be raised at a special session of that body, either at the request of a member state or following consideration by the O.A.S. Permanent Council. Thus, since the Council acts for the Assembly when it is not in session,[96] the Inter-American Court would appear to be free to call the Council's attention to cases that might justify emergency measures such as, for example, threats of non-compliance with provisional measures adopted by the Court. This information might prompt the Council to convene a special session of the Assembly or to take some other measures it deems appropriate.[97]

b. *The Inter-American Court's Advisory Jurisdiction.* The jurisdiction of the Inter-American Court of Human Rights to render advisory opinions is more extensive than that of any other international tribunal in existence today. It is spelled out in article 64 of the American Convention, which reads as follows:

> 1. The member states of the Organization may consult the Court regarding the interpretation of this Convention or of other treaties concerning the protection of human rights in the American states. Within their spheres of competence, the organs listed in Chapter X of the Charter of the Organization of American States, as amended by the Protocol of Buenos Aires, may in like manner consult the Court.
> 2. The Court, at the request of a member state of the Organization, may provide that state with opinions regarding the compatibility of any of its domestic laws with the aforesaid international instruments.

Article 64 indicates, first, that standing to request an advisory opinion from the Court is not limited to the states parties to the American Convention; any O.A.S. member state may seek it. Second, the advisory jurisdiction is not limited to interpretations of the American Convention: it also extends to interpretations of any other treaty 'concerning the protection of human rights in the American states'. Third, all O.A.S. organs, including the Inter-American Commission on

95 American Convention, art. 65.
96 *See* O.A.S. Charter art. 91.
97 *See id.* arts. 56, 59, & 60.

Human Rights, have standing to request advisory opinions.[98] Fourth, the member states of the O.A.S may also seek opinions from the Inter-American Court regarding the compatibility of their domestic laws with the American Convention or any of the aforementioned human rights treaties.

Article 64 leaves many questions unanswered, and the Inter-American Court has not as yet had an opportunity to deal with any of them. It is by no means clear, for example, what is meant by 'treaties concerning the protection of human rights in the American states'. This is not a concept that has an accepted juridical meaning within the inter-American system, and the *travaux préparatoires* of the American Convention do not help explain it. The phrase might have reference to human rights treaties concluded exclusively by American States or adopted within the framework of the inter-American system; it might also apply to human rights treaties, whether bilateral or multilateral, universal or regional, accepted by one or some American states. Despite the fact that the O.A.S. Charter deals with many different subjects, is it a 'treaty concerning the protection of human rights' to the extent that it also contains human rights provisions, thus enabling the Court to interpret those provisions? The answers to these questions are by no means self-evident. They are also very important, for they will determine *inter alia* whether the Court is deemed to have the power in appropriate cases to interpret a United Nations human rights treaty or the human rights provisions of a bilateral commercial treaty, for example, or whether its advisory jurisdiction applies only to treaties concluded within the framework of the O.A.S.

It is also not clear whether there are any limits on the scope of the Inter-American Court's power to render advisory opinions. Assume, for example, that a complaint has been filed with the Inter-American Commission against State *X* and that it has not accepted the jurisdiction of the Inter-American Court. If during the proceedings before the Commission a disagreement arises between State *X* and the Commission concerning the interpretation of a provision of the American Convention, may the Commission request the Court to render an advisory opinion on that legal issue even if State *X* objects? State *X* would presumably argue that this was not an advisory opinion but a

[98] In identifying the organs of the O.A.S. that have standing to seek an advisory opinion, art. 64 of the American Convention refers to Chapter X of the O.A.S. Charter. That chapter identifies the following organs: the General Assembly; the Meeting of Consultation of Ministers of Foreign Affairs; the Councils (consisting of the Permanent Council of the Organization, the Inter-American Economic and Social Council, and the Inter-American Council for Education, Science, and Culture); the Inter-American Juridical Committee; the Inter-American Commission on Human Rights; the General Secretariat; the Specialized Conferences; and the Specialized Organizations. *See* O.A.S. Charter art. 51.

disguised contentious case and that the Commission was resorting to it to get around *X*'s failure to recognize the Court's jurisdiction.[99] The strength of this contention may well depend on the weight that should be given to the claims that article 64 is unambiguous in imposing no limits whatsoever on the right to request advisory opinions; that such opinions may only deal with questions of law; that they are by definition not binding on any state; and that, consequently, they should not be equated with decisions rendered in contentious cases. It is not necessary to adopt one or the other of these arguments to recognize that the Court's advisory jurisdiction could significantly strengthen the Commission's capacity to deal with complex legal issues arising under the Convention. If it is recalled, moreover, that all O.A.S. organs, and not only the Commission, have standing to request advisory opinions from the Court, it is not unreasonable to assume that the political organs of the O.A.S. might find it politically useful in certain cases to resort to the Court.

Article 64(2) permits O.A.S. member states to seek an opinion from the Court on the extent to which their domestic laws are compatible with the Convention or with any other 'American' human rights treaty. This provision might have a number of important uses. Governments might resort to it to obtain the Court's opinion on pending legislation. States considering the ratification of the American Convention might invoke it to ascertain whether, given certain domestic laws, they should do so with specific reservations. National tribunals might use this provision to consult the Court before interpreting or applying the American Convention or the other human rights treaties covered by article 64. That approach, if adopted, would contribute very significantly to the uniform application of the Convention by national tribunals. This conclusion raises the question whether national courts may request an advisory opinion directly from the Inter-American Court or whether they have to go through their governments. The language of article 64(2) appears to suggest that the request must come from the state, *i.e.*, the government, rather than directly from national tribunals. If this interpretation is correct, governments should be encouraged to establish a domestic procedure, which would facilitate the transmittal of these requests and regulate the manner of their presentation to the Court. The matter could also be regulated by a special agreement between the Court and the govern-

[99] South Africa made a similar argument before the International Court of Justice in the *Namibia* case, but the Court rejected it. Advisory Opinion on Legal Consequences for States of the Continued Presence of South Africa in Namibia, [1971] I.C.J. 16. *See also* W. Bishop, International Law 74–76 (3d ed. 1971), where other precedents bearing on this subject are discussed.

ment. Article 27 of its Statute authorizes the Court to conclude such agreements.

Resort to the advisory jurisdiction of the Court, whether it be by the Inter-American Commission, the other O.A.S. organs, or the member states, has a number of advantages that its contentious jurisdiction does not provide. The latter can only be invoked by and against states that have recognized the Court's jurisdiction; no such requirement applies to its advisory jurisdiction. Although the Court's decision in a contentious case is binding, which is of course not true of an advisory opinion, that distinction may not be of great practical significance. Compliance and non-compliance by states with their international obligations depend less on the formal status of a judgment and its abstract enforceability. Much more important is its impact as a force capable of legitimating governmental conduct and the perception of governments about the political cost of non-compliance. States may find it as difficult in some cases to disregard an advisory opinion as a binding decision. The Inter-American Court may therefore be able to play an important role even if its contentious jurisdiction is not widely accepted by the states parties to the American Convention. Much will depend on the extent to which the advisory power is resorted to by O.A.S. organs and the member states; much will also depend on the wisdom and prestige of the Court.

C. THE O.A.S. CHARTER AND HUMAN RIGHTS

A member state of the O.A.S. which has not ratified the American Convention on Human Rights is subject to the human rights regime that has its constitutional basis in the O.A.S. Charter.[100] This regime has evolved over the past three decades and achieved full constitutional legitimacy in 1970 with the entry into force of the 'Protocol of Buenos Aires', which amended the 1948 O.A.S. Charter in a number of important respects.[101] The entry into effect in 1978 of the American Convention on Human Rights resulted in some further institutional and legal modification in the Charter-based regime.

1. *The Evolution of the Charter-Based Regime*

a. *Under the 1948 Charter*. The 1948 O.A.S. Charter contained very few provisions relating to human rights and all of them were phrased

[100] *See generally Revised OAS Charter*, *supra* note 2; Farer & Rowles, *supra* note 44.

[101] The Protocol of Buenos Aires was signed on Feb. 27, 1967, and entered into force on Feb. 27, 1970. 21 U.S.T. 607, T.I.A.S. No. 6847. The original O.A.S. Charter was signed at Bogotá in 1948, and entered into force in 1951. 2 U.S.T. 2394, T.I.A.S. No. 2361, 119 U.N.T.S. 3. On the Protocol of Buenos Aires, *see* Sepúlveda, *The Reform of the Charter of the Organization of American States*, 137 Recueil des Cours 83 (1972); Robertson, *Revision of the Charter of the Organization of American States*, 17 Int'l & Comp. L.Q. 346 (1968).

in very general terms. The most important reference to human rights appeared in article 5(j), which has been retained in the amended Charter as article 3(j). In this provision the American States 'reaffirm' and 'proclaim' as a principle of the Organization 'the fundamental rights of the individual without distinction as to race, nationality, creed or sex'. But the 1948 Charter did not define the meaning of 'the fundamental rights of the individual', nor did it establish a mechanism to promote or protect them.[102] The American Declaration of the Rights and Duties of Man was proclaimed at the same Bogotá conference that produced the 1948 Charter but the American Declaration was adopted in the form of a simple conference resolution[103] and did not form part of the Charter itself. Moreover, whereas the American Declaration proclaimed that '[t]he international protection of the rights of man should be the principal guide of an evolving American law',[104] the Bogotá conference went on record with an understanding that the American Declaration had not been incorporated by reference into the Charter.[105] The Inter-American Juridical Committee reinforced this position with a 1949 ruling that the American Declaration 'does not create legal contractual obligations' and lacked the status of 'positive substantive law'.[106]

Following the Bogotá conference, sporadic attempts were made in the O.A.S. to establish some institutional mechanisms for dealing with human rights problems.[107] These efforts produced no tangible results until 1959, when the Fifth Meeting of Consultation of Ministers of Foreign Affairs, relying on article 5(j) of the O.A.S. Charter, adopted a resolution[108] mandating the creation of 'an Inter-American Commission on Human Rights, composed of seven members, elected, as individuals, by the [O.A.S.] Council . . .' The resolution provided further that 'the Commission, which shall be organized by the Council . . . and have the specific functions that the Council assigns to it, shall be

[102] For the drafting history of this provision, *see* A. Schreiber, The Inter-American Commission on Human Rights 13–20 (1970) [hereinafter cited as Schreiber].

[103] Res. XXX, Final Act of the Ninth International Conference of American States, Bogotá, Colombia, 30 Mar.–2 May 1948, at 48 (Pan American Union 1948), *reprinted in* Handbook, *supra* note 3, at 17.

[104] American Declaration, preambular para. 3.

[105] Department of State, Report of the Delegation of the United States of America to the Ninth International Conference of American States, Bogotá, Colombia, March 30–May 2, 1948, at 35–36 (Publ. No. 3263, 1948).

[106] Inter-American Juridicial Committee, Report of the Inter-American Council of Jurists Concerning Resolution XXXI of the Bogotá Conference September 26, 1949, *reprinted in* Pan American Union, Human Rights in the American States 163, 164–65 (prelim. ed. 1960).

[107] *See* Schreiber, *supra* note 102, at 22–27.

[108] Res. VII, Fifth Meeting of Consultation of Ministers of Foreign Affairs, Santiago, Chile, 12–18 Aug. 1959, Final Act, O.A.S. Doc. OEA/Ser.C/II.5, at 10–11 (1950); *reproduced in* Sohn & Buergenthal, *supra* note 2, at 1281–82.

charged with furthering respect for [human] rights'. The O.A.S. Council adopted the Statute of the Commission and elected its members in 1960, and the Commission began its activities that very year.[109] The Statute described the Inter-American Commission as an 'autonomous entity' of the O.A.S. having the function 'to promote respect for human rights'.[110] The definition was provided in article 2, which declared that '[f]or the purpose of this Statute, human rights are understood to be those set forth in the American Declaration of the Rights and Duties of Man'. The 'non-binding' American Declaration thus became the basic normative instrument of the Commission.

The Statute adopted by the Council in 1960 gave the Inter-American Commission only very limited powers. These were spelled out in article 9:

> In carrying out its assignments of promoting respect for human rights, the Commission shall have the following functions and powers:
> (a) to develop an awareness of human rights among the peoples of America;
> (b) to make recommendations to the governments of the member states in general, if it considers such action advisable, for the adoption of progressive measures in favor of human rights within the framework of their domestic legislation and, in accordance with their constitutional precepts, appropriate measures to further the faithful observance of those rights;
> (c) to prepare such studies or reports as it considers advisable in the performance of its duties;
> (d) to urge the governments of the member states to supply it with information on the measures adopted by them in matters of human rights;
> (e) to serve the Organization of American States as an advisory body in respect of human rights.

In a formal interpretation adopted at its first session, the Commission determined that article 9(b) of its Statute empowered it 'to make general recommendations to each individual member state, as well as to all of them'.[111] This interpretation enabled the Inter-American Commission to condemn, in general terms, violations of human rights in specific countries and, for that purpose, to make use of the powers granted it in paragraphs (c) and (d) of article 9. These powers would

[109] The 1960 Statute of the Inter-American Commission on Human Rights with subsequent amendments [hereinafter cited as Statute], is reproduced in Basic Documents, *supra* note 3, at 194. *See also* [1960] Annual Report of the [O.A.S.] Secretary General, O.A.S. Doc. OEA/Ser.D/III.12, at 19–20.

[110] Statute, art. 1.

[111] IACHR, Report on the Work Accomplished During its First Session, Oct. 3–28, 1960, O.A.S. Doc. OEA/Ser.L/V/II.1, doc. 32, at 10 (1961) [hereinafter cited as IACHR, First Report].

not have been of much use without article 9(b) and the interpretation placed on it by the Commission.

Relying on this interpretation, the Inter-American Commission embarked upon studies investigating 'situations relating to human rights' in various O.A.S. member states; it began to address recommendations to governments found to be engaging in large-scale violations of human rights; and it started to issue reports documenting violations of human rights in specific countries.[112] In order to prepare these country studies, the Commission examined complaints, heard witnesses, and, in some cases, carried out on-the-spot investigations in different countries. These 'visits' were based on article 11 of the Statute, which authorized the Commission to 'move to the territory of any American state when it so decides by an absolute majority of votes and with the consent of the government concerned'.[113]

At its first session in 1960, the Inter-American Commission also ruled, however, that its Statute did not authorize it 'to make any individual decisions regarding written communications . . . it receives involving the violation of human rights in American states, although, for the most effective fulfillment of its functions, the Commission shall take cognizance of them by way of information'.[114] This ruling prevented the Commission from examining and taking action on individual petitions. But it could rely and use these communications as a source of information in preparing country reports as well as in deciding whether to make a particular country the subject of an investigation.

The powers of the Inter-American Commission were expanded in 1965 by a resolution of the Second Special Inter-American Conference.[115] This resolution was restated in the Inter-American Commission's Statute as article 9(*bis*), which reads as follows:

> The Commission shall have the following additional functions and powers:
> (a) to give particular attention to observance of the human rights referred to in Articles I, II, III, IV, XVIII, XXV, and XXVI of the American Declaration of the Rights and Duties of Man;
> (b) to examine communications submitted to it and any other available information; to address the government of any American state for information deemed pertinent by the Commission; and to make

[112] *See* Farer & Rowles, *supra* note 44, at 54–55; Thomas & Thomas, *The Inter-American Commission on Human Rights*, 20 Sw. L.J. 282, 287–305 (1966). *See also* Sohn & Buergenthal, *supra* note 2, at 1293–340, where some of the country studies are reproduced.

[113] *See, e.g.*, Schreiber & Schreiber, *The Inter-American Commission on Human Rights in the Dominican Crisis*, 22 Int'l Organization 508 (1968).

[114] IACHR, First Report, *supra* note 111, at 9.

[115] Res. XXII, Second Special Inter-American Conference, Rio de Janeiro, Brazil, Nov. 17–30, 1965, Final Act, O.A.S. Doc. OEA/Ser.C/I.13, at 32–34 (1965).

recommendations, when it deems this appropriate, with the objective of bringing about more effective observance of fundamental human rights;

(c) to submit a report annually to the Inter-American Conference or to the Meeting of Consultation of Ministers of Foreign Affairs, which should include: (i) a statement of progress achieved in realization of the goals set forth in the American Declaration; (ii) a statement of areas in which further steps are needed to give effect to the human rights set forth in the American Declaration; and (iii) such observations as the Commission may deem appropriate on matters covered in the communications submitted to it and in other information available to the Commission;

(d) to verify, as a condition precedent to the exercise of the powers set forth in paragraphs (b) and (c) of the present article, whether the internal legal procedures and remedies of each member state have been duly applied and exhausted.

The Inter-American Commission relied on this provision to devise an individual petition system that served to complement its other efforts, particularly the country studies and on-the-spot investigations which over the years have developed into its most important activities. The petition system applied only to the human rights that were singled out in article 9(a)(*bis*). It dealt with complaints alleging violations of the right to life, liberty, and personal security (article I); equality before the law (article II); freedom of religion (article III); freedom of expression (article XVIII); freedom from arbitrary arrest (article XXV); and due process of law (article XXVI).[116]

b. *Under the Revised O.A.S. Charter*. Until 1970, the human rights system of the O.A.S. was based on a very weak constitutional foundation. The Inter-American Commission's Statute lacked an express treaty basis and derived its existence from O.A.S. conference resolutions of uncertain legal force.[117] This situation changed dramatically with the entry into force of the Protocol of Buenos Aires, which effected extensive amendments of the O.A.S. Charter.[118] The newly revised Charter changed the status of the Inter-American Commission from an 'autonomous entity of the OAS' into one of the principal organs of the O.A.S.[119] Its functions were defined as follows in article 112 of the amended Charter:

[116] Some of the individual petitions considered by the Inter-American Commission are reproduced in Sohn & Buergenthal, *supra* note 2, at 1340–56. Additional ones are reproduced in the Commission's annual reports. *See, e.g.*, Annual Report of the Inter-American Commission on Human Rights to the General Assembly, O.E.A. Doc. OEA/Ser.P/AG/doc. 1101/79, at 28 (1979).

[117] *See generally Revised OAS Charter*, *supra* note 2, at 833–34.

[118] The text of the 1948 O.A.S. Charter together with the amended version are reproduced in L. Sohn, Basic Documents of the United Nations 125 & 140 (1968). Also *see* note 101 *supra*.

[119] O.A.S. Charter art. 52(e).

There shall be an Inter-American Commission on Human Rights, whose principal function shall be to promote the observance and protection of human rights and to serve as a consultative organ of the Organization in these matters.

An inter-American convention on human rights shall determine the structure, competence, and procedure of this Commission, as well as those of other organs responsible for these matters.

Although the Protocol of Buenos Aires entered into force in 1970—one year after the American Convention on Human Rights was adopted—it was drafted in 1967. At that time the American Convention was not yet in existence. The drafters of the Protocol consequently attached a transitory provision to the revised O.A.S. Charter, in which they provided that '[u]ntil the inter-American convention on human rights, referred to in [article 112], enters into force, the present Inter-American Commission on Human Rights shall keep vigilance over the observance of human rights'.[120]

These provisions of the revised O.A.S. Charter gave institutional legitimacy to the Inter-American Commission by recognizing it as a treaty-based O.A.S. organ. Moreover, through the transitory provision, the Commission's Statute became an inherent part of the O.A.S. Charter itself.[121] The revised Charter thus effectively legitimated the powers that the Commission exercised under article 9 and 9(*bis*) of its Statute and it recognized the normative character of the American Declaration of the Rights and Duties of Man as a standard by which to judge the human rights activities of all O.A.S. member states.[122]

c. *Effect of the American Convention.* The entry into force of the American Convention on Human Rights in 1978 also changed the status of the Inter-American Commission in relation to those O.A.S. member states that have not ratified the American Convention. To understand the post-1978 status of the Inter-American Commission as a Charter organ, it must be recalled, first, that article 112 of the O.A.S. Charter provides that 'the structure, competence, and procedure' of the Commission shall be determined by 'an inter-American convention on human rights', and second, that article 150 stipulates that until the American Convention enters into force 'the present Inter-American Commission on Human Rights shall keep vigilance over the obser-

[120] *Id.* art. 150.

[121] Farer & Rowles, *supra* note 44, at 49–50. *See also* Professor Farer's testimony supporting U.S. ratification of the American Convention on Human Rights, *Hearings before the Senate Foreign Relations Comm. on International Human Rights Treaties*, 96th Cong., 1st Sess., at 98 (1979).

[122] *See* Statute, art. 2.

vance of human rights'. By ratifying the O.A.S. Charter, all O.A.S. member states thus agreed, whether or not they ratified the American Convention, that 'the structure, competence, and procedure' of the Inter-American Commission *qua* O.A.S. Charter organ shall be determined by reference to the American Convention once it enters into force. It follows that as soon as the American Convention enters into effect, article 112 became fully applicable and the transitory arrangements envisaged in article 150 lapsed. The American Convention and the Statute of the Commission adopted pursuant to it now consequently determine 'the structure, competence, and procedure' of the Commission as a Charter organ.

To enable the new Inter-American Commission to perform the functions of a Convention organ as well as a Charter organ, the American Convention distinguishes, in defining the Commission's functions, between 'member states' and 'States Parties'.[123] Moreover, article 41 of the American Convention, which enumerates the powers of the Inter-American Commission, adopts verbatim most of the provisions of article 9 of the Commission's old Statute.[124] Although language comparable to that of article 9(*bis*) is not to be found in the American Convention, the omission does not appear to have been intended to deprive the new Commission of article 9(*bis*) power when dealing with states that have not ratified the American Convention. This conclusion finds support in the fact that there is one very important difference between the wording of article 41(b) of the American Convention and article 9(b) of the old Statute. The former gave the Inter-American Commission the power 'to make recommendations to the governments of the member states', whereas article 9(b) uses the same language but adds the phrase 'in general'. The old Commission interpreted the phrase 'in general' in article 9(b) to mean that it could address general recommendations to each O.A.S. member state or to all of them,[125] but the limitation concerning 'general recommendations' was understood to bar individual resolutions for specific cases. The omission of the phrase 'in general' from article 41(b) of the American Convention is thus very significant. Beyond codifying the previous interpretation of article 9(b) of the Statute and empowering the Inter-American Commission to adopt general and individual recommendations, it authorizes Commission action in the form of specific resolutions relating to individual cases.

The fact that article 41 is silent about communications, as is article

[123] *See*, *e.g.*, American Convention, arts. 41–44. Thus, for example, all functions of the Inter-American Commission enumerated in art. 41, except for art. 41(f), apply to 'member states'. Art. 41(f) applies only to states parties.

[124] *Compare* the texts of art. 41 of the American Convention *with* art. 9 of the Statute.

[125] *See* text accompanying note 111 *supra*.

9(*bis*), is of little significance. Although the Inter-American Commission recognized in 1960 that article 9 of the Statute did not empower it 'to make any individual decision regarding the written communications that it receives', it determined that it was authorized under article 9(b) and (c) 'to take cognizance of them by way of information'.[126] The Commission was prevented from doing more, that is, examining the communication and rendering a decision in an appropriate resolution, by its lack of power to adopt specific recommendations. Article 41(b) of the American Convention rectifies this omission and empowers the Commission *qua* O.A.S. Charter organ to do under article 41 what it was authorized to do under articles 9 and 9(*bis*) of its pre-Convention Statute.[127]

The new Statute of the Inter-American Commission on Human Rights, which was drafted by the Commission and approved by the O.A.S. General Assembly in 1979[128] following a thorough article-by-article review,[129] indicates that the O.A.S. General Assembly proceeded on the assumption that the new Commission, when acting as a Charter organ, possesses all of the powers that the old Commission had under its Statute. Three provisions of the new Statute—articles 18, 19, and 20—deal with the powers of the Commission. Article 18 enumerates the powers of the Commission 'with respect to the member states of the Organization of American States'. It restates the functions of the Inter-American Commission that are spelled out in article 41 of the American Convention and adds a stipulation authorizing the Commission 'to conduct on-site observations in a state, with the consent or at the invitation of the government in question.'[130] Article 19 of the new Statute applies only 'to the States Parties to the American Convention on Human Rights' and lists the functions that the Com-

[126] IACHR, First Report, *supra* note 111, at 13. The full text of the ruling is reproduced in Sohn & Buergenthal, *supra* note 2, at 1288–89.

[127] This conclusion is borne out by the *travaux préparatoires* of the American Convention. Art. 32 of the Draft Convention referred to the Statute of the Inter-American Commission and the resolution of the Second Special Inter-American Conference, *viz*., to arts. 9 and 9(*bis*) of the Statute, in defining the functions of the Commission. This provision was deleted in favor of art. 41, not because the drafters wanted to limit the Commission's power, but because they thought it 'inappropriate for the Convention to establish the structure and functions of the Commission by reference to other instruments . . .' Conferencia Especializada, *supra* note 3, at 372.

[128] Statute of the Inter-American Commission on Human Rights, O.A.S. Doc. OEA/Ser.P, AG/doc. 1180 (1979), *reprinted in* Handbook, *supra* note 3, at 95 [hereinafter cited as 1979 Statute]. The O.A.S. General Assembly adopted this Statute in accordance with the provisions of art. 39 of the American Convention, which provides that '[t]he Commission shall prepare its Statute, which it shall submit to the General Assembly for approval'.

[129] *See* Informe del Relator de la Primera Comisión—Asuntos Jurídicos y Políticos, O.A.S. Doc. OEA/Ser.P, AG/doc. 1198/79, at 15–18 (1979).

[130] 1979 Statute, art. 18(g). Art. 11 of the old Statute of the Commission authorized such visits without denominating them 'on-site observations'.

mission exercises in relation to them. This provision is followed by article 20, which provides that:

> In relation to those member states of the Organization that are not Parties to the American Convention on Human Rights, the Commission shall have the following powers, in addition to those designated in Article 18:
> a. to pay particular attention to the observance of the human rights referred to in Articles I, II, III, IV, XVIII, XXV, and XXVI of the American Declaration of the Rights and Duties of Man;
> b. to examine communications submitted to it and any other available information, to address the government of any member state not a Party to the Convention for information deemed pertinent by this Commission, and to make recommendations to it, when it finds this appropriate, in order to bring about more effective observance of fundamental human rights, and
> c. to verify, as a prior condition to the exercise of the powers granted under subparagraph b. above, whether the domestic legal procedures and remedies of each member state not a Party to the Convention have been duly applied and exhausted.

Note that the above quoted provision is virtually identical to the text of article 9(*bis*) of the old Statute from which only one paragraph has been omitted.[131] By incorporating the text of article 9(*bis*) into the new Statute, its drafters intended to put all states not parties to the Convention on notice that the new Commission had retained the powers that were conferred on it by article 9(*bis*).

The new Statute also declares in article 1(2) that

> for the purpose of the present Statute, human rights are understood to be:
> (a) the rights set forth in the American Convention on Human Rights, in relation to the States parties thereto;
> (b) the rights set forth in the American Declaration of the Rights and Duties of Man, in relation to the other member states.

Paragraph (b) of this provision reaffirms the interpretation that the human rights referred to in various provisions of the O.A.S. Charter, notably in articles 3(j) and 112, must be defined by reference to the American Declaration, which thus establishes standards applicable to all O.A.S. member states. The American Convention on Human Rights recognizes this normative status of the American Declaration when it provides that 'no provision of this Convention shall be interpreted as . . . excluding or limiting the effect that the American Declaration of the Rights and Duties of Man . . . may have'.[132] It should be emphasized in this connection, that the Inter-American

[131] The omitted paragraph is art. 9(c)(*bis*), which dealt with the Commission's annual reporting requirement.

[132] American Convention, art. 29(d).

Commission may on occasion have to look to the American Convention for guidance in interpreting the American Declaration. This conclusion results from the fact that the American Declaration 'proclaims very general principles which are ill-suited for adjudicatory purposes. The Commission may find it useful, therefore, to draw on the language of the American Convention . . . to give juridical precision to the American Declaration.'[133]

2. *The Practice of the Commission as a Charter Organ*

The principal activities of the Inter-American Commission on Human Rights acting as an O.A.S. Charter organ have consisted of the preparation of country studies and the processing of individual complaints. Although the Commission also has broad promotional authority—article 41(a) of the American Convention requires the Commission 'to develop an awareness of human rights among the peoples of America'—it has thus far made very limited use of this power.[134] The Inter-American Commission has yet to undertake a systematic effort to promote human rights in the hemisphere by developing programs to encourage human rights education and research, for example. The neglect of its promotional activities may be attributed, in part at least, to its limited financial resources and its relatively small staff,[135] which appear to have forced it to make difficult choices in deciding upon which activities it should concentrate. Events in the hemisphere have also affected that choice because in recent years the Commission has been called upon with increasing frequency to investigate one human rights trouble spot after another. These so-called 'on-site' observations have left little time for other activities.

a. *Country Studies and 'On-Site' Observations.* As soon as it assumed office in 1960, the Inter-American Commission began to receive complaints charging violations of human rights in different O.A.S. member states. Although its Statute did not authorize specific action relating to these petitions, article 9 permitted the Commission to prepare

[133] Buergenthal, *supra* note 3, at 134. *See also* IACHR, Report on the Status of Human Rights in Chile: Findings of 'On the Spot' Observations in the Republic of Chile, O.A.S. Doc. OEA/Ser.L/II.34, doc. 21, Corr. 1 (1974), where the Commission looked to art. 27 of the American Convention—the derogation clause—to demonstrate that even a national emergency did not authorize the suspension by Chile of certain fundamental human rights guaranteed in the American Declaration. *Id.* at 2–3.

[134] The Inter-American Commission had the same power under art. 9(a) of its old Statute, but it never really developed a systematic plan or program to implement it.

[135] Farer & Rowles, *supra* note 44, at 52, reported in 1978 that 'until 1977 staffing had been frozen at four lawyers, despite a caseload that had increased nearly 1000% since 1973. The staff has recently expanded and there are now established slots for nine lawyers in addition to the Executive Secretary.' They also report that the budget of the Commission for 1978 represented slightly less than 2% of the regular O.A.S. budget for that year.

studies and reports, and to adopt general recommendations. Article 11 enabled it to hold meetings away from its headquarters. These two provisions of the Statute provided the Commission with the legislative authority to develop the system of country studies and 'on-site' observations.

A country study, that is, a report examining the human rights conditions in a specific country, was initiated, as a rule, if a large number of complaints began to be received by the Inter-American Commission charging that government with serious and large-scale violations of human rights. The first such reports were prepared in the early 1960s and dealt with Cuba, Haiti, and the Dominican Republic.[136] Both Cuba and Haiti refused to allow the Commission to visit their countries; the Dominican Republic permitted the Commission to enter, and it became the first country to be the subject of an 'on-site' investigation.[137]

In its initial country study of Cuba, the Commission established the precedent of hearing witnesses and receiving evidence. In that particular case, it held hearings in Miami and interviewed many refugees. During its visits to the Dominican Republic, the Commission travelled extensively in that country, held hearings, met with government and opposition leaders, with representatives of various church, business, and union groups, and with private individuals; it also set up temporary offices in the country where it accepted written and oral complaints. The *modus operandi* adopted by the Commission during its visits to the Dominican Republic in the 1960s became a model that is followed by the Commission to this day. Thus, during the more recent 'on-site' observations in Nicaragua,[138] El Salvador,[139] and Argentina,[140] the Commission employed basically the same fact-finding approach it had used in the Dominican Republic.

The 'on-site' investigations are usually arranged by an exchange of letters and cables between the chairman of the Inter-American Commission and the government concerned. As a rule, the Commission requests permission to visit a particular country,[141] but some govern-

[136] For information on these reports, *see* IACHR, The Organization of American States and Human Rights 1960–67, at 39–53 (1972). The Haitian and Dominican reports are reproduced in Sohn & Buergenthal, *supra* note 2, at 1293–1339.

[137] The first visit to the Dominican Republic took place in Oct. 1961.

[138] IACHR, Report on the Situation of Human Rights in Nicaragua: Findings of the 'on-site' Observations in the Republic of Nicaragua, Oct. 3–12, 1978, O.A.S. Doc. OEA/Ser.L/V/II.45, doc. 16, Rev. 1 (1978).

[139] IACHR, Report on the Situation of Human Rights in El Salvador and Observations of the Government of El Salvador in the Report, O.A.S. Doc. OEA/Ser.P, AG/doc. 1086/79 (1979).

[140] IACHR, Report on the Situation of Human Rights in Argentina, O.A.S. Doc. OEA/Ser.L/V/II.49, doc. 19 (1980).

[141] Art. 11 of the old Statute of the Commission plainly required such permission. Arts. 48(1)(d) and 48(2) of the American Convention, when read together, appear not to require

ments have lately begun to invite the Commission on their own initiative.[142] For many years, the Commission did not have a specific set of rules applicable to such visits. This meant that the ground rules had to be negotiated on an *ad hoc* basis. This situation changed in 1977 when the Commission adopted a 'Resolution on On-Site Observation',[143] which spelled out the undertaking a government had to give before the Inter-American Commission or one of its sub-committees would visit the country. These standards have been included, with some additions, in the Commission's new Rules of Procedure.[144] Article 54 of the rules of procedure requires the host government to put at the disposal of the Commission all facilities necessary for the accomplishment of its mission and to pledge that it will impose no punitive measures against individuals who cooperated with or supplied information to the Commission. The right of members of the Commission and its staff to travel freely in the host country, to meet with any individuals whatsoever, and to visit prisons are provided for in article 55 of the rules of procedure. This provision also establishes the government's obligation to assure the safety of the Commission and its staff, and to provide the Commission with whatever documents it may request.

The very presence of the Inter-American Commission in a country has at various times contributed to the improvement of conditions in it. The most dramatic example is provided by the role of the Commission performed during the Dominican civil war, when it saved hundreds of lives and obtained the release from detention camps and prisons of large numbers of political detainees.[145] A more recent example of the salutory effect of the presence of the Commission consists of its activities in Colombia in the spring of 1980, when it negotiated the release of various diplomats being held hostage in

permission in ordinary cases as far as states parties are concerned. However, art. 18(g) of the Commission's new Statute specifies that the Commission may 'conduct on-site observations in a state, with the consent or at the invitation of the government in question'. *See* text accompanying and note 130 *supra*.

[142] This was done, for example, by the Government of Panama. *See* IACHR, Report on the Situation of Human Rights in Panama, O.A.S. Doc. OEA/Ser.L/V/II.44, doc. 38, Rev. 1, at 1–3 (1978).

[143] The resolution was adopted at the 42d session of the Commission, held during Oct. 31–Nov. 12, 1977, and is reproduced in IACHR, Handbook of Existing Rules Pertaining to Human Rights, O.A.S. Doc. OEA/Ser.L/V/II.23, doc. 21, Rev. 6, at 40 (1978). The same publication also contains the Commission's 'Regulations Regarding On-Site Observations', adopted on 15 Oct. 1975. *Id.* at 39.

[144] *See* Regulations, *supra* note 51, arts. 51–55.

[145] *See* IACHR, Report of the Activities of the Commission on Human Rights in the Dominican Republic, June 1–Aug. 31, 1965, O.A.S. Doc. OEA/Ser.L/V/II.12, doc. 14, Rev. (1965). *See also* Sandifer, *The Inter-American Commission on Human Rights in the Dominican Republic, June 1965 to June 1966*, in J. Carey, The Dominican Republic Crisis, 1965, at 115 (1967); Sohn & Buergenthal, *supra* note 2, at 1325.

Colombia in return for the government's agreement, which was demanded by those holding the hostages, that the Commission be permitted to monitor the military trials of suspected terrorists.[146]

The impact of the Commission's country studies and 'on-site' investigations depends on various considerations, including the publication of the report and the action that the O.A.S. is willing to take after the report has been published. Governments like to prevent the publication of well-documented reports charging them with large-scale violations of human rights. They are also willing at times to stop the criticized practices if that will reduce the adverse impact of a report or stop its publication. That is why the Commission's power to publish its country studies and investigation reports can be a very effective method to promote compliance.

The procedure which the Inter-American Commission follows in these cases is to prepare a draft report,[147] which analyzes the conditions in the country by reference to the human rights that are proclaimed in the American Declaration and sets out the Commission's findings and recommendations. The draft report is then submitted to the government for its comments and a date is fixed within which the government is requested to present its observations. The government's response is analyzed by the Commission with a view to determining whether the report should be amended in light of the information brought to the Commission's attention by the government. After reassessing its findings, the Commission decides whether to publish the report. The rules of procedure of the Commission require the publication of the report if the government does not respond to the request for observations.[148] The Inter-American Commission need not publish it if the government replies and either agrees to comply with recommendations or demonstrates that it is not committing any violations. The reports that have been published by the Commission in the past few years have usually reproduced in full the observations of the governments. In most of these cases the governments disagreed with some or a majority of the findings of the Commission.[149]

In addition to the publication of the report, the Inter-American Commission may also transmit it for consideration by the O.A.S. General Assembly, which holds one regular session per year. The Commission may include the particular country study in whole or in part in its annual report to the Assembly or it may transmit it as a

[146] The Commission lawyers were still in Bogotá, Colombia, in the fall of 1980.

[147] *See* Regulations, *supra* note 51, art. 58.

[148] *Id.* art. 58(d).

[149] *But see* IACHR, Report on the Situation of Human Rights in Panama, *supra* note 142, at 119–22.

separate document. Because debates in the Assembly generally attract considerable public attention, reference to and discussion by the Assembly of a country report, followed by an appropriate resolution, can have a significant impact on the behavior of a government charged with violations of human rights and may lead to an improvement of conditions in the country. These considerations probably explain why for a number of years there seemed to be tacit agreement among O.A.S. member states not to discuss the annual report that the Inter-American Commission submitted to the Assembly. Instead, they would routinely and without debate adopt a resolution in which the General Assembly resolved 'to take note of the annual report of the Inter-American Commission on Human Rights and to thank the Commission for the important work it has been doing'.[150]

This situation began to change in the mid-1970s. The first break with tradition occurred in 1975 when the O.A.S. General Assembly had before it the Commission's annual report for the year 1974 as well as its report on 'The Status of Human Rights in Chile'. Although the Assembly once again passed its usual resolution on the annual report,[151] it also adopted a separate resolution dealing with the Chilean report,[152] which was preceded by a lengthy and well-publicized debate. The change was described as follows by William S. Mailliard, the U.S. Representative to the O.A.S.:

> [T]his was the first occasion when the Inter-American Human Rights Commission reports were not merely noted and filed away. In the past the nations of the hemisphere strongly preferred not to point the finger at any one government, at least in part, for fear that they could be on the receiving end of accusations the next time. The real breakthrough then is this: We have now established a precedent which can insure that the status of human rights in the hemisphere receives full and frank airing at the annual OAS General Assembly.[153]

At the next annual O.A.S. General Assembly session, the Assembly adopted a much stronger resolution dealing with the Commission's report concerning violations of human rights in Chile,[154] besides passing another resolution dealing with various specific issues that the Commission had raised in its annual report for the year 1975.[155] This

[150] *See, e.g.*, O.A.S. General Assembly Res. 154 (IV-0/74); O.A.S. General Assembly Res. 83 (II-0/72).

[151] O.A.S. General Assembly Res. 192 (V-0/75).

[152] *Id.* 190 (V-O/75).

[153] *Hearings* [*on Human Rights Issues at the Sixth Regular Session of the Organization of American States General Assembly*] *before the Subcomm. on Int'l Organizations of the House Comm. on Int'l Relations*, 94th Cong., 2d Sess., at 3 (1976).

[154] O.A.S. General Assembly Res. 243 (VI-0/76).

[155] *Id.* 242 (VI-0/76).

practice has continued, and specific human rights issues raised by annual reports of the Commission have been discussed and acted upon in recent O.A.S. General Assembly sessions. Although O.A.S. General Assembly resolutions, as a matter of law, are recommendations only, they are acts emanating from the highest organ of the O.A.S. and consequently carry considerable moral and political weight. Governments take these considerations into account when they have to decide how to react to recommendations made by the Commission in one of its country studies. Ultimately, as in all efforts to enforce internationally guaranteed human rights, the effectiveness of the Commission's 'country-study' practice depends on its prestige and credibility, on the public opinion pressure that is likely to be exerted to support its recommendations, and on the resolutions that the O.A.S. General Assembly is willing to adopt to back the Commission.[156]

b. *Individual Communications*. Prior to the entry into force of the American Convention, the Inter-American Commission examined and acted on only those private communications that alleged a violation of one of the 'preferred' freedoms enumerated in article 9(*bis*) of its Statute.[157] This policy was based on the assumption that the power which this provision conferred on the Commission with regard to communications was intended to apply only to those fundamental rights. Although it is debatable whether this restrictive interpretation was in fact compelled by the text of article 9(*bis*), it is clear that the Inter-American Commission today assumes that the entry into force of the American Convention significantly expanded its powers for dealing with petitions concerning O.A.S. member states that have not ratified the Convention. Its new rules of procedure, adopted after the American Convention and the Commission's new Statute entered into force, contain stipulations that allow the Commission to act on *all* communications lodged against a non-state party, provided only that the petitioner alleges the violation of a right that is proclaimed in the American Declaration.[158] Moreover, for the purposes of examining the admissibility of petitions, these rules make no distinction between

[156] At the session of the O.A.S General Assembly held in Nov. 1980, certain governments, led by Argentina, successfully blocked the adoption of O.A.S. General Assembly resolutions, based on thorough Commission reports, charging them with serious violations of human rights. Eventually, a single watered-down resolution, applying to all states, was adopted. This action amounted to a significant setback for the Inter-American Commission, in particular, and O.A.S. human rights efforts, in general. For the text of the resolution, *see* O.A.S. General Assembly Res. of 27 Nov. 1980 (Annual Report and Special Reports of the Inter-American Commission on Human Rights), O.A.S. Doc. OEA/Ser.P, AG/doc. 1348/80, Rev. 1 (1980). It is too early to say whether this development signals a weakening of the support for human rights that had gradually built up in recent years in the O.A.S. General Assembly.

[157] *See* text accompanying notes 115–16 *supra*.

[158] *See* Regulations, *supra* note 51, art. 49.

complaints involving states that are parties to the American Convention and those that are not.[159] The admissibility requirements and the proceedings applicable to communications filed under the Convention consequently also govern complaints involving violations of the American Declaration, notwithstanding the fact that the latter complaints are dealt with by the Commission pursuant to the authority it derives from the O.A.S. Charter.

The Commission's new rules of procedure distinguish between complaints filed under the American Convention and those that are based on the American Declaration only when they have reached the post-admissibility stage.[160] A complaint filed against a state that is not a party to the American Convention, which has been ruled admissible and not resolved by means of a friendly settlement,[161] is not subject to the reporting stages applicable to petitions lodged under the Convention. Instead, after the Inter-American Commission has examined the complaint, it adopts a resolution containing the facts of the case, its conclusions, and whatever recommendations it deems appropriate.[162] The resolution, which must also specify by what date the recommendations are to be complied with, is transmitted to the defendant state and the petitioner.[163] Prior to the expiration of the date, the defendant state has an opportunity to request the Commission to re-examine its findings and recommendations.[164] It may also submit whatever additional evidence it deems relevant to support its motion.[165] The petitioner may be heard at this stage as well. If the Commission modifies the resolution after the rehearing, it may fix a new date for compliance. If the defendant state fails to comply with the recommendations by the date which the Commission fixed, it has the right to publish the resolution in its annual report to the O.A.S. General Assembly or in whatever other manner it deems advisable.[166]

Because a state that has not ratified the American Convention is not subject to the jurisdiction of the Inter-American Court of Human Rights, a complaint dealt with by the Commission acting exclusively as a Charter organ cannot be referred to the Inter-American Court for adjudication. But this is not to say that such cases can under no circumstances reach the Court. The Inter-American Court's advisory

[159] *See id.* arts. 29–40.

[160] *Id.* art. 50.

[161] *Id.* art. 42. Despite the fact that art. 42(1) refers to the American Convention, it appears also to apply to complaints involving the American Declaration. Judging from the context, the failure to refer to the Declaration seems to have been an oversight.

[162] *See* Regulations, *supra* note 51, art. 50(1).

[163] *Id.* art. 50(2).

[164] *Id.* art 50(3).

[165] *Id.*

[166] *Id.* arts. 50(4) & 50(5).

jurisdiction, for example, is not limited to states parties to the American Convention nor to questions regarding the interpretation of that Convention. Since any O.A.S. member state and any O.A.S. organ may seek advisory opinions from the Court and since the subject of the request may relate to treaties 'concerning the protection of human rights in the American states',[167] the Inter-American Commission, the O.A.S. General Assembly, or a member state might apply for an advisory opinion concerning legal issues arising in a case under consideration by the Commission acting as a Charter organ.[168] Here the Court might be asked to address questions about the powers of the Commission as a Charter organ, the human rights obligations of O.A.S member states that have not ratified the American Convention, and, possibly, the normative relationship between the American Declaration and the O.A.S. Charter.

Finally, it should be asked whether the procedures developed by the Inter-American Commission for dealing with individual complaints have been effective. The answer, regrettably, is that they have not proved very effective. For one thing, contrary to its practice involving country studies, the O.A.S. General Assembly has rarely considered the Commission's decisions in individual cases. Secondly, the Commission appears in the past few years to have devoted less and less time to individual complaints. It has no doubt been motivated by the realization that, given the attitude of the O.A.S. General Assembly, it can have much more significant impact by concentrating on country studies. Conditions in the hemisphere have also forced the Inter-American Commission to embark on an increasing number of country studies and on-site investigations, and these have been a drain on its staff resources. But whatever the reasons, there has been little institutional pressure on the Assembly to concern itself with individual cases. Therefore, since states know that they will rarely, if ever, be called to account for their actions in individual cases, it is easy for them to disregard the Commission's resolutions in such cases. One might consequently question the wisdom of the Commission's decision to make the petition system applicable to all rights proclaimed in the American Declaration. (Would it not make more sense to limit it only to violations of some of the most fundamental rights? This approach,

[167] American Convention, art. 64(1).

[168] *See*, in this connection, section I.B.2.b. *supra*. If such a request for an advisory opinion related exclusively to the American Declaration, the Inter-American Court would have to decide whether and under what circumstances, if any, the Declaration can be treated as a 'treaty' within the meaning of art. 64(1). A draft resolution sponsored by Costa Rica and a number of other states, which would have had the O.A.S. General Assembly request an advisory opinion from the Inter-American Court regarding the competence of the Inter-American Commission to prepare reports on the human rights situation in Cuba, failed to obtain the necessary number of affirmative votes during the 1980 O.A.S. General Assembly session.

which was reflected in article 9(*bis*) of the Commission's old Statute, enabled the Commission to concentrate on important cases.) The Commission's failure to be more selective in choosing the types of cases it deals with as a Charter organ weakens the entire O.A.S. petition system, including the petition machinery provided for under the American Convention. Both depend for their enforcement on the O.A.S. General Assembly, which has little interest in and patience for dealing with too many individual petitions. Of course, if the Assembly could be persuaded to establish, as one of its subsidiary organs, a special human rights committee to review the Commission's reports for each session of the Assembly and advise the Assembly on the measures it should adopt, the petition system might gradually acquire 'teeth'. Such a committee might also enhance the overall capacity of the Assembly to enforce decisions of the Inter-American Commission and the Inter-American Court and thus significantly strengthen the entire inter-American rights system.

D. CONCLUSIONS

This is not the best time to write about the inter-American system for the protection of human rights. The system is in a period of transition and so is the political milieu in which it operates. The new Convention-based regime is only now beginning to function and there is very little practice and no case law to draw on.[169] The extensive practice of the Charter-based regime, while still relevant and of value for purposes of analysis, is becoming increasingly less important because the regime's institutional framework has been modified with the entry into force of the American Convention, which more and more states are ratifying.

The political realities of the Americas and the fact that the region lacks political stability also quite obviously affect the protection of human rights in the hemisphere. The political instability of the region, whose causes are many and which is reflected in cyclical and often violent vacillations between representative democracy and military dictatorship, makes it hazardous to predict the future effectiveness of the inter-American human rights system.

The system depends for its effectiveness and survival on the member states of the Organization of American States and their willingness to support a strong regional machinery for the protection of human rights. The attitude of the major powers of the region, particularly the United States, is also very important. In the past few years, the United States has been the strong proponent of an effective inter-American human rights system, and that has helped to strengthen the system considerably. The mere fact, moreover, that the American Convention

[169] [Ed. note: *See* note 86 *supra*.].

has entered into force and that fifteen states have ratified it is an encouraging development. It is also evidence that the political transformation occurring in the region is bringing governments to power which are more responsive to demands for the enjoyment of basic human rights. If this trend continues, the American Convention and the institutions it has established could come to play a significant role in promoting and protecting human rights in the hemisphere. But whether it will remains to be seen.

II. Teaching Suggestions

In a general course on the international protection of human rights, it would be very helpful to discuss the two regional systems for the protection of human rights—the European and inter-American systems—as part of one teaching unit. By exploring the similarities and differences of these two systems, the instructor would have an opportunity to consider which of these two systems might be better suited for adaptation in other regions of the world. Here one may want to discuss the legal, political, economic, and linguistic prerequisites for effective regional systems.

A

The fact that the inter-American human rights system consists of two regimes—one based on the American Convention, the other derived from the O.A.S. Charter—must be a starting point of any discussion dealing with it. (In introducing this subject, it would be useful to provide a rudimentary description of the organizational structure of the O.A.S.) Which regime should be discussed first—the Convention or the Charter-based one—is a matter of personal preference. In this chapter, I started with the Convention-based regime because I wanted to focus on a number of important substantive and institutional problems arising under the American Convention and because it seemed to me that this approach might make it easier for students to understand how the two regimes interact. An instructor interested in exploring the process of international institution-building would probably want to start with the Charter-based regime and focus on its evolution.

In discussing the Convention-based system, it makes sense, after providing a general overview of the American Convention, to examine the powers and functions of the principal Convention institutions—the Inter-American Commission and the Inter-American Court—and to analyze a selected number of difficult substantive law problems that arise under the American Convention. (Almost every provision of the

American Convention presents one or more interesting analytic problems, and my recommendation would be that the criterion for their selection should be the students' and instructor's interest.) When dealing with the Inter-American Commission, it might be useful to explore, *inter alia*, the different functions the third-stage and fourth-stage reports perform and the problems this dual report procedure might create. In this connection, it might be asked whether the procedure favors the individual petitioner or the government and whether, given the voting requirements, the procedure is subject to political abuse. The fact that the American Convention makes private petitions obligatory and inter-state ones optional, thus reversing the traditional approach, also makes an interesting topic for comparative discussion and policy analysis.

When considering the role of the Inter-American Court, the differences between its contentious and advisory jurisdiction merit thorough discussion. Of particular importance, in this connection, are the functions the Court's advisory opinions might perform. The many legal ambiguities surrounding the Court's advisory jurisdiction are worthy of analysis. (What are the advantages and disadvantages of the ambiguities?) This topic leads easily into a discussion of the role international adjudication might play in the implementation of human rights.

B

The most interesting aspect of the Charter-based regime is its evolution and gradual transformation from a system of promotion to one of protection. Unlike most other human rights regimes, this one was not created by a human rights convention; it derived its normative standards from the American Declaration of the Rights and Duties of Man, which had been proclaimed as a 'mere' declaration. The manner in which the Inter-American Commission on Human Rights gradually achieved constitutional and institutional legitimacy is in and of itself an interesting lesson in international institution-building.

Despite the emphasis that has been placed in the literature on the individual petition system as it was developed by the Inter-American Commission on Human Rights, it is clear that its country studies and 'on-site' observations have been the backbone of the Charter-based regime. What factors would explain this situation is a topic worthy of discussion. Equally important is the question whether the 'on-site' observation model should be duplicated in other regional systems, particularly in regions that are likely to suffer large-scale violations of human rights similar to those that have victimized the Western Hemisphere. A related issue is whether the Charter-based system should concentrate on large-scale violations and/or on the more individual egregious violations of human rights instead of seeking to enforce, through individual complaints, all rights that are proclaimed in the American Declaration.

C

A topic that acquires special importance in assessing the effectiveness of the inter-American system for the protection of human rights concerns the role that the political organs of the O.A.S., particularly the O.A.S. General Assembly, play in the enforcement process. One might want to compare the O.A.S. General Assembly with the Committee of Ministers and Assembly of the Council of Europe, discuss the respective functions they perform, and consider to what extent they promote or hinder the enforcement of human rights decisions. It should also prove extremely interesting to explore the role that the Inter-American Court of Human Rights might play in the enforcement processes of the Charter-based system.

III. Syllabus

I. *Introduction*
- A. The Organization of American States: General Introduction.
- B. Regional Systems for the Protection of Human Rights: An Overview.

II. *The American Convention on Human Rights: Substantive Problems*
- A. In General.
- B. Selected Problems of Interpretation. (Topics choice of instructor.)
  1. The Self-Executing Character of the Convention.
  2. The Federal-State Clause.
  3. The Right of Derogation.

III. *The American Convention on Human Rights: Institutions*
- A. The Inter-American Commission on Human Rights.
  1. Its Functions.
  2. Individual and Inter-State Complaints.
- B. The Inter-American Court of Human Rights.
  1. The Court's Contentious Jurisdiction.
  2. The Court's Advisory Jurisdiction.

IV. *The O.A.S. Charter and Human Rights*
- A. Evolution of the Charter-Based Regime.
  1. Under the 1948 O.A.S. Charter.
  2. Under the Revised O.A.S. Charter.

3. Effect of the American Convention.

B. The Practice of the Inter-American Commission as a Charter-Based Organ.

1. Country Studies and 'On-Site' Observations.
2. Individual Communications.

V. *The Inter-American and European Systems Compared*

A. Effectiveness and Political Realities.
B. Models for Other Regional Systems.

IV. Minisyllabus

I. *The Organization of American States: General Introduction*

II. *The American Convention on Human Rights*

A. In General.
B. Selected Problems of Interpretation. (Topics choice of instructor.)

III. *The American Convention on Human Rights: Institutions*

A. The Inter-American Commission on Human Rights.

1. Its Functions.
2. Individual and Inter-State Complaints.

B. The Inter-American Court of Human Rights.

1. The Court's Contentious Jurisdiction.
2. The Court's Advisory Jurisdiction.

IV. *The O.A.S. Charter and Human Rights: The Practice of the Inter-American Commission as a Charter-Based Organ*

A. Country Studies and 'On-Site' Observations.
B. Individual Communications.

V. Bibliography

Buergenthal, *The American Convention on Human Rights: Illusions and Hopes*, 21 Buffalo L. Rev. 121 (1971).

—— *The Revised OAS Charter and the Protection of Human Rights*, 69 Am. J. Int'l L. 828 (1975).

—— *The Inter-American Court of Human Rights*, 76 Am. J. Int'l L. 231 (1982).

T. Buergenthal, R. Norris & D. Shelton, Protecting Human Rights in the Americas: Selected Problems (1982).

Cabranes, *Human Rights and Non-Intervention in the Inter-American System*, 65 Mich. L. Rev. 1147 (1967).

—— *The Protection of Human Rights by the Organization of American States*, 62 Am. J. Int'l L. 889 (1968).

Farer & Rowles, *The Inter-American Commission on Human Rights*, in International Human Rights Law and Practice 48 (J. Tuttle ed. 1978).

Fox, *Doctrinal Development in the Americas: From Non-Intervention to Collective Support for Human Rights*, 1 N.Y.U. J. Int'l & Pol. 44 (1968).

—— *The American Convention on Human Rights and Prospects for United States Ratification*, 3 Human Rights 243 (1973).

Frowein, *The European and American Conventions on Human Rights—A Comparison*, 1 Human Rights L. J. 44 (1980).

Garcia-Bauer, *Protection of Human Rights in America*, in 1 René Cassin Amicorum Discipulorumque Liber 75 (1969).

R. Goldman, The Protection of Human Rights in the Americas: Past, Present and Future (5 N.Y.U. Center for International Studies Policy Papers No. 2, 1972).

Gros Espiell, *L'Organisation des Etats Americains*, in Les Dimensions Internationales des Droits de l'Homme 600 (K. Vasak ed. 1978).

Norris, *Bringing Human Rights Petitions before the Inter-American Commission*, 20 Santa Clara L. Rev. 733 (1980).

—— *Observations in Loco: Practice and Procedure of the Inter-American Commission on Human Rights*, 15 Texas Int'l L. J. 46 (1980).

Sandifer, *The Inter-American Commission on Human Rights in the Dominican Republic, June 1965 to June 1966*, in The Dominican Republic Crisis, 1965, at 115–41 (J. Carey ed. 1967).

—— *Human Rights in the Inter-American System*, 11 How. L. J. 508 (1965).

Scheman, *The Inter-American Commission on Human Rights*, 59 Am. J. Int'l L. (1965).

A. Schreiber, The Inter-American Commission on Human Rights (1970).

L. Sohn & T. Buergenthal, International Protection of Human Rights 1267–374 (1973).

Symposium [*on*] *The American Convention on Human Rights* 30 Am. U. L. Rev. 1–187 (1980).

Thomas & Thomas, *Human Rights and the Organization of American States*, 12 Santa Clara Law. 319 (1972).

—— —— *The Inter-American Commission on Human Rights*, 20 Sw. L. J. 282 (1966).

K. Vasak, La Commission Interamericaine des Droits de l'Homme (1968).

VI. Minibibliography

Buergenthal, *The Revised OAS Charter and the Protection of Human Rights*, 69 Am. J. Int'l L. 828 (1975).

—— *The American and European Conventions on Human Rights: Similarities and Differences*, 30 Am. U. L. Rev. 155 (1980).

—— *The Inter-American Court of Human Rights*, 76 Am. J. Int'l L. 231 (1982).

Farer & Rowles, *The Inter-American Commission on Human Rights*, in International Human Rights Law and Practice 48 (J. Tuttle ed. 1978).

Fox, *The American Convention on Human Rights and Prospects for United States Ratification*, 3 Human Rights 243 (1973).

Frowein, *The European and the American Conventions on Human Rights—A Comparison*, 1 Human Rights J. 44 (1980).

A. Schreiber, The Inter-American Commission on Human Rights (1970).

Thomas & Thomas, *Human Rights and the Organization of American States*, 12 Santa Clara Law. 319 (1972).

K. Vasak, La Commission Interamericaine des Droits de l'Homme (1968).

Chapter 13

The European Convention on Human Rights*

Rosalyn Higgins[1]

I. Legal and Policy Considerations

A. CONCEPTUAL ISSUES

The law of the European Convention on Human Rights[2] has to be understood at two levels: as an increasingly important body of procedural and substantive law, and as part of the wider fabric of international efforts for the promotion of human rights. It is both inward looking and outward looking. It is this dual facet (that which is special to Europe, and that which is of global significance) that must be reflected in a worthwhile course on the European Convention. Too often, university courses on the European Convention on Human Rights merely explain the structure of the institutions and then propel the students into a random study of some leading cases or a brief selection of case studies. There is no sense of the place of the European Convention in the global struggle for human rights.

The relationship between the precepts of the U.N. Universal Declaration of Human Rights[3] and the text of the European Convention is important. The Universal Declaration deals both with political and civil rights, and with economic and social rights. So far as the former are concerned, the Universal Declaration covers the right to life, liberty, and security of person;[4] slavery and servitude;[5] torture and cruel, inhuman, or degrading treatment or punishment;[6] entitlement to 'recognition everywhere as a person before the law';[7] effective remedies by competent national tribunals;[8] arbitrary arrest, detention, or exile;[9] fair trial and determination of rights and obligations;[10]

[1] This study was completed in April 1981.

[2] European Convention for the Protection of Human Rights and Fundamental Freedoms, 213 U.N.T.S 221, *reprinted in* Basic Documents on Human Rights 242 (2d ed. I. Brownlie 1981) [hereinafter cited as Brownlie].

[3] G.A. Res. 217A. U.N. Doc. A/810, at 71 (1948).

[4] *Id.* art. 3.

[5] *Id.* art. 4.

[6] *Id.* art. 5.

[7] *Id.* art. 6.

[8] *Id.* art. 8.

[9] *Id.* art. 9.

[10] *Id.* art. 10.

privacy and protection of reputation;[11] freedom of movement;[12] asylum from persecution;[13] entitlement to nationality;[14] freedom to marry and found a family, based on consent;[15] the ownership of property and the prohibition against arbitrary deprivation of property;[16] freedom of thought, conscience, and religion;[17] freedom of assembly and association (including the right not to belong to an association);[18] the right to take part in government either directly or through representatives, and universal suffrage by secret ballot.[19] There is in penal matters a presumption of innocence.[20]

The European Convention includes many of these rights. The notions underlying articles 3, 4, 5, 6, 8, 9, 10, 18, and 20 of the Universal Declaration are also found in the European Convention. Sometimes the formulation of the right closely follows that used in the Universal Declaration: this is true, for example, of the prohibition of torture and cruel, inhuman, or degrading treatment or punishment. Sometimes there has been an alteration, or a change of emphasis. Thus article 8 of the European Convention drops the notion of protection of reputation and honor and uses the term 'respect' instead.[21] Again, the European Convention's clause on freedom of association[22] omits the provision found in the Universal Declaration which provides that no one may be compelled to belong to an association. This takes account of the existence of the 'closed shop' system of labour unions in certain European countries. Further, the European Convention's clause on the right to marry[23] is more limited than that of the Universal Declaration. The presumption of innocence in penal matters becomes part of the right to a fair trial.[24]

Certain Universal Declaration provisions, such as the ownership of property,[25] freedom of movement, asylum from persecution, the right

[11] *Id.* art. 12.
[12] *Id.* art. 13.
[13] *Id.* art. 14.
[14] *Id.* art. 15.
[15] *Id.* art. 16.
[16] *Id.* art. 17.
[17] *Id.* art. 18.
[18] *Id.* art. 20.
[19] *Id.* art. 21.
[20] *Id.* art. 11(1).
[21] *See* J. Fawcett, Application of the European Convention on Human Rights 186 (1969) [hereinafter cited as Fawcett] which finds the term 'respect' (for private and family life, home, and correspondence) tame, belonging to the world of manners rather than of law. 'Respect' contrasts with 'inviolability' or 'legal protection from', which could have been employed.
[22] Art. 11.
[23] Art. 12.
[24] Art. 6.
[25] *But see* First Protocol to the European Convention, art. 1, *reprinted in* Brownlie, *supra* note 2, at 257.

to participate in government and public life,[26] and the right to universal suffrage by secret ballot, find no mention in the European Convention.

Importantly, many of the rights that are repeated in the European Convention—whether in identical, similar, or somewhat different form—have qualifying clauses attached to them which limit their applicability. In particular, such clauses—which have figured prominently in the case law—are to be found in articles 5–11 of the European Convention.[27]

The Universal Declaration also contains an important list of economic and social rights.[28] These are not found at all in the European Convention, which limits itself to civil rights.[29] The International Covenant on Economic, Social and Cultural Rights[30] gives such matters the status of legal rights for the states parties.[31] Eastern Europe and much of the Third World regard economic and social aspirations as just as much of a human right as civil and political rights. These states charge that the West cynically disregards economic and social rights—and indeed that the capitalist political system makes 'the right to work', for example, or 'the right to housing' impossible to attain. The dilemma is that the full achievement of those economic and social rights entails a loss of individual liberties which is unacceptable to the western liberal democracies. The liberal democracies, knowing that these economic and social standards cannot be fully attained within their own political and economic structures, perceive them as 'aspirations' rather than legal rights. The developing countries further argue that the civil and political rights are 'secondary' to the economic and social rights—that the right of free expression, for example, means little to a man who is at starvation level—and, indeed, that the provision of these civil and political rights in a developing country is

[26] *But see* First Protocol, art. 3.

[27] These clauses are analyzed in Fawcett, *supra* note 21, at 57–227. For the difference between such qualifying clauses and derogation clauses, *see* Higgins, *Derogations Under Human Rights Treaties*, 48 Brit. Y.B. Int'l L. 281 (1976–77) [hereinafter cited as Higgins].

[28] *See* arts. 22, 23, 24, 25, 26, & 27 of the Universal Declaration, which cover such matters as social security, the rights to work, equal pay, just remuneration, holidays with pay, public assistance with housing and medical needs, etc. The non-discrimination clause of the Universal Declaration, art. 2, applies to both economic and social, and civil and political rights. The European Convention contains a clause, art. 14, which requires non-discrimination in respect of the rights contained therein, *i.e.*, civil rights.

[29] But there has been recent discussion and study on whether the European Convention should be amended to include social or economic rights. *See* Jacobs, *The extension of the European Convention to include Economic, Social and Cultural Rights*, 3 Human Rights Rev. 163 (1978); and draft Protocol to extend the rights, Doc. 5039, 7 Feb. 1983.

[30] G.A. Res. 2200, 21 U.N. GAOR, Supp. (No. 16) 49, U.N. Doc. A/6316 (1966).

[31] The Economic Covenant does not, however, have any enforcement or supervisory machinery, and is in that sense more cautious than the International Covenant on Civil and Political Rights, *id.* at 52.

counterproductive to the restructuring of society in a manner necessary to provide the 'more basic' economic and social rights.

In an ideal world, regional arrangements should buttress universal standards. In the field of human rights, however, the coexistence of the universal and the regional models is an uneasy one. The International Covenant on Civil and Political Rights embodies a considerable number of rights not found in the European Convention.[32] The European Convention contains a smaller number of rights not reflected in the Political Covenant.[33] Equally important, even where a right is embodied in both texts it may be couched in different terms.[34] Also significant is that the derogation clauses in each instrument, while they overlap to a certain extent, are differently drafted and not identical in the matters covered.[35] Other incompatibilities may be noted: the scope of the Political Covenant is narrower, being limited to individuals within the territory of a party and subject to its jurisdiction,[36] whereas the rights defined in the European Convention are secured by the contracting parties 'to everyone within their jurisdiction'.[37] Thus there are two sets of instruments whose texts do not fully coincide, and with very different implementing procedures. If the Political Covenant covers more rights, the implementing procedures of the European Convention are much stronger. It may further be noted that article 27(1)(b) of the European Convention would seem to preclude the European Commission of Human Rights from finding an application to it admissible if substantially the same matter has already been handled under the Political Covenant.

The parties to the European Convention have decided that, in respect of matters covered by the European Convention, they will use the regional rather than the universal machinery. Parties to the European Convention will be free to choose to use the procedure of the Political Covenant in respect of rights not covered by the European Convention.[38] For the moment, therefore, the possibility has receded

[32] *See* arts. 1, 6(4), 6(5), 10(1), 10(2)(b), 10(3), 14(4), 14(3)(a), 14(3)(g), 14(5), 14(6), 14(7), 16, 20, 23(3), 24, 25(b), 25(c), 26, & 27 of the Political Covenant.

[33] *See* European Conventions, arts. 2(2) & 16; First Protocol, art. 1; Fourth Protocol, arts. 3(1) & 4, *reprinted in* Brownlie, *supra* note 2, at 262.

[34] *Compare* art. 7 of the Political Covenant *with* art. 3 of the European Convention; art. 17 of the Political Covenant *with* art. 8 of the European Convention; art. 18(2) of the Political Covenant *with* art. 9 of the European Convention; art. 2(3) of the Political Covenant *with* art. 13 of the European Convention; art. 2 of the Political Covenant *with* art. 14 of the European Convention.

[35] *Compare* art. 4 of the Political Covenant *with* art. 15 of the European Convention.

[36] Political Covenant, art. 2(1).

[37] European Convention, art. 1. However, the Human Rights Committee can receive petitions from individuals subject to the jurisdiction of the state concerned, pursuant to art. 1 of the Optional Protocol to the International Covenant on Civil and Political Rights, G.A. Res. 2200, 21 U.N. GAOR, Supp. (No. 16) 59, U.N. Doc. A/6316 (1966).

[38] *See generally* Committee of Ministers Res. (70) 17, *reprinted in* Eissen, *The European*

of a state party to the European Convention using the procedure provided for in article 41 of the Political Covenant against another party to the European Convention, and the more obvious jurisdictional clashes seem to have been avoided. For the time being, the problems of coexistence remain theoretical.

Any course on human rights must make clear the areas in which the European Convention is modelled on the Universal Declaration; where they part company; and the extent to which the U.N. Covenants draw on or differ from the European Convention. This cannot be done by textual comparisons alone. An understanding of the philosophical, political, and economic background is also required.

The European Convention, then, covers the following rights, limited in scope but potentially effective in their enforcement: the right to life;[39] prohibition against torture and inhuman or degrading treatment or punishment;[40] prohibition against slavery, servitude, and forced or compulsory labour;[41] liberty and security of person;[42] fair and public hearings by an independent and impartial tribunal in the determination of civil rights and obligations or criminal charges;[43] prohibition of retrospective criminal liability;[44] respect for private and family life, home and correspondence;[45] freedom of thought, conscience, and religion;[46] freedom of expression;[47] freedom of peaceful assembly and association;[48] and the right to marry and found a family.[49] Other provisions serve to strengthen the efficacy of these rights, or to encourage governments (who are responsible for state security and who are anxious about frivolous litigation) to become parties to the European Convention. Thus article 13 speaks of the requirement of an effective remedy before a national authority.[50] Article 14 contains the

Convention on Human Rights and the United Nations Covenant on Civil and Political Rights: Problems of Coexistence, 22 Buffalo L. Rev. 181, 204–05 (1972); Directorate of Human Rights, Council of Europe, Proceedings of the Colloquy about the European Convention on Human Rights in Relation to other International Instruments for the Protection of Human Rights, Athens, Sept. 21–22, 1978 (Strasbourg 1979).

[39] Art. 2.
[40] Art. 3.
[41] Art. 4.
[42] Art. 5
[43] Art. 6.
[44] Art. 7.
[45] Art. 8.
[46] Art. 9.
[47] Art. 10.
[48] Art. 11.
[49] Art. 12.
[50] It is controversial whether this means that legal action *on the European Convention* should be available within the national legal systems of states parties. *See* 'Tyrer' Case [1978], Y.B. Eur. Conv. on Human Rights 612 (Eur. Ct. on Human Rights). *See also* Fawcett, *supra* note 21; A. Robertson, Human Rights in Europe 105–07 (2d ed. 1977) [hereinafter cited as Robertson].

vitally important provision that the enjoyment of the rights guaranteed by the European Convention shall be without discrimination as to sex, race, color, language, religion, political or other opinion, national or social origin, association with a national minority, property, birth, or other status. There is no right of non-discrimination *as such*, but rather non-discrimination in the securing of rights under the Convention. Article 15 provides, under carefully controlled conditions, for derogation from certain obligations in times of war or public emergency threatening the life of the nation.[51]

Article 17 warns that the European Convention may not be interpreted as implying for any state, group, or person any right to engage in any activity or perform any act aimed at the destruction or limitation of any of the rights or freedoms enumerated in the Convention.

There are various protocols to the European Convention. The First Protocol and the Fourth Protocol provide the opportunity for states to extend the rights guaranteed under the European Convention. The First Protocol protects a person from the deprivation of his or her possessions[52] 'except in the public interest and subject to the conditions provided for by law and by the general principles of international law.'[53] Article 2 provides that no person shall be denied the right to education, and that the state shall respect the right of parents to ensure education and teaching in conformity with their own religious and philosophical convictions.[54] Article 3 provides for the holding of free elections at reasonable intervals by secret ballot. However, there is no explicit reference to universal suffrage.[55] This Protocol, concluded in 1952, has been ratified by nineteen states to date.[56]

[51] No derogation may be made from art. 2 (except in respect of deaths resulting from lawful acts of war), or from arts. 3, 4(1), or 7. *See generally* Higgins, *supra* note 27.

[52] The text avoids reference to entitlement to own property. It is couched in terms of peaceful enjoyment of possessions. *Cf.* Universal Declaration, art. 17. For some case law under this clause, *see* Application 551/59, [1960] Y.B. Eur. Conv. on Human Rights 244 (Eur. Comm'n of Human Rights); Application 3039/67, [1967] Y.B. Eur. Conv. on Human Rights 506 (Eur. Comm'n of Human Rights); Application 5849/72, [1975] Y.B. Eur. Conv. on Human Rights 374 (Eur. Comm'n of Human Rights).

[53] First Protocol, art. 1.

[54] The leading case on art. 2 of the First Protocol is the 'Belgium Linguistics' Case [1968], 2 Y.B. Eur. Conv. on Human Rights 832 (Eur. Ct. of Human Rights). *See also* 'Case of Kjeldsen, Busk Madsen and Pedersen', [1976] Y.B. Eur. Conv. on Human Rights 502 (Eur. Ct. of Human Rights). It will readily be appreciated that claims under art. 2 of the First Protocol are often coupled with a claim under art. 14 of the European Convention, *i.e.*, non-discrimination.

[55] *Compare* art. 3 of the First Protocol *with* art. 21(3) of the Universal Declaration *and* art. 25 of the Political Covenant. There was a finding of a breach of art. 3 of the First Protocol in the 'Greek' Case, [1969] 1 Y.B. Eur. Conv. on Human Rights 175–80 (Eur. Comm'n of Human Rights).

[56] Austria, Belgium, Cyprus, Denmark, Federal Republic of Germany, France, Greece, Iceland, Ireland, Italy, Luxembourg, Malta, Netherlands, Norway, Portugal, Sweden, Turkey, and United Kingdom.

The Fourth Protocol[57] was concluded in 1963 and entered into effect in 1968. It provides for freedom from imprisonment for civil debts;[58] freedom of movement and of residence, and freedom to leave any country, including one's own;[59] freedom from exile and the right to enter the country of which one is a national;[60] and prohibition of a collective expulsion of aliens.[61] This Protocol has been ratified by eleven states to date.[62]

The Second Protocol[63] allows the European Court of Human Rights to give advisory opinions if certain conditions are fulfilled.[64] The Third Protocol[65] revised the original text of article 29 of the European Convention itself to deal with the grounds on which petitions already accepted may be rejected by the European Commission, and made small textual amendments to articles 30 and 34. The Fifth Protocol[66] amends the original articles 24 and 40 of the European Convention relating to terms of office for the European Commission, the Committee of Ministers, and the European Court. Thus the European Convention itself now exists with its text amended through the later Protocols.

In the European system it was decided to proceed with the serious promotion of a limited number of rights. For a proper understanding of the reasons for, and significance of, this decision the teacher will want a full discussion of the merits and demerits of a regional approach to human rights. There will also need to be some analysis of why the European Convention is limited to a small number of civil rights. The right to vote, for example, is not included in the Convention at all.[67] Freedom of movement only appears as a right in

[57] *See* note 33 *supra*.

[58] Fourth Protocol, art. 1.

[59] *Id.* art. 2.

[60] *Id.* art. 3.

[61] *Id.* art. 4.

[62] Austria, Belgium, Denmark, Federal Republic of Germany, France, Iceland, Ireland, Luxembourg, Norway, Portugal, and Sweden. The United Kingdom has not ratified the Fourth Protocol due to a lack of certainty as to the compatibility of its immigration policy with art. 3 of the Protocol.

[63] *Reprinted in* Brownlie, *supra* note 2, at 258.

[64] The Second Protocol has been ratified by eighteen states to date and came into effect in 1970, although its procedures have not yet been used.

[65] *Reprinted in* Brownlie, *supra* note 2, at 260.

[66] *Reprinted in id.* at 264.

[67] *But see* art. 3 of the First Protocol, whereby the parties 'undertake to hold free elections at reasonable intervals by secret ballot, under conditions which will ensure the free expression of the opinion of the people in the choice of the legislature.' This has been held to imply a right to vote. *See* Applications 6745/74 and 6746/74, W, X, Y, and Z v. Belgium, [1975] Y.B. Eur. Conv. on Human Rights 236, 244 (Eur. Comm'n of Human Rights); Application 6573/74, Decisions and Reports No. 6, at 87, 89.

an additional protocol to which not all Convention members are parties.[68] Why is this?

The question of the absolute or relative quality of human rights, referred to above in the context of civil/political and economic/social rights, arises in another context—namely whether certain human rights are applicable in times of war or other national emergency. It is possible to deal with this after dealing with the various substantive rights under the European Convention, but my own view is that it is better dealt with in the 'conceptual' part of the syllabus.

Necessarily, a discussion of derogation will focus on article 15 of the European Convention. Article 15 provides:

> (1) In time of war or other public emergency threatening the life of the nation any High Contracting Party may take measures derogating from its obligations under this Convention to the extent strictly required by the exigencies of the situation, provided that such measures are not inconsistent with its other obligations under international law.
>
> (2) No derogation from Article 2, except in respect of deaths resulting from lawful acts of war, or from Articles 3, 4 (paragraph 1) and 7 shall be made under this provision.
>
> (3) Any High Contracting Party availing itself of this right of derogation shall keep the Secretary-General of the Council of Europe fully informed of the measures which it has taken and the reasons therefor. It shall also inform the Secretary-General of the Council of Europe when such reasons have ceased to operate and the provisions of the Convention are again being fully executed.

In principle, human rights may be derogated from if there is war or other major emergency, but the measures of derogation must be limited to those strictly necessary to meet the situation. The European Convention case law—especially the *'Lawless' Case*[69] and *Ireland v. United Kingdom*[70]—is illuminating on this point.

A contrast may be drawn between the reference to 'time of war' in article 15(1) and the total omission of that phrase in comparable article 4 of the Political Covenant.[71]

Article 15(2) makes it clear that there are certain human rights that are absolutely fundamental and that cannot be derogated from even in time of war or national emergency. These include the right to life (save for lawful wartime deaths), the prohibition against torture or degrading treatment (though compulsory labour, article 4(2), may per-

[68] Fourth Protocol, art. 2.

[69] [1961] Y.B. Eur. Conv. on Human Rights 430, 432 (Eur. Ct. of Human Rights) [hereinafter cited as *Lawless*].

[70] [1978] Y.B. Eur. Conv. on Human Rights 602, 608 (Eur. Ct. of Human Rights) [hereinafter cited as *Ireland*].

[71] *See* Higgins, *supra* note 27, at 289.

haps be permitted in wartime), and the prohibition against retrospective penalties. Again, this list of nonderogable human rights may be contrasted with the (wider) list in article 4(2) of the Political Covenant. The students will want to discuss why these particular rights, rather than others, can never be derogated from, and what the legal significance of that fact is. Is it indicative that these rights—and these alone—are *jus cogens*?

It is important that students get a feel for how the European institutions have handled the difficult question of derogations. Who determines whether the measures taken are those strictly needed to meet the exigencies of the situation? The practice indicates that while the European Court reserves the decision to itself, it will be prepared to leave the derogating state a 'margin of appreciation' in choosing between alternative methods compatible with the European Convention. This difficult question of margin of appreciation has come up (in the context of article 15) in the *'Lawless' Case*,[72] the *'Cyprus' Case*,[73] and the *Ireland v. United Kingdom*[74] case.

Attention can also be drawn to the way in which the procedural requirements of article 15(3) allow the European institutions to exercise a measure of control over derogations. The question of whether states can still avail themselves of article 15(1) if they have not done all that is required of them under article 15(3) is not wholly settled by the case law.[75]

This is an appropriate moment in the course to contrast the provisions of article 15 on derogations with the qualifying clauses that are attached to several of the substantive rights guaranteed by the European Convention. These will necessarily have to be analyzed in detail at a later stage of the course, but it should be clearly explained at this juncture that these qualifying clauses are available to governments at all times, and not just during war or national emergency and that therefore the questions of notification of appropriate measures and the reasons for them do not arise.

The class is now well prepared to turn to a very important topic: the relationship of the European Convention to the domestic law of the parties. In some of the member states the Convention has been made part of the local law. In yet others its terms are incorporated into constitutional laws; or constitutional laws contain terms that are similar.[76] Indeed in some states—for example Germany—there is both

72 *Lawless*, *supra* note 69.

73 [1958–1959] Y.B. Eur. Conv. on Human Rights 174 (Eur. Comm'n of Human Rights).

74 *Ireland*, *supra* note 70, at 608.

75 *See* Higgins, *supra* note 27, at 290.

76 For an excellent survey, *see* Buergenthal, *The Effect of the European Convention on Human Rights on the International Law of Member States*, in The European Convention on Human Rights, Int'l & Comp. L.Q. Supp. No. 11, at 82 (1965).

a constitutional provision *and* the Convention is part of statute law. What is unique is for a country to have no written constitution and not to have incorporated the Convention into its national law. This is the situation with respect to the United Kingdom. Although the United Kingdom is party to the European Convention and accepts the two special procedures which gives states and individuals effective remedies, the Convention has not been made part of the law of the land. Accordingly, a person with a human rights claim against the United Kingdom may pursue it at the European institutions in Strasbourg, but not in English courts.[77] The United Kingdom government has been unhappy about the amount of adverse publicity generated by actions against it in Strasbourg; but it has resisted suggestions that the European Convention be made part of English law or that a Bill of Rights be enacted. There has, however, been keen debate on the issue of incorporation.[78]

At the same time, it should be said that the distinction between local law and European Convention law is not as rigid as it sometimes seems. In certain cases in the United Kingdom the courts have been willing to pay close attention to the European Convention, and they have offered their views as to whether a particular course of action on the part of the Executive would or would not be acceptable under the Convention. Thus in *Malone v. Metropolitan Police Commissioner*,[79] which concerned telephone tapping, the plaintiff claimed, *inter alia*, that interception of his phone calls violated article 8 of the European Convention. The judge found that as the European Convention was not justiciable in the English courts, the court could make no declaration in relation to it. But he was nonetheless prepared to say, referring to the leading European Convention case on the topic, 'I . . . find it impossible to see how English law could be said to satisfy the requirements of the Convention, as interpreted in the *Klass* case . . .' He

[77] It should be noted that it is possible for an applicant to pursue his or her case at Strasbourg even if there is no remedy available as a matter of law under the relevant domestic legal system. In the 'Amerkrane' Case, for example, [1973] Y.B. Eur. Conv. on Human Rights 356 (Eur. Comm'n of Human Rights), no remedy in any country would have been available. I am grateful to Mr. T. McNulty for pointing this out.

[78] *See, e.g.*, Draft Bill of Rights, H.L. Bill 100, 6 Dec. 1979; Hansard, 402 H.L. at col. 999 (1979); Hansard, 403 H.L. at cols. 287, 297 & 502 (1979).

[79] [1979] 2 W.L.R. 700.

[80] Art. 8 provides:

1. Everyone has the right to respect for his private and family life, his home and his correspondence.
2. There shall be no interference by a public authority with the exercise of this right except save as is in accordance with the law and is necessary in a democratic society in the interests of national security, public safety or the economic wellbeing of the country, for the prevention of disorder or crime, for the protection of health or morals, or for the protection of the rights and freedoms of others.

identified the requirements enunciated in the *'Klass' Case*[81] and thought that the English common law certainly fell short on one of those elements.

Students should be made aware that it is not correct to assume that the European Convention is ineffective if it is not incorporated into domestic law. This assumption is not true for a variety of reasons. First, as indicated above, domestic case law may often make reference to the requirements of the European Convention, even if the Convention may not—as in the United Kingdom—in formal terms be the basis of a cause of action. Second, the judgments of the European Court are binding, and that fact depends not at all upon the question of enforcement. Those countries accepting the jurisdiction of the Court are bound to give effect to its judgments. Third, countries will often amend their legislation or introduce new legislation during the course of proceedings before the European institutions so as to ensure that by the time the Court pronounces judgment there will be no grounds for complaint. However, the amendments may be claimed to be 'wholly independent' of any proceedings in which the institutions of the Convention are engaged.[82] Fourth, parties to the European Convention will have the European institutions very much in mind when drafting any new national legislation.

Before embarking on a study of the case law of the European Convention, it is necessary to have a clear understanding of the Convention's machinery and its operation.

B. THE MACHINERY

The European Commission of Human Rights has the same number of members as there are parties to the European Convention. The European Convention operates under its own Rules of Procedure and can deal with either inter-state cases or with individual petitions. Article 24 of the European Convention allows any state party to refer a case against another state party to the European Commission. Article 25—a crucial article—provides that the parties may recognize the competence of the European Commission to receive petitions 'from any person, non-governmental organization or group of individuals claiming to be the victim of a violation by one of the High Contracting Parties of the rights set forth in this Convention'. This operation of article 25 has been agreed to by the great majority of parties[83] to

[81] [1978] Eur. Conv. on Human Rights 622 (Eur. Ct. of Human Rights).

[82] *See, e.g.*, the legislation introduced by Belgium between the findings of the Commission and the judgment of the Court in the 'De Becker' Case, [1962] Y.B. Eur. Conv. on Human Rights 320 (Eur. Ct. of Human Rights).

[83] These do not include Cyprus, Greece, or Malta.

the Convention and is in many ways a test of a country's willingness to have its human rights commitments publicly examined. When a petition is received under article 25, the European Commission will not be able to deal with it if local remedies have not been exhausted.[84] Article 27 further directs that the Commission shall not deal with any petition which is anonymous, substantially the same as another already examined, 'manifestly ill founded', or an abuse to the right of petition.

There is interesting case law relevant to each of these requirements, and students will need to spend some time familiarizing themselves with the concept of abuse of petition.[85] It can also be difficult for students to understand when the European Commission rejects a claim upon examination of the merits rather than declaring it 'manifestly ill founded'.

When the Commission does declare a petition admissible, it investigates the facts and places itself at the disposal of the parties to secure a friendly settlement. Such friendly settlement must be on the basis of respect for the European Convention.[86] Thus the Commission has to act as guardian of the treaty, and the general practice is, for example, that money settlements are only to be regarded as an appropriate friendly settlement if there is no chance of a repetition of the alleged offense (*e.g.*, if new legislation or administrative directions are issued by the government concerned). If it succeeds in achieving a friendly settlement,[87] the Commission draws up a report and sends it to the states concerned and to the Committee of Ministers and the Secretary General of the Council of Europe. This brief report is published.[88] But if no friendly settlement is achieved, the Commission draws up a

[84] *See* art. 26. The local remedies requirement is not tied to art. 25, and could, as a matter of textual construction, relate also to inter-state actions under art. 24. It is now clear from the case law that the local remedies rule applies when the applicant state does no more than denounce a violation or violations allegedly suffered by 'individuals' whose place, as it were, is taken by the State. On the other hand and in principle, the rule does not apply where the applicant State complains of a practice as such, with the aim of preventing its continuation or recurrence, but does not ask the Commission or the Court to give a decision on each of the cases put forward as proof or illustrations of that practice. Ireland v. United Kingdom (Eur. Ct. of Human Rights 1978), *reprinted in* 17 Int'l Legal Materials 680, para. 159 (1978).

[85] 'Abuse of petition' turns not on who the applicant is, but on what he or she seeks to achieve. *See* Application 1270/61, [1962] Y.B. Eur. Conv. on Human Rights 126 (Eur. Comm'n of Human Rights). *See also* European Convention, art. 17.

[86] European Convention, art. 28(b).

[87] *See, e.g.*, Knechtl v. United Kingdom, [1970] Y.B. Eur. Conv. on Human Rights (Eur. Comm'n of Human Rights); Simon-Herold v. Austria, [1971] Y.B. Eur. Conv. on Human Rights 352 (Eur. Comm'n of Human Rights); 'Amerkrane' Case, [1973] Y.B. Eur. Conv. on Human Rights 356 (Eur. Comm'n of Human Rights). The last case is, in the view of the author, a settlement which is very hard to square with the requirement that it be in accordance with respect for the rights protected in the European Convention.

[88] European Convention, art. 30.

detailed report on the facts, and states whether or not it finds a breach of the Convention.[89] This is transmitted to the parties and to the Committee of Ministers, but is not published at that stage.[90] Publication is treated as a sanction.

Within three months after the transmittal of this report, the Commission, the state party whose national is alleged to be a victim, the state party which referred the case to the Commission (*i.e.*, in an inter-state dispute), or the state party against which the complaint has been lodged has the right to take the case on to the European Court of Human Rights.[91]

In an inter-state application, the decision to take the matter to the European Commission has already involved, for the applicant state concerned, political decisions at the hightest level. A finding of admissibility by the Commission together with a failure to secure a friendly settlement is thus extremely likely to proceed to the European Court. The Commission itself will be inclined to refer a case that it regards as having important implications for the Convention; and the respondent state will choose to proceed to the Court when it regards the issue as one of principle and believes that it has good answers to the report of the Commission. States in this position will often choose to pre-empt the possibility that the Commission will refer the case by speedily referring it themselves.

If the question is *not* referred to the European Court within this time period, the Committee of Ministers of the Council of Europe decides whether there has been a violation of the Convention.[92] If the Committee considers that there has been a violation, it prescribes a time period during which measures required by its decision must be taken.[93] If satisfactory measures are not taken within this time period the Committee decides upon further measures and usually publishes the report of the Commission.[94] The decisions of the Committee are binding upon the parties.[95]

[89] *Id.* art. 31(1).

[90] *Id.* art. 31(2).

[91] *Id.* art. 48.

[92] *Id.* art. 32(1). The Committee of Ministers has adopted rules of procedure for the exercise of its responsibilities under art. 32 of the Convention. *See* Rules Adopted by the Committee of Ministers for the Application of Article 32 of the European Convention on Human Rights, *reprinted in* Appendix, Council of Europe, Collection of Resolutions Adopted by the Committee of Ministers in Application of Article 32 of the European Convention for the Protection of Human Rights and Fundamental Freedoms, 1959–1981, Council of Europe Doc. H. (81) 4 (1981) [hereinafter cited as Article 32 Resolutions]. For criticism of the role entrusted to the Committee of Ministers, *see* Higgins, *The Execution of Decisions of Organs Under the European Convention on Human Rights*, [1978] Revue Hellénique de Droit International 1 [hereinafter cited as Higgins, *Execution*].

[93] European Convention, art. 32(2).

[94] *Id.* art. 32(3).

[95] *Id.* art. 32(4).

If the case is to go to the Court, article 46 becomes crucial. This too, like article 25, is an 'optional clause', providing for jurisdiction in a manner comparable to article 36(2) of the Statute of the International Court of Justice, *i.e.*, parties may at any time declare that they recognize as compulsory *ipso facto* and without special agreement the jurisdiction of the European Court, such declarations being either unconditional or on condition of reciprocity.

If a basis for jurisdiction exists,[96] the Court will proceed to decide whether there has been a breach of the Convention.[97] The judgment of the Court is final and binding.[98] Two facts should particularly be pointed out. First, the judgment is binding whether or not the European Convention has been incorporated into domestic law. Second, the European Commission appears before the Court to present the applicant's case whether or not the Commission itself upheld the entirety of the applicant's case. The applicant's lawyer can assist the Commission if requested by the latter, and in respect of cases referred after January 1, 1983, can also directly represent the applicant.

The Court does not normally specify in any detail that amendments to national legislation or administrative regulations are needed. Rather, it identifies a breach, and the national authorities must then do whatever is necessary to bring themselves back into compliance with the Convention. It is for the Committee of Ministers to supervise the execution of the judgment, though in practice they have not rigorously inspected the compatibility of new legislation with the findings of the Court.[99]

The supervision of the execution of the judgments of the Court is carried out by the Committee of Ministers by virtue of article 54 of the European Convention and the special rules of procedure drawn up in relation thereto. The usual pattern has been for the Committee of Ministers to receive a report from the state adjudged by the Court to be in breach of the Convention. The rules of procedure allow the Committee to grant liberal extensions of time for the submission of such reports.[100] These reports will specify what action the state concerned

[96] Optional competence under art. 46 has been recognized by Austria, Belgium, Denmark, Federal Republic of Germany, France, Iceland, Ireland, Italy, Luxembourg, The Netherlands, Norway, Portugal, Sweden, Switzerland, and United Kingdom.

[97] European Convention, art. 50.

[98] *Id.* art. 52.

[99] *See* Robertson, *supra* note 50, at 236–67; Morgan, *Article 32: What Is Wrong?*, 1 Human Rights Rev. 157 (1976); Higgins, *Execution*, *supra* note 92.

[100] *See* Rule 2 & 3, Rules Adopted by the Committee of Ministers Concerning the Application of Article 54 of the European Convention on Human Rights, *reprinted in* Council of Europe, Collection of Resolutions Adopted by the Committee of Ministers in Application of Article 54 of the European Convention for the Protection of Human Rights and Fundamental Freedoms, 1976–1981, Council of Europe Doc. H (81) 5 (1981) [hereinafter cited as Article 54 Resolutions].

has taken in order to bring itself back into compliance with the Convention. The Committee of Ministers usually notes such reports and declares its duties under article 54 fulfilled. Disturbingly, it does not carry out (nor, being a political body, is it equipped to carry out) any quasi-judicial analysis as to whether the reported legislative changes do indeed achieve their stated purpose of terminating the breach found by the Court and making its repetition impossible in the future. In other words, there is an operational assumption that altered legislation equals compliance. The correctness of that assumption may have to be tested by subsequent litigants.

Notwithstanding this built-in inadequacy in the functioning of the Committee of Ministers, the judgments of the European Court are undeniably efficacious, in that states which are the subject of adverse findings by the Court have virtually without exception[101] been prepared to take the action necessary to bring themselves back into a position of compliance with the Convention. It should be emphasized to students that compliance does not always entail altering legislation as such. It may be that it is an administrative practice that is found to be contrary to the European Convention, and this may be remedied by a revision of administrative directives. Thus, after the adverse findings in the *'Golder' Case* the United Kingdom government altered prison regulations to remove the right of the prison authorities to control the communication of a prisoner with his or her lawyer.[102]

Certain cases call for particular comment so far as giving effect to the judgment of the Court is concerned. In the case of *Ireland v. United Kingdom*,[103] the latter state simply reported to the Committee of Ministers the measures that it had already taken before the case opened before the European Court. The United Kingdom had pointed out to the Court that these measures (to prohibit the use of the so-called 'five interrogation techniques') had already been put into effect before the case ever came before the Commission. Before the Court, the United Kingdom added weight to this fact by making a solemn declaration that these interrogation techniques would not be reintroduced in any circumstances. The Court declined to find that these events made the case 'moot' or that it was improper to proceed to judgment; but the Committee of Ministers found these same facts sufficient for a finding that the United Kingdom had given effect to the

[101] The exception is the implementation of the judgment in the 'Belgian Linguistics' Case [1968], 2 Y.B. Eur. Conv. on Human Rights 832 (Eur. Ct. of Human Rights). Some four years elapsed before Belgian constitutional reforms, and the effect of these reforms is not wholly clear in relation to the breach of art. 2 of the First Protocol and art. 14 of the European Convention.

[102] *See* Committee of Ministers Res. (79) 35, *reprinted in* Article 54 Resolutions, *supra* note 100. *See generally* text accompanying notes 171–72 *infra*.

[103] *Ireland*, *supra* note 70.

Court's conclusion that the 'five interrogation techniques' were contrary to article 3 of the European Convention.[104]

In the case of *Tyrer v. United Kingdom*,[105] where judicial birching of a minor in the Isle of Man was found to be contrary to article 3 of the European Convention, the government of the United Kingdom did not itself have the constitutional authority to prohibit judicial birching in the Isle of Man; nor was it able to persuade the Isle of Man legislature to take such action. Instead, it reported to the Committee of Ministers that it had notified all those who had the potential authority in the Isle of Man to order the punishment of a minor for a criminal offense by birching that this would be unlawful under the Convention. The Committee of Ministers declared that the judgment of the Court was to be regarded as executed.[106]

Notwithstanding the inadequacy of the execution mechanism, the judgments of the Court are very efficacious in securing human rights. While compliance with the judgments of the European Court is the norm, it must be stressed that compliance is only a small part of the efficacy of the European Convention system. Friendly settlement upon terms acceptable to the Commission[107] and what we may term 'anticipatory compliance' (alteration of legislative or administrative practice after a finding of admissibility and prior to a judgment of the Court) are an equally important part of the picture. Again, governments now have the European Convention very much in mind when drafting new legislation, and it will be a matter of self-interest for them to endeavor to ensure that new laws will not involve them in applications to the European Commission.

This survey of the institutions should leave the reader with a clear understanding of the following:

1. the criteria of admissibility of cases by the European Commission;
2. the optional procedures for individual petition and for jurisdiction of the European Court;
3. inter-state applications;
4. the friendly settlement procedure;
5. the interplay between the Commission, the Committee of Ministers, and the Court; and
6. the timing of publication of the Commission's reports and proposals.

The reader now has a sufficient conceptual understanding, and

[104] *Id.* at 606.
[105] *See* note 50 *supra*.
[106] Committee of Ministers Res. (78) 39, *reprinted in* Article 54 Resolution, *supra* note 100.
[107] European Convention, art. 28(b).

enough of an introduction to the institutions and source materials, to begin an examination of the substantive rights guaranteed by the European Convention. It is obviously a matter of choice as to whether one endeavors to cover them all (perhaps rather lightly), or whether, having briefly gone through articles 2–12, one selects certain articles for detailed examination. Certain rights seem to me to be central to an understanding of the European Convention—for example, protection against torture and degrading or inhuman treatment, the right to liberty and security of person, the entitlement to a fair trial, and the right to freedom of expression. It is also a useful technique to reserve a couple of seminars for rights that correspond to 'burning issues of the moment'.

In the ensuing sections, key issues and leading cases concerning those articles which would be an essential component of any course on the European system, *i.e.*, the rights protected in articles 3, 5, 6, and 10 of the European Convention, are discussed.

C. CASE STUDIES

1. *Case Study. Freedom from Torture and Inhuman or Degrading Treatment or Punishment*

Article 3 of the European Convention provides: 'No one shall be subjected to torture or to inhuman or degrading treatment or punishment.' There are no qualifying clauses at all and it is clear from article 15(2) that no derogations to article 3 are permissible. There are, as should be the case in liberal democracies, few applications under this article, but among the most important ones are the *'Greek' Case*, *Ireland v. United Kingdom*, and *Tyrer v. United Kingdom*, each of which merits detailed study.

There have been only a few cases where torture was directly in issue. In the early years of the European Convention, when Cyprus was still under British rule, Greece claimed that there were forty-nine cases of torture or maltreatment amounting to torture. The case was deemed admissible in respect of twenty-nine of those claimed.[108] However, when a political settlement was reached in Cyprus the parties requested that the proceedings be terminated. The Committee of Ministers decided that no further action was called for, and the Report of the European Commission has never been published.[109]

In 1967, Denmark, Norway, Sweden, and The Netherlands instituted proceedings against Greece. The Greek government had claimed to be able to derogate from many of the articles in the European

[108] [1958–1959] Y.B. Eur. Conv. on Human Rights 174–80 (Eur. Comm'n of Human Rights).
[109] *See* Committee of Ministers Res. (59) 32, *reprinted in* Article 32 Resolutions, *supra* note 92.

Convention by virtue of the provisions for a national emergency in article 15. The applicant governments claimed that Greece had violated articles 5, 6, 8, 9, 10, 11, 13, and 14 of the European Convention. After the applications had been declared admissible new allegations were added concerning article 3 and article 7 of the Convention. Irrespective of the complex arguments about the position of Greece with respect to article 15, and the question of the margin of appreciation,[110] it was clear that no derogations could be made from article 3. The European Commission engaged in the most extensive investigation of the facts it has ever undertaken, travelling to Greece, interviewing many witnesses, and visiting many localities. Professor A.H. Robertson writes of the Commission's Report:

> [M]ore than 300 pages of the report were devoted to the question of torture. It is impossible to read the report without being impressed by the objective manner in which the Commission required corroboration of the allegations made, offered the government every opportunity to rebut the evidence produced and even examined the possibility that (as alleged) many of the accounts of torture were deliberately fabricated as part of a plot to discredit the government.[111]

The Commission made detailed findings of torture (and thought there was strong *prima facie* evidence in respect of certain investigations which its investigatory sub-committee had not been allowed to complete). It further found that torture for political reasons was an administrative practice of the Athens security police, which the government had declined to control.[112]

The case was not referred to the European Court, but the Committee of Ministers, acting under article 32, found Greece in violation of various articles of the European Convention, including article 3.[113] The *'Greek' Case*, while reflecting appalling facts and while raising interesting points of law on derogations, gave rise to no particularly difficult points of law on the question of torture. But it seems salutary that charges of torture under the European Convention should merit the weightiest of investigations in respect of this most serious of offenses.

In *Ireland v. United Kingdom*,[114] Ireland submitted an application concerning the Northern Ireland situation, charging the United Kingdom with violations of articles 1, 2, 3, 5, 6, and 14. The European

[110] *See* Higgins, *supra* note 27, at 314.

[111] Robertson, *supra* note 50, at 41.

[112] [1969] 1 Y.B. Eur. Conv. on Human Rights 504–05 (Eur. Comm'n of Human Rights). This volume of the *Yearbook* is given over entirely to the *'Greek' Case*.

[113] *See* Committee of Ministers Res. DH (74) 2, *reprinted in* Article 32 Resolutions, *supra* note 92.

[114] *See* note 70 *supra*.

Commission, having declared the application admissible as regards articles 3, 5, and 14, endeavored to obtain a friendly settlement. It could not do this and therefore proceeded with a detailed investigation of the case—hearing witnesses *in camera* and providing them with anonymity, and security where necessary. In this report, the Commission found that derogations by the United Kingdom were properly applicable in respect of article 5 and that article 6 did not apply on the facts. Nor did it uphold the claim under article 14 that detention had been discriminatory. The focus of its attention was article 3. Here the main question was whether certain interrogation techniques constituted torture and an administrative practice. The Commission found they did and the case was submitted to the European Court.

Even by the time the European Commission pronounced on admissibility, the United Kingdom government had already issued an instruction to the Home Office that the practices complained of should cease. When the matter was referred to the European Court the United Kingdom did not contest the Commission's findings. Further, the Attorney General gave a solemn understanding before the Court that these 'five techniques' would not in any circumstances be reintroduced.

The Court was not, however, prepared to treat the issue as moot or disposed of.[115] It stated that the responsibilities assigned to it under the European Convention extended to pronouncing on non-contested allegations of violations under article 3. The Court then proceeded to find (although the United Kingdom had not itself contested the Commission's findings) that the five techniques did not amount to torture, although they did constitute a practice of inhuman and degrading treatment that was a breach of article 3.

The European Court was thus reserving a right to pronounce on all torture claims; but it still distinguished torture from inhuman and degrading treatment under article 3. Only the most appalling and dire acts of maltreatment would constitute the former.

The question still remains of how loosely or tightly 'inhuman or degrading treatment' will be interpreted. In the *'Tyrer' Case*,[116] the applicant, a resident of the Isle of Man, had pleaded guilty to assault occasioning actual bodily harm to a fellow pupil at his school. The Isle of Man Court ordered three strokes of the birch, under Isle of Man legislation. Tyrer complained, among other things, that the judicial birching contravened article 3 of the European Convention. He claimed damages and asked for repeal of the legislation concerned.

[115] *Compare* this *with* Northern Camerouns Case [1963], I.C.J. *and* Nuclear Tests Case [1974), I.C.J.

[116] [1978] Y.B. Eur. Conv. on Human Rights 612 (Eur. Ct. of Human Rights) [hereinafter cited as *Tyrer*].

The Commission found in its Report of 14 December 1976 that the judicial corporal punishment inflicted on Tyrer was degrading and in breach of article 3. The European Court affirmed this view.[117] It agreed with the Commission that the corporal punishment did not amount to torture, as there was no suffering of the level inherent in this notion.[118] For the 'degrading' aspect of article 3 to apply, said the Court, the applicant must be humiliated not merely by virtue of the fact that he has been criminally convicted, but by the execution of the punishment. Notwithstanding that the Isle of Man legislation allowed for appeal against sentence and that there is a prior medical examination with the birching carried out in the presence of a doctor (who may order the punishment to be stopped) and of a parent, it offended article 3. Since there could be no derogation from article 3, even if law and order in the Isle of Man depended upon its retention (which the Court did not accept), birching would not be compatible with the European Convention.

The sole dissent was by Judge Sir Gerald Fitzmaurice. He said that torture and inhuman treatment do not have a monolithic and absolute character, and that the absence of a definition meant that in any particular case the tribunal must take account of all the circumstances. Quite simply, he was unable to accept the Court's proposition that the *very nature* of judicial corporal punishment was contrary to article 3, notwithstanding the adequacy of safeguards in its administration. Sir Gerald recognized that modern opinion had come to regard corporal punishment as an *undesirable* form of punishment, but pointed out that that does not automatically turn it into degrading punishment. He felt it did not degrade young offenders, although he was careful to reserve his position as to adult offenders.[119]

There are presently pending applications concerning the use of corporal punishment not as judicial punishment but as a disciplinary measure in Scottish schools.[120]

[117] The European Court has been asked by the Attorney General for the Isle of Man to strike the case off its list as Tyrer, when he acquired full age, had attested that he wished to withdraw the complaint. The Court decided that as the complaint raised questions of a general character under the European Convention, it could not accede to this request.

[118] *Tyrer*, *supra* note 116, at 614.

[119] The Isle of Man legislation, in respect of which the United Kingdom does not intervene because of constitutional convention, has not in fact been changed. Summary Jurisdiction Act, 1960, 8 Eliz., §§ 8, 10 (1960). The United Kingdom informed the Committee of Ministers that it had communicated the decision of the European Court to all persons on the Isle of Man authorized to pass a sentence of birching. The Committee of Ministers simply took note of the information. Committee of Ministers Res. (78) 39, *reprinted in* Article 54 Resolutions, *supra* note 100. *See* text accompanying notes 106–06 *supra.*

[120] Campbell and Cosans v. United Kingdom [1978], Y.B. Eur. Conv. on Human Rights 396 (Eur. Comm'n of Human Rights). [Ed. note: After this chapter was completed, the European Court unanimously held that the possible use of the tawse (a leather strap applied to the palm) in

The question of inhuman treatment has sometimes arisen in the context of expulsions. For example, in *Amerkrane v. United Kingdom*, Lt. Colonel Amerkrane was, without opportunity to contest it before the courts, transferred back to Morocco from Gibraltar, where he had fled after being convicted of attempting to kill the King of Morocco. It was claimed that the very fact of transferring him back to Morocco caused him to suffer inhuman treatment. Lt. Colonel Amerkrane was executed, and the claim, which was brought by his wife, was settled. She received a very large cash settlement.[121] The Commission had before it a similar claim by an African against Belgium. The applicant does not posses any documentation proving identity or nationality, and he claims that orders to leave Belgium amount to inhuman and degrading treatment under article 3 because he cannot legally go to any other country.[122]

A further group of article 3 applications center on claims by prisoners as to their conditions of imprisonment. In *Mahler v. Germany*,[123] the question of the compatibility of solitary confinement with article 3 was raised but not answered as it was found that the confinement had not actually been solitary. Friendly settlement ended *Simon-Herold v. Austria*[124] which had raised the question of whether it was inhuman and degrading treatment for a poliomyelitis sufferer, detained on remand, to be placed in a lunatic asylum. The government of Austria sent out a directive, of which the Commission took note, stating that there was a risk of violating article 3 if persons were put in institutions solely for security reasons.

2. *Case Study. Liberty of the Person*

A second central area of study has to be the question of liberty of the person. This concept has been particularly well-developed under the European Convention. Article 5 provides:

1. Everyone has the right to liberty and security of person. No one shall be deprived of his liberty save in the following cases and in accordance with a procedure prescribed by law:
   (a) the lawful detention of a person after conviction by a competent court;
   (b) the lawful arrest or detention of a person for non-compliance with

Scottish schools as a method of corporal punishment did not violate art.3. 15 Eur. Hum. Rts. Rep. 293 (1982).

[121] *See also* note 87 *supra*

[122] Application 5961/72, [1973] Y.B. Eur. Conv. on Human Rights 356 (Eur. Comm'n of Human Rights).

[123] Application 6038/73, 44 Recueil de Decisions 115 (1973).

[124] Application 4340/69, [1971] Y.B. Eur. Conv. on Human Rights 352 (Eur. Comm'n of Human Rights).

the lawful order of a court or in order to secure the fulfilment of any obligation prescribed by law;

(c) the lawful arrest or detention of a person effected for the purpose of bringing him before the competent legal authority on reasonable suspicion of having committed an offence or when it is reasonably considered necessary to prevent him committing an offence or fleeing after having done so;

(d) the detention of a minor by lawful order for the purpose of educational supervision or his lawful detention for the purpose of bringing him before the competent legal authority;

(e) the lawful detention of persons for the prevention of the spreading of infectious diseases, of persons of unsound mind, alcoholics or drug addicts, or vagrants;

(f) the lawful arrest or detention of a person to prevent his effecting an unauthorised entry into the country or of a person against whom action is being taken with a view to deportation or extradition.

2. Everyone who is arrested shall be informed promptly, in a language which he understands, of the reasons for his arrest and of any charge against him.
3. Everyone arrested or detained in accordance with the provisions of paragraph 1(c) of this article shall be brought promptly before a judge or other officer authorised by law to exercise judicial power and shall be entitled to trial within a reasonable time or to release pending trial. Release maybe conditioned by guarantees to appear for trial.
4. Everyone who is deprived of his liberty by arrest or detention shall be entitled to take proceedings by which the lawfulness of his detention shall be decided speedily by a court and his release ordered if the detention is not lawful.
5. Everyone who has been the victim of arrest or detention in contravention of the provisions of this article shall have an enforceable right to compensation.

Article 5(1)(a), (c), and (e) have received judicial attention. A considerable amount of case law now also exists on article 5(3), with the concepts of an 'officer authorized by law to exercise judicial power' and 'trial within a reasonable time' being particularly well-scrutinized. This is an area that merits detailed study since the right to liberty of the person is so fundamental and the built-in provisions for the exercise of judicial and other legitimate state functions so carefully worded. The issues that have arisen are basic to any democratic society. The interplay between article 5(3) and article 6(1) should also be considered.[125]

What does the phrase 'entitled to trial within a reasonable time or to release pending trial' found in article 5(3) mean? In the '*Neumeister*'

[125] *See* text accompanying notes 144–48 *infra*.

Case,[126] the European Court said that detention has to be reasonable and if it is not the accused must be released.[127]

What is a 'reasonable time' within which an accused must be brought to trial? In a series of cases, the answer to this question has been refined. There is no fixed period of time that one can designate as reasonable, no moment beyond which the time can be termed unreasonable.[128] What is reasonable depends upon all the circumstances. In the '*Wemhoff*' *Case*,[129] a German national, a broker, was arrested on November 9, 1961 for breaches of trust. He was ordered to be detained on remand. The reasons cited were the seriousness of the alleged crime, and fear that he might abscond and/or attempt to suppress evidence if left at liberty. The original warrant was succeeded by two detention orders of December 28, 1961 and January 8, 1962, which referred to suspicion of fraud as well as breach of trust. In the first half of 1963, two appeals were made to the Regional and Appeals Court respectively concerning the detention, the District Court having already turned down an application. These appeals were unsuccessful. The Court of Appeal thought that since Wemhoff would receive an appreciatively higher sentence if found guilty than had formerly been thought, the risk of absconding was even greater, notwithstanding that Wemhoff's lawyer had offered to deposit his client's identity papers. In January 1964, Wemhoff lodged an application with the European Commission of Human Rights.

A detailed indictment was filed in April 1964, and in July 1964 a new detention order was issued. Wemhoff's trial opened on November 9, 1964, by which time his application to the Commission had been declared admissible. The Commission was unable to secure a friendly settlement.

In April 1965, Wemhoff was found guilty and sentenced to six years and six months penal servitude, as well as a fine. The period of detention on remand was counted as part of the sentence. Pending appeal of his case, Wemhoff again several times sought his provisional release, and offered bank guarantees to be provided by his father. Release was not granted. In December 1965, his appeal was also rejected, and the time he had spent in detention since judgment at first instance was also counted towards his sentence. In November 1966, after serving two-thirds of his sentence, Wemhoff was conditionally released.

The European Commission found that Wemhoff had not been

[126] [1968] Y.B. Eur. Conv. on Human Rights 812 (Eur. Ct. of Human Rights).

[127] *See also* text accompanying notes 134–37 *infra*.

[128] *See* 'Matznetter' Case, [1969] Y.B. Eur. Conv. on Human Rights 406 (Eur. Ct. of Human Rights); *see* text accompanying notes 138–40 *infra*.

[129] [1968] Y.B. Eur. Conv. on Human Rights 796 (Eur. Ct. of Human Rights).

brought to trial 'within a reasonable time' and that this was so notwithstanding the fact that the period of detention was counted as part of the sentence. The detention on remand had been a lawful detention under article 5(1)(c), but contravened the 'reasonable time' requirements of article 5(3).

The Commission suggested seven criteria for establishing whether a person lawfully detained was not being brought to trial within a reasonable time: (i) the actual length of the detention; (ii) the length of detention on remand in relation to the nature of the offense; (iii) the effects on the detained person; (iv) the conduct of the accused, with special reference to whether he contributed to delays, and to whether he requested bail; (v) the difficulties and complexity of the case; (vi) the manner in which the necessary investigation was conducted; and (vii) the conduct of the judicial authorities.

The matter proceeded to the European Court. The Court did not feel able to adopt the seven criteria of the Commission, saying that it 'must judge whether the reasons given by the national authorities to justify continued detention are relevant and sufficient to show that detention was not contrary to Article 5(3)'. It is hard to see how in making such a judgment the Court will not in fact (even if not in form) be mindful of the elements listed by the Commission. The Court thought that the anxiety of the German courts about suppression of evidence was justified. As to danger of flight, the Court found that the likelihood of a long sentence was not enough. Further, 'the effect of such fear diminishes as detention continues' and as the balance of such sentence which the accused may expect to have to serve is reduced.[130]

The Court found that where fear of flight is the only reason for detention, release pending trial must be ordered if financial guarantees were adequate. Therefore, there could only have been a breach of article 5(3) if the detention between November 1961 and April 1965 had been due to slowness of investigation, or too long a period between the end of investigation or the beginning of trial, or to the length of the trial. The Court found that no fault lay with the judicial authorities, and that '[t]he exceptional length of the investigation and of the trial are justified by the exceptional complexity of the case and by further unavoidable reasons for delay'.[131] The Court therefore overruled the Commission, and found by six votes to one that there was no breach of article 5(3).

Clearly, this case is an important clarification of the component elements of the notion of 'unreasonable time' under article 5(3), so far as questions relating to the conduct of the accused, fear of flight,

[130] *Id.* at 806.
[131] *Id.* at 808.

interference with evidence, adequacy of financial guarantees for bail, and slowness of investigation and/or of trial are concerned. But the Court also dealt with another important point of interpretation. The Commission had agreed with the German government that the period of detention in respect of which 'reasonable time' was to be judged ran from the date of arrest to the opening of the trial. The Court thought this too restrictive a view.[132] Emphasizing that it was giving interpretative priority to the aims and purposes of the European Convention rather than to minimizing the obligations of the parties, the Court decided that the protection against unduly long detention did not cease with the opening of the trial but continued up to the delivery of judgment. The Court further found that this meant judgment by a court of first instance, rather than a final judgment. Here the Court found article 5(1)(a) compelling, because a person convicted at first instance is lawfully deprived of liberty within the meaning of that clause. It was in principle lawful to hold such a person. The implication of the Court's findings is that conviction is *per se* enough for post-trial detention—there is no need to show, *e.g.*, fear of flight. The Court observed that if the post-trial detention became 'unreasonably long' a possible remedy would lie in article 6(1)[133] even if not in article 5(3).

The *'Neumeister' Case*[134] raised similar points. The applicant was an Austrian national suspected of defrauding the exchequer through customs fraud. He was arrested on August 11, 1959. In January 1960 his examination before an Investigating Judge began. He was provisionally released on parole in May 1961, and resumed work (though he had had to sell his previous company at a reduced price). In July 1961 he and his family went to Finland on holiday and in February 1962 he went to the Saar for several days on business. In 1962, however, he was denied permission to holiday again in Finland—though Neumeister claimed that permission *was* given to him by the Investigating Judge in spite of the wish of the Public Prosecutor that permission not be given. In July 1962 he was arrested on a warrant referring to the danger of flight. In a series of court cases Neumeister challenged his detention on remand, urging that he had had the

[132] The French and English texts lead to different conclusions—the latter refers to 'trial' while the former uses the word '*jugée*'. The European Court stated that the use of the term 'trial' referred to the whole of proceedings before the court, not just their beginning. In other words, 'entitled to trial' was not necessarily limited to 'entitled to be brought to trial'. The French text, which is of equal authority to the English one, permitted of only one interpretation. The obligation to release an accused person within a reasonable time continues until that person has been '*jugée*'—until the day of judgment. *Id.* at 798–99.

[133] Art. 6(1) refers to the right to a fair and public hearing 'within a reasonable time' for the determination of civil rights and liberties.

[134] [1968] Y.B. Eur. Conv. on Human Rights 812 (Eur. Ct. of Human Rights) [hereinafter cited as *Neumeister*].

opportunity to abscond, but had never done so. He also pointed out that his business interests were in Vienna, his wife had just opened a dress shop, and that he had already served nine months on remand, which fact argued against the dangers of flight. He offered to deposit with the court his identity papers and passport. The Austrian courts, however, noted the inadequacy of financial guarantees, and pointed to confessions incriminating Neumeister made by a fellow-accused.

Neumeister contended that statements made by a co-accused could not form the basis for detention on remand. He also urged that article 5(3) of the European Convention precluded the fixing of bail at such a high level that the prisoner's release became impossible in practice. The European Commission—once again using the 'seven criteria' as a guideline (the Commission handed down the decisions in *Wemhoff* and *Neumeister* on the same day)—found that several of the criteria pointed to the detention being unreasonably long, though on the seventh criterion (the conduct of the judicial authorities), the evidence was open to different evaluations. It found a violation of article 5(3).

On this case the Court agreed with the Commission. It was significant that while Neumeister's second period of detention was caused by the statements of his co-accused, he was not interrogated again during the fifteen month period that followed. And although the danger of flight had perhaps not decreased, the assessment of that danger still had to take account of other factors, such as his job, family ties, etc. Moreover, while the European Court declined to pronounce on whether the security offered by Neumeister was 'sufficient', it did note that article 5(3) made it inappropriate to fix the required security solely in relation to the amount of the loss imputed to him.[135] The Court therefore found that Neumeister's detention until September 16, 1964 constituted a violation of article 5(3).

The question of identifying the relevant period to be judged as reasonable or not arose also in this case, but in a somewhat different manner from *Wemhoff*. Neumeister had had two periods of detention. The European Court could not consider whether the first period as such was incompatible with the European Convention because, *inter alia*, Neumeister had not submitted an application to the European Commission until after the six month time limit laid down in article 26 of the Convention had expired.[136] This period of imprisonment had in any event been a fairly short period—two months and seventeen days. The second period lasted over two years and two months. However, the Austrian government argued that the European Court should not

[135] *Id.* at 822.

[136] Art. 26 provides that '[t]he Commission may only deal with the matter . . . within a period of six months from the date on which the final decision [of the domestic authorities] was taken.'

consider Neumeister's detention *subsequent* to the day on which he filed his application with the Commission, as the application could only relate to facts that had taken place before this date. Once again, the Court showed that in a human rights instrument strict rigidity was not a suitable canon of interpretation:

> In his Application of 12th July 1963 Neumeister complained not of an isolated act but rather of a situation in which he had been for some time and which was to last until it was ended by a decision granting him provisional release, a decision which he sought in vain for a considerable time. It would be excessively formalistic to demand that an Applicant denouncing such a situation should file a new Application with the Commission after each final decision rejecting a request for release.[137]

The Court for these reasons found that it should examine the period of detention through to his provisional release.

The following year the Court had to deal with the '*Matznetter*' *Case*.[138] This concerned fraud charges against an Austrian tax consultant. Matznetter was arrested on May 15, 1963 and in December 1963 sought his release, noting that there was no real danger of absconding: he was an amputee with other severe disabilities, he had no funds abroad nor could transfer any, and he was of good record. The Austrian courts found a continued danger nonetheless—he had connections abroad, and a good financial position in spite of debts. There was also reference to the possibility of repeating the offenses. Matznetter continued his appeals on the question of provisional release, and by December 1964 was making the point that he had served the greater part, if not the whole, of any possible sentence because, as a first offender, he could reasonably expect an early release.

Matznetter had made his application to the European Commission on April 3, 1964. The Commision particularly noted that the preliminary investigation did not proceed at an adequate pace. Matznetter had to wait six months before appearing before the Investigating Judge (at his own request), who had to deal not only with this difficult case, but also with others. The Commission found a violation of article 5(3), but this was not upheld by the European Court. The Court confirmed its view in *Neumeister* that it could examine facts subsequent to the application; and that time in detention after the lodging of an application was to be taken into account in determining what delay was 'reasonable'. The Court thought the unusual length of the investigation was justified by the exceptional complexity of the case. Although there was significant delay in the investigatory procedure, the Court

[137] *Neumeister, supra* note 134, at 816.

[138] [1969] Y.B. Eur. Conv. on Human Rights 406 (Eur. Ct. of Human Rights).

declared itself satisfied that explanations given by the Austrian government were 'credible'.[139] The arguments of the Austrian government on this point really related to the continued need to restrict Matznetter on grounds of danger of absconding. Such justifications of the delay (in contradistinction to the need to detain during such delay) turned on the heavy work load of the Investigating Judge and the efforts made by the Austrian government to provide assistance for him. The Court said, '[W]hile an accused person held in custody is entitled to have his case given priority and conducted with special diligence this must not stand in the way of the proper administration of justice'.[140] But slow investigation because of overwork is, in the view of this author not to be assimilated to 'the proper administration of justice'. This judgment provides a good teaching opportunity to discuss the relationship of international obligations to the *bona fide* realities of domestic life.

On the same day, the European Court handed down its judgment in the *'Stögmüller' Case.*[141] Stögmüller, an Austrian national, was arrested on March 3, 1958 on suspicion of having committed offenses under the Usury Act. His preliminary investigation began on March 10, 1958. On April 21, 1958 he was provisionally released. In June 1958 further information was laid against him alleging fraud and related offenses. In the summer of 1959 Stögmüller changed his occupation and became a pilot. He sold his company. He flew to many international airports, always returning. However, he did not attend a regional examination by the Investigating Judge, going instead to Greece, though Stögmüller did make sure that his whereabouts were known and asked for an adjournment of the examination. When he returned at the end of August he offered himself for examination, but the Judge stated that he now would not have the time to examine him until September. Three days later (August 24, 1961) his arrest was ordered, on the grounds that he had gone abroad to Greece without permission, thus breaking the conditions of his provisional release. Stögmüller was detained from August 25, 1961 to August 26, 1963. In July 1966 the preliminary investigation—in which hundreds of witnesses were interviewed and twenty thousand pages written—was concluded. The interrogating judge conceded that when Stögmüller changed his occupation, the likelihood of repetition of offenses ended, but the danger of absconding increased.

The European Court found that while reasonable suspicion is a relevant consideration for lawful arrest under article 5(1)(a), it was not

[139] *Id.* at 434.
[140] *Id.*
[141] [1969] Y.B. Eur. Conv. on Human Rights 364 (Eur. Ct. of Human Rights).
[142] [1971] Y.B. Eur. Conv. on Human Rights 838 (Eur. Ct. of Human Rights) [hereinafter cited as *Ringeisen*].

of itself enough to prolong detention under article 5(3). It thought that there was little danger of the offenses being repeated and the fact that Stögmüller had always returned from his trips and had family left behind in Austria made the likelihood of absconding small. The mere opportunity to cross frontiers was not enough to make it likely that he would abscond. Austria was found in breach of article 5(3).

In July 1971 the Court handed down its decision in the '*Ringeisen*' *Case.*[142] Here an Austrian citizen was charged with certain real property frauds and with fraudulent bankruptcy. His first period of detention was from August 5, to December 23, 1963 and the second from March 15, 1965 to March 20, 1967. The first period alone fell outside of the European Court's review as Ringeisen's application to the European Commission in July 1965 was more than six months later. But, importantly, the Court said that 'these four and a half months of the first detention must be added to the period which followed for the purpose of assessing the reasonableness of the whole period of detention . . .'[143]

The Court found unpersuasive government arguments about the possibility of Ringeisen tampering with witnesses, noting that he had already been at liberty for five months since his arrest. Nor did it accept that he was likely to commit further offences. The Court held by five votes to two that his detention between May 14, 1965 to January 1966 was in violation of article 5(3).

On January 14, 1966 Ringeisen was convicted of fraud. His counsel requested that he be released pending appeals to this case. He again made a request for release in the fraudulent bankruptcy case. Both sets of requests were refused, and appeals were made in respect of each. He was eventually released in the fraudulent bankruptcy proceedings on March 20, 1967. The European Commission had asked the European Court to review its dictum in the '*Wemhoff*' *Case* that post adjudication detention is not covered by article 5(3) but only by article 6(1). Alternatively, the Court was asked to interpret its earlier dictum in such a way that 'reasonable delay' remains subject to article 5(3) until the conviction becomes final under the domestic law of the state concerned. The Court found it unnecessary to respond to this request because the detention from May 12, 1965 until March 15, 1967 (relating to the appeals procedure in the fraud conviction) fell within the limits of the remand in custody in the fraudulent bankruptcy case which ran from March 15, 1965 to March 2, 1967. The Court held by the narrower majority of four votes to three that the detention from January 1966 to March 1967 continued the breach of article 5(3).

The Court has given different meanings to 'reasonable time' in

[143] *Id.* at 856.

article 6(1) and article 5(3). It is therefore necessary to look at proceedings under the European Convention about the length of judicial proceedings.

Article 6(1) provides:

> In the determination of his civil rights and obligations or of any criminal charge against him, everyone is entitled to a fair and public hearing within a reasonable time by an independent and impartial tribunal established by law . . .

In the *'Huber' Case*,[144] the applicant, who was a co-accused with Neumeister, was arrested in February 1961 in Switzerland and released in May 1961 on grounds of ill health; he was re-arrested in March 1962 and extradited to Austria in September 1962. He was released from custody in July 1965. Various charges were dropped, but he was convicted of one charge of fraud in July 1968. The European Commission declared his application inadmissible save as regards the length of the criminal proceedings. The case thus proceeded forward with article 6(1) as the main issue. The Commission eventually adopted its report in February 1973.[145] Neither the Commission nor Austria decided to take the case to the European Court; it therefore went to the Committee of Ministers. In spite of the Commission's view that there had been a violation of article 6(1), the Committee of Ministers found that no further action was called for.[146] The Committee of Ministers was no doubt greatly influenced by the fact that the European Court had, in the *'Neumeister' Case*, found there was *no* breach of article 6(1) (although it had found a breach of article 5(3)).

In 1978 the European Court gave its judgment in the *'König' Case*.[147] König was the owner and director of a clinic in Germany, and his licence to manage the clinic was withdrawn in 1967 on grounds of professional misconduct. He appealed unsuccessfully to various bodies and tribunals. He then claimed before the European Commission that proceedings before the Frankfurt Administrative Tribunal were unreasonably lengthy. The Commission, and eventually the European Court, upheld his claim. However, the Court rejected the stated view of the German government and the Commission that time starts to run from the date of filing of appeals with the court of first instance. In this case the Court found that time began to run on the day on which the applicant lodged an objection to the withdrawal of his authorization to practise. Although Dr. König had himself to

[144] [1971] Y.B. Eur. Conv. on Human Rights 548 (Eur. Comm'n of Human Rights).

[145] *Reprinted in* [1975] Y.B. Eur. Conv. on Human Rights 324, 326 (Eur. Comm'n of Human Rights).

[146] Committee of Ministers Res. DH (75) 2, *reprinted in* Article 32 Resolutions, *supra* note 92.

[147] [1978] Y.B. Eur. Conv. on Human Rights 618 (Eur. Ct. of Human Rights).

some extent contributed to the length of proceedings, the Court still found that the period was unreasonably long within the meaning of article 6(1).[148]

There have been other cases concerning article 5 of the European Convention that should be pointed out. It is the second part of article 5(3) which is concerned with the right to trial within a reasonable time. The first part of article 5(3) provides that '[e]veryone arrested or detained in accordance with the provisions of paragraph 1(c) of this article shall be brought promptly before a judge or other officer authorised by law to exercise judicial power. . . .'

Thus in the '*Schiesser*' *Case*,[149] the applicant had been placed in detention on remand by the District Attorney of Winterthur on suspicion of theft. Following earlier precedents, the European Court found that an 'officer' under article 5(3) was a person who was independent of the executive and the parties. He or she could still be subordinate to other judges or officers provided that they themselves enjoy similar independence. The 'officer' must also hear the individual concerned. As well as this procedural guarantee, the term also implies a substantive guarantee—that the 'officer' will employ legal criteria in deciding whether or not there are grounds for detention.

Comparable issues have arisen in relation to the meaning of the word 'court' in article 5(1)(a) of the European Convention.[150] Thus in the '*Engel*' *Case*,[151] which concerned detention by the Dutch military authorities under military disciplinary provisions, the term 'court' was held to apply to organs which had a judicial character, exemplified by their independence of the executive and the parties to the case, and which offered procedural guarantees. In this, the European Court was following its stated view in the '*Neumeister*' *Case*.[152] In the '*Eggs*' *Case*,[153] the European Commission's Report had to deal with the application of a Swiss national serviceman who received a disciplinary sanction of five days strict arrest for refusing to carry out certain orders. The penalty was confirmed by the Camp Commander and an appeal by Eggs to the Chief Military Prosecutor was unsuccessful. Eggs claimed that his deprivation of liberty had not been ordered by a trial court. The Commission found that the organization of military service

148 *Id.* at 622. This case also raises difficult questions about whether a 'civil' right is involved in the withdrawal of a medical license by the state authorities. The present author has difficulty in following the logic of this part of the judgment. *See id.* at 620.

149 [1979] Y.B. Eur. Conv. on Human Rights 432 (Eur. Ct. of Human Rights).

150 Art. 5(1)(a) allows deprivation of liberty during 'the lawful detention of a person after conviction by a competent court'.

151 [1976] Y.B. Eur. Conv. on Human Rights 490 (Eur. Ct. of Human Rights) [hereinafter cited as *Engel*].

152 *See Neumeister*, *supra* note 134, at 828–30.

153 Eggs v. Switzerland, Application 7431/76.

in Switzerland guaranteed the independence of military justice in general. Nonetheless, there was a merging of powers in the sense that the Chief Military Prosecutor could dismiss a case in his capacity as director of public prosecutions, but still be required to deal with it as the appeals authority in disciplinary proceedings. He therefore could *not* be likened to a court and the strict arrest was contrary to article 5(1). The matter went not to the European Court but to the Committee of Ministers. The Committee of Ministers noted that modifications to the Swiss Military Penal Code were to take effect in January 1980, the main aim of which was to substitute a judge for the Chief Military Prosecutor as the appeal authority. The Committee of Ministers therefore contended itself with noting[154] this fact, together with the report of the Commission.

When a person of unsound mind has committed an offense, his or her detention will also be considered under article 5(1)(a);[155] but the most directly relevant clause will be article 5(1)(e), which speaks of the permitted lawful detention of persons of unsound mind. The case law under article 5(1)(a) in this context has been growing.[156]

The first European Court decision in this area was the '*Winterwerp*' *Case*.[157] In May 1968 Winterwerp was committed to a psychiatric hospital for three weeks by order of the local Dutch burgomaster. This detention was extended by the public prosecutor, and was later renewed periodically on the application of his wife and at the request of the public prosecutor. Winterwerp was unaware of these proceedings and was not represented at them. He thus was unable to argue the law or to challenge the medical evidence. He did apply four times for release. The first request in 1969 was dismissed by the Regional Court. Later requests were dismissed by the public prosecutor, without reference to the Regional Court. Winterwerp claimed, *inter alia*, that his deprivation was not 'lawful' under article 5(1). The Commission found there was no breach of this article, and the European Court confirmed this. Both held that Winterwerp's detention fell under article 5(1)(e) (detention of persons of unsound mind), and that the deprivation of liberty had been carried out by a procedure prescribed by law. The Court also agreed with the Commission that a mental patient's right to treatment cannot be derived from article 5(1)(e).

[154] Committee of Ministers Res. DH (79) 7, *reprinted in* [1979] Y.B. Eur. Conv. on Human Rights 454.

[155] For an interesting criticism, *see* Muchlinski, *Mental Health Patients' Rights and the European Human Rights Convention*, 5 Human Rights Rev. 90 (1980), who argues that unless the offender was sane at the time of the offense but became insane in prison, there is a causal link between the illness and the detention.

[156] *See, e.g.* Application 4741/71, 43 Recueil de Decisions 14 (1973); Application 5624/72, 45 Recueil de Decisions 115 (1973) (two early cases).

[157] [1979] Y.B. Eur. Conv. on Human Rights 426 (Eur. Ct. of Human Rights).

The European Court and the Commission found that there had been a violation of article 5(4). This clause provides that a person deprived of liberty by arrest or detention 'shall be entitled to take proceedings by which the lawfulness of his detention shall be decided speedily by a court and his release ordered if the detention is not lawful'. The Court indicated that article 5(4) provides the right to have both the substantive and the formal lawfulness of detention verified by a court. Neither the burgomaster nor the public prosecutor could be regarded as having the characteristic of a 'court'.[158] The District Court and Regional Court clearly were 'courts' but the availability of procedural guarantees was still essential. A detained person should have access to a court, either personally or through representation.[159] Further, the later claims for discharge had not been referred by the public prosecutor to the courts. Accordingly, there was a violation of article 5(4).

There has been considerable current interest in the so-called United Kingdom Mental Health Case presently under consideration. In Application 6998/75, the applicant was ordered to be detained in a hospital for the criminally insane under the United Kingdom Mental Health Act, 1959, after pleading guilty to a charge of wounding with intent. He was subsequently conditionally discharged by the Home Secretary which meant that he could be recalled at any time on the decision of the Home Secretary and the responsible medical officer. Three years later he was recalled and returned to the hospital. He had committed no criminal offense but his probation officer said that his 'condition was giving cause for concern'. He applied unsuccessfully for habeas corpus.

The government contends that this is lawful detention under article 5(1)(a) of the European Convention. The applicant contends that article 5(1)(a) is inapplicable, and that the matter falls to be determined under article 5(1)(e)—that is to say, that his detention was related to his mental state rather than to the commission of any offense. It now remains to be seen whether the opinion of the applicant's probation officer is a sufficient basis for the Home Secretary to have exercised his discretion to recall the applicant. In short, the discretion that the Home Secretary possesses in these matters is probably in principle in conformity with the European Convention: what is at issue is whether its exercise is in the circumstances of this application in conformity with the European Convention.[160]

The interpretation of article 5(4) has arisen in various cases. Of

[158] *Id.* at 428.

[159] *Id.* at 430.

[160] [Ed. note: After this chapter was completed, the case, X v. United Kingdom, was decided on 5 Nov. 1981 by the European Court. *See* 14 Eur. Hum. Rts. Rep. 188 (1982). *annexed to* Eur. Comm'n of Human Rights Press Release B (81) 50 (1981).]

particular interest are the so-called '*Vagrancy*' *Cases*.[161] Three applicants had been detained under a Belgian Act of 1891 for the suppression of vagabondage and begging. They claimed that as their detention was ordered by a magistrate acting in an administrative capacity, their right to a court hearing in the lawfulness of their detention was denied. The European Court upheld this claim. Although the magistrate is a 'court', his functions in relation to vagrancy are administrative. Article 5(4) requires judicial supervision even in relation to vagrancy. There was found to be no breach of article 5(1)(e).[162]

A somewhat curious invocation of the notion of vagrancy occurred in *Guzzardi v. Italy*.[163] After being acquitted for lack of proof of charges of kidnapping, certain detention measures were ordered against Guzzardi under the Mafia Act of 1965. The Milan Regional Court ordered the applicant to reside in a specified locality (the island of Asinara) under supervision for three years. The Italian government claimed that there was no detention under article 5; but even if there were, it satisfied the conditions laid down in article 5(1)(e) on vagrancy. The European Commission was careful to point out that having to reside within a specified area did not necessarily amount to a deprivation of liberty.[164] But the nature of the restriction that applied to him did in fact amount to a deprivation of liberty under article 5(1) of the European Convention. Although the definition of 'vagrancy' offered in the '*Vagrancy*' *Cases* was not the only possible one, action had been taken against Guzzardi under the Mafia Act and he could not be described as a vagrant. His detention therefore did not fall under article 5(1)(e)—or indeed any of the categories in article 5.[165]

3. *Case Study. The Rights to a Fair Trial*

A further major area of the European Convention relates to the right to a fair trial guaranteed in article 6. This article provides:

1. In the determination of his civil rights and obligations or of any criminal charge against him, everyone is entitled to a fair and public hearing within a reasonable time by an independent and impartial tribunal

[161] 'De Wilde, Ooms and Versyp' Cases, [1971] Y.B. Eur. Conv. on Human Rights 788 (Eur. Ct. of Human Rights).

[162] Art. 5(3) was inapplicable because it refers back to art. 5(1)(c) with its mention of 'an offence' and vagrancy was not an 'offence' under Belgian law. The applicants were therefore not detained under art. 5(1)(c) but under art. 5(1)(e).

[163] Application 7367/76. Report of Eur. Comm'n, 7 Dec. 1978.

[164] But it might amount to a restriction upon movement under Fourth Protocol, art. 2. *See also* 'Engel' Case, [1976] Y.B. Eur. Conv. on Human Rights 490, 494 (Eur. Ct. of Human Rights); 'Greek' Case, [1969] 1 Y.B. Eur. Conv. on Human Rights 133 (Eur. Comm'n of Human Rights).

[165] On 6 Nov. 1980, the European Court delivered a decision in *Guzzardi v. Italy*. [Ed. note: On Apr. 30, 1981, the Committee of Ministers adopted Resolution DH (81) 6 on the 'Guzzardi' Case. Committee of Ministers Res. DH (81) 6, *reprinted in* Article 54 Resolution, *supra* note 100.

established by law. Judgment shall be pronounced publicly but the press and public may be excluded from all or part of the trial in the interests of morals, public order or national security in a democratic society, where the interests of juveniles or the protection of the private life of the parties so require, or to the extent strictly necessary in the opinion of the court in special circumstances where publicity would prejudice the interests of justice.

2. Everyone charged with a criminal offence shall be presumed innocent until proved guilty according to law.
3. Everyone charged with a criminal offence has the following minimum rights:
   (a) to be informed promptly, in a language which he understands and in detail, of the nature and cause of the accusation against him;
   (b) to have adequate time and facilities for the preparation of his defence ;
   (c) to defend himself in person or through legal assistance of his own choosing or, if he has not sufficient means to pay for legal assistance, to be given it free when the interests of justice so require;
   (d) to examine or have examined witnesses against him and to obtain the attendance and examination of witnesses on his behalf under the same conditions as witnesses against him;
   (e) to have the free assistance of an interpreter if he cannot understand or speak the language used in court.

It will be seen that a fair trial is guaranteed for both civil and criminal cases and that article 6(1) applies to each. Articles 6(2) and 6(3) provide procedural guarantees applicable to criminal proceedings—but even if these are met there may not be a fair trial under article 6(1). In other words, the guarantees of articles 6(2) and 6(3) are necessary but not exhaustive.[166] Qualifications on the right to a fair trial are limited only to the circumstances enumerated in article 6(1) as to when a trial need not be public. Otherwise no qualifications are permitted, save for such as could be justified under article 15, *i.e.*, derogations in times of war or national emergency.

The *'Ringeisen' Case*[167] is important not only in the context of article 5 but also for an understanding of article 6. It has been made clear in the jurisprudence of the European Convention that 'civil rights and obligations' as found in article 6(1) is a term with an autonomous meaning, and is not solely a reference to rights that are recognized under domestic law. In the *'Ringeisen' Case* it was made clear that a right could be a 'civil right' under article 6(1) even if it was a public law right rather than a private law right.[168] The European Court held that

[166] *See* 'Pfunders' Case (Austria v. Italy), [1963] Y.B. Eur. Conv. on Human Rights 790 (opinion of Eur. Comm'n of Human Rights) (before Committee of Ministers).

[167] *Ringeisen, supra* note 142. *See also* text accompanying and following notes 142–43 *supra*.

[168] *Ringeisen, supra* note 142, at 850. For a useful discussion, *see* F. Jacobs, The European

article 6(1) was applicable, but that it had not been violated. The test for the applicability of article 6(1) is not that both parties should be private parties, but that the pre-existing relations between individuals under private law are in some way affected. Thus, notwithstanding '*Ringeisen*', the Commission has held that article 6(1) (the right to a fair hearing) is not applicable to proceedings regarding a pension claim to set aside a planning decision.[169]

The '*Delcourt*' *Case*[170] has made it clear that article 6(1) applies not only in proceedings at first instance, but also through the appeals process (and, indeed, in applications to appeal).

The question of the right of access to the courts has been fundamental. In *Knechtl v. United Kingdom*,[171] the United Kingdom government had contended that article 6(1) does not guarantee a right to initiate proceedings, but rather contains procedural rights before a court once those proceedings have been initiated. The applicant was a prisoner who had sought to commence legal action for the loss of his leg in prison, contending it was due to the negligence of the prison authorities. The United Kingdom argued that even if article 6(1) did provide a right to commence proceedings before a court, that right must necessarily be limited in the case of prisoners. The case reached a friendly settlement, so these issues were not resolved, though similar ones arose in the '*Golder*' *Case*.[172] In this case the applicant was in prison in the United Kingdom when rioting broke out. He was originally charged with participation in this, though the charges were not pursued. Golder, protesting that he had not been involved, wanted reference to the charge removed from his record book, and he also wanted to instigate libel charges against the prison officer who made the charge. He was particularly anxious that the reference to the riot and his alleged part in it might hinder his chances of parole. His letters were intercepted by prison authorities (in accordance with the Prison Rules, 1964) and the Home Secretary denied him permission to consult a solicitor. As to this last matter, Golder claimed a breach of article 6(1). As in *Knechtl*, the United Kingdom asserted that article 6(1) does not confer a right to access to the courts; and that even if it did, that right was not available to convicted prisoners. The government argued

Convention on Human Rights 79 (1975). The European Commission had held art. 6(1) to not be applicable to the situation in '*Ringeisen*'—a view overturned by the European Court.

[169] *See, e.g.*, Application 5428/72, 44 Recueil de Decisions 49 (1973); 'König' Case, [1978] Y.B. Eur. Conv. on Human Rights 618 (Eur. Ct. of Human Rights). In the latter case, the European Court seems to have focused on the private, *i.e.*, commercial, nature of König's medical practice, rather than on the role of the public authorities in permitting medical practice. On the particular facts of the case, this is a curious choice of focus.

[170] [1970] Y.B. Eur. Conv. on Human Rights 1100 (Eur. Ct. of Human Rights).

[171] [1970] Y.B. Eur. Conv. on Human Rights 730 (Eur. Comm'n of Human Rights).

[172] [1975] Y.B. Eur. Conv. on Human Rights 290 (Eur. Ct. of Human Rights).

that article 5(4) explicitly provided for the right of access. If article 6(1) also provides access it would be expected to say so explicitly. To interpret article 6(1) as giving a right of access made article 5(4) redundant.

The European Court held that any ambiguity in article 6 had to be interpreted in such a way as to give effect to the purposes and objectives of the European Convention, rather than in a manner to limit the obligations of the parties. It thought that although article 6(1) does not specifically state the existence of a right of access to the courts, the right to institute proceedings in civil matters is one aspect of the right to a court,[173] Even without reference to the *travaux préparatoires*, the Court was prepared to find that article 6(1) secures to everyone the right to have any claim relating to civil rights and obligations brought before a court or tribunal. As to the 'implied limitation' argument, the Court was not prepared to advance a general theory. It merely said that Golder was entitled in the circumstances to consult a solicitor, and that it was not for the Home Secretary to appraise the prospects of the action contemplated. Article 6(1) thus applied and had been violated.

The 'implied limitation' question arose also in the '*Engel' Case*.[174] In this case, certain Dutch soldiers had been placed under arrest for certain actions of military indiscipline.[175] Was the military charge a 'criminal charge' under article 6(1)? The European Court thought it no more than a starting point to know whether the provisions determining the charge belonged to the criminal or disciplinary law of the state concerned. The nature of the offenses was the more important test. The Court agreed with the Dutch government that the offense was essentially disciplinary. But the Court then slid (through a process of logic that is not entirely clear to this author) into stating that the heavier punishment was of a sort associated with criminal offenses (*i.e.*, significant deprivations of liberty). Article 6 therefore applied to some of the applicants but not to Engel. As the hearing before the Supreme Military Court was *in camera*, in circumstances not justified in any way by the government as an exception to the general rule of public trial, there was a violation.

In a not dissimilar recent case, *Eggs v. Switzerland*,[176] the European Commission dealt with disciplinary measures imposed on a Swiss serviceman which were challenged under articles 5 and 6. The Commission held[177]—adopting the Court's tests in the '*Engel' Case*—that a

[173] *Id.* at 292.
[174] *Engel*, *supra* note 151.
[175] There were separate arguments raised about the freedom of members of the armed forces to print publications undermining military discipline. *See* text accompanying note 187 *infra*.
[176] Application 7431/76. *See* text accompanying notes 153–54 *supra*.
[177] Report of Eur. Comm'n, Mar. 4, 1978.

refusal to obey an order to perform fatigues did not affect the interests of society protected by criminal law, and that the severity of the penalty did not lead to the view that the offense was criminal. Article 6(1) was here found to be inapplicable.

In an interesting case, *Airey v. Ireland*,[178] the European Court held that the applicant was denied effective right of access to the courts to seek judicial separation by virtue of the fact that she could not afford the costs involved and no legal aid for separation proceedings was available. The Court was careful to confirm an earlier line of doctrine, *viz.* that the European Convention does not *per se* lay down a requirement for the provision of legal aid. But in these circumstances legal aid was essential if the applicant was to have access to the courts.

The *'Leudicke, Belkacem and Koç' Case*[179] raises pertinent questions relating to article 6(3). The applicants were non-Germans brought to trial for criminal offenses in Germany. They had each received interpreters for whom no charge had been made during the course of trial. But after conviction the applicants were ordered to pay for the interpreters. The German government argued that the entitlement under article 6(3)(e) to 'free assistance' was in respect of a person 'charged with a criminal offence'. After conviction they were no longer persons charged with criminal offenses,[180] and under German legislation became liable for costs. The European Court rejected this, holding that article 6(3)(e) guaranteed the right to free interpretation without having to repay the costs to persons who could not speak or understand the language of the court. Further, and importantly, that right extends also to all documentation or statements necessary for the accused to understand in order to have a fair trial.[181]

4. *Case Study. The Rights to Free Speech*

No course on the European Convention can reasonably omit special study of the right of freedom of speech under that instrument. Article 10 provides:

> 1. Everyone has the right to freedom of expression. This right shall include freedom to hold opinions and to receive and impart information and ideas without interference by public authority and regardless of frontiers. This article shall not prevent States from requiring the licensing of broadcasts, television or cinema enterprises.

[178] [1979] Y.B. Eur. Conv. on Human Rights 420 (Eur. Ct. of Human Rights).

[179] [1978] Y.B. Eur. Conv. on Human Rights 630 (Eur. Ct. of Human Rights).

[180] This argument would mean that an *acquitted* person would in principle equally have to pay, as that person too would no longer be 'charged with a criminal offence'.

[181] For an excellent analysis of this judgment, *see* Duffy, *The Luedicke, Belkacem and Koç Case*, 4 Human Rights Rev. 98 (1979).

2. The exercise of these freedoms, since it carries with it duties and responsibilities, may be subject to such formalities, conditions, restrictions or penalties as are prescribed by law and are necessary to a democratic society, in the interests of national security, territorial integrity or public safety, for the prevention of disorder or crime, for the protection of health or morals, for the protection of the reputation or rights of others, for preventing the disclosure of information received in confidence, or for maintaining the authority and impartiality of the judiciary.

As early as the *'De Becker' Case*[182] the European Commission had had to address itself to the compatibility of national legislation with the right to freedom of expression. It examined article 123 *sexies* of the Belgian Penal Code (which punished the applicant for wartime journalism in collaboration with the Nazis) by imposing upon him a prohibition against publishing or writing for publication. It was found that the breadth of this prohibition (which went beyond publication of political matters and continued in effect years after the end of the war) was contrary to article 10 of the European Convention. New legislation was introduced before the matter went to the European Court, and that body agreed, after reviewing the situation, to strike the case from its list.[183]

In *Pers N.V. v. Netherlands*,[184] a magazine publisher wanted to be able to include information on radio and TV programs but was prevented from doing so by the Copyright Act and the Broadcasting Act. The government pointed to the fact that there existed in The Netherlands seven broadcasting channels which jointly published details of broadcasting, and that even if there was a restriction on the applicant's freedom to publish, it was for the purpose of protecting the rights of others. The European Commission adopted a report[185] and the matter went to the Committee of Ministers. The Committee of Ministers agreed with the Commission[186] that there was no interference with the applicant's rights under article 10(1), as the freedom to impart information was limited to information produced, provided, or organized by the person claiming the right. In other words, article 10 does not cover information not yet in one's possession. The Committee of Ministers commented that article 10(1) was not directed to the protection of the commercial interests of particular newspapers.

In *'Engel'*,[187] Dutch soldiers claimed, *inter alia*, that in suffering

182 [1962] Y.B. Eur. Conv. on Human Rights 320, 324–26 (Eur. Ct. of Human Rights).
183 *Id.* at 336.
184 *See* [1973] Y.B. Eur. Conv. on Human Rights 124 (Eur. Comm'n of Human Rights).
185 Report of Eur. Comm'n, July 6, 1976.
186 Committee of Ministers Res. DH (77) 1, *reprinted in* Article 32 Resolutions, *supra* note 92.
187 *See* text accompanying notes 151 & 174–75 and note 151 *supra*.

disciplinary punishment for the publication of certain materials their freedom of expression had been denied. Was the restriction necessary in a democratic society for the protection of order? The European Court held that it must take into account the specific characteristics of military life, and also that The Netherlands goverment had a margin of appreciation in deciding how those characteristics should best be protected. It is in that context that one must read the otherwise curious dictum that 'there was no question of depriving them of their freedom of expression but only of punishing the abusive exercise of that discretion'. The European Court found there was no breach of article 10(2).

In the *'Handyside' Case*[188]—where the question of margin of appreciation was at issue again—the European Court was concerned with the reference to the limitation based on 'protection of morals' in article 10(2). Handyside was a publisher who planned to publish and distribute in the United Kingdom 'The Little Red Schoolbook'. It was seized prior to publication under the Obscene Publications Act and Handyside was convicted and fined. Handyside claimed before the European Commission that the action taken against the book and him was contrary to various articles of the European Convention, including article 10. The book—directed at schoolchildren—had in fact circulated without legal restraint in several other countries which were parties to the European Convention.

The United Kingdom claimed that its legislation was not in substance different from comparable legislation in other Western European states, that the legislation was necessary to protect the young, and that it fell within the limitation of article 10(2) which referred to the protection of morals. The Commission was narrowly divided in its findings, with the majority finding significant the fact that the book was intended for schoolchildren. It found that the interference had been necessary for the protection of morals of the young and was reasonably necessary in a democratic society. The dissenting members thought that their task was not to review the decision of the English court but rather to assess the book in the light of the Convention in order to ascertain whether an infringment fell under Article 10(2).

The European Court held that there was no violation of article 10. While the relevant national legislation did not reveal a uniform European concept of morals, the national authorities had a margin of appreciation (available alike to the domestic legislature, as to judicial and other bodies that have to interpret the law) in assessing pressing social needs. The European Court acknowledged that the very notion

188 [1976] Y.B. Eur. Conv. on Human Rights 506 (Eur. Ct. of Human Rights).

of a 'democratic society' meant that there was freedom of expression for unpopular or shocking ideas as well as for ideas that were inoffensive: but the 'encouragement to indulge in precocious activities harmful for [children] or even to commit certain criminal offences' gave sufficient reason for the United Kingdom to rely on the limitation of article 10(2).

The *'Handyside' Case* introduced a range of issues that were also to be relevant in *'The Sunday Times' Case*.[189] In both cases there was at issue one of the limitations available under article 10, the question of 'margin of appreciation'[190] for the state in deciding that such a limitation needed to be relied on, and the particular difficulties that arise when the European Commission and the European Court deal with matters that arise out of judicial decisions at the national level. *'The Sunday Times' Case* arose out of legal actions against the Distillers Company, the manufacturers of thalidomide, by parents of thalidomide children. *The Sunday Times* had conducted a campaign supporting the thalidomide victims, a campaign critical to Distillers and the terms of settlement that it had eventually offered. Litigation was still pending when an injunction was granted by the High Court to prevent *The Sunday Times* from publishing an article which argued that Distillers showed insufficient concern about the dangers of the product at various stages. The Court of Appeal was prepared to allow publication, but the House of Lords unanimously affirmed the judgment of the High Court. The House of Lords addressed itself to the argument that the article constituted a contempt of court given that litigation was still outstanding. Their Lordships thought that public policy required a balancing of interests which might conflict—freedom of speech and the administration of justice. The latter required that citizens should have access to duly established courts, that they should be able to rely upon decisions free from bias, and that once a matter was submitted to a court of law the court's functions should not be usurped. The House of Lords felt that *The Sunday Times* was usurping the court's function and conveying a message to all who would read the article that an examination of the issues would show Distillers to have been negligent.[191]

The European Commission and the European Court were at pains to point out that they were not 'judging the House of Lords' but rather

[189] [1979] Y.B. Eur. Conv. on Human Rights 402 (Eur. Ct. of Human Rights).

[190] *See* Morrisson, *Margin of Appreciation in Human Rights Law*, 6 Revue des Droits de l'Homme 263 (1963).

[191] It might be thought that this was a less than robust attitude, given that the Distillers case was not to be heard before a jury, and the judges were presumably capable of ignoring articles in the press when weighing the evidence. This author also finds curious the suggestion of usurpation of the court's function.

scrutinizing whether the restriction imposed on *The Sunday Times* could be justified under article 10(2). The law of contempt, though not enshrined in a statute, was still a restriction 'prescribed by law'—albeit a rather unclear case law. But given the professional training in impartiality that judges receive, *The Sunday Times* article would not influence a competent judge. Nor did the newspaper's views purport to be a legal assessment of the merits of the Distillers case under the laws of England; it was journalism rather than a usurpation of the functions of the court.[192]

II. Teaching Suggestions

Ideally, all courses on regional human rights machinery and jurisprudence should be prefaced by a general overview of human rights in international law. There should be several classes devoted to what one could term the conceptual aspects of human rights. Before embarking on substantive materials the students should understand the classical relationship of the individual to the state under international law—whether his or her own state or another state. This is the moment for a historical survey of the theory of individual/state relationships: Locke, Mill, Rousseau, and Austin could be usefully explained and selected readings assigned. Other more contemporary writings could also be studied (see Bibliography).[193]

An appreciation is necessary of the limits of 'regular' international law in advancing the rights of the individual against governments. Why do we need a special body of law termed 'human rights'? In what ways is international law unable to provide full protection for the individual? General international law affords little direct assistance to the individual in claims against his or her own government. And the individual is still constrained in asserting direct benefits under a treaty.[194] At best, the individual will be able in domestic courts to cite international instruments to which his or her state is party, and which have a bearing on the rights being asserted. If these international treaties have not been transformed (through statutory instruments or

[192] *See also* Duffy, *The Sunday Times Case: Freedom of Expression, Contempt of Court and the European Convention on Human Rights*, 5 Human Rights Rev. 17 (1980). This author has also found it useful to compare the (still modest) views of the European Convention on freedom of expression with the rather different case law in the United States on first amendment questions.

[193] In addition, *see* ch. 3 *supra*.

[194] Where a treaty provides for rights *in rem*, it may be possible for an individual to directly assert benefits, but he or she may still need to persuade the state of nationality to pursue the matter on his or her behalf. The Permanent Court thought that the matter turned on the intentions of the parties to the treaty. *See* Jurisdiction of the Courts of Danzig [1928], P.C.I.J., ser. B, No. 15. And even in the case of clearly expressed intentions, the treaty will need to be made part of the law of the land before the individual will have direct municipal rights under it. The direct applicability of certain parts of the EEC Rome Treaty affords an example.

constitutional equivalent) into part of the domestic law of the land, the courts may consider that relevant in deciding whether the plaintiff can rely on them.[195] Above all, classical international law does not provide the individual claimant with any access to an international court against his or her *own* government. The individual is treated as lacking the procedural capacity to pursue such a claim at the international level, and the international tribunals generally make no provision for individual claims.[196]

An individual who wishes to pursue a claim against a foreign government is hardly in a better position. If the complaint is actionable in the courts of the state against which the complaint lies, the claimant is likely to pursue the case there[197]—but if the state's action is lawful under its own laws it is unlikely the case will succeed. An individual claimant does not have the legal capacity to bring an action on the international level and the international law rule of nationality of claims severely circumscribes the chances of finding someone else whose government would be willing to bring the claim. So the claimant must persuade his or her government of the rightness of the claim, and, through the link of nationality, the government must perceive the harm done to the individual as an international legal wrong done to it. The case will not be pursued unless the government finds it diplomatically and politically expedient to do so. And then, if all those hurdles are surmounted, there must be a sufficient basis of jurisdiction for the matter to proceed before an international tribunal.[198]

It is therefore useful for the student to be given some understanding of the question of international minimum standards in the treatment of aliens, as well as an outline of the law of state responsibility and the exhaustion of local remedies rule. The student will need to understand the operation of the nationality of claims rule and the way in which this combination of international legal precepts can leave the individual exposed.[199] This is also the time to introduce the notion of domestic

[195] *See generally* text accompanying notes 75–82 *supra*.

[196] Thus art. 34(1) of the Statute of the International Court of Justice provides: 'Only states may be parties in cases before the Court.'

[197] The ability of a person to pursue a claim against a state depends on a variety of factors including the jurisdictional rules of the forum and whether the state is exempt from legal action under domestic law.

[198] If the case is to go before the International Court of Justice, there must be jurisdiction on the basis of art. 36 of the Statute of the Court, either by virtue of both parties having made a declaration recognizing the Court's competence under art. 36(2), with no reciprocally applicable reservations, or by virtue of a jurisdictional clause in an applicable treaty, or by *ad hoc* reference to the Court.

[199] On the nationality of claims rule, *see* D. O'Connell, 2 International Law 734–46, 1116–24 (1965). For comments on the ways in which this rule leaves the individual vulnerable, *see* Higgins, *Conceptual Thinking About the Individual in International Law*, 4 Brit. J. Int'l Stud. 1, 7–8 (1978).

jurisdiction: in most claims by individuals against their own governments it will be beyond the reach of other governments to lend assistance, in part because of the nationality of claims rule, but also because of the insistence by the allegedly offending government that the matter is within its own jurisdiction. Most legal matters that concern the state and its citizens will be regarded as within the domestic jurisdiction of that state[200] and not a matter of legitimate international concern.

The great significance of the concept of human rights is that it provides some prospects for mitigating this exposure of the individual in the face of the state. Classical international law cannot fulfill this function. Human rights law is a special branch of international law, one of whose salient features is that it can provide an individual with access to international institutions whether the complaint is against his or her own state or against another state.[201] Human rights law imposes obligations upon states in respect of their treatment of individuals, whether nationals or not; and it gives those individuals procedural capacity to defend their rights. The enormous significance of those acts cannot be exaggerated. Herein lies the importance for an individual to be able to classify a claim as a human rights claim. There are other important psychological and political functions performed by designating a legal claim as a human rights claim; in the ordering process of competing claims, the claim of entitlement as a human right assumes a certain priority.[202] It not only becomes a matter of legitimate international concern, beyond the domestic jurisdiction of any one state, but it assumes a special significance and weight.

One can, of course, simply define human rights as those legal rights that have found their way into the major human rights instruments. This may be pedagogically convenient, but it is hardly satisfactory intellectually. It assumes that no human rights exist outside of treaty law, and it ignores the important process of identifying what legal rights have come to be codified as human rights, and why. A discussion on this topic will give the student some understanding of the transmutation of certain claims from political aspiration to perceived human rights. The U.N. organs are a fruitful laboratory for this process, as is the negotiating-conference material of the major international instruments. Such a discussion would provide the student

[200] This flows from the legal precept that states have jurisdiction over persons and events within their territory as an attribute of state sovereignty. Thus questions of private law and remedies will *prima facie* fall within this category, as will matters of constitutional and administrative law.

[201] The European Convention allows complaints against states parties to be filed with the European Commission by persons of *any* nationality. *See* European Convention, art. 25(1).

[202] For an excellent analysis of this aspect of human rights claims, *see* Bilder, *Rethinking International Human Rights: Some Basic Questions*, 2 Revue des Droits de l'Homme 557 (1969).

with a salutary survey of a range of U.N. materials and could lead to a look at some of the *travaux préparatoires* of the European Convention on Human Rights.[203] Of particular interest is the debate over the balance to be struck between civil and political rights on the one hand and economic and social rights on the other. Are the latter 'realistic'? Does the preference for political and civil rights in the West reflect inadequacies in the social structure of those states? How has the matter been handled in the various major international instruments? Where are the pressures for the alternative views?

There is one other important topic which is sometimes left to be dealt with as an incidental to the case law in which it arises, but which properly belongs among the conceptual issues which must be addressed before the student can begin to come to grips with the details of the European Convention. To what extent is the notion of human rights an absolute or a relative one? Are our views of human rights the product of our own culture? Do the rights that westerners regard as essential (right of liberty, right to a fair trial, freedom of expression) reflect a certain structure of society or are they witness to an objective truth? Do many of the designated rights require a certain stage of development to have been reached and are they in fact luxuries that only the developed world can afford? Is it realistic to expect adherence to these rights by states that are still seeking to make effective their nationhood, and that desperately fear all centrifugal tendencies? These questions obviously are not directly addressed in the case law of the European Convention, but there is no avoiding them. The student will need to understand why the global human rights picture is such a curious collage of different instruments (some universal, some regional) that attempts different things. The student will also need some explanation as to why the Universal Declaration found binding legal form in two, rather than one, Covenants—and why the enforcement and scrutinizing procedures of the Covenants differ.[204]

III. Syllabus

A. The Conceptual Issues

1. The emergence of the modern state. The place of the individual therein. The role of international law in delineating that relationship.

   L. Sohn & T. Buergenthal, The International Protection of Human Rights 1–21 (1973).

[203] *See* 1–4 Collected Editions of the Travaux Préparatoires of the European Convention on Human Rights (1975–1977).

[204] *See* ch. 10 *supra*.

McDougal, *Human Rights and World Public Order*, 63 Am. J. Int'l L. 237 (1969).

L. Henkin, The Rights of Man Today, ch. 1 (1979).

Milne, *The Idea of Human Rights: A Critical Enquiry*, in Human Rights: Problems, Perspectives and Texts, ch. 2 (F. Dowrick ed. 1979).

2. The extent to which the relationship between the state and the individual is an unchanging or relative one. Are there 'absolute' rights? The process of specifying human rights. Human rights and political ideology. Human rights and diverse conditions. Human rights and economic development.

   Bilder, *Rethinking International Human Rights: Some Basic Questions*, 2 Revue des Droits de l'Homme 557 (1969).

   McDougal, *Human Rights and World Public Order: Principles of Content and Procedure for Clarifying General Community Policies*, 14 Va. J. Int'l L. 387 (1974).

   F. Dowrick, Human Rights: Problems, Perspectives and Texts, ch. 1, *supra*.

   R. Higgins, Human Rights: Prospects and Problems (1979).

   Eze, *Les Droits de l'Homme et le Sous-developpement*, 12 Revue des Droits de l'Homme 5 (1979).

   Mower, *Human Rights in Black Africa: A Double Standard?*, 9 Revue des Droits de l'Homme 39 (1976).

3. Nationality and the protection of human rights. Nationality of claims. Minimum standards in the treatment of aliens. Outlines of the law of state responsibility and local remedies rule. Inadequacy of the traditional approach.

   Sohn & Buergenthal, *supra*, 62–116, 124–36.

   Weis, *Diplomatic Protection of Nationals and International Protection of Human Rights*, 4 Revue des Droits de l'Homme 642 (1971).

   McDougal, Lasswell & Chen, *Nationality and Human Rights: The Protection of the Individual in External Arenas*, 83 Yale L.J. 900 (1974).

   CASES: Tunis and Morocco Nationality Decrees, [1923] P.C.I.J., ser. B.
   Nottebohm, [1955] I.C.J.
   Barcelona Traction, [1970] I.C.J.

4. Derogations from accepted standards.
   a. In peace.

Higgins, *Derogations Under Human Rights Treaties*, 48 Brit. Y.B. Int'l L. 281 (1976–1977).

Tremblay, *Les Situations d'Urgence qui Permittent en Droit International de Suspendre les Droits de l'Homme*, [1977] Cahiers de Droit 3.

Garibaldi, *General Limitations on Human Rights: The Principle of Legality*, 17 Harv. Int'l L.J. 503 (1976).

Warbrick, *The Protection of Human Rights in National Emergencies*, in Human Rights: Problems, Perspectives and Texts, ch. 7, *supra*.

Daes, *Restrictions and Limitations on Human Rights*, in 3 René Cassin Amicorum Discipulorumque Liber 79 (1971).

Jacobs, *The Restrictions on the Exercise of Rights and Freedom Guaranteed by the European Convention on Human Rights*, 4 International Colloquy on the European Convention on HumanRights, Council of Europe Doc. H/Coll (75) 5(1975).

CASES: 'Lawless' Case, [1961] Y.B. Eur. Conv. 14 (Eur. Comm'n).

Greece v. United Kingdom (First Cyrpus Case), [1958–1959] Y.B. Eur. Conv. 182 (Eur. Comm'n).

Greece v. United Kingdom (Second Cyprus Case), [1958–1959] Y.B. Eur. Conv. 186 (Eur. Comm'n).

'Greek' Case, [1969] 1 Y.B. Eur. Conv. (Eur. Comm'n).

b. In armed conflict.

Respect for human rights in armed conflict, Report of of the U.N. Secretary-General, U.N. Doc. A/7720 (1969).

S. Bailey, Prohibitions and Restraints in War, chs. 3 & 4 (1972).

Final Act, Diplomatic Conference on the Reaffirmation and Development of International Humanitarian Law Applicable in Armed Conflicts, Comnd. No. 6927 (1977).

Sandoz, *La Place des Protocols Additionnels aux Conventions de Guerre du 12 Aout 1945 dans le Droit Humanitaire*, 12 Revue des Droits de l'Homme 135 (1979).

B. The Machinery

1. The optional clauses. Petitions. The organs.

Sohn & Buergenthal, *supra*, at 1008–1238.

Schwelb, *On the Operation of the European Convention of Human Rights*, 18 Int'l Organization 558 (1964).

—— *Abuse of the Right of Petition*, 3 Revue des Droits de l'Homme 313 (1970).

Fawcett, *Application of the European Convention on Human Rights*, World Today (Apr. 1972).

—— *Spread of the Ombudsman System in Europe*, World Today (Oct. 1975).

2. The European Convention and national law.

Golsong, *The European Convention before Domestic Courts*, 38 Brit. Y.B. Int'l L. 445 (1962).

Dale, *Human Rights in the United Kingdom: International Standards*, 25 Int'l & Comp. L.Q. 292 (1976).

P. Merlens, Le Droit de Recours Effectif Devant les Instances Nationales en cas d'un Violation d'un Droit de l'Homme (1973).

Bill of Rights, 6 Dec. 1979 (H.L. Bill 100); Hansard, 402 H.L. (8 Nov. 1979); Hansard, 403 H.L. (22 Nov., 29 Nov., 6 Dec. 1979).

Fawcett. *A Bill of Rights for the United Kingdom*, 1 Human Rights Rev. 57 (1976).

Mann, *Britain's Bill of Rights*, 94 L.Q. Rev. 512 (1978).

3. Admissibility. Exhaustion of local remedies. 'Manifestly ill-founded'. Friendly settlement. Reports of the European Commission. Reference to the European Court. Execution of the decisions of the Court. 'Just satisfaction.' The notion of a 'victim'.

Cancado Trinidade, *Exhaustion of Local Remedies in the Jurisprudence of the European Court of Human Rights: An Appraisal*, 10 Revue des Droits de l'Homme 141 (1977).

—— *The Burdens of Proof with regard to the Exhaustion of Local Remedies*, 9 Revue des Droits de l'Homme 81 (1976).

Higgins, *The Execution of Decisions of Organs. Under the European Convention on Human Rights*, [1978] Revue Hellénique de Droit International 1.

4. The European Convention and other international instruments.

a. The restriction of the European Convention to civil rights;

cf. the U.N. Covenants and the Universal Declaration of Human Rights.

Jacobs, *The Extension of the European Convention on Human Rights to include Economic, Social and Cultural Rights*, 3 Human Rights Rev. 163 (1978).

b. Overlapping jurisdiction and liabilities.

Tardu, *Coexistence des Procedures Universelles en Regionalles de Plainfe Individuelle dans la Domaine des Droits de l'Homme*, 4 Revue des Droits de l'Homme 585 (1971).

Schermers, *The Communities Under the European Convention on Human Rights*, [1978] Legal Issues Eur. Integration 1.

Robertson, Human Rights in Europe 286–91 (2d ed. 1977).

Problems arising from the co-existence of the United Nations Covenants on Human Rights and the European Convention on Human Rights, Report of the Committee of Experts on Human Rights to the Committee of Ministers, Council of Europe Doc. H (70) 7 (1970).

Proceedings of the Colloquy about the European Convention on Human Rights in Relation to other International Instruments for the Protection of Human Rights, Athens, Sept. 21–22, 1978 (Strasbourg 1979).

C. Case Studies: The Rights Protected

1. Torture or inhuman or degrading treatment or punishment (article 3).

CASES: 'Greek' Case, [1969] 1 Y.B. Eur. Conv. (Eur. Comm'n).

Ireland v. United Kingdom [1978] Y.B. Eur. Conv. 602 (Eur. Ct.).

Tyrer v. United Kingdom, [1978] Y.B. Eur. Conv. 612 (Eur. Ct.).

Amerkane v. United Kingdom, [1973] Y.B. Eur. Conv. 356 (Eur. Comm'n).

Spjut, *Torture under the European Convention on Human Rights*, 73 Am. J. Int'l L. 267 (1979).

O'Boyle, *Torture and Emergency Powers under the European Convention on Human Rights: Ireland v. the United Kingdom*, 71 Am. J. Int'l L. 674 (1977).

2. Liberty of the person (article 5).
   a. Mental health patients' rights.
      CASES: Winterwerp v. Netherlands, [1979] Y.B. Eur. Conv. 426 (Eur. Ct.).
      X v. United Kingdom, Eur. Ct. Press Release C (81) 58 (Nov. 5, 1981).
   b. Pre-trial detention.
      CASES: 'Wemhoff' Case, [1968] 2 Y.B. Eur. Conv. 796 (Eur. Ct.).
      'Neumeister' Case, [1968] 2 Y.B. Eur. Conv. 812 (Eur. Ct.).
      'Matznetter' Case, [1969] Y.B. Eur. Conv. 406 (Eur. Ct.).
      'Stögmüller' Case, [1969] Y.B. Eur. Conv. 364 (Eur. Ct.).
      'Ringeisen' Case, [1971] Y.B. Eur. Conv. 838 (Eur. Ct.).
      'Huber' Case, [1971] Y.B. Eur. Conv. 548 (Eur. Comm'n).
      'Schiesser' Case, [1979] Y.B. Eur. Conv. 432 (Eur. Ct.).
      'Engel' Case, [1976] Y.B. Eur. Conv. 490 (Eur. Ct.).
      'König' Case, [1978] Y.B. Eur. Conv. 618 (Eur. Ct.).
      'Vagrancy' Cases, [1971] Y.B. Eur. Conv. 788 (Eur. Ct.).

3. Fair trial and access to courts (article 6).
   CASES: 'Ringeisen' Case, [1971] Y.B. Eur. Conv. 838 (Eur. Ct.).
   'Delcourt' Case, [1970] Y.B. Eur. Conv. 1100 (Eur. Ct.).
   Knechtl v. United Kingdom, [1970] Y.B. Eur. Conv. 730 (Eur. Comm'n).
   'Engel' Case, [1976] Y.B. Eur. Conv. 490 (Eur. Ct.).
   Eggs v. Switzerland, Report of Eur. Comm'n, 4 Mar. 1978.
   'Airey' Case, [1979] Y.B. Eur. Conv. 420 (Eur. Ct.).
   'Luedicke, Belkacem and Koç' Case, [1978] Y.B. Eur. Conv. 630 (Eur. Ct.).

'Golder' Case, [1975] Y.B. Eur. Conv. 290 (Eur. Ct.).

Harris, *The Application of Article 6(1) of the European Convention on Human Rights to Administrative Law*, 47 Brit. Y.B. Int'l L. 157 (1974–1975).

Duffy, *The Luedicke, Belkacem and Koç Case*, 4 Human Rights Rev. 98 (1979).

Del Russo, *Prisoners' Rights of Access to the Courts: A Comparative Analysis of Human Rights Jurisprudence in Europe and the U.S.*, 13 J. Int'l L. & Econ. 1 (1978).

4. Freedom of expression (article 10).

CASES: 'De Becker' Case, [1962] Y.B. Eur. Conv. 320 (Eur. Ct.).

Pers v. Netherlands, Report of Eur. Comm'n, 6 July 1976.

'Engel' Case, [1976] Y.B. Eur. Conv. 490 (Eur. Ct.).

'Handyside' Case, [1976] Y.B. Eur. Conv. 506 (Eur. Ct.).

'The Sunday Times' Case, [1979] Y.B. Eur. Conv. 402 (Eur. Ct.).

Duffy, *The Sunday Times Case: Freedom of Expression, Contempt of Court and the European Convention on Human Rights*, 5 Human Rights Rev. 17 (1980).

Fiengold, *The Little Red Schoolbook and the European Convention on Human Rights*, 3 Human Rights Rev. 21 (1978).

5. Non-Discrimination/Protection of minorities (article 14).

CASES: 'Belgian Linguistics' Case, [1968] 1 Y.B. Eur. Conv. 832 (Eur. Ct.).

International Convention on the Elimination of All Forms of Racial Discrimination, 660 U.N.T.S. 195.

Bruegel, *A Neglected Field: The Protection of Minorities*, 4 Revue des Droits de l'Homme 413 (1971).

Dinstein, *Collective Human Rights of Peoples and Minorities*, 25 Int'l & Comp. L.Q. 102 (1976).

6. Privacy and family life (article 8).

CASES: 'Klass' Case, [1978] Y.B. Eur. Conv. 622 (Eur. Ct.).

Malone v. Metropolitan Police Commissioner, [1979] 2 W.L.R. 700.

Alam and Khan v. United Kingdom, [1967] Y.B. Eur. Conv. 478 (Eur. Comm'n) (admissibility);

[1968] 1 Y.B. Eur. Conv. 788 (Eur. Comm'n) (friendly settlement).

East African Asians v. United Kingdom (unpublished). But see Joint Council for Welfare of Immigrants, 'The Unpublished Report' (Dec. 1979).

Privacy and Human Rights (A. Robertson ed. 1973).

IV. Minisyllabus

In Europe it is now customary for human rights courses, while making due reference to the United Nations' role and human rights machinery, to focus primarily on the European Convention on Human Rights. There are two reasons for this. First, the European Convention now provides a case law in the field that is as yet unmatched for interest. Second, because of their impact on the domestic legal plane, the decisions of the European Commission and the European Court are widely reported in the European press, and thus attract the notice of students. The first reason is sufficiently objective and weighty that in this writer's view any serious course on human rights must include close study of the European Convention. But it is appreciated that outside of continental Europe the balance may be different, and the main emphasis may be on, for example, the U.N. instruments or the Inter-American system for human rights.

But even a severely curtailed course-module on the European Convention (say two or three two-hour sessions) must contain certain elements if it is to have even marginal value. The student must above all be made aware of the essential nature of the European model—of like-minded democratic states agreeing on effective machinery to protect a limited number of rights. The central place of individual petitions, the parallel role of inter-State applications, and the role of the European Commission in admissibility and friendly settlement also need clear explanation. Care should be taken to distinguish qualifications on protected rights from derogation, and the nature of the institutional control over each must be examined. The student must also appreciate that certain rights do not admit of derogation or qualification. The following is a suggested short syllabus.

1. The parties to the European Convention.
2. The rights protected therein.
3. The additional rights in the First Protocol and the Fourth Protocol, and the parties thereto.
4. The machinery.
   Optional clauses (articles 25 and 46).

Inter-state applications (article 24).
The European Commission.
Admissibility, with particular reference to the exhaustion of local remedies.
Articles 26 and 27 explained.
Investigation and friendly settlement (article 28).
The Committee of Ministers.
Its functions under articles 32 and 54.
The European Court.
Who may refer and when.

5. Jurisprudence—the rights protected (a brief selection).
Torture: *Ireland v. United Kingdom.*
Fair trial/access to courts: *'Engel' Case.*
'Golder' Case.
Freedom of expression: *'The Sunday Times' Case.*
Privacy: *'Klass' Case.*
(Inevitably, taking any one of these cases in isolation, without also dealing with the other case law on the topic, distorts and to that extent misleads.)

V. Bibliography

All students will require a copy of the European Convention and the Protocols. Extremely useful for teaching purposes is *Human Rights in International Law: Basic Texts*, Council of Europe Doc. H (79) 4 (1979), published by the European Commission Secretariat. It contains not only the European Convention and its six Protocols, but also other leading human rights instruments, thus greatly facilitating comparative examination. Students must rapidly learn to find their way around the *Yearbook of the European Convention on Human Rights* which contains general information and extracts from decisions of all the organs. Importantly, it also includes selected decisions of national courts on the European Convention and extracts from proceedings of national parliaments. It has a useful bibliography. So far twenty-two volumes have been published. (It should also be explained to students that a special volume exists on the *'Greek' Case.*) But not all decisions find their way into the *Yearbook*. The paperback series of *Decisions and Reports* will lead to lesser known materials. Other essential primary source materials are: *Collected Texts*, which includes the Rules of Procedure of the European Commission, of the European Court, and Rules of the Committee of Ministers, as well as the state of ratifications; the Explanatory Reports on the Second to Fifth Protocols, Council of Europe Doc. H (71) 11 (1971).

Finally, so far as fairly current materials are concerned, it is advisable for universities offering courses on the European Convention to receive the 'blue book' versions of Commission Reports and Court Judgments. These arrive *seriatim* from Strasbourg in speedy fashion, making it unnecessary to await the publication of Court Judgments in the *Series A* bound form, or the Commission's Reports in the *Yearbook*. (Students should also be aware that when a case goes on to the Court, the judgment will contain a fairly detailed resumé of the Commission's report.)

Students will find *Stocktaking*, which is a periodic survey of decisions and case law in respect of all the rights, invaluable. Two useful new publications are the *Collection of Resolutions Adopted by the Committee of Ministers in Application of Article 32, 1959–1981*, Council of Europe Doc. H (81) 4 (1981), and *Collection of Resolutions Adopted by the Committee of Ministers in Application of Article 54, 1976–1981*, Council of Europe Doc. H (81) 5 (1981).

Leading Textbooks

S. Castberg, The European Convention on Human Rights (1974).
The European Convention on Human Rights, Int'l & Comp. L.Q. Supp. No. 11 (1965).
J. Fawcett, The Application of the European Convention on Human Rights (1969).
F. Jacobs, The European Convention on Human Rights (1975).
Mélanges Offerts à Polys Modinos: Problèmes des droits de l'Homme et de l'implication européenne (1968).
L. Mikaelsen, European Protection of Human Rights (1980).
F. Monconduit, La Commission Européene des Droits de l'Homme (1965).
C. Morrisson, The Developing European Law of Human Rights (1976).
1–3 René Cassin Amicorum Discipulorumque Liber (1968–1971).
L. Sohn & T. Buergenthal, International Protection of Human Rights, ch. 7 (1973).
K. Vasak, La Convention Européene des Droits de l'Homme (1964).
G. Weil, The European Convention on Human Rights: Background, Development and Prospects (1963).

Source Materials

Collected texts.

[European Convention; 6 Protocols; Rules of Procedure of the European Commission and the European Court of Human

Rights; Rules of the Committee of Ministers for the Application of Articles 32 and 54; state of ratifications.]
Publications of the European Court of Human Rights.
[Series A—decisions and judgments.
Series B—pleadings, oral arguments, and documents.]
Yearbook of the European Convention on Human Rights.
[General information; extracts from decisions of the European Commission and Court.]
1–5 Collected Edition of the Travaux Préparatoires of the European Convention on Human Rights.
Collection of Decisions of National Courts relating to the European Convention on Human Rights.
[Plus 4 supplements to date.]
Activities of the Council of Europe in the field of Human Rights.
[Annual survey.]
Stocktaking on the European Convention on Human Rights.
[A periodic survey of the results achieved; invaluable.]

VI. Minibibliography

J. Fawcett, The Application of the European Convention on Human Rights (1975) [use when going through the listed rights and articles relating to admissibility].
A. Robertson, Human Rights in Europe (2d ed. 1977) [especially for an understanding of how the European Commission works].
F. Jacobs, The European Convention on Human Rights (1975).
Schwelb, *On the Operation of the European Convention on Human Rights*, 18 Int'l Organization 558 (1964).
Buergenthal, *The Effect of the European Convention on Human Rights on the International Law of Member States*, in the European Convention on Human Rights, Int'l & Comp. L.Q. Supp. No. 11, at 82 (1965).
Higgins, *Derogations Under Human Rights Treaties*, 48 Brit. Y.B. Int'l L. 281 (1976–1977).

Index

ABORTION 123–4
ABUSE
of rights 93
ACCESS
to public service 191–3
ACKERMAN, B. 94n
ACTON, LORD 194n
ADELMAN AND MORRIS 224n
ALSTON 219n, 220n, 221n, 224n, 244n, 245n
AMALRIK, ANDRÉ 73n
AMERICA, *see* UNITED STATES OF AMERICA
AMERICAN CONVENTION ON HUMAN RIGHTS
adherents to 440–1
arbitrary arrest, detention, exile, prohibition of 137
assembly, freedom of 188–9
asylum, right to 153
Chile and 444
conscience, freedom of 159–60
duties under 442
equality before the law 132
European Convention on Human Rights and 441, 442, 450, 455; *see also* EUROPEAN CONVENTION ON HUMAN RIGHTS
ex post facto laws 146, 147
fair trial 141, 142
generally 439–42
government, right to take part in 192, 193
innocence, presumption of 144
institutions 451–70; Inter-American Commission on Human Rights 452–60; Inter-American Court of Human Rights 460–70; Organization of American States Charter 470–87
International Covenant on Civil and Political Rights and 446, 450–1
interpretation and application 381, 442–51; derogation, right of 448–52; Federal State Clause, the 445–8; Inter-American Court of Human Rights and 447; *Missouri* v. *Holland*, principle in 446–7; self-executing character 442–5
life, liberty and security of person 121
movement, freedom of 150, 151
nationality, right to a 154
nondiscrimination in application of law 132
Organization of American States and 440, 451–4
privacy 148, 149
property, right to own 157
recognition, legal 130
religion, freedom of 159–60
remedy, right to a 134, 135, 136
self-determination 195
slavery and servitude 124
thought, freedom of 159–60
torture, cruel, inhuman, or degrading treatment or punishment 126, 166
AMERICAN DECLARATION ON THE RIGHTS AND DUTIES OF MAN
assembly, freedom of 189
government, right to take part in 192, 193
religious freedom 178
AMNESTY INTERNATIONAL 405, 408, 409, 427–8
in Afghanistan 414
APARTHEID 317, 385
International Convention on the Suppression and Punishment of the Crime of 379
United Nations and 385–7
ARGENTINA 93
ARISTOTLE 77
ARMAND HAMMER CONFERENCES ON PEACE AND HUMAN RIGHTS 99n
ARMED CONFLICT 345–68
capital punishment in 350
civilians and 349
conscientious objectors 352
duties in 354–6
emergency situation in 351
European Convention on Human Rights and 502
freedom of assembly in 353–4
generally 345–8
Geneva Conventions, the 345–50
hostages 349
immigration and 353
implementation and supervision of human rights 356–62
medical experimentation, freedom from 354
military service 352–3

peacetime and wartime, interplay of rights in 350–4
prisoners of war 352
Red Cross, International Committee of 359–62
teaching human rights and, *see* TEACHING, armed conflict, human rights in
torture 352
war crimes 358–9
ARREST
arbitrary 131–9, 515–28
freedom from 91
unlawful, U.S.A. in 38–9
ASSEMBLY, FREEDOM OF 173–4, 188–9
wartime, in 353–4
ASSOCIATION, FREEDOM OF 174, 190–1
International Labour Organisation Committee on 290–2
ASYLUM
right to 152–3
AXINN 99n

BAXTER, JUDGE 118n
BEARD, C. and M. 29n
BENEFITS
apportionment of 103
BENTHAM, JEREMY 88–9, *see also* UTILITY
BERGER 17n
BERLIN, I. 81n, 83n
BILL OF RIGHTS, AMERICAN, *see* UNITED STATES OF AMERICA, rights in, Bill of Rights
BILL OF RIGHTS, THE INTERNATIONAL
basic documents 207n
economic, social, cultural well-being and 207
BIRCHING 510
BITKER 307n
BRAZIL
growth strategy and 254
BROWNLIE, IAN 4n, 6n, 9n, 11n
BUERGENTHAL, THOMAS 3n, 12n, 327n, 439–49n

CAHN, PROFESSOR EDMUND 93–4
CAPACITY, LEGAL 131
CAPITALISM
'libertarian' 94
CARTER, PRESIDENT 137n, 139n, 143n, 156n, 440n
CASE STUDIES 511–36
fair trial, right to a 528–32
free speech, right to 532–6
liberty of the person 515–28
mental health 527–8
torture, inhuman or degrading treatment or punishment 511–15
work, right to 231–42
CASTBERG, F. 123n
homosexuality, on 149n
CHAKARAVARTI, R. 172n
CHARTER
Economic Rights and Duties of States, of, *see* CHARTER OF ECONOMIC RIGHTS AND DUTIES OF STATES
Organization of American States, of, *see* ORGANIZATION OF AMERICAN STATES, Charter
CHARTER OF ECONOMIC RIGHTS AND DUTIES OF STATES
property ownership and 158
CHILE
American Convention on Human Rights and 444
Commission on Human Rights and, United Nations 388–9
nongovernmental organizations and 424
CICERO 363
CIVIL RIGHTS 115–69, *see also* RIGHTS; UNIVERSAL DECLARATION OF HUMAN RIGHTS
arrest, arbitrary, prohibition of 136–9
asylum 152–3
conscience, freedom of 158–60
detention, prohibition of 136–9
equality before the law 132–3
exile, prohibition of 136–9
ex post facto laws and 145–7
fair trial, right to 139–44
family, right to found 155–6
innocence, presumption of 144
international human rights course, in 161–5
life, liberty, and security of person 120–4
marry, right to 155–6
'minimodule', as 165–7
movement, freedom of 149–52
nationality, right to a 153–4
nondiscrimination in application of law 132–3
privacy 147–9
property, right to own 156–7
recognition, legal 130–1
religion, freedom of 158–60
remedy, right to a 133–6
slavery and servitude, prohibition of 124–6
teaching, *see* TEACHING, civil rights
thought, freedom of 158–60
torture, cruel, inhuman or degrading treatment or punishment 126–30
CLAUDE 3n
COMMISSION OF CHURCHES ON INTERNATIONAL AFFAIRS 408
COMMISSION ON HUMAN RIGHTS,

EUROPEAN, *see* EUROPEAN COMMISSION ON HUMAN RIGHTS
COMMISSION ON HUMAN RIGHTS, INTER-AMERICAN 454–60
COMMISSION ON HUMAN RIGHTS, UNITED NATIONS, *see* UNITED NATIONS, Commission on Human Rights
COMMISSION TO STUDY THE ORGANIZATION OF PEACE, NEW ASPECTS OF THE INTERNATIONAL PROTECTION OF HUMAN RIGHTS 14n
COMMITTEE, UNITED NATIONS HUMAN RIGHTS, *see* UNITED NATIONS HUMAN RIGHTS COMMITTEE
COMMUNISM
freedom of movement and 151
Marxism and 82
priority of rights and 73
rights and privileges, view of 72
COMPARATIVE ANALYSIS OF THE INTERNATIONAL COVENANTS ON HUMAN RIGHTS AND INTERNATIONAL LABOUR CONVENTIONS AND RECOMMENDATIONS 234n
COMPARATIVE SURVEY OF FREEDOM
categories of freedom 21–2
definition of freedom in 21
COMPLAINTS
Inter-American Commission on Human Rights and 454–60
International Labour Organisation members, against 288–90
United Nations procedures for 379–94
CONCERN 97–8
CONFLICT
armed, *see* ARMED CONFLICT
human rights instruments and systems, of 22–3
values in system of rights, of 39–45
CONSCIENCE, FREEDOM OF 158–60, 174–81, *see also* RELIGION, freedom of
CONSCIENTIOUS OBJECTORS 352
CONVENTION
Apartheid, on the Suppression and Punishment of the Crime of 379
Employment Policy, 1964, *see* EMPLOYMENT POLICY CONVENTION OF 1964, THE
Consent to marriage, on, *see* CONVENTION ON CONSENT TO MARRIAGE, MINIMUM AGE FOR MARRIAGE, AND REGISTRATION OF MARRIAGES
Discrimination, racial, on, *see* CONVENTION ON THE ELIMINATION OF ALL FORMS OF RACIAL DISCRIMINATION
Discrimination, women, against, *see* CONVENTION ON THE ELIMINATION OF ALL FORMS OF DISCRIMINATION AGAINST WOMEN
Geneva, *see* GENEVA CONVENTIONS
Hague, *see* HAGUE CONVENTIONS
Human Rights, on, *see* AMERICAN CONVENTION ON HUMAN RIGHTS; EUROPEAN CONVENTION ON HUMAN RIGHTS
Vienna, *see* VIENNA CONVENTION ON THE LAW OF TREATIES, THE
CONVENTION ON CONSENT TO MARRIAGE, MINIMUM AGE FOR MARRIAGE, AND REGISTRATION OF MARRIAGES 156
CONVENTION ON THE ELIMINATION OF ALL FORMS OF DISCRIMINATION AGAINST WOMEN 327–30
marriage and 156
CONVENTION ON THE ELIMINATION OF ALL FORMS OF RACIAL DISCRIMINATION 322–7
force, coming into 181
COUNCIL OF EUROPE, THE
human rights instruments, adoption of 22
nongovernmental organizations and 407
COVENANT
Civil and Political Rights, on, *see* INTERNATIONAL COVENANT ON CIVIL AND POLITICAL RIGHTS
Economic, Social and Cultural Rights, on, *see* INTERNATIONAL COVENANT ON ECONOMIC, SOCIAL, AND CULTURAL RIGHTS
League of Nations, of 176–7
CRANSTON, M. 73n, 74n
CRUEL TREATMENT, *see* TREATMENT, cruel
CULTURE 213, *see also* ECONOMIC, SOCIAL, AND CULTURAL RIGHTS

DECLARATION
intolerance and religious freedom, on, *see* DECLARATION ON ALL FORMS OF INTOLERANCE AND OF DISCRIMINATION BASED ON RELIGION OR BELIEF
Universal, of Human Rights, *see* UNIVERSAL DECLARATION OF HUMAN RIGHTS

DÉCLARATION DES DROITS DE L'HOMME ET DU CITOYEN 183
DECLARATION ON THE ELIMINATION OF ALL FORMS OF INTOLERANCE AND OF DISCRIMINATION BASED ON RELIGION OR BELIEF 160, 330–1
DECLARATION ON THE ELIMINATION OF ALL FORMS OF RACIAL DISCRIMINATION
  adoption of 181
DECLARATION ON THE GRANTING OF INDEPENDENCE TO COLONIAL COUNTRIES AND TERRITORIES 196
DECLARATION ON THE PROTECTION OF ALL PERSONS FROM BEING SUBJECTED TO TORTURE AND OTHER CRUEL, INHUMAN, OR DEGRADING TREATMENT OR PUNISHMENT 127n
DEFINITION
  human rights, of 70–4
DEGRADING TREATMENT, *see* TREATMENT, degrading,
DEMOCRACY
  information, freedom of, and 182
  test of 173
DEROGATION
  American Convention on Human Rights and 448–52
DETENTION 136–9, 515–28
  unlawful in U.S.A. 38–9
DE TOCQUEVILLE 41
DEVELOPMENT
  social welfare approach to 227–31, 239
DIGNITY 87
  theory of human rights based on 95–7
DINSTEIN, YORAM 2n, 17n, 18n, 19n, 123n, 345–68
DISCRIMINATION, *see also* EQUALITY; NONDISCRIMINATION
  basic instruments, interpretation and application 332–4
  Declaration on Religious Discrimination 330–1
  employment, *see* EMPLOYMENT, discrimination in
  enforceability 325–7
  International Covenant on Civil and Political Rights 320–2
  International Covenant on Economic, Social and Cultural Rights 318–20
  Racial Discrimination, Convention on the Elimination of all Forms of 322–5
  sex, on grounds of, *see* SEX DISCRIMINATION
  strictures against 309
  teaching, *see* TEACHING, race, sex, religious discrimination
  United Nations Charter and 309–11, 313–18
  Universal Declaration of Human Rights and 309–10, 311–18
  Women, Convention on the Elimination of all Forms of Discrimination against 327–30
DOCTRINE
  laissez-faire 94–5
DUTY, LEGAL
  armed conflict and 1–2
DWORKIN, RONALD 71n, 80n, 97–8

ECONOMIC AND SOCIAL COUNCIL, THE
  International Covenant on Economic, Social and Cultural Rights 218, 219–23
ECONOMIC, SOCIAL AND CULTURAL RIGHTS 205–71
  core legal documents 208–23; International Covenant on Economic, Social, and Cultural Rights, the 210–23; United Nations Charter, the 209; Universal Declaration of Human Rights, the 209, 210
  development doctrine, the 223–31; growth strategy, failure of 226–7; liberal view, the 224–6; welfare-orientated 227–31
  health, right to 242–5
  International Bill of Rights and 207, 208
  introduction to 205–8
  New International Economic Order, the 247–55; basic needs approach and 249–51; global compact and 251–3
  teaching, *see* TEACHING, Economic, Social and Cultural Rights
  Third World, in 208
  United Nations development policy 245–7
  work, right to, case study 231–42; employment policy and development strategy 235–42; Employment Policy Convention of 1964 236–7; International Labour Organisation, and the Economic Covenant 232–5; scope 232; unemployment and the Third World 235–6; World Employment Conference of 1976 236–42
  World Bank and 246–7
EDEL 74n, 75n, 78n
EDUCATION
  discrimination in, remedies for 381–2
  human rights, about 2
  right to 213
EISSEN 393n
EL SALVADOR 442n, 450n

ELECTIONS 191–3
EMERGENCY, STATE OF 351–2
European convention on Human Rights and 502
EMIGRATION
repression of 93
EMPLOYMENT, *see also* EMPLOYER; INTERNATIONAL LABOUR ORGANISATION
discrimination in 279
Employment Policy Convention of 1964 236–7
policy, International Labour Organisation and 235–42
World Employment Conference of 1976 237–9
EMPLOYER
International Labour Organisation, involvement in 279–80
ENGELS, F. 81n
EQUALITY 101–3
American concept of 42–3
basic liberties and 102
exercises relating to 101–5
law, before 132–3
respect and concern, of 97–8
EUROPEAN COMMISSION ON HUMAN RIGHTS
emergency, state of 351–2
ex post facto laws and 146
free speech, right to 533–6
liberty of person 517–18
nongovernmental organizations 425
petitions to 505–9
privacy and 149
torture and 128–9
EUROPEAN CONVENTION ON HUMAN RIGHTS 11, 495–549
aliens, expulsion of, and 501
American Convention on Human Rights and 441, 442, 450
arbitrary arrest, detention, exile, prohibition of, 137, 515–28
assembly, freedom of 188, 499
association, freedom of 191, 499
asylum, right to 153
case studies 511–36; fair trial, right to 528–32; free speech, right to 532–6; liberty of the person 515–28; torture, inhuman or degrading treatment or punishment 511–15
conceptual issues 495–505
conscience, freedom of 159–60, 499
derogation from 502–3
education, right to 500
elections and 500
equality before the law and 132, 499
exile, freedom from 501
ex post facto laws and 146, 499
expression, freedom of 499, 532–6
fair trial 141–2, 499, 528–32
free speech, right to 499, 532–6
government, right to take part in 192, 193
innocence, presumption of 144, 499
labour, compulsory and 125–6, 499
life, liberty, and security of person 121, 499, 515–28
machinery 505–11
marry and found a family, right to 155–6, 499
movement, freedom of 150, 151, 501
nationality, right to a 154, 501
nondiscrimination in application of law and 132, 499
petitions under 505–8
Political Covenant and 498–9
privacy 148, 499, 504–5
property, right to own 157
Protocols 500–1
recognition, legal 130
religion, freedom of 159–60, 499
remedy, right to a 134–6
scope 499–505
self-determination 195
slavery and servitude 124, 499
teaching, *see* TEACHING, European Convention on Human Rights, the
thought, freedom of 159–60, 499
torture, cruel, inhuman or degrading treatment or punishment 126, 166, 499, 511–15
United Kingdom and 504–5
Universal Declaration of Human Rights and 495–8
violations of 381
EUROPEAN COURT OF HUMAN RIGHTS, THE
arbitrary arrest, detention, exile and 139
emergency, state of, and 351–2
fair trial, right to 528–32
free speech, right to 532–6
privacy and 149
person, liberty of 515–28
references to 381, 507–10
remedy, right to 135–6
torture, cruel, inhuman or degrading treatment or punishment 128–9, 513–15
EUROPEAN ECONOMIC COMMUNITY (EEC)
representation against, 287
EUTHANASIA 123–4
EXILE 136–9
EXPRESSION, FREEDOM OF 181–8, 532–6, *see also* FREE SPEECH

FAIR TRIAL
case study 528–32
European Court of Human Rights and 528–32
right to 139–44
FALK, R. 124n
FAMILY
right to found a 155–6, 165
FARER AND ROWLES 452n, 475n, 479n
FAWCETT, J. 123
implementation, on 135–6
impartiality, on 141n
FOOD AND AGRICULTURE ORGANIZATION, THE 240
FOX 440n, 443n
FREEDOM, *see also* LIBERTY
arrest, from 91 *see also* ARREST
assembly, of peaceful 188–9 *see also* ASSEMBLY, FREEEDOM OF
association, of 190–1, *see also* ASSOCIATION, FREEDOM OF
Comparative Survey of, the, *see* COMPARATIVE SURVEY OF FREEDOM
conscience, of 158–60, 174–81, *see also* RELIGION, freedom of
definitions of in Comparative Survey of Freedom 21
denial of 8
expression, of 181–8, 532–6, *see also* EXPRESSION, FREEDOM OF,
information, of, *see* INFORMATION, FREEDOM OF
medical experimentation, from 354
movement, of 149–52
norm, as a 87
opinion, of 181–8
persecution, from 152–3
person, of 91, 515–28
political and civil 20–1
religious 158–60, 174–81, *see also* RELIGION; consensus on, impossibility of 16
scale of 21–2
seizure, from 91
thought, of 158–60, 174–81
FREE SPEECH 181–8, *see also* EXPRESSION, FREEDOM OF
case study 532–6
FROWEIN 33n
FREUD, SIGMUND 102n
FULLER, L. 80n

GALTUNG 249n
GASTIL 18n
GENEVA CONVENTIONS, THE 345–50, 352, 353, 356, *see also* ARMED CONFLICT
application and supervision 356–62
military service 353
prisoners of war 358
protected persons 357
Protecting Powers 359–62
Red Cross, International Committee of 359–62
torture and 352
war crimes 358–9
GOLDTHORPE 229n
GOODWIN-GILL, G. 353n
GOVERNMENT
take part in, right to 173, 191–3
GREEN 403n
GREENBERG, JACK 10n, 76n, 307–43
GROTIUS
natural law, theory of 77–8

HABEAS CORPUS, RIGHT OF
U.S.A., in 44
HAGUE CONVENTIONS, THE 345–7, *see also* ARMED CONFLICT
HAILSHAM, Q. 54n
HARRIS 141
HART, H. L. A. 80–1
HASSAN 122n
HEALTH
Alternative Approaches to Meeting Basic Health Needs in Developing Countries 242n
mental, case study on 527–8
primary health care 243–4, 245
right to 213
World Health Organization and 242–5
HELSINKI ACCORDS, THE 310, 314, 334
HELSINKI WATCH, THE 334
HENKIN, ALICE 9n, 12n
HENKIN, L. 25–67, 115–16
HIGGINS, ROSALYN 16n, 117, 119, 495–547
HUMAN RIGHTS, *see also* RIGHTS; TEACHING, human rights
acceptance of, status of 18
aid and nongovernmental organizations 425–6
American constitution and 54–5
American rights and, *see* UNITED STATES OF AMERICA, rights in
armed conflict, in, *see* ARMED CONFLICT
civil rights and, *see* CIVIL RIGHTS
concept of 74–5
conventions, U.S.A. and 50–4
countries' records in 18–22; U.S.A. 18–19; U.S. Department of State, reports by 20–1
definitions 70–4
derogation from,

Cyprus Case 503
Ireland v. *United Kingdom* 502–3
Lawless Case 502
economic, social and cultural, *see* ECONOMIC, SOCIAL AND CULTURAL RIGHTS
education and, *see* EDUCATION
emergency, in a state of 351–2
geography of 18–22
global protection of 115–439
implementation and supervision of 369–401; European and Inter-American Courts of Human Rights, references to 381; fact finding and conciliation 381–4; international 373–94; International Court of Justice, reference to 379–80; International Labour Organisation and 371, 380; national measures 369–72; periodic reporting, United Nations and 373–9; Political Convention and 370; United Nations and 372, 373–401; complaints procedure 379–94
International Bill of, *see* INTERNATIONAL BILL OF HUMAN RIGHTS
International Labour Organisation and, *see* INTERNATIONAL LABOUR ORGANISATION
international nongovernmental organization, protection by, *see* NONGOVERNMENTAL ORGANIZATIONS, human rights, protection by
jurisprudence, *see* JURISPRUDENCE
law of, *see* LAW
meaning of 70–4
peacetime and wartime, in 350–4
political, *see* POLITICAL RIGHTS
philosophy of 107
protection of, inter-American system of 439–93
regional protection 439–549
setting, the 1–113
sources of 75–105; marxism 81–3; modern theories 85–101; dignity, based on 95–7; justice, based on 90–4; natural rights, based on 85–8; respect and concern, equality of 97–8; Revisited State of Nature and Minimalist State 94–5; utility, value of 88–90; undeveloped 99–101; natural law 77–9; positivism 79–81; religion 75–7; sociological 83–5; theory to practice, from 101–5
Soviet Constitution and 72
teaching, *see* TEACHING, human rights,
United Nations Committee on, *see* U.N. HUMAN RIGHTS COMMITTEE
Universal Declaration of, *see* UNIVERSAL DECLARATION OF HUMAN RIGHTS
U.S. and international, a comparison of 6
violation of, *see* VIOLATION of human rights
war and, *see* ARMED CONFLICT
HUMAN RIGHTS LAW: A RESEARCH GUIDE TO THE LITERATURE 4n
HUMPHREY, JOHN P. 171–203, 315n

ILLEGITIMACY
rights and 155–6
IMMIGRATION
armed conflict and 353
IMPLEMENTATION
human rights, of 155; domestic 10
emphasis on, in book, 6–11
INDIGENOUS PEOPLES 408
INDIVIDUAL, *see also* PERSON
asylum of 152–3
autonomy of 77–9
rights of, *see* CIVIL RIGHTS; HUMAN RIGHTS; RIGHTS
rights, recognition of 84
INFORMATION, FREEDOM OF 181–8, *see also* EXPRESSION, FREEDOM OF; OPINION, FREEDOM OF
INHUMAN TREATMENT, *see* TREATMENT, inhuman
INNOCENCE
presumption of 144
INSTRUMENTS
proliferation of 22–3
INTER-AMERICAN COMMISSION ON HUMAN RIGHTS, THE
complaints to 454–60
functions 452–4
Organization of American States' Charter and 472–5, 479–87; country studies 479–84; industrial communications 484–7; 'on-site' investigations 480–4
reports by 458, 459
torture and 130
INTER-AMERICAN COURT OF HUMAN RIGHTS, THE
American Convention on Human Rights and 447
jurisdiction 460–70; advisory 467–70; contentious 460–7
references to 381
INTERNATIONAL ASSOCIATION OF DEMOCRATIC LAWYERS, THE 409–10
INTERNATIONAL BILL OF HUMAN RIGHTS, THE 22
INTERNATIONAL COMMISSION OF JURISTS, THE 407–8, 409, 413

INTERNATIONAL CONVENTION ON THE ELIMINATION OF ALL FORMS OF RACIAL DISCRIMINATION, THE 9–10, 322–5
complaints under 382
obligations under 371–2
INTERNATIONAL COURT OF JUSTICE, THE
reference to 379–80
INTERNATIONAL COVENANT ON CIVIL AND POLITICAL RIGHTS, THE (POLITICAL COVENANT) 4, 71, 116–24
American Convention on Human Rights and 446, 450–1
arrest, arbitrary, detention, exile and 136–8
association, freedom of 190, 191
assembly, freedom of 188, 189
asylum, right to 153
complaints' procedure 383
conscience, freedom of 159–60
discrimination, race, sex, religious 320–2, 325–7
Economic, Social and Cultural Rights, International Covenant on, and 211–12, 213
ensuring rights 36
equality before the law 132
fair trial 141–4
innocence, presumption of 144
marry and found family, right to 155–6
movement, freedom of 150, 151, 152
nationality, right to a 154
nonderogable rights and 16–17
obligations under 370; derogation from 44
political rights in 171, 172, 174
priority of human rights 160–1
privacy, right to 147–8
religious freedoms and 16, 159–60
remedy, right to a 134
reports on rights under 377
rights under and U.S.A. 40–1
self-determination 195–6
thought, freedom of 159–60
INTERNATIONAL COVENANT ON ECONOMIC, SOCIAL, AND CULTURAL RIGHTS, THE 8, 210–23
American rights and 42–3
available resources clause in 217n
background to 210–12
definition of rights 72–3
discrimination, race, sex, religious 318–20, 325–7
Economic and Social Council and 219–23
evaluation of country performance by 240–2
health and 219–23, 242–5
implementation 213–19; generic, international 217–19; progressive realization of 213–17
International Labour Organisation and 219–23
political rights in 171
primary health care and 243–4, 245
programs under 230–1
reports on rights under 376
resources and 215
rights specific to 212–13
self-determination and 195–6
United Nations' development policy and 245–7
UNESCO and 219–23
World Health Organization and, the 219–23, 242–5
work, right to 232–5
World Bank and, the 246–7
INTERNATIONAL DEFENSE AND AID FUND (IDAF), THE 405n
INTERNATIONAL FEDERATION OF HUMAN RIGHTS, THE 413
INTERNATIONAL LABOUR OFFICE, THE 227n, 228n, 235n
INTERNATIONAL LABOUR ORGANISATION (ILO), THE,
association, freedom of, and 191, 290–3; Committee on, the 290–2; Fact-Finding and Conciliation Commission on 292–3
basic needs and 239–40
complaints procedure 380
Conventions and Recommendations, Committee of Experts on Application of 281–3
Conventions and Recommendations, Conference Committee on Application of 284
discrimination and 310
Discrimination (Employment and Occupation) Convention 1958 and 279
Employment Policy Convention of 1964 and 236
generally 273–6
human rights and 273–305
instruments, nature and scope of 296–7
leverage by 2
nongovernmental organizations and 407
objectives 273
obligations of members 371
organs of, main 295
procedures, contentious 286–90; complaints against members 288–90; representations against members 286–7
procedures, non-contentious 293
promoting human rights, methods of 296
social welfare rights and 219

rights protected by 8–9
supervision by, permanent 276–86; employers' and workers' organizations and 279–80; information required by 276–7; reports 277–9; supervisory bodies 280–6
supervisory machinery 297–9
teaching, *see* TEACHING, International Labour Organisation
World Employment Conference of 1976 and 236–42
work, right to, and 231–42
INTERNATIONAL LEAGUE OF HUMAN RIGHTS 407, 413
INTOLERANCE, DECLARATION ON THE ELIMINATION OF ALL FORMS OF, *see* FREEDOM; PERSECUTION; RELIGION

JACOBS 126n, 147n, 148n
JAMES, WILLIAM 84
JENKS 9n, 18n, 232n, 275n
JUDICIAL REVIEW
U.S.A., in 37–8
JURISPRUDENCE 69–113
American system of 32n
definition of human rights 70–4
domestic systems of 70n
nature of rights 70–4
privilege 71–2
religion 75–7
slavery and servitude and 72
sources of human rights 75–85; marxism 81–3; modern theories 85–101, based on dignity 95–7, on justice 90–4, on natural rights 85–8, on respect and concern, equality of 97–8, on Revisited State of Nature and Minimalist State 94–5, undeveloped 99–101, and based on utility, value of 88–90; natural law 77–9; positivism 79–81; sociological 83–5
Soviet view of rights 72
teaching, *see* TEACHING, jurisprudence
theories 69, *see also* JURISPRUDENCE, sources of human rights, modern theories.
JUS COGENS, STATUS OF 118
JUSTICE
Cahn, Edmund, and 93–4
theories of human rights based on 90–4

KANT, I. 87, 93, 95
KOMMERS, 11n

LABOUR, *see* INTERNATIONAL LABOUR ORGANISATION; WORK
LAUTERPACHT, H. 78n, 356n
LAW
equality before 132–3
ex post facto 145–7
humanitarian 10; armed conflict and 1
human rights and practice 2–3
nations, of 78
natural, *see* NATURAL LAW
nondiscrimination in application 132–3
rights provided by, U.S.A. in 45–9
treaties, of 337
LEAGUE OF ARAB STATES, THE 6
LIBERTY, *see also* FREEDOM
civil, in Third World 20
conscience, of 91
denial of 98
equal citizenship and 91
equality and 98
movement, of, *see* FREEDOM, movement, of,
person, of 515–28
right to a 97, 120–4, 162, 163
worth of 91
LIFE, RIGHT TO 120–4, 163
LILLICH, RICHARD B. 3n, 115–69, 317n
LOCKE, JOHN
human beings, view of 78–9

MACAULAY, LORD 175n
MARRIAGE
convention on, *see* CONVENTION ON CONSENT TO MARRIAGE, MINIMUM AGE FOR MARRIAGE AND REGISTRATION OF MARRIAGES
right of 155–6, 165
United Nations and 375
MARSHALL, CHIEF JUSTICE JOHN 37
MARX, KARL, *see* MARXISM
MARXISM
source of human rights, as 81–3
MCDOUGAL, CASSWELL, CHEN, PROFS, *see also* DIGNITY 95–7, 115
MELDEN, A. 71n
MERON, THEODOR 1–24
MICHELMAN 85n
MILL, JOHN STUART 88n
MONTEALEGRE, H. 449
MONTREAL STATEMENT, THE 117n
MOSKOWITZ, M. 69n, 106n
MOVEMENT, FREEDOM OF 149–52, 165
MOYNIHAN, DANIEL PATRICK 73n

NATIONAL CONFERENCE ON SOVIET JEWERY, THE 334
NATIONALITY
right to a 153–4, 165

NATURAL LAW 77–9
NAZIS, THE 80–1
legal atrocities by 122
nationality, right to, and 153
NEED, basic
development, as approach to 227–31; International Labour Organisation, effect on 239–42; New International Economic Order and 249–51, 253–55
human fulfilment of 20
U.S.A. and 44
NEW INTERNATIONAL ECONOMIC ORDER (NIEO) 104, 158, 247–5
basic needs approach and 249–51
global compact and 251–3
Third World and 247–53
NONDISCRIMINATION 132–3, *see also* DISCRIMINATION
NONGOVERNMENTAL ORGANIZATIONS (NGOs)
aid and human rights 425–6
Amnesty International 405
Brazil, communications to 424
Chile, communications to 424
diplomatic interventions and missions 412–14
fact-finding techniques 408–10
genocide and 425
human rights, protection of, by 403–38; implementation 410–28
information on human rights from 20
International Labour Organisation and 423–4
investigative procedures and 420–5
local activities 426–8
norms, contribution to 429–30
prominent international 405–6
slavery and 425
status 406–7
structure and characteristics 406–8
teaching, *see* TEACHING, Nongovernmental Organizations,
violations, public discussion of 415–20
NORMS
elaboration of, progress in 13–14
freedom as 87
NOZICK, ROBERT 94–5

O'CONNELL, D. 70n
OLDFROM, 87n
OPINION, FREEDOM OF 181–8
OPPORTUNITY 102
ORGANIZATION
African Unity, of, *see* ORGANIZATION OF AFRICAN UNITY
American States, of, *see* ORGANIZATION OF AMERICAN STATES
ORGANIZATION OF AFRICAN UNITY, THE 6
ORGANIZATION OF AMERICAN STATES, THE 22
American Convention on Human Rights and 440, 451–4, 459–60
Charter 452, 453–4, 470–87; American Convention on Human Rights and 475–9; evolution of 470–9; Inter-American Commission on Human Rights and 479–87
Inter-American Court of Human Rights, opinion of 467–70
non-compliance and 467
nongovernmental organizations and 407
OWNERSHIP
property, of, right to 156–8

PAGELS 76n
PAINE, THOMAS 52n
PEACE
crimes against 355
human rights and 2
wartime and human rights in 350–4
PEACETIME, *see* PEACE
PERSECUTION
freedom from 152–3
PERSON
'before the law' 131
security of, *see* SECURITY
PHILOSOPHY, *see* THEORIES and under respective philosophers
POLITICAL COVENANT, *see* INTERNATIONAL COVENANT ON CIVIL AND POLITICAL RIGHTS
POLITICS 17–18
POTOBSKY, VON 291n
POLITICAL RIGHTS 171–203
assembly, freedom of 188–9
association, freedom of 190–1
conscience, freedom of 174–81
elections, periodic and genuine 191–3
European Convention on Human Rights and 498–9
expression, freedom of 181–8
generally 171–4
government, access to 191–3
information, freedom of 181–8
opinion, freedom of 181–8
public service, access to 191–3
religion 174–81
self-determination 193–6
teaching, *see* TEACHING, political rights,
thought, freedom of 174–81
United Nations Documents on 202–3
POSITIVISM 79–81

POUND, ROSCOE 84–5
POVERTY
U.S.A., in 47–9
PRESS, THE
freedom of 182, *see also* EXPRESSION, FREEDOM OF, INFORMATION, FREEDOM OF,
United Nations Subcommittee on Freedom of Information and the 183, 187
PRESUMPTION
innocence, of 144
PRIMARY HEALTH CARE 243–4
PRISONER OF WAR, *see* ARMED CONFLICT
PRZETACZNIK 120n
PRIVACY
right to 147–9
PRIVILEGES 71–2
PROCEDURE
association, freedom of, International Labour Organisation and 290–3
contentious, International Labour Organisation and 286–90
PROHIBITION
arbitrary arrest, detention, exile, of 136–9
ex post facto laws, of 145–7
PROPERTY
right to own 156–8
PROTECTION
families, of 213
standards, of 6
PUBLIC OPINION 19
Ex-President Carter's view of 19n
PUBLIC SERVICE
access to, right to 191–3
PUFENDORF 77
PUNISHMENT
cruel, inhuman, or degrading 126–30

RACIAL DISCRIMINATION 307–43
apartheid and 317
basic instruments, interpretation and application 332–4
Economic Covenant and 318–20
enforceability 325–7
Political Covenant and 320–2
Racial Discrimination Convention, the 322–5
strictures against 309
teaching, *see* TEACHING, race, sex, religious discrimination
United Nations Charter and 309-11,313–18
Universal Declaration of Human Rights and 309–10, 311–18
RAMCHARAN 13n
RAWLS, JOHN 90–3, *see also* JUSTICE
RECOGNITION, LEGAL 130–1
RED CROSS, INTERNATIONAL COMMITTEE OF 359–62, 405, 408, 414
missions by 414
REDLICH 3n
RELIGION
discrimination on grounds of 307–43; basic instruments, interpretation, and application 332–4
Declaration on 330–1
Economic Covenant and 318–20
enforceability 325–7
Political Covenant and 320–2
strictures against 309
teaching, *see* TEACHING, race, sex, religious discrimination
United Nations Charter and 309–11, 313–18
Universal Declaration of Human Rights and 309–10, 311–18
freedom of 158–60, 174–81
repression of 93
source of human rights, as 75–7
REMEDY
right to a 133–6
U.S.A., in 36–9
REPORT
on human rights; U.S. Department of State, by 20–1; United Nations periodic 373–9
RESOURCES
social welfare and 215
sovereignty over 158
teaching human rights, for 3–4
RESPECT 97–8
rights, for retained 33
rights, for, U.S.A., in 34–6
RICHARDS 89n
RIGHTS
assembly, of 188–9
association, of 190–1
asylum, to 152–3
core, *see* RIGHTS, natural,
Civil and Political, International Covenant on, *see* INTERNATIONAL COVENANT ON CIVIL AND POLITICAL RIGHTS
collective 111
content of 39–45
culture, to fruits of 213
definition of 6, 70–4
derogation, to, American covenant and 448–52
distinction between 17
economic 12, 20 *see also* CHARTER OF ECONOMIC RIGHTS AND DUTIES OF STATES; INTERNATIONAL

COVENANT ON ECONOMIC SOCIAL AND CULTURAL RIGHTS
education, to, *see* EDUCATION, right to,
elections, to periodic and genuine 191–3
ensuring 34–6
equality, of 132–3, *see also* EQUALITY
European Covenant, covered by 499
fair trial, to 139–44, 165, 528–32
fundamental 33–4
government, to take part in 172, 191–3
group 171–2
health, to, *see* HEALTH, right to
human, *see* HUMAN RIGHTS
'international' 25
International Labour Organisation, protected by 8
justice, of 90–4
liberty, to 120–4
liberty and security of person, to 97, 515–28
life, to 120–4, 162, 163
marry and found a family, to 155–6, 165
meanings of within book 15–17
movement, to freedom of 149–52, 165
nationality, to a 153–4, 165
natural, theories based on 85–8
nondiscrimination in law, to 132–3
nonderogable 12, 16–17
political, *see* POLITICAL RIGHTS
priority of 73
privacy, to 147–9
privileges and 71–2
property, to own 156–8, 165
protection of 34–6
public service, to access to 191–3
recognition, to legal 130–1, 164
remedies and, in the U.S.A. 36–9
remedy, to a 133–6
respect for 34–6
science, to fruits of 213
security of person, to 120–4
self-determination, to 193–6, 374
social 12, *see also* ECONOMIC, SOCIAL AND CULTURAL RIGHTS; INTERNATIONAL COVENANT ON ECONOMIC, SOCIAL AND CULTURAL RIGHTS
social welfare, *see* ECONOMIC, SOCIAL AND CULTURAL RIGHTS; INTERNATIONAL COVENANT ON ECONOMIC, SOCIAL AND CULTURAL RIGHTS
standard of living, to adequate 213, 216n
social security, to, *see* SOCIAL SECURITY, right to,
Soviet view of 72
Third World, in, *see* THIRD WORLD
United States of America, in, *see* UNITED STATES OF AMERICA, rights in
work, to, *see* WORK, right to
RIGHTS OF MAN, THE 52n

SCARMAN, LORD 54n
SCHACHTER 18n, 26n, 54n, 131n, 314n, 315n
SCHREIBER, A. 471n, 473n
SCHWARTZENBERGER, G. 395n
SCIENCE 213
SEARCH
unreasonable, U.S.A., in 37
SECURITY
person, of, right to, 121–4
social, *see* SOCIAL SECURITY
SEIZURE
U.S.A., in, remedy for 37
SELF-DETERMINATION, RIGHT TO 193–6
SERVITUDE 124–6
International Covenant on Civil and Political Rights and 72
SEX DISCRIMINATION 307–43
basic instruments, interpretation and application of 332–4
cases 333n, 336–9
enforceability 325–7
International Covenant on Civil and Political Rights and 320–2
International Covenant on Economic, Social and Cultural Rights and 318–20
strictures against 309
teaching, *see* TEACHING, race, sex, religious, discrimination,
United Nations Charter and 309–11, 313–18
Universal Declaration of Human Rights and 309–10, 311–18
Women, Convention on the Elimination of All Forms of Discrimination against 327–30
SHAME
sense of, importance of 2
Wolf on 2n
SHARP 23n
SHESTACK, JEROME J. 69–113, 403n
SHUE, 15n, 225n
SIDORSKY 100n
SKINNER, B.F. 101
SLAVERY 124–6
America and 41
International Covenant on Civil and Political Rights and 72
Nongovernmental Organizations and 425
United Nations and 375
SOCIAL SECURITY

right to 213
U.S.A., in 47
SOCIAL WELFARE, *see* ECONOMIC, SOCIAL AND CULTURAL RIGHTS
SOCIOLOGY
approach to human rights, as 83–5
SOHN, LOUIS B. 3n, 8n, 12n, 309n, 369–401
SOPHOCLES 77
SOUTH AFRICA 131
apartheid and the United Nations 385
SOVEREIGNTY
resources, over 158
SOVIET UNION, THE
movement, freedom of 150, 151
SPEECH, FREE, *see* FREE SPEECH
SPJUT, 128n
STANDARDS
protection of 6
STATE
Arab, League of, *see* LEAGUE OF ARAB STATES authority of 79–81
minimalist 94–5
newly independent, armed conflict and human rights in 2
STATELESSNESS 153–4
STREETEN AND BURKI 227n, 228n
STRONG 15n
SUPERVISION
human rights, of, systems of 22–3
SYSTEM
human rights, supervision of 22–3
TARDU, M. 23n, 393n, 457n
TEACHING
armed conflict, human rights in 362–8; bibliography 366–8; full course, a 362–4; minibibliography 368; minisyllabus 366; module course 363–5; syllabus 365–6
civil rights 161–9; articles 169–70; bibliography 168–9; international human rights course in 161–5; minibibliography 170; 'minimodule', as 165–7; minisyllabus 168; syllabus 167–8
economic, social, and cultural rights 255–71; basic needs approach 257; bibliography 263–71; minibibliography 271; minisyllabus 259–63; syllabus 258–9
European Convention on Human Rights, the 536–49; bibliography 547–9; case studies 543–6; minibibliography 549; minisyllabus 546, 547; suggestions 536–8; syllabus 539–46
human rights 1–25; acceptance of, status of 18; art, state of the 1–4; conflicts and 22–3; definition and meaning 15–17; geography of 12–18; implementation of, and 6–11; introduction to 5–24; legal and policy considerations 5; overview of 1–25; pedagogical tactics 11–14; politics: the art of the possible 17–18; present state of and available resources 3–4; reasons for 1–3; substantive convergence of book 14–15; UNESCO International Congress on, 1978, *see* UNESCO INTERNATIONAL CONGRESS ON TEACHING HUMAN RIGHTS; UNESCO teaching manual, the 4
Inter-American System for the protection of human rights 488–93; bibliography 491–2; minibibliography 493; minisyllabus 491; syllabus 490–1
International Labour Organisation 294–305; activity, area of 295–6; bibliography 301–4; instruments, nature and scope of 296–7; minibibliography 304–5; minisyllabus 301; organs of, main 295; promotion of human rights, methods of 296; purpose 294–5; supervisory machinery 297–9; syllabus 299–301
International Nongovernmental Organizations 430–8; bibliography 435–8; materials 433; minibibliography 438; minisyllabus 435; set problem 431–3; syllabus 434–5
jurisprudence 105–13; bibliography and minibibliography 112–13; minisyllabus 111–12; suggestions 105–7; syllabus 107–11
political rights 197–203; bibliography 201–2; minibibliography 203; minisyllabus 201; syllabus 200–1; United Nations documents 202–3
race, sex, religious discrimination 334–43; bibliography 341–3; cases 336–9; minibibliography 343; minisyllabus 340–1; syllabus 339–40
social welfare, *see* TEACHING, economic, social, and cultural rights
United Nations implementation and supervision 395–401; bibliography 400–1; minibibliography 401; minisyllabus 399; syllabus 398–9
United States of America and international rights 55–67; bibliography 62–7; cases 58; minibibliography 67; minisyllabus 62; syllabus 57–62
THANT, U. 418n
THEORIES 101–5
dignity, based on 95–7
human rights, of, domestic and international 108

justice, based on 90–4
justificatory 108–10
Marxist, *see* MARXISM
modern 85–101
positivism, *see* POSITIVISM
practice and 101–5
respect and concern, equality of 97–8
revisited state of nature and minimalist state 94–5
sociological 83–5
theology as basis for 76
undeveloped 99–101
utility, value of 88–90
THIRD WORLD, THE
civil liberties in 20
Economic Covenant and 222
economic, social and cultural rights in 205–69
New International Economic Order and 104, 247–53
priority of rights in 73
repression in 224–5
social welfare law in 223–4
THOME 229n
THOUGHT, FREEDOM OF 158–60, 174–81
TORTURE 126–30, 511–15
armed conflict and 352
case study 511–15
Filartiga v. *Peña-Irala*, case of 165–6
TREATMENT
cruel, inhuman, or degrading 126–30
case study 511–15
TREATY
Missouri v. *Holland*, principle in 446–7
Vienna Convention 357
TREVELYAN, G. 175n
TRIAL, FAIR, *see* FAIR TRIAL
TRUBEK, DAVID M. 3n, 8n, 17n, 205–71

UNEMPLOYMENT
Third World, in 235–6
UNITED NATIONS (U.N.), THE
apartheid and 385–7
complaints procedures 379–94; Court of Human Rights, references to 381; International Court of Justice, reference to 379–80; fact-finding and conciliation 381–4; inter-state 379–84; private 384–92
country reports 20–21
development policy and social welfare 245–7
discrimination and, *see* UNITED NATIONS CHARTER, discrimination and
Economic and Social Council of 373, 378
Human Rights Committee, *see* U.N. HUMAN RIGHTS COMMITTEE
implementation and supervision of human rights 369–401; conflict between procedures 393–4; international 373–94; national measure 369–72; periodic reporting systems 373–9; teaching, *see* TEACHING, United Nations, implementation and supervision by
Information and the Press, Sub-Commission on Freedom of 183, 187
marriage, right to etc. 375
Minorities, Sub-Commission on the Prevention of Discrimination and Protection of 373
movement, freedom of 150
occupied territories and 387–8
organizations, system of 8
rights in the Third World and 12
Secretary-General 418n
self-determination, right to 374
slavery and 375
social welfare policies 230
system of implementation 10
torture, cruel, inhuman or degrading treatment and 127, 130, 166
women, status of, and 373, 385
UNITED NATIONS CHARTER, THE
discrimination, race, sex, religious 309–11, 313–18
reports and complaints under 19
self-determination and 195
social welfare law and 209
torture, *Filartiga* v. *Pẽna-Irala*, and 165–6
trusteeship system 177
violations of 391
UNITED NATIONS COMMITTEE FOR TRADE AND DEVELOPMENT 152
UNITED NATIONS CONFERENCE ON FREEDOM OF INFORMATION 186–7
UNITED NATIONS EDUCATIONAL, SCIENTIFIC AND CULTURAL ORGANIZATION (UNESCO)
discrimination and 310
fact-finding and conciliation 381–2
information and communications and 187–8
nongovernmental organizations and 407
teaching manual, the 4
UNITED NATIONS GENERAL ASSEMBLY, THE
information, freedom of 183
self-determination 194
UNITED NATIONS HUMAN RIGHTS COMMITTEE
arbitrary arrest, detention, exile, and 138,

139
Chile and 388–9
Israeli occupied territories and 387–8
privacy and 149
torture and 166
status and financing 378
Sub-Committee on the Prevention of Discrimination and Protection of Minorities, communications to 421
UNITED STATES OF AMERICA
amendment of Constitution of 50
Association of the Bar of the City of New York 334
Civil War Amendments 35–8
conventions, principal human rights of 50–4
economic and social benefits in 48
education, financing 48n
education, right to, *Rodriguez,* case of 49n, 50n
fair trial in 141, 142
harmonization and 53–4
human rights, record in 18–19
Lawyers Committee for International Rights, the 334
'localism' in 49
movement, freedom of 150, 151–2
need, basic human, and 44
'Petite' policy the, 40n
protection of human rights and 439–93; American Covention on Human Rights, the 439–70; *see also* AMERICAN CONVENTION ON HUMAN RIGHTS; Inter-American Commission on Human Rights, *see* INTER-AMERICAN COMMISSION ON HUMAN RIGHTS; Inter-American Court of Human Rights, *see* INTER-AMERICAN COURT OF HUMAN RIGHTS; teaching, *see* TEACHING, Inter-American System of Protection of Human Rights
racial discrimination in 307–9, 312–18, 323–4
religious discrimination in 331
reports by the Department of State of 20–1
rights in 25–67; Articles of Confederation 28; Bill of Rights 29, 31, 34, 35, 41; conceptions of 29–34; conflict with international rights and 40–5; Congress and 27, 35; Constitution, the 27–9, 30, 31, 34, 35, 36, 38; content of 39–45; Declaration of Independence and 27–9; ensuring 34–6; judicial review 37, 38; law and policy considerations 27–55; non-constitutional 45–9; protecting 34–6; respecting 34–6; state legislatures, granted by 27; theory of 29–30, 32; remedies and 36–9; teaching, *see* TEACHING, United States of America, rights in and international rights
slavery and 26n
social security in 47
Supreme Court, the, *see* U.S. SUPREME COURT, THE
Universal Declaration of Human Rights and 116
United Nations Charter and 313–18
United States Diplomatic and Consular Staff in Tehran, case concerning 118
welfare state in 43–4
women, discrimination against 330
UNIVERSAL DECLARATION OF HUMAN RIGHTS 1948
adoption of 117
arrest, arbitrary, prohibition of 136–9
association, freedom of 190–1
assembly, right of 173–4, 188–91
asylum 152–3
conscience, freedom of 158–60, 174
detention, prohibition of 136–9
discrimination, race, sex, religious 309–10, 311–18
elections, periodic and genuine 192–3
equality 42, 132–3
European Convention and 495–8
exile, prohibition of 136–9
ex post facto laws and 145–7
information, freedom of 183–6, 188
innocence, presumption of 144–5
fair trial 139–44
government, right to take part in 191–3
life,liberty and security of person, right to 120–4
family, right to found a 155–6
marry, right to 155–6
movement, freedom of 149–52
nationality, right to a 153–4
nondiscrimination in application of law 132–3
opinion and expression, freedom of 178
political rights in 171–81
privacy, right to 147–9
priority of human rights in 161–2
property, right to own 156–8
public service, access to 192–3
recognition, legal 130–1
religion, freedom of 158–60, 174
remedy, right to a 133–6
Secretariat Outline 177
self-determination and 195
slavery and servitude, prohibition of 124–6
social welfare law and 209–10
thought, freedom of 158–60, 174

torture, cruel, inhuman or degrading treatment or punishment 126–30, 166
U.S.S.R. 72n, 126n
U.S. SUPREME COURT, THE
fair trial and 142
UTILITY
Bentham, Jeremy, and 88–9
egalitarian character of 97
value of 88–90

VAGRANCY 528
VALUE
utility, of 88–90
VIENNA CONVENTION ON THE LAW OF TREATIES, THE 357
VIENNA FINAL DOCUMENT, THE 12, 13n
VIOLATIONS OF HUMAN RIGHTS
education and 2
public discussion of 415–20
war, leading to 2
VON GLAHN, G. 345n

WALDHEIM, KURT 43n
WAR, *see* ARMED CONFLICT; WORLD WAR I; WORLD WAR II
WARREN, CHIEF JUSTICE 275
WARTIME, *see* ARMED CONFLICT
WEISSBRODT, DAVID 54n, 403–38
WELFARE
development and 227–31
social
development doctrine 223–31; rights, *see* ECONOMIC, SOCIAL AND CULTURAL RIGHTS
state, *see* WELFARE STATE
WELFARE STATE
U.S.A., in 43–4
WOLF, FRANCIS 273–305
WOMEN
discrimination against, *see* SEX DISCRIMINATION, status of, U.N. Commission on 373
WORK, *see also* EMPLOYMENT, WORKER
conditions of 213
right to 15, 213, 231–42; employment policy and development strategy 235–42; Employment Policy Convention of 1964 236–7; International Labour Organisation and the Economic Covenant 232–5; implementation by the International Labour Organisation of 15
scope 232
unemployment and the Third World 235–6
World Employment Conference of 1976 236–42
WORKERS
International Labour Organisation, involvement in 279–80
WORLD BANK, THE
social welfare and 246–7
WORLD COUNCIL OF CHURCHES, THE, 408
WORLD EMPLOYMENT CONFERENCE OF 1976, THE 237–42
WORLD HEALTH ORGANIZATION (WHO), THE 242–5
Economic Covenant and 219–23, 242–5
primary health care and 243–4, 245
WORLD PEACE COUNCIL 409
WORLD WAR I
Polish minority treaty 176
rights in, *see* ARMED CONFLICT
self-determination after 193, 194–5
WORLD WAR II
employment policy after 235
information, freedom of 183
international human rights after 347
rights in, *see* ARMED CONFLICT
treaties after 177

YOUNG-ANAWATY 17n